The Holocaust a

C000126719

Robert Eaglestone argues that postmodernism, especially understood in the light of the work of Emmanuel Levinas and Jacques Derrida, is a response to the Holocaust. This way of thinking offers new perspectives on Holocaust testimony, literature, historiography, and post-Holocaust philosophy. While postmodernism is often derided for being either playful and superficial or obscure and elitist, Eaglestone argues and demonstrates its commitment both to the past and to ethics.

Dealing with Holocaust testimony, including the work of Primo Levi and Eli Wiesel, with the memoirs of, 'second generation' survivors and with recent Holocaust literature, including Anne Michael's *Fugitive Pieces*, Jonathan Safran Foer's *Everything is Illuminated* and the false memoir of Benjamin Wilkomirski, *The Holocaust and the Postmodern* proposes a new way of reading both Holocaust testimony and Holocaust fiction. Through an exploration of Holocaust historiography, the book offers a new approach to debates over truth and memory. Eaglestone argues for the central importance of the Holocaust in understanding the work of Emmanuel Levinas and Jacques Derrida, and goes on to explore what the Holocaust means for rationality, ethics, and for the idea of what it is to be human. Weaving together theory and practice, testimony, literature, history, philosophy, and Holocaust studies, this interdisciplinary book is the first to explore in detail the significance of the Holocaust for postmodernism, and the significance of postmodernism for understanding the Holocaust.

The Holocaust
and
the Postmodern

ROBERT EAGLESTONE

OXFORD
UNIVERSITY PRESS

OXFORD
UNIVERSITY PRESS

Great Clarendon Street, Oxford OX2 6DP

Oxford University Press is a department of the University of Oxford.
It furthers the University's objective of excellence in research, scholarship,
and education by publishing worldwide in

Oxford New York

Auckland Bangkok Buenos Aires Cape Town Chennai
Dar es Salaam Delhi Hong Kong Istanbul Karachi Kolkata
Kuala Lumpur Madrid Melbourne Mexico City Mumbai Nairobi
São Paulo Shanghai Taipei Tokyo Toronto

Oxford is a registered trade mark of Oxford University Press
in the UK and in certain other countries

Published in the United States
by Oxford University Press Inc., New York

British Library Cataloguing in Publication Data
Data available

Library of Congress Cataloging in Publication Data
Data available

ISBN 978-0-19-926593-0 (Hbk.)   978-0-19-923937-5 (Pbk.)

3 5 7 9 10 8 6 4 2

Typeset by Laserwords Private Limited, Chennai, India
Printed in Great Britain
by
Biddles Ltd,
King's Lynn, Norfolk

Acknowledgements

I have to thank many people for their help and support in writing this book: Phil Agulnik, Janice Allen, John Armstrong, Tim Armstrong, Jennifer Bavidge, Tamas Benyei, Andrew Bowie, Matthew Broadbent, Susan Brown, Robert Burns, Bryan Cheyette, Josh Cohen, Claire Colebrook, Penny Crawford, Simon Critchley, Tommy Crocker, Holly Crocker, Jane Cowell, Colin Davis, Maire Davis, Lucy Dallas, Sarah Dimmerlow, William Eaglestone, Carol Eckersley, Michael Eskin, Rebecca Ferguson, Patrick Finney, Erica Fudge, Malcolm Geere, Tom Glennon, Patricia Glennon, Tony Hariss, Nick Hoare, Alex Hollingsworth, Robert Hampson, Judith Hawley, Ann Hobbes, Barry Langford, Betty Jay, Will Large, Peter Longerich, Simon Malpas, Sean Matthews, Martin McQuillan, Peter Middleton, Robert Mighall, Lawrence Normand, Jennifer Neville, Sue Pitt, Daphne Pollen, Jean Rayner, Jonathan Rée, Jo Reilly, R. R. Rockingham-Gill, Allen Samuels, Jo Sockett, Sara Salih, Clifton Spargo, Gavin Stewart, Ralph Strehle, Philip Smallwood, Helen Smith, Andrew Taylor, Richard Tennant, Sarah Tennant, Liz Thompson, Julian Thomas, Helen Tindale, Ralph Strehle, Nadia Valman, Robert Vilain, Tom Webster, Bernard Weiss, Angie Wilson, Lucie Wenigerova, and Ika Willis. To all of these, and to others I have not listed, I'm very grateful. I'd also like to thank my colleagues at Royal Holloway and the students on the courses I have taught on the MA in Holocaust Studies there. Participants at a number of seminars, conferences, and panels have also given very useful feedback: thanks to those at the Royal Holloway Centre for Research in the Holocaust and Twentieth Century History/Wiener Library workshops and at seminars hosted by the International Youth Meeting Centre in Oświęcim/Auschwitz Foundation, the Modern Language Association, the International Association for Philosophy and Literature, the Society for European Philosophy, Heythrop College, the Institute of Historical Research Philosophy of History Seminar, Chichester College of Higher Education, University of Wales, Lampeter, Middlesex University, Manchester University, and Manchester Metropolitan University.

I'd especially like to thank Adam Roberts, Dan Stone, and Sue Vice for reading, discussing, and disagreeing with me about parts of the book. The several anonymous readers for Oxford University Press all made significant and useful comments, and I'd like to thank them too. Intellectual life is made up of argument, thought, and response, and without this from all of the people I've mentioned, and others I have not recorded here, much of this would not have emerged. All errors are, of course, mine.

I'd like to thank the Library Staff at Royal Holloway, University of London, Senate House, the Wiener Library, and the British Library (especially in Humanities 2), and the library staff of the United States Holocaust Memorial Museum in Washington. At OUP I'd like to thank Sophie Goldsworthy for her support and encouragement and the other staff at the press, especially Elizabeth Prochaska and Emily Jolliffe.

I am especially grateful for a Research Fellowship from Leverhulme Trust fellowship in 2001 and to a sabbatical term granted me by Royal Holloway.

Most of all, I'd like to thank my parents Alex and Clare Eaglestone, my wife Geraldine Glennon, and my son Alex and daughter Isabella for their constantly generous love and support.

Versions of some chapters have appeared elsewhere: a version of Chapter 1 appears in *Critical Quarterly*, 45 (2003); of Chapter 2 in *Immigrants and Minorities*, 21 (2003); of Chapter 6 in *Groniek: Historisch Tijdschrift*, 160 (2003); of Chapter 10 in *Angelaki*, 7 (2002). A version of Chapter 8 appears as my *Postmodernism and Holocaust Denial* (Cambridge: Icon, 2001). Some of the issues in Chapter 5 were aired in John J. Joughin and Simon Malpas (eds.), *The New Aestheticism* (Manchester: Manchester University Press, 2003) and in 'Truth, Aesthetics, History' for the *Bucknell Review* (2004).

Contents

Contents

Abbreviations

LL   Jorge Semprun, *Literature or Life*, tr. Linda Coverdale (London: Viking, 1997)

MHEJ   Saul Friedländer, *Memory, History and the Extermination of the Jews of Europe* (Bloomington: Indiana University Press, 1993)

NM   Philippe Lacoue-Labarthe and Jean-Luc Nancy, 'The Nazi Myth', *Critical Inquiry*, 16 (Winter 1990)

OA   Stanley Milgram, *Obedience to Authority: An Experimental View* (New York: Harper Row, 1974)

OBBE   Emmanuel Levinas, *Otherwise than Being: Or, Beyond Essence*, tr. Alphonso Lingis (The Hague: Martinus Nijhoff, 1981)

OCF   Jacques Derrida, *On Cosmopolitanism and Forgiveness*, tr. Mark Hughes (London: Routledge, 2001).

OG   Jacques Derrida, *Of Grammatology*, tr. Gayatri Chakravorty Spivak (London: Johns Hopkins University Press, 1976)

OM   Christopher Browning, *Ordinary Men: Reserve Police Battalion 101 and the Final Solution* (London: Harper Collins, 2nd edn., 1998)

PH   Mark Roseman, *The Past in Hiding* (London: Allen Lane, 2000)

PSM   Isaiah Berlin, *The Proper Study of Mankind*, ed. Henry Hardy and Roger Hausheer (London: Pimlico, 1998)

RA   Giorgio Agamben, *Remnants of Auschwitz*, tr. Daniel Heller-Roazen (New York: Zone Books, 1999)

RN   Saul Friedländer, *Reflections on Nazism: An Essay on Kitsch and Death*, tr. Thomas Weyr (Bloomington: Indiana University Press, revised edn., 1993)

RTH   Hilary Putnam, *Reason, Truth and History* (Cambridge: Cambridge University Press, 1981)

TI   Emmanuel Levinas, *Totality and Infinity: An Essay on Exteriority*, tr. Alphonso Lingis (London: Kluwer Academic Publishers, 1991)

TTW   Saul Friedländer, 'Trauma, Transference and "Working through" in Writing the History of the *Shoah*' , *History and Memory*, 4 (1992), 39–59

WA   Anne Karpf, *The War After* (London: Minerva, 1996)

WMC   Saul Friedländer, *When Memory Comes*, tr. Helen R. Lane (New York: Discus Books, 1980)

Introduction
The Holocaust and the Postmodern

In August 1944, when 20,000 corpses had to be burned on some days, the open pits broke the bottleneck. Thus the capacity for destruction was approaching the point of being unlimited. Simple as this system was it took years to work out in the constant application of administrative techniques. It took millennia in the development of Western culture.[1]

Christopher Browning, a leading American historian of the Holocaust, writes:

I believe that the Holocaust was a watershed event in human history—the most extreme case of genocide that has yet occurred. What distinguishes it from other genocides are two factors: first the totality and scope of intent—that is, the goal of killing every last Jew, man, woman and child, throughout the reach of the Nazi empire; and second, the means employed—namely, the harnessing of the administrative/bureaucratic and technological capacities of a modern nation state and western scientific culture.[2]

This statement is peculiar in that it draws on two different discourses. It argues that the scope, intent, and means of the Holocaust are within the range of the discipline of history. It is the result of scrutinizing and weighing up documents, accounts, and archives. It suggests that the Holocaust can be compared with other historical cases of mass murder and genocide (its position as 'the most extreme case' distinguishes it from those other cases). But how could one prove or disprove the claim that that the Holocaust was a watershed in human history? The claim sounds right, but which archive or methodology reveals this? This is not to criticize Browning, but to show that this claim and countless others like it about the Holocaust do not only rely on the historical record or archive but on something wider, more significant, and, precisely because it is so all-pervasive, very much harder to pin down: a

---

[1] Raul Hilberg, *The Destruction of the European Jews* (London: Holmes & Meier, 1985), 251.

[2] Christopher R. Browning, *Nazi Policy, Jewish Workers, German Killers* (Cambridge: Cambridge University Press, 2000), 32.

sense of 'who we are' and 'how the world is for us' and how the event of the Holocaust has utterly changed this. It also embodies the sense, laconically implied by Hilberg, that the Holocaust and Western culture and thought were and are somehow deeply interconnected.

This sense, which is not necessarily at all religious or sublime, under-lies Jean-François Lyotard's detailed rebuttal to French Holocaust deniers, *The Differend*. In a much-cited passage he writes of how this feeling is like an earthquake which 'destroys not only lives, buildings, objects but also the instruments used to measure the earthquakes directly and indirectly. The impossibility of quantitatively measuring it does not prohibit, but rather inspires in the mind of the survivors the idea of a great seismic force.'[3] This has often been taken as suggesting that we cannot know about the Holocaust and must remain silent. However, as Geoffrey Hartman writes, the 'after shocks are measur-able; we are deep into the process of creating new instruments to record and express what happened': these instruments are 'born of trauma'.[4] Indeed, Lyotard's own work and that of other philosophers, thinkers, historians, and critics described as postmodern are some of those instru-ments, perhaps the most acute. This is part of the aim of this book: to show that postmodernism in the West begins with thinking about the Holocaust, that postmodernism—understood as poststructuralism, a still developing tradition of post-phenomenological philosophy—is a response to the Holocaust. Following from that, this book also aims to show how these ways of thinking, precisely because they begin with the Holocaust, both measure and offer new perspectives on a range of issues in our understanding of the Holocaust and its aftermath.

Emil Fackenheim wrote with scorn of those philosophers who keep on acting as if there 'is no difference between the six million and one child dying of cancer'.[5] The issue is, I think, not that the individual philosophers, or theologians or literary critics or historians, are unaware of the Holocaust—how could they be?—but that our way of

---

[3] Jean-François Lyotard, *The Differend: Phrases in Dispute*, tr. Georges Van Den Abbeele (Manchester: Manchester University Press, 1988), 56.

[4] Geoffrey Hartman, *The Longest Shadow* (Basingstonke: Palgrave Macmillan, 2002), 1. The different names of the events—Holocaust, Shoah, Churban—all with their different histories and deeply rooted frameworks, are themselves signs of this: signs of coming to terms with the events in different ways. This book follows standard academic practise of referring to the events as the 'Holocaust', though this already shows how the events have been 'normalized'.

[5] Emil Fackenheim, *To Mend the World: Foundations of Jewish Thought* (New York: Schocken Books, 1982), 11.

thinking, criticizing, doing history itself, the discourses that our debates inhabit and the horizons which orient these debates, are still striving to respond to the Holocaust. Postmodern thought, especially that of Emmanuel Levinas and Jacques Derrida or inspired by them, marks the most profound attempt to do this.[6] This point of view will raise hackles with those who understand postmodernism as being centrally concerned with, on one hand, playfulness, pastiche, irony, a superficiality beyond caring about truth and falsity, and so on, and, on the other hand, academic obscurantism and elitism, removed from wider, more worldly concerns. It will raise worse than hackles with those who see postmodernism as an excessive valorization of irrationalism or overburdened with the legacy of Martin Heidegger and his strong philosophical connections to Nazism. Indeed, sometimes in good faith and sometimes not, the Holocaust has been invoked as a 'test case' for postmodern ideas: this is not simply because it is seen, perhaps rather tastelessly, as a good example on which to test ideas, but because it is never far from our thoughts, even if we are never quite sure how to think about it. However, these understandings of the postmodern fail to take into account both its central and consistent commitment to ethics and its rigorous, rational side: that is, postmodernism does not reject rationality, but is aware of the limits and processes of rationality. I will explore this in my analysis of the work of Emmanuel Levinas and Jacques Derrida.

Two interwoven strands of ethical thought develop in the work of these thinkers. The first, I suggest, is a grounding of a new form of hope and humanism, a humanism beyond humanism, based on a sense of the 'fundamentally fragile, corporeal existence' and on an awareness of 'the trace', of that otherness which escapes the limits of systems of thought and language but is made manifest in them.[7] The second, and

---

[6] Other commentators have suggested this. Dominick LaCapra wrote that one 'crucial undertaking of postmodern and poststructuralist approaches may . . . be to explore more clearly their own relation to the Shoah in all its intricate dimensions' (*Representing the Holocaust: History, Theory, Trauma* (New York: Cornell University Press, 1994), 223) and again 'postmodernism can also be defined as post-Holocaust; there's an intricate relation between the two' (*Writing History, Writing Trauma* (London: Johns Hopkins University Press, 2001), 179. Lawrence Langer's opposition to 'pre-empting the Holocaust', to using 'its grim details to fortify a prior commitment to an ideal of moral reality, community responsibility, or religious belief that leaves us with space to retain faith in their pristine value in a post-Holocaust world', seems to embody a sense of this, too (Lawrence Langer, *Pre-empting the Holocaust* (London: Yale University Press, 1998), 1).

[7] Paul Gilroy, *Between Camps* (London Penguin, 2000), 117.

linked to the first, is both an awareness and consequent rejection of the metaphysics of comprehension. The metaphysics of comprehension can be understood as both the desire for and the methods by and through which Western thought, in many different ways, comprehends, seizes, or consumes what is other to it and so reduces the other to itself, to the same: 'oh, omnivorous philosophy!' Levinas cites Pascal. It appears in very basic assumptions: for example, in how we read, in how history is done, and in how and why philosophy is done. Postmodernism focuses on both the act of comprehending, seizing, covering up, and on the resistance to that act—to the emergence, if only momentarily, of otherness. These senses of the trace, of the human, and of the resistance to the metaphysics of comprehension appear in different ways in different contexts. I will illustrate this in debates over 'normalization' in history, in how testimony is understood, in discussions of Holocaust literature, and in relation to the limits and powers of philosophy.

Postmodernism's concern with reason, its rules, and its limits leads to a concern with the edges and outsides of discourses: where the philosophical, literary, historical meet, where what can be spoken of and what cannot meet. As I argue in Chapter 5 and in Part III of this book, this concern does not make Derrida or Levinas irrationalists or mystics. Instead, engaging with what is outside reason, their work moves between or around these themes of reason and that which is outside reason. Moreover, a concern with edges and limits of disciplines and discourses, where one discourse shades into another, where philosophy becomes autobiography, for example, or where fiction challenges how it is to be understood, means that this sort of thinking is sensitive to the ways in which many different sorts of claims are made and discourses are used in the same text, often in the same sentence.

In showing how postmodernism is a response to the Holocaust, and how this in turn appears in or clarifies current debates, four major themes emerge: what is called in historical controversies 'normalization'; the process of identification in both literary, cultural, and political life; the idea of 'genre' or 'discipline' or 'phrase-regimens' or 'language games'; and truth. These themes recur in different registers—literary, historical, philosophical—and they interweave and overlap. Perhaps, indeed, they may be different ways of discussing the same phenomenon, unnamable in itself save within the different disciplines.

The term 'normalization' is used by Saul Friedländer. For him, this represents the ways in which the assumed neutrality or objectivity of discourses, such as the discipline of history, has a meaning beyond that detachment: they place the reader or writer 'in a situation not unrelated to the detached position of an administrator of extermination: interest is fixed on an administrative process . . . words used for record keeping. And that's all.'[8] This issue of normalization is one of the ways that the metaphysics of comprehension, embedded in Western thought, is made manifest in relation to the Holocaust (and to other events and issues) and so is precisely one of the things that postmodernism seeks to question.

In a parallel way, this book is also concerned with identity and more centrally with the process of identification. In the summer of 2001, I attended a conference on Holocaust museums. Three eminent historians disagreed: one insisted that a particular museum made the visitors identify too much with the victims, the second that it made them identify too much with the perpetrators, and a third suggested that the museum led the visitors to identify themselves with bystanders during the Holocaust. I wondered if the real problem was with the idea of identification itself, what it means, what it does. I begin with a discussion of this in literature because it is a process that underlies much in literature—some see it as the central power and vital moral moment at the heart of the literary, for example—and it has corollaries in philosophy and in history. But it is not only a literary process. While the content of the process varies considerably from time to time and from place to place there are some things that are clear about the process itself. Identification is simultaneously personal and communal: one identifies or fails to identify oneself both as a person and through or with a national and communal identity. It is simultaneously both imposed from without and developed from within. It is simultaneously performed by us with conscious and unconscious agency, and, in many different ways, taught to us or enacted on us by outside forces. It is central not only in aesthetics but also politics. The process of identification, too, is part of the metaphysics of comprehension, delimiting, and identifying. The fact that the process itself seems unavoidable, though the actual identifications may change for better or for worse (as Jews became identified as 'non-Aryans', for example), shows how much the metaphysics of comprehension is part of 'who we are'. However, this vital issue is rarely addressed in an explicit way, though

---

[8] Saul Friedländer, *Reflections on Nazism: An Essay on Kitsch and Death*, tr. Thomas Weyr (Bloomington: Indiana University Press, rev. edn., 1993), 90.

it plays a key role in debates over identity. It has an strong ethical significance, especially in relation to the Holocaust, not least in that, as a process, it often leads to the 'consumption' and reduction of otherness, the assimilation of others' experience into the one's own frameworks. Postmodernism is concerned with identifying who and how we are in the West, and, after the Holocaust, with questioning that process.

Literature seeks literary answers, history historical answers, and philosophy philosophical answers. This foregrounds the nature and idea of 'genre', 'discourse', 'phrase regimen', 'Language game', or 'discipline', words which all seem to name, at first, the subrules that govern forms of thinking, writing, and creating. But genre is not simply a system of pigeonholes, invented by academics, into which to put texts: it is more than textual convention. Genre is not just a way of writing: it is simultaneously a way of reading, too. Genres form horizons of understanding, interpretation, and reading, where text, readership, and knowledge come together. A genre is a way of looking at a text, implicitly connecting texts with contexts, ideas, expectations, rules of argument, and so on. Genres are vital in the act of creating texts and, more importantly, the knowledges from which texts emerge. Great works, of course, span, defy, and so invent genres. Works define genres, bodies of knowledge, and their rules: likewise genres, bodies of knowledge, and their rules define works. Over time, new works change the nature of the genres in which they appear, or inaugurate new genres. In the case of Holocaust testimony, it is certainly true that there are accounts of horrors before (Pliny on Pompeii for example, Conrad's narrator Marlowe on the 'Grove of Death' in the Congo Free State) and it is true that these are testimonial. But they tend to be subsumed into, for example, historical accounts (an eyewitness report, an oral history) or literary accounts (novels). Literary, historical, and philosophical writing since 1945 are involved in a new genre, testimony, with its own form, its own generic rules, its own presuppositions. In the light of this, pre-Holocaust texts, from before Browning's 'watershed', can perhaps be reread or reimagined or recriticized as works of testimony, and new similarities and differences can be analysed.

Finally, this book engages with issues of truth. The more ideas about truth are taken for granted and not discussed (in literary studies and in history, for example), the more significant, perhaps, is their role. Whether implicitly or explicitly, truth has been central not only to the major debates in philosophy, but the humanities in general. Often, the participants in these debates, when in dialogue, sound as if they have missed each other entirely: this is sometimes because they have been unclear about the ways in which they have been referring to or relying on their different concepts of truth. It seems important to me to have at least some rough account of how truth works, although one could easily spend a lifetime investigating this central and fascinating problem. A rough idea at least, perhaps, helps disentangle an array of problems. Andrew Bowie writes that

> the philosophical question of truth can either become reduced to the attempt to give an adequate explanation of how it is we can generate valid evidence [for testable facts and theories about human or non-human nature] . . . or it becomes a location of ways of thinking which have no obvious place in a world where calculability and pragmatic success increasingly dominate public discourse about truth . . . [a location which] confronts us with the deepest questions about our self-understanding.[9]

In this book, and as in the citation from Browning above, I argue that these two versions of truth—truth as explanation, corresponding to evidence and states of affairs, and truth as in some way revealing of ourselves, of 'who and how we are'—not only operate at the same time, but have a complex interrelationship. More than this, Levinas asks what underlies truth, and answers by arguing that truth itself, even the form of truth not amenable to 'calculation and pragmatic success', relies on ethics, on justice. And ethics, in the sense of both justice and the sense of *éthos*, who and how we are, finally make up the subject of this book in too large a way to be codified into a theme.

While all these themes, normalization, the process of identification, the idea of 'genre', and truth are interwoven in complex and different ways, and emerge and re-emerge throughout, the book is divided into three parts. The first, 'Reading and the Holocaust', concentrates on testimony and literature: the aim of this section is not to discuss the facts of testimony and literature but rather its consequences and contexts. It concerns the consequences of the form and genre of Holocaust testimony for the reading and understanding of that testimony. Literature, and art in general, is like having a tiger by the tail. While it can often mislead us in terrible ways, we are always already enmeshed in and by it, not least because of its capacity to shape us and tell us who we are and what the world is like. Part of our response must be to understand

---

[9] Andrew Bowie, *From Romanticism to Critical Theory* (London: Routledge, 1997), 164–5.

this, watch, and judge it. However, it also has another significance: as Derrida writes on Celan, philosophy 'finds itself, rediscovers itself, in the vicinity of the poetic, indeed of literature'.[10] I begin by looking at how works of testimony are often consumed in the same way as fiction. This happens principally through the day-to-day process of identification, in which a reader identifies with—becomes or relives in some way—the events of a book: the significance of this process, thought of as naive, is often overlooked. While it occurs when people read testimony, it is ethically and epistemologically dubious. To prevent this consumption, and so respond to these texts in the way they demand rather than the way we presuppose, and to respond to the sense of the Holocaust as a watershed event, I argue that Holocaust testimonies are to be understood as a new genre in their own right. In a sense, this is only to find out why it is that, for example, Primo Levi is fascinating but not pleasurable to read. To see testimony in this way—as a new genre— seems importantly to parallel the intuitions of survivors and writers of testimony. More than this, it also allows enabling questions to be asked of these texts. Chapter 2 looks in detail at the specific generic qualities of testimonies, concentrating on the textual ways in which they eschew easy identification and so comprehension by readers. Chapter 3 turns to issues of memory and postmemory and discusses the ways in which the children of survivors have written about identifying with the memory of the Holocaust and what this might mean. This process involves a com- plex identification with the parents that does not comprehend their experience, identity, or suffering: as one writes 'I must be near *and* I must be far.' Chapter 4 turns to recent Holocaust fiction, and traces these themes of normalization and identification.

The second section, 'Holocaust Metahistories', is not the work of a historian, and turns not to history but to metahistory. While I take this term from Hayden White's work, it is not because White's work is postmodern (Ankersmit describes him as an 'unrelenting structuralist') but rather because I develop some of his ideas following the line of thought laid out by Levinas and Derrida.[11] Metahistory, here, is part of the contemporary philosophy of history. History has been the dom- inant genre for engaging with the Holocaust. It is a caricature that

---

[10] Jacques Derrida, 'Shibboleth: For Paul Celan', tr. Joshua Wilner, in *Wordtraces: Reading of Paul Celan*, ed. Aris Fioretos (London: Johns Hopkins University Press, 1994), 3–72, 48.

[11] F. R. Ankersmit, *Historical Representation* (Stanford: Stanford Universtity Press, 2001), 252.

others in the humanities deride historians and argue that the intellectual breakthroughs have come, for example, from literary studies and
from philosophy. However, apart from the continuing, rigorous,
detailed, and vitally important archival research, in the area of the representation and understanding of the Holocaust, historians have made
many significant extra-historical claims, and in general established the
terms of the argument, leaving other disciplines engaged with the
Holocaust behind. Despite this, much still remains opaque, and cannot
be resolved by 'adding more facts': as Saul Friedländer writes, if 'the
jigsaw does not work out, the reason may not be that some of the pieces
are missing but that we have set it up wrongly'.[12] Moreover, as the
chapters in the second section of this book argue, the establishment of
historical facts and development of interpretations are inextricably
intertwined with philosophical issues.

Here, turning to metahistory—which does not deny the reality of the
historical past, as some have suggested—might serve some use. This section attempts to move beyond the seemingly intractable (and often rather
clichéd) debates between 'empiricists' and 'postmodernists' by coming to
the debate from a different angle which supports much of what the
empiricists cherish (the 'rules' of history and evidence) while seeing them
in the context of a wider contemporary philosophical discussion over the
nature of history. Much of the debate over the relationship between postmodernism and history has been made difficult because of a confusion
over its terms, especially over the nature of truth. This is not surprising,
as, in some significant ways, the debate represents the confluence of a
post-phenomenological European thought with a tradition of Anglo-
American historical empiricism and both these traditions maintain very
different understandings about how to understand truth. Centrally, the
issue is not 'Is the past real?' but rather 'What sort of claims to truth
about the past are historians making?' Chapter 5 builds on the themes of
Part I, and suggests that there are two different, and complementary,
understandings of truth at work in the discipline of history and that the
history of the Holocaust brings this to the fore. One understanding of
truth is comprehensive and positivistic, the other is existential, involved
with ethics and a sense of 'how the world is for us'. These two understandings of truth—both are unavoidable in modernity—are in tension
with each other, sometimes productively, sometimes negatively. The next

---

[12] Saul Friedländer, 'Some Reflections about the Historicization of National
Socialism', *Reworking the Past: Hitler, the Holocaust and the Historian's Debate*, ed.
Peter Baldwin (Boston: Beacon Press, 1990), 88–101, 99.

chapter explores this in the work of Saul Friedländer. Friedländer's work is a negotiation between and development of a positivist, 'scientific' historical truth and an existential ethical truth of the past, often described in his discourse as memory: these two are interwoven with each other, sometime supportive, sometimes at odds. The next chapter, as a metahistorical case study, looks at the very heated debate in the late 1990s over Daniel Goldhagen's *Hitler's Willing Executioners*. Contrasting Goldhagen's work with the work of Christopher Browning, some of which covers similar ground, reveals that their disagreement, and much of the furore, stemmed not so much from the historical record as from their different ideas of what it is to be human: an existential, ethical sense of truth. The final chapter of Part II looks at Holocaust denial, and especially at the Irving/Lipstadt libel trial of 2000. It shows how these two understandings of truth run together and so how the discipline of history depends on 'genre conventions', and argues that postmodernism offers very strong tools to use against deniers.

The last section, 'The Trace of the Holocaust', turns to philosophy. One particular philosophical tradition, the European post-phenomenological tradition stemming from Kant, has a very wide influence: thus, postmodernism. This spread has also, of course, been a dilution, and involved a loss of specificity and rigour. In order to focus the debate, I have looked in detail at what I take to be two of the most important figures in this diverse and heterogeneous tradition, Levinas and Derrida. The work of both of these thinkers is very usefully seen as saturated with the Holocaust, and both seek to bring into philosophical discourse that which lies outside it and to engage with the various problems that this movement involves. As a result of this context, neither are therapeutic philosophers: they do not aim principally to resolve problems in thought or to offer self-development. Quite to the contrary: both are insomniac or, worse, wounding philosophers, aiming shake their readers and audiences from slumber. The first chapter in this section looks in detail at the work of Emmanuel Levinas, and argues that his philosophy, throughout and in every way, from particular words and sentences to his overall aims, is a response to the Holocaust. It goes on to show the effect this has on how his philosophy works and how it achieves and fails to achieve the ends it sets itself. Chapter 10 turns to Derrida's thought. By developing his use of an idea from Levinas, the trace, it shows how his thought is imbued with the thought of the Holocaust, and how that in turn shapes his responses to the task of philosophy and to his aims. Chapter 11 looks at attempts to explain Nazism and to refute it though 'philosophical histories' and accounts of 'perpetrator philosophy'. This too reveals the limits of philosophical discourse. The final chapter turns to the idea of the human. Beginning with Heidegger, it looks at ways in which the human has been thought after the Holocaust, and outlines how it might be possible to think about a humanism beyond humanism.[13] The conclusion turns to issues to which this overall discussion might lead.

In conversation with Foucault, Gilles Deleuze argued that 'practice is a set of relays from one theoretical point to another, and theory is a relay from one practice to another. No theory can develop without eventually encountering a wall, and practice is necessary for piercing this wall.'[14] Still thinking in these opposites, a more anglophone intellectual tradition would probably reverse the second sentence, thus, 'no practice can develop without eventually encountering a wall, and theory is necessary for piercing this wall'. Yet the point remains that the categories of theory and practice are often seen as being at odds with one another and yet are inescapably entwined, which itself suggests that such a divide is really only an analytical device. In this spirit, I have taken as a guide what the philosopher Jonathan Rée calls philosophical history. Not the 'history of philosophy' (a study of canonical texts, forced into dry, professorial narratives) but a way of thinking about 'the world in terms of what it can mean to us, to each of us, in whatever specific situations we happen to find ourselves' . He calls for accounts that are 'mobile, complicated, stratified, detailed', making use of the

rememorative methods of autobiography and the evocative polyphonies of fiction, as well as the exacting demands of historical research and philosophical criticism. Like any other fundamental intellectual inquiry, its results may not lend themselves to abstract summary. It will always be taking us on journeys whose purpose and payoff may not be apparent till we reach the end, or even later; down paths which, instead of leading us somewhere new, simply help us understand . . . where we have been all along.[15]

Attempting something like this has led me not only to interleave 'theory' and 'practice', but also to bring together, where possible, the different genres this book discusses: literary, testimonial, historical, philosophical,

[13] Both Levinas and Derrida are highly aware of Heidegger's past and engage precisely with his Nazism and his silence, which they do not seek to avoid, exculpate, or ignore. This is discussed in more detail in Ch. 5 and in the third section of the book.
[14] Gilles Deleuze in Michel Foucault, *Language, Counter-Memory, Practice*, ed. Donald Bouchard, tr. Donald Bouchard and Sherry Simon (New York: Cornell University Press, 1977), 206
[15] Jonathan Rée, *I See a Voice* (London: Harper Collins, 1999), 384.

to highlight how, in this field, similar debates emerge in different ways in different disciplines. I have also tried to trace affinities and occasional resemblances between thinkers, historians, and critics. For example, it seems to me that, in this area, Adorno, despite his very considerable differences, is an illuminating parallel to Derrida and Levinas. This is not to suggest that there is a 'meta-philosophy', overarching discipline, or grand unifying theory, but it is to stress interrelationships and to attempt to break down the more common intellectual barriers.

Holocaust studies has given rise to 'specialisations and subspecialisations' and Dan Michman is right when he argues that the 'assumption that there exists a truly shared field of research . . . in which researchers from different locations exchange "goods" freely, amid borderless cross-influence and [cross]-fertilisation . . . is almost a fiction'.[16] In a version of Holocaust studies wider than the strictly historical studies Michman is discussing, I have attempted this 'almost' but (it seems to me) necessary fiction. In this context, trying to write a work that is cross- or inter-disciplinary will often unavoidably involve clarifying for some what is obvious to others. For example, most historians in the field will be more than familiar with the details of the Goldhagen/Browning debate and feel, rightly in this limited context, that it is passé: some critics and philosophers will not be so well-informed. The gain here—the connections and insights—seems to me to outweigh the loss, but I apologize none the less. Different disciplinary languages—historical, philosophical both analytic and continental, literary critical, and theoretical—raise difficulties too, and postmodernism is also an area sometimes filled with its own argot. I have tried throughout to avoid unnecessary jargon. Moreover, sometimes, a less acute phrase that illuminates is better than a very precise one that may serve to obscure.

The book is a reflection on the Holocaust but central to its argument is the idea that, however fully or poorly understood, the event of the Holocaust is already a horizon which orients our time, certainly in the West, even now, three or four generations afterwards. Thus, this book describes the circular process by which postmodern thought is shaped explicitly or implicitly by the Holocaust and how it engages with and shapes how we understand the Holocaust.

---

[16] Raul Hilberg, *Sources of Holocaust Research* (Chicago: Ivan R. Dee, 2001), 204. Dan Michman, *Holocaust Historiography; A Jewish Perspective* (London: Valentine Mitchell, 2003), 359.

I

Reading and the Holocaust

1

'Not Read and Consumed in the Same Way as Other Books': Identification and the Genre of Testimony

Texts that testify do not simply report facts but, in a different way, encounter—and make us encounter—strangeness . . . the concept of the testimony . . . is in fact quite unfamiliar and estranging . . . the more we look closely at texts, the more they show us that, unwittingly, we do not even know what testimony is and that, in any case, it is not simply what we thought we knew it was.[1]

How can one write about a situation and not identify with all its characters? And how can one identify with so many victims? Worse, how can one identify with the executioner? How could a victim say 'I' in the place of his killer?[2]

INTRODUCTION

Maurice Blanchot writes that the accounts of Holocaust survivors are 'not read and consumed in the same way as other books'.[3] If this is the case, how and why is it so? Why is Primo Levi fascinating to read, but not pleasurable? Elie Wiesel famously claimed that the Holocaust 'invented a new literature, that of testimony' and this chapter takes this

---

[1] Shoshona Felman and Dori Laub, *Testimony: Crises of Witnessing in Literature, Psychoanalysis, and History* (London: Routledge, 1992), 7.

[2] Elie Wiesel, 'The Holocaust as Literary Inspiration', in *Dimensions of the Holocaust* (Evanston, Ill.: Northwestern Univerity Press, 1990), 7.

[3] Maurice Blanchot, *Friendship*, tr. Elizabeth Rottenberg (Stanford, Calif.: University of Stanford Press, 1997), 110.

remark—often thought to be hyperbolic—as its guide.[4] It concerns the affect of testimony.[5] Central to reading's affect is the common or garden process of identification: it is the grasping, or comprehending, of another's experience as one's own by 'putting one's self in their place'. Identification is the staple of much fiction—verbal and visual—and of the so-called 'human interest angle' in the news media, yet the texts that witness the Holocaust question this taken-for-granted process. It is precisely this questioning of identification and the context in which it occurs that explains the general experience voiced by Blanchot and others, and that, with the events from which it emerges, makes testimony a new genre.[6]

'PLANET AUSCHWITZ'

The events of the Holocaust are often described as incomprehensible, as ungraspable to those who did not experience them. Raul Hilberg writes that survivors seem to have 'a special kind of knowledge': they

> have referred to it in expressions like 'planet Auschwitz' and in such sentences as 'Those who were not there cannot imagine what it was like'. Clearly, they were there, and thus they are set apart or set themselves apart from anyone who did not share their fate. The outsider can never cross this divide and can never grasp their experience.[7]

These sorts of remarks are frequently found in Holocaust testimony. Elie Wiesel, for example, argues that those 'who did not live through the event will never know it . . . between our memory and its reflection there stands a wall that cannot be pierced. The past belongs to the dead and the survivor does not recognise himself in the world linking him to them.'[8] Andrea Reiter suggests this is because there is no stock of

---

[4] Wiesel, 'Holocaust as Literary Inspiration', 7.

[5] On the importance and difficulty of affect, in an aesthetic context but with some parallels to the discussion below, see Peter de Bolla, *Art Matters* (London: Harvard University Press, 2001).

[6] Raul Hilberg, with a historian's eye, divides testimony into four categories: 'Legal testimony, interviews of specific persons, oral history and memoir literature'. Raul Hilberg, *Sources of Holocaust Research* (Chicago: Ivan R. Dee, 2001), 44. My argument below centrally concerns what he names memoir literature, though—in as much as all these forms use narrative, reflect generic forms, and raise questions about form and identification—it applies to them all.

[7] Raul Hilberg, *Perpetrators Victims Bystanders: The Jewish Catastrophe 1933–1945* (London: Harper Perennial 1992), 187.

[8] Wiesel, 'Holocaust as Literary Inspiration', 7.

shared life experiences which the author and reader share, which, as a consequence, excludes the reader.[9] However, the failure to grasp the experience is usually seen to lie not so much in absence of a shared life practice *per se* but as a result of a break between language and reference itself. Wiesel continues: 'We speak in code, we survivors, and this code cannot be broken, cannot be deciphered, not by you no matter how much you try.'[10] For Primo Levi, too, it is language that is at the core of the problem: he writes that just

as our hunger is not that feeling of missing a meal, so our way of being cold has need of a new word. We say 'hunger', we say 'tiredness', 'fear', 'pain', we say winter and they are different things. They are free words, created and used by free men who live in comfort and suffering in their homes. If the Lagers had lasted longer a new, harsh language would have been born; and only this language could express what it means to toil the whole day in the wind, with the temperature below freezing, wearing only a shirt, underpants, cloth jacket and trousers, and in one's body nothing but weakness, hunger and knowledge of the end drawing nearer.[11]

One of Charlotte Delbo's comrades makes the same point about survivors and superficial words:

All of those I met since I came back do not exist. . . . They belong to another universe and nothing will allow them to rejoin ours. Sometimes it seems that they're about to rejoin us. Then they utter one of these superficial words, one of their empty words, and they plunge headlong into their world, that of the living.[12]

Jorge Semprun, whose work, like these others, is characterized by tension between his understanding and the failure of others to understand, meets three Allied officers at Buchenwald, just after his liberation and reflects:

they can't really understand. They probably know what the words mean. Smoke: you know what that is, you think you know. Throughout historic memory, there have been smoking chimneys. Sometimes country hearths,

[9] See Andrea Reiter, *Narrating the Holocaust*, tr. Patrick Camiler (London: Continuum, 2000).

[10] Wiesel, 'Holocaust as Literary Inspiration', 7.

[11] Primo Levi, *If This is a Man and The Truce*, tr. Stuart Woolf (London: Abacus, 1979), 129. See also Bryan Cheyette, 'The Ethical Uncertainty of Primo Levi', in Bryan Cheyette and Laura Marcus (eds.), *Modernity, Culture and the Jew* (London: Polity Press, 1998).

[12] Charlotte Delbo, *Auschwitz and After*, tr. Rosette C. Lamont (London: Yale University Press, 1995), 265.

domestic firesides: the smoke of household gods. This smoke, however, is beyond them, And they will never really understand. Not these people, that day. Nor all the others, afterward, They will never know—they cannot imagine, whatever their good intentions may be.[13]

These writers and survivors, and many others, believe that it is not possible for those who did not survive to understand, in a truthful way, the events of the Holocaust. Language is not enough. This is not mystical nor does it suggest that the Holocaust is unapproachable or sublime: it is only to suggest that there is an insurmountable difficulty in understanding the existential truth of the events using 'free words'.

This difficulty is not to do with the naming of the horrors. Paul Fussell writing about trench warfare and Elaine Scarry writing about pain have shown that language is rich in terms to describe wounding, pain, and terror. Although some accounts of the Holocaust are censored or self-censor the worst, many—and not just recently written ones—describe the horrors without blanching. Olga Lengyel's *Five Chimneys*—first published in 1947 with editions in 1959 and 1995— discusses medical experiments, murdered babies, rape and abusive sex in the camp without evasion or euphemism. As Semprun writes, the 'horror itself was not the Evil—not its essence at least . . . One could have spent hours testifying to the daily horror of the camp without touching upon the essence of this experience.'[14]

It is not, or not only, the pain and suffering that is incomprehensible. This is not special to Holocaust testimony: any representation of physical pain or other sensations is not those sensations. Pain can be described but, through description, it cannot be experienced by another. Jean Améry writes that it

would be totally senseless to try and describe here the pain that was inflicted on me. Was it 'like a red hot iron in my shoulders' and another 'like a dull wooden stake that had been driven into the back of my head'? One comparison would only stand for the other, and in the end we would be hoaxed by turn in the hopeless merry-go-round of figurative speech. The pain was what it was. Beyond that there is nothing to say.[15]

---

[13] Jorge Semprun, *Literature or Life*, tr. Linda Coverdale (London: Viking, 1997), 10–11.

[14] Ibid. 87.

[15] Jean Améry, *At the Mind's Limits*, tr. Sidney Rosenfled and Stella Rosenfeld (London: Granta Books, 1999), 33. See also Andrea Reiter, *Narrating the Holocaust*, tr. Patrick Camiler (London: Continuum, 2000), 17.

The hunger Levi describes, the 'thirst of the morning and the thirst of the evening, the thirst of the day and the thirst of the night' that Delbo suffers, are not just extremes: they seem to be hunger and thirst of a different sort.[16]

What is incomprehensible is given different names. For Wiesel, *Night*: 'Never shall I forget that night . . . which has turned my life in to one long night.'[17] For Semprun, with his philosophical training, it is something like a Kantian radical evil or, developed from Heidegger, a being-with-towards-death. For Levi, it is an 'awakening' into a 'grey and turbid nothing . . . the dawn command of Auschwitz . . . "Wstawàch"'.[18] Kitty Hart, returning to Auschwitz for the first time in 1978, writes that the past and present 'got hopelessly jumbled up. All I could be sure of was that I belonged here. And anyway, there wasn't anywhere else in the world. Never had been, never would be.'[19] These different terms and accounts, and those given to it by others, name this incomprehension at what lies beyond language and mark the limits of comprehension by those who were not there.

PRIMO LEVI'S SMILE

Yet survivor testimony opens a problem. We who come after the Holocaust and know about it only through representations are frequently and with authority told that it is incomprehensible. However, the representations seem to demand us to do exactly that, to comprehend it, to grasp the experiences, to imagine the suffering, through identifying with those who suffered. And readers and audiences do identify strongly with testimony accounts.

Levi recalls 'with a smile' a discussion in a 'fifth grade class room'.[20] 'An alert-looking little boy . . . asked me the obligatory question: "But how come you didn't escape?".' Remembering that in the cinema the 'incarcerated hero is always a positive character, always trying to escape' and that this is 'constantly reinforced by romantic (*The Count of Monte Cristo*) and popular literature', he patiently explains that, in

---

[16] Delbo, *Auschwitz and After*, 70.

[17] Elie Wiesel, *Night*, tr. Stella Rodway (London: Penguin, 1981), 43, 45.

[18] Levi, *If This is a Man*, 379–80.

[19] Kitty Hart, *Return to Auschwitz* (London: Panther, 1983), 233.

[20] Primo Levi, *The Drowned and the Saved*, tr. Raymond Rosenthal (London: Abacus, 1989), 123, 127.

the camps, the prisoners were demoralized, hungry, and maltreated. With shaved heads and filthy clothes they would be instantly recognizable, they had no knowledge of the local area and anyway had nowhere to flee to in the hostile state which had deprived them of rights. Moreover, escape led to repercussions—usually death—for those left behind. The boy is unconvinced, and asks for a map of the Lager. He then

> presented to me the plan he had worked out: here at night, cut the throat of the sentinel; then put on his clothes; immediately after this run over there to the power station and cut off the electricity, so the search light would go out and the high tension fence would be deactivated; after that I could leave without any trouble. He added seriously: 'If it should happen to you again, do as I told you; you'll see that you'll be able to do it.'

Used to romantic prison fictions, the boy identifies himself with the captive Levi and imagines a storybook escape. Anca Vlasopolos, a Romanian daughter of an Auschwitz survivor who later emigrated to the US, describes how she began to hear stories about Auschwitz at about 5 years old: 'I listened to them as to adventure tales, with a sense of excitement as the plot rose and with sorrow or relief at the denouement, but I believe on the whole with emotions not unlike those elicited by my reading of *The Three Musketeers* or *The Count of Monte Cristo*.'[21] For the young Vlasopolos, as in adventure stories, she identifies with the fate of the characters.

It is not only children who make these sort of identifications. Daniel Schwarz finds himself identifying with victims of the Holocaust, an identification strengthened through his Jewish heritage: in 'our nightmares, we are deported and suffer the horrors of these camps. . . . I dream of myself within shtetls, camps and confined circumstances, as a participant in the very world I am writing about.'[22] For M. E. Heinemann, 'willingness to grant authenticity to Holocaust literature', including testimony, depends on 'eliciting reader involvement and emotional response'.[23] Mary Lagerwey's *Reading Auschwitz* picks up on the act of identification: visiting the site of the camp, she writes of how she walked around in a daze. 'The wind whips through my wool coat. I am very cold, and I imagine what the wind would have felt

---

[21] Anca Vlasopolos, *No Return Address: A Memoir of Displacement* (New York: Colombia University Press, 2000), 25–6.

[22] Daniel Schwarz, *Imagining the Holocaust* (New York: St Martin's Griffin, 1999), 5.

[23] M. E. Heinemann, *Gender and Destiny: Women Writers and the Holocaust* (Westport, Conn.: Greenwood Press, 1986), 117.

like for someone here fifty years ago without a coat, boots or gloves.'[24] Likewise, Dina Wardi imagines her grandparents 'standing naked in the snow in a queue of people marching to their death. The feeling of terrible humiliation and anxiety caused by this picture was so strong I couldn't bear it, and I had to detach myself emotionally from the scene.'[25] The graduate students in Martin Gilbert's *Holocaust Journey* expressed similar feelings, discussing the emotional 'responses to the atrocities and horror, and empathy with the victims' as well as a 'geographical' connection engendered by visiting the sites of mass death.[26] Visiting the site of Birkenau, one of Gilbert's students is overcome by the sheer physical experience: 'What could it have been like to have been here, for even one day? The enormity of the camp, where the endless lines of barracks and searchlights and barbed wire stretch as far as the eye can see, overwhelms me.'[27] The US Holocaust Memorial Museum offers identity cards to 'personalise the concept of victims' and ensure that 'visitors do not learn at a distance; rather they are brought inside the story' through the gaining of an exhibition 'twin' or 'companion'.[28] Edith Wyschogrod, in a essay that ends a testimony, cites Gautama the Buddha in asking 'Could this too happen to me?'.[29] Gitta Sereny, while interviewing Franz Stangl, developed an intense— if less focused— fear: 'in the weeks I worked with Stangl I barely slept; in the years afterwards, when I prepared and wrote *Into that Darkness*, a nightmare of harm coming to my young daughter—the kind of harm Stangl so graphically described to me—pursued me virtually every night'.[30] Froma Zeitlin writes that the 'haunted terrain' of the Holocaust is the 'one on which we ourselves continue to record, recall, re-vision and *re-enact*' (my italics) our responses.[31] Some people,

[24] Mary D. Langerwey, *Reading Auschwitz* (London: Sage, 1998), rear cover and preface.

[25] Dina Wardi, *Memorial Candles: Children of the Holocaust*, tr. Naomi Goldblum (London: Tavistock/Routledge, 1992), 4.

[26] Martin Gilbert, *Holocaust Journey: Travelling in Search of the Past* (London: Weidenfeld & Nicolson, 1997), 404.

[27] Gilbert, *Holocaust Journey*, 400–1. No searchlights remain, and the barracks are mostly ruins.

[28] Tim Cole, *Images of the Holocaust: The Myth of the 'Shoah Business'* (London: Duckworth, 1999), 161–2.

[29] Morris Wyszogrod, *A Brush with Death: An Artist in the Death Camps* (Albany, NY: State University of New York Press, 1999), 246.

[30] Gitta Sereny, *The German Trauma: Experiences and Reflections 1938–2000* (Harmondsworth: Allen Lane, 2000), 93.

[31] Froma I. Zeitlin, 'The Vicarious Witness: Belated Memory and Authorial Presence in Recent Holocaust Literature', *History and Memory*, 10/2 (1992), 5–42, 5.

Jewish and non-Jewish, claim that they are reincarnations of Holocaust victims: if no more, this certainly shows the strength of feeling about, and identification with, Holocaust victims.[32] Theodore Adorno, describing the 'recurring dreams' that plagued him, had the feeling that 'I am no longer really alive, but am just the emanation of a wish of some victim of Auschwitz.'[33]

These sorts of responses are not the result of a childish naivety. They are the result of the process of identification. Identification is, very simply, the way in which the reader or audience 'identifies' herself or himself with the textually created characters in the narrative. The boy in the fifth grade identifies with Levi in his story of himself, and confuses an action adventure for a testimony. The others—who know that life testimony is not an action adventure—still identify themselves, willingly or unwillingly, with or as victims. Levi writes that this shows the 'gap that exists and grows wider every year between things as they were down there and things as they are represented by the current imagination fed by approximate books, films and myths . . . I would like here to erect a dyke against this trend.' For Levi and for others, this is not simply an epistemological problem about other minds: it is an ethical concern. For Wiesel, Delbo, and others, it is both that identification *cannot* happen in any meaningful way ('a wall that cannot be pierced', a code that 'cannot be broken', all 'of those I met since I came back do not exist . . . They belong to another universe and nothing will allow them to rejoin ours') and that it *should not* happen. Levi continues: it is

part of our difficulty or inability to perceive the experience of others, which is all the more pronounced the further these experiences are from ours in time, space or quality. We are prone to assimilate them to those related ones, as though the hunger in Auschwitz were the same are that of someone who has skipped a meal, or as though escape from Treblinka were similar to an escape from any ordinary gaol.[34]

Through the process of identification, this incomprehensible event seems to become comprehensible and so—to import a word from a parallel debate in historiography—normalized, part of experience. Identification is not, *pace* the work of Dominick LaCapra, 'acting-out' leading to a 'working-through' precisely because it relies on the illicit

---

[32] See Yonassan Gershom, *Beyond the Ashes: Cases of Reincarnation from the Holocaust* (Virginia Beach, Va.: A. R. E. Press, 1992).

[33] Theodor Adorno, *Metaphysics: Concepts and Problems*, ed. Rolf Tiedemann, tr. Edmund Jephcott (Cambridge: Polity, 2000), 110.

[34] Levi, *The Drowned and the Saved*, 128.

and impossible grasping or comprehension of another's real and represented experience as one's own. However—and this is the seeming aporia to be discussed here—it is precisely the representation or mediation of experience, in the forms that seem to allow and encourage identification, that leads to this illicit comprehension, this grasping, of these experiences of survivors. This identification happens, despite a wish for them not to happen, because of basic assumptions about narratives and reading, because we expect identification to happen when we read prose narratives. In order to 'erect a dyke', or even only to understand what is happening, it is necessary not simply to dismiss identification as a 'childish naivety' but to explore the processes of identification.

IDENTIFICATION AND READING

> A book is not shut in by its contours, is not walled up as in a fortress. It asks nothing better than to exist outside itself, or to let you exist in it. In short, the extraordinary fact in the case of a book is the falling away of the barriers between you and it. You are inside it; it is inside you; there is no longer either outside or inside.[35]

While the process of identification is often considered to be naive, it seems to be the case that, for most people, even for those employed to read and teach literary and other prose narratives, identification is part of how and why we read: 'an embarrassingly ordinary process', one so common and taken for granted that critics often neglect to examine it, like the spectacles forgotten at the end of one's nose.[36] And, like these forgotten spectacles, it works best when it is not noticed. When it is cloying, mawkish, or over-heroic, or when readers find texts sexist or racist or unacceptable ('Am I that name?') a 'dissonance' appears.[37] Identifications can often fail to happen, by accident or by design, and

---

[35] Georges Poulet, 'Criticism and the Experience of Interiority', in Richard Macksey and Eugenio Donato (eds.), *The Language of Criticism and the Science of Man* (London: Johns Hopkins University Press, 1970), 57.

[36] Diana Fuss, *Identification Papers* (London: Routledge, 1995), 1. This will be abbreviated to *IP* in the text. An exception to this is the work of Karl Morrison: see e.g. his '*I am You': The Hermeneutics of Empathy in Western Theory, Literature and Art* (Princeton: Princeton University Press, 1988).

[37] See e.g. Denise Riley, '*Am I That Name?': Feminism and the Category of 'Women' in History* (Basingstoke: Macmillan, 1988).

are different from person to person, from text to text. Yet, when it works, as Diana Fuss writes, identifications 'are the origin of some of our most powerful, enduring and deeply felt pleasures . . . the source of considerable emotional turmoil, capable of unsettling or unmooring the precarious groundings of our everyday identities . . . Identifications are erotic, intellectual and emotional. They delight, fascinate, confuse, unnerve, and sometimes terrify' (*IP* 2). Identification is a central and major—but not always necessary—part of our experience of reading. Many critics pass over identification despite the fact that much contemporary work in literary studies is concerned with issues around the construction of identity—personal, political, and communal—which, in relation to reading, must be involved with the process of identification. In part, this is because much of the teaching of literature is—perhaps rightly—aimed at destroying precisely that comfortable sense of identification that reading can offer. This goes hand in hand with the movement of much of the canonically great literature of the twentieth century against both realism and the clearer encouragement to identify that realism offers.

Identification, like many processes that affect us deeply and personally, is also very hard to describe. It is clear that it happens, but not so clear why or how. It is not monolithic or concrete: acts of identification are complex and able to 'reverse and disguise themselves, to multiply and contravene each other, to disappear and to reappear years later' (*IP* 2). This is not to say that descriptions of identity formation are not useful: Judith Butler's basically Hegelian paradigm, for example, suggests that identity is constructed through parody of texts—literary, living—which is to say identity is a sort of parody. But this does not explain why or how it happens. These sorts of accounts do not explain how identification works, how it gets from text to subject, or how it has such power. Indeed, in perhaps the most likely place to find such an explanation, the discourse of psychoanalysis, Fuss finds the

psychoanalytic literature on identification . . . littered with taxonomic qualifiers that seek to identify, with greater and greater precision, modes and types of identifications: primary and secondary, feminine and masculine, imaginary and symbolic, maternal and paternal, idiopathic and hetereopathic, partial and total, centrifugal and centripetal, narcissistic and regressive, hysterical and melancholic, multiple and terminal, positive and negative. (*IP* 4)

Fuss goes on to suggest that this 'often incongruous proliferation of kinds of identification points to a theoretical difficulty psychoanalysis must routinely confront in laying hold of its object, a difficulty, that is in identifying identification' (*IP* 4).[38] Freud discusses introjection, imitation, and regression as the movement of identification; Abraham and Totok, too, discuss introjection and incorporation; the psychologist Theodore Reik expands this schema into a four-stage process through which a subject identifies with an object.[39] Mary Jacobus approaches these issues by using 'British object relations psychoanalysis, particularly the version of object relations theory associated with contemporary post-Kleinian thinking', aiming to explore 'the question of how things get, so to speak, from the outside to the inside—simultaneously establishing the boundary between them and seeming to abolish it'.[40] However, these terms and approaches offer no more than another description (often highly metaphorical, despite the seeming scientific intent) of this ordinary process in psychological or psychoanalytical language. Likewise, 'sympathy' and 'empathy' seem not to explicate this process: Thomas McCarthy discusses the scholarly debate over the terms and he concludes that the distinction between them is 'arbitrary' and focuses on

the central idea in both . . . that human beings are capable of understanding and responding feelingly to another person's experience, and what is important is not so much how this takes place cognitively and emotionally or the name we assign it, as that it can and does take place and that this interpersonal medium is the context for the ongoing creation of the self.[41]

While he argues that this 'must be understood as a historical, communicative and linguistic event', this does not explain how or why it happens.[42]

This process we cannot identify or explain clearly is extremely important: as Philippe Lacoue-Labarthe argues, identification is the

[38] Fuss argues that, though psychoanalysis has a specific interest in this, the issue is bought into psychoanalysis through the 'tradition of French Hegelianism' which 'provides a larger philosophical framework in which to understand psychoanalysis's continued interest in the problem of identification' (*IP* 4).

[39] Robert Katz, *Empathy: Its Nature and Uses* (London: Free Press of Glencoe, 1963). These stages are 'identification' where the subject 'drifts' into the object; 'incorporation' where the subject takes the experience as their own; 'reverberation', a 'concrete imaging of the other side without losing sight of one's own experience'; and finally 'detachment'. Ibid. 44.

[40] Mary Jacobus, *Psychoanalysis and the Scene of Reading* (Oxford: Oxford University Press, 1999), 9, 19.

[41] Thomas J. McCarthy, *Relations of Sympathy: The Writer and Reader in British Romanticism* (Aldershot: Scolar Press, 1997), 19.

[42] Ibid. 107.

only term 'we possess to designate what is at stake in the mimetic process' and has been at the heart of Western thinking about literature.[43] Plato, the most significant point of origin for thinking about literature, was well aware of the powers and dangers of identification. Among his reasons for banishing the poets in *The Republic*, Socrates argues that, since 'we soon reap the fruits of literature in life . . . prolonged indulgence in any form of literature leaves its mark on the moral nature of a man'.[44] Any literature that needs readers or performers to identify with 'women, young or old . . . women in sickness or love or childbirth . . . bad or cowardly characters . . . madmen . . . horses neighing or bulls bellowing' will be forbidden.[45] This is an admission of the power of identification in literature for good and bad. Later still, Socrates discusses how poetry is able to corrupt even the best and that the power of identification is so strong that it must be mastered by reason. While everybody in the audience is moved by the grief of characters on stage or in poetry, they should face up to these emotions and 'bear them in silence like men, and . . . regard the behavior we admired on the stage as womanish'.[46] (Identification is clearly gendered, too.) As its 'terrible power' seems unavoidable, Plato does not eschew identification. Rather, his dialogues are a form of theatre which teach moral enquiry by appealing to the intellect alone. Plato seems to want the readers and audience to learn to identify with—and so become like— the character he felt was the best: Socrates.[47]

Identification is central, in a different way, for Aristotle too. Catharsis is achieved through pity and fear: 'pity is aroused by someone who unreservedly falls into misfortune, and fear is evoked by our recognizing that it is someone like ourselves who encounters this misfortune'.[48] Much follows from this for Aristotle: the demand for dramatic unity, for example, stems from the need to follow the events that befall the key identified character. More than this, Martha

---

[43] Philippe Lacoue-Labarthe, *Heidegger, Art and Politics: The Fiction of the Political*, tr. Chris Turner (Oxford: Blackwell, 1990), 82.

[44] Plato, *The Republic*, tr. H. D. Lee (London; Penguin, 1955), 134.

[45] Ibid. 135. Plato's attitude to woman has been commented on many times: it is interesting how it emerges here over issues of identification.

[46] Ibid. 382.

[47] 'There is one man with whom all European philosophers identify, even if they reject all his ideas, and that man is Socrates; a philosopher who does not identify with this archetype does not belong to our civilization.' Leszek Kołakowski, *Metaphysical Horror*, ed. Agnieszka Kołakowska (London: Penguin, 2001), 1.

[48] Aristotle, 'On the Art of Poetry' in *Classical Literary Criticism*, tr. T. S. Dorsch (London: Penguin, 1965), 48.

Nussbaum—as a neo-Aristotelian philosopher—argues that identification is central for the moral significance of literature. Nussbaum suggests that readers identify with characters and, in a way, enact their stories. It is this enactment which generates the response that makes us people 'on who nothing is lost': more sensitive and able to respond to other people's pain and the moral demands placed on us. The text is an 'adventure of the reader', almost as if a text were an educational or therapeutic role-playing exercise.[49] For example, in one of her essays on *The Golden Bowl*, Nussbaum suggests that 'we carefully follow Maggie, seeing the world through her intelligent eyes'.[50] Nussbaum's work is an Aristotelian version of the idea that literature makes us more imaginative and sensitive, opens our eyes, and makes us aware of other people's points of view, an idea that underlies many central developments in the realist novel.

The issue of 'identification' and its power emerges with renewed force with the rise of the realist novel and the growth and popularity of the prose narrative in general. The debate between Richardson and Fielding, played out in the novels themselves, is over whether the novels' characters should model and so inspire (by identification) moral behaviour or show a range of behaviours and let the reader follow their own mind and judgement (that is, identify and praise whom they choose). For Barthes, novels of love, archetypally *Young Werther*, rely on identification: 'the hero is real (because he is created out of an absolutely projective substance in which every amorous subject collects himself)'. [51] The reality of this projection is what led to young men killing themselves out of love, identifying themselves (overmuch) with Werther. The corruptions of the novel lie behind the love affairs in Stendhal's *The Red and the Black*, as the daughters and wives strive to imitate the heroines about which they have read. Conversely, the narrating voice of George Eliot takes the reader to task for lacking sympathy and identification: just as readers of *Middlemarch* want to condemn Causabon, for example, or sigh angrily at Fred Vincy, the narrative voice warns us away from this and gives us their point of view. *Tout comprenner, tout pardonner.* At the novel's core is Dorothea's action of sympathetic compassion, an allegory, in the de Manian sense, of how readers should read the novel: readers should

---

[49] Martha Nussbaum, *Love's Knowledge: Essays on Philosophy and Literature* (Oxford: Oxford University Press, 1990), p. 143.   [50] Ibid. 144–5.

[51] Roland Barthes, *A Lover's Discourse*, tr. Richard Howard (London: Penguin, 1990), 219.

read in the sympathetic way Dorothea acts—we should be to all the characters (and everyone) the way Dorothea is to them. If only, the novel seems to imply, we could be like this all the time, how much nicer the world would be. Part of the work of the novelist—and especially the realist novelist— is the education of sympathy. Realism seems the easiest form in which this happens: but this does not mean that identification is unique to realism. The famous discussion between Henry James and Robert Louis Stevenson over the role and workings of fiction is specifically about identification.

Despite being at the centre of the Western experience of literature and reading, and described in a plethora of different ways, the process of identification is barely understood. Yet much rests on it: ideas about our enjoyment of literature in general and for many, such as Martha Nussbaum and Wayne Booth, the possibility of the moral power of literature. Centrally, in this context, identification is that against which Levi and others want to build a dyke: it is identification which leads to the illicit 'grasping' and 'assimilation' (to use Levi's word) of Holocaust survivor testimony. Survivors do not believe that they can or should be identified with, even through their testimony. Moreover, the process of identification underlies debates about the representation of the Holocaust. Discussions about the Holocaust in relation to form and media, over the idea of trauma and about imagery, circle around this process and seem to take it for granted.

IDENTIFICATION IN HOLOCAUST REPRESENTATION

Form

Debates over the form and media of testimony are based on issues of identification. In her influential article on testimony, Barbara Foley argues that narrative forms, whether fictional or historical, cannot describe or cover the depth of the experience of the Holocaust. She suggests that this is because the conventions of writing lead to the 'assimilation' of the Holocaust. Holocaust 'autobiography frequently furnishes an inadvertent parody of the conventional journey toward self-definition and knowledge', she argues, but 'the realist novel presupposes ethical humanist resolutions that are incommensurate with the totalitarian horrors of the text's represented world'.[52] For Foley the

---

[52] Barbara Foley, 'Fact, Fiction, Fascism: Testimony and Mimesis in Holocaust Narratives', *Comparative Literature*, 34 (1982), 330–60, 333.

generic conventions of memoirs and their usual teleologies prevent them conveying the incomprehensibility: in contrast, for example, a diary lacks a teleology and so seems gives the impression of being more historically true. She argues that it is the way in which Holocaust memoirists 'incorporate aspects of novelistic technique' into their representation that ensures the 'grounds of communication are established between writer and reader'.[53] One of the key principles of 'novelistic technique' is the creation of an identification which underlies, for example, a *Bildungsroman* or even a parody of one, whether it is, as Foley says, 'inadvertent' like *Night* or intentional like *The Red and the Black*. James Young pushes this argument further: he suggests that it is not, or not only, novelistic techniques or the stylization of art which makes the properly incomprehensible falsely comprehensible, but the nature of narrative itself. He suggests that 'violent events—perceived as aberration or ruptures in the cultural continuum—demand their retelling, their narration back into traditions and structures they would otherwise defy'.[54] However, on being put into a narrative, these events

necessarily re-enter the continuum, are totalised by it, and thus seem to lose their 'violent' quality. In as much as violence is 'resolved' in narrative, the violent event seems also to lose its particularity—i.e. its facthood—once it is written . . . .. once written events assume the mantle of coherence that narrative necessarily imposes on them, the trauma of their unassimilability is relieved.[55]

However, it is not the literary conventions *per se* (Foley) nor just the very effect of narrative itself in any form (Young) that makes it possible for readers to think they have grasped the experience the texts describe. Rather, this grasping itself—which lies behind narrative and literary conventions—relies on the process of identification, of taking the other as oneself.

Lawrence Langer is also very concious of this and offers another solution. Aware that written memoirs have a number of literary strategies available that make the description of events more familiar, less threatening, and so easier to assimilate, he argues that video testimonies evade these difficulties. Unlike reading, video testimonies are full of gaps and pauses, gestures, facial expressions, evidence of hesitation which foregrounds the 'incompatibility between the impromptu

---

[53] Ibid. 342.
[54] James Young, *Writing and Rewriting the Holocaust: Narrative and the Consequences of Interpretation* (Bloomington: Indiana University Press, 1990), 15.
[55] Ibid. 15–16.

self that endured atrocity and the self that sought reintegration into society after liberation', the conflict between the memories of who survivors were and who they are when giving testimony.[56] These 'principles of incoherence' mean that these testimonies are stripped of literary pretensions and a teleology: the 'raw material of oral Holocaust narratives, in content and manner of presentation, resist the organising impulse of moral theory and art . . . A kind of unshielded truth emerges from them, through which we salvage an anatomy of melancholy for the modern spirit.'[57] One of the distinctive qualities of oral testimony is its immediacy, its seeming lack of mediation.

This argument has been highly contentious, however. Geoffrey Hartman points out that, while TV and film are certainly different from verbal or literary media, they are still a medium, one that 'conveys the illusion not of making absent things more present but present things more present (than they are or can be)'.[58] Choices about filming and production, as well as the very existence of the medium as a medium, a form of representation and mediation, suggest that for all their seeming raw and unshielded qualities these video texts are still texts and not unmediated experience, as Dori Laub's analysis of witnessing these acts of testimony makes clear.[59] It is not so much literary conventions that mislead readers or audiences into grasping the events but the process of identification. Moreover, just as there are strategies that arise, both implicitly or explicitly, in written narratives, there may be strategies that arise in the verbal and filmed telling of testimonies, as yet not clearly understood, which (*pace* Foley and Young) lead to the assimilation of these texts. For example, Gadi BenEzer, in a study of the stories of Ethiopian Jews, noted thirteen recurring 'trauma signals', which implies that the ways in which they are retold will be bound up with specific cultural ideas and expectations and so suggests that there may be an unfocused and implicit way (or genre) of mediating trauma that supervenes on the nature of narrative and language itself, rather than being a conscious literary fashioning.[60] It seems questionable to

---

[56] Lawrence Langer, *Holocaust Testimonies: The Ruins of Memory* (London: Yale University Press, 1991), 148.

[57] Ibid. 204.

[58] Geoffrey Hartman, 'Tele-Suffering and Testimony in the Dot Com Era', in Barbic Zelizer (ed.), *Visual Culture and the Holocaust* (London: Athlone Press, 2001), 111–26, 111.

[59] Felman and Laub, *Testimony*, 57–92.

[60] See Gadi BenEzer, 'Trauma Signals in Life Stories', in Karnly Rogers *et al.* (eds.), *Trauma and Life Stories* (London: Routledge, 1999). The thirteen signals are: self-report (i.e. naming an event as traumatic, often focusing on one particular moment); a 'hidden'

suggest that video testimony offers a more immediate rather than different relation to the experience of the Holocaust. Video testimony, too, relies on identification.

Trauma

The issue of identification also underlies discussions of Holocaust texts as trauma. The term trauma originally only applied to actual physical wounds. Freud and others developed it as a metaphor to refer to psychic or mental wounds that they would, to some degree, cure just as doctors healed severe bodily damage. In turn, it has become a metaphor for the testimony texts survivors produce, and so a way of understanding them.

Judith Lewis Herman's influential *Trauma and Recovery* outlines the origin of the study of psychological trauma, from Freud and Breuer's studies of hysteria to the work on First World War shellshock to more recent studies on the effects of domestic and sexual violence. She argues that the 'core experiences of psychological trauma are disempowerment and disconnection from others'.[61] As a consequence, she suggests that all traumatic syndromes have basic features in common and the 'recovery process follows a common pathway' which involves 'establishing safety, reconstructing the trauma story, and restoring the connection between survivors and their community': a narrative of loss and return.[62] This narrative, with its insistence on the sense of the self in society is centrally to do with identity and identification, and 'how one is in the world'. However, the problems for discourses that attempt to utilize the idea of trauma for Holocaust testimonies are threefold.

First, as Langer writes, the 'clinical formula' of trauma 'will not serve the truth' of the survivors: their memories are not 'symptoms, nor in telling their tales do they seek some form of reintegration into their community—a goal that they have long since achieved'. More than this, he argues, 'forgetting would be the ultimate desecration, a "cure" the ultimate illusion'.[63] Testimonies are not, or are not simply, part of

event (not narrated at first but which emerges during discussion); long silence; loss of emotional control; emotional detachment or numbness; repetitive reporting; losing oneself in the traumatic event; intrusive images; forceful argumentation of conduct within an event; cognitive–emotional disorientation; inability to tell a story at all; changes in voice; changes in body language.

[61] Judith Lewis Herman, *Trauma and Recovery* (London: Routledge, 1992), 155.
[62] Ibid. 3.
[63] Lawrence Langer, *Preempting the Holocaust* (London: Yale University Press, 1998), 68.

a talking cure.[64] Second, the misapplication of therapeutic terms to the understanding of literary texts involves the placing of a framework of interpretation meant for people onto a series of generic strategies, representations, and mediations. Noticing that trauma theory picks up on a lexicon of 'trauma, transference, melancholia, mourning and working-through', Kerwin Lee Klein writes that these

preferred terms come from those sections of the tradition most closely identified with Freud's vision of psychoanalysis as an empirical science and a medical treatment of ill individuals. But Freud's therapeutic discourse was also his most redemptive, and stressing the therapeutic Freud loads some of the weakest seams in psychoanalysis, for 'talking cure' moves away from Freudian tradition as cultural hermeneutics toward psychiatry as a medical science, and clinical efficacy is not a place where psychoanalysis has covered itself in glory.[65]

Trauma theory offers not only misapplied science but also an illusory redemption. To go further, one might argue that trauma in this redemptive sense—wounding followed by recovery—is essentially comic: testimony texts are not. Third, using these terms can, in fact, risk stripping any agency from the survivor, revictimizing the survivor as (only) a traumatized victim. Since these testimony texts described as traumatic are, in no small part, about the conflict between agency and lack of agency (some even to the point of assuming—incorrectly—an unfair amount of choice and so blame: Olga Lengyel begins by blaming herself for the 'destruction of my own parents and of my two small sons'), this secondary stripping of agency seems dubious, to say the least.[66] This risk seems to betray the good intentions inherent in the use of 'trauma' as a concept in understanding testimonies.

Arguing that trauma is 'not so much a symptom of the unconscious as it is a symptom of history', Caruth warns that the 'crucial problem'

---

[64] This does not meant that analysis or therapy might not be a vital tool for reducing the pain that survivors feel: it is rightly and completely beyond my purview to suggest something like this. My comments are only about the ways that testimonies are understood. For discussion of this, see the work of survivor and novelist Ka-Tzetnik 135633 (Yehiel De-Nur), who testified at the Eichmann trial and underwent therapy in Holland with the supervised use of LSD with Professor Jan Bastiaans. His account of this is *Shivitti: A Vision*, tr. Eliyah Nike De-Nur and Lisa Herman (San Francisco: Harper Row, 1989). On this, see also Omer Bartov, *Mirrors of Destruction: War, Genocide and Modern Identity* (Oxford: Oxford University Press, 2000), 202 ff.

[65] Kerwin Lee Klein, 'On the Emergence of Memory in Historical Discourse', *Representations*, 69 (2000), 127–50, 141.

[66] Olga Lengyl, *Five Chimneys* (London: Panther, 1959), 1.

is 'how to help relieve suffering, and how to understand the nature of the suffering, without eliminating the force and truth of the reality that trauma survivors face and quite often try to transmit to us'.[67] In terms of dealing with survivor testimony (and not, I stress, of attempting to relieving the pain of survivors), it seems mistaken to fuse the suffering with its representation: to respond to the 'force and truth' of testimony is one needful thing, to respond to the pain of survivors is another, equally needful thing. The risk seems to be that the term trauma (already twice metaphorical), if it is invoked with all the rest of the analytic and therapeutic tools, will overcode the accounts of the Holocaust with a discourse of healing analysis or therapy, and so pass over both the epistemological and ethical impossibility of comprehending the survivors' testimony by seeming to grasp and resolve it, and 'work through' or finish with the ethical obligation to recall the events. To read testimonies as traumatic texts is to identify with them, perhaps in a sophisticated way, and then wrongly to resolve, assimilate, or normalize them—to make their 'troubles . . . as a drop of rain in the sea'.[68]

Imagery

Debates over form and media and over the use of an analytic vocabulary to engage with testimony invoke ideas of identification implicitly. However, this tension between the impossibility of identification and the seemingly ineluctable identification that stems from mediation comes clearly to the fore in a brief exchange between Norma Rosen and Michael Bernstein over Holocaust imagery. Rosen, a novelist and critic, is well aware of the power of narrative to create identifications, both for ourselves and for others. In her 1987 essay 'The Second Life of Holocaust Imagery', she writes that we 'cannot see a full grown retarded man without thinking of Faulkner's Benjy . . . ; cannot see a poor storekeeper staying open long empty hours without remembering Malamud's Morris Bober in *The Assistant*'.[69] For her, this is not simply the result of too much reading but part of our humanity, as 'an analogy making species': 'What we connect and how we connect it are

[67] Cathy Caruth, *Trauma: Explorations in Memory* (London: Johns Hopkins University Press, 1995), 5, vii.

[68] Herman, *Trauma and Recovery*, 236.

[69] Norma Rosen, *Accidents of Influence: Writing as a Woman and a Jew in America* (Albany, NY: State University of New York Press, 1992), 49.

vital keys to our understanding and can be discussed and at times cor-
rected. That we connect is a given.'[70] She continues

One of our human goals, we are frequently reminded, is to try to understand
the suffering of others. Sympathised with, yes, but can someone else's suffering
be felt? The answer is obvious. Anyone's suffering can be understood and felt
only through one's own suffering. But what if one's own suffering, terrible as
it is, does not approach the sufferings of another? Then the law of human communication is unchanged. We must still work from what we know and try to
connect it to what we do not.

This means that

for a mind engraved with the Holocaust, gas is always that gas. Shower means
their shower. Ovens are those ovens. A train is a freight car crammed with suf-
focating children: it arrives at the suburban station in a burst of power and
noise, there is a moment of hideous hallucination that is really only remembering, and then one steps into the train and opens a newspaper . . . Such images .
. . continue to come unbidden to the mind.[71]

Like the examples cited at the beginning of the chapter, she identifies
with victims and survivors through their accounts, both through choice
and through an uncontrollable compulsion.[72] The issue is not that the
Holocaust is, as it were, in the forefront of her mind (as Jacques
Derrida said in an interview, 'I think that today nothing at all can be
burnt, not even a love-letter, without thinking about the Holocaust'),
but that she understands this through the process of identification.[73]

   Alan Berger writes of this: 'is there not a real danger in trying to
appropriate for oneself symbols of an experience that the witnesses

---

[70] Rosen, *Accidents of Influence* 50.

[71] Ibid. 50, 52. For another, more positive reading of this same sentence, see James
Berger, *After the End: Representations of the Post-Apocalypse* (London: University of
Minnesota Press, 1999), 230–1.

[72] The identification process for Rosen stems from a very profound experience: an
identification with a photograph of a Jewish boy, sent to her parents, in the hope that
they would be able to shelter him from the Nazis in the US. It was not possible, the 'photo
was put away somewhere. The boy no doubt died somewhere else.' ('Notes toward a
Holocaust Fiction', in *Accidents of Influence*, 110). Again, this is to stress the power and
importance of identification.

[73] Cited Gideon Ofrat, *The Jewish Derrida*, tr. Peretz Kidron (Syracuse, NY: Syracuse
University Press, 2001), 152.. It is from an interview in Hebrew in *Teoria Vebikoret*, 15
(1999), 5–17. Because it is an interview, it is impossible to tell whether the 'H' in
Holocaust is meant to be capitalized: Derrida usually does not capitalize it (see
Ch. 10).

themselves contend is beyond the imagination?'[74] Indeed, Rosen is the source of the phrase 'Witness through the Imagination'.[75] Michael Bernstein goes further: he suggests that Rosen's position is 'an extra-ordinarily misplaced and even pernicious response'.[76] Despite her qualifications, he writes, 'it is difficult to read the text and rhetoric of the whole passage [cited above] except as symptomatic of an almost clinically excessive identification with the suffering of others'.[77] While Bernstein is acutely aware of the 'affective force of identification', he argues—in an article that develops the phrase 'witness through the imagination' into 'witness by adoption'—that 'no amount of empathy can make one a witness to events at which one was not present': such identifications are simply not possible.[78] The desire to 'witness through the imagination' is linked, for Bernstein, with the idea that texts are unmediated and the idea that reading a testimony is, in some way, the same as actually being there. He writes:

one of the most pervasive myths of our era, a myth perhaps partially arising out of our collective response to the horrors of the concentration camps, is the absolute authority given to first person testimony. Such narratives . . . are habitually regarded as though they were completely unmediated, as though language, gesture and imagery could become transparent if the experience expressed is sufficiently horrific.[79]

He goes on to describe the ways in which all texts are mediated and shaped: by conscious or unconscious desires on behalf of the testifier, for example, or by fitting or being fitted into the 'specific ideological/narrative framework'—what Young calls the 'epistemolo-gical climate in which they existed'—of the writer or readers.[80] Not only is he 'deeply sceptical about both its intrinsic plausibility' but he also argues that its 'cultural consequences' are questionable: ' "testi-monies through emotional identification" inevitably merge into the

---

[74] Alan Berger, 'Theological Implications of Second Generation Literature', Efraim Sicher (ed.), in *Breaking Crystal: Writing and Memory after Auschwitz* (Chicago: University of Illinois Press, 1998), 251–74, 256.

[75] Rosen, *Accidents of Influence*, 107. For its use, see, e.g. Lillian Kremer, *Witness through the Imagination* (Detroit: Wayne State University Press, 1989).

[76] Michael André Bernstein, *Foregone Conclusions: Against Apocalyptic History* (London: University of California Press, 1994), 54.

[77] Ibid. 54.

[78] Ibid. 49. Michael André Bernstein, 'Unspeakable No More', *Time Literary Supplement* (3 Mar. 2000), 7–8, 8.

[79] Bernstein, *Foregone Conclusions*, 47.

[80] Ibid. 49. See: Young, *Writing and Rewriting*, 26.

general clamour of a culture that is only just beginning to question the revelatory power of the catastrophic and the extreme'.[81]

In contrast to this, Michael Bernard-Donals and Richard Glejzer in *Between Witness and Testimony* offer an opposite yet, in its very opposition, an oddly similar view to Rosen. Arguing that 'there is no sense in which any testimony can adequately describe either the lives that preceded the disaster or the disaster itself', they deny any possible identification.[82] Instead, a work from or about the Holocaust, like Abraham Lewin's diary, does not shed light on the events but rather 'forces open those worlds we might imagine' and opens 'a confrontation with what the human mind can and cannot do'.[83] However, it is precisely the total inability to identify, the 'nonknowledge' that these texts create, that makes them 'redemptive', in that in what they 'cannot say . . . we see the disaster as it affects us individually, as it destroys the narratives and the memories we have created to contain both our "selves" and the name of the Shoah'.[84] The moment of 'redemption, the process of releasing the divine spark and human ethical and creative activity' occurs at the seemingly sublime moment of the absolute impossibility of identification.[85] So, it is precisely because 'for a mind engraved with the Holocaust', the gas is always *not* that gas, the shower, *not* their shower that 'redemption' is possible. This opposite approach to Rosen's still valorizes the idea and the moment of identification, and—just as Rosen's moments offer an over-identification and so some sense of fulfilment—so these 'anti-identifications' offer redemption.[86]

Bernstein's powerful argument against the valorization of identification, and Levi's which lies behind it, is right in that texts are mediated and untroubled identification is highly questionable: there are no real 'witnesses through the imagination'. However, Rosen's argument, those accounts of the centrality of identification such as Nussbaum's, as well as the examples given at the beginning of the chapter, are symptomatic of something profound and powerful: that identification does happen when we read, that it is a potent and—espe-

[81] Bernstein, 'Unspeakable No More', 8.

[82] Michael Bernard-Donals and Richard Glejzer, *Between Witness and Testimony: The Holocaust and the Limits of Representation* (Albany, NY: SUNY Press, 2001), 21.

[83] Bernard-Donals and Glejzer, *Between Witness and Testimony*, 47.

[84] Ibid. 173, 47.   [85] Ibid. 8.

[86] LaCapra makes a similar point: 'Unproblematic identification—more generally, a binary logic of identity and difference—furthers victimisation, including at times the constitution of the self as surrogate victim.' Dominick LaCapra, *Writing History, Writing Trauma* (London: Johns Hopkins University Press, 2001), 219.

cially in the case of Rosen—sincere force. Despite the impossibility of understanding, and the admonitions made against identifying with the victims, Holocaust testimonies are read and the readers do identify with narrators and other characters, precisely because that is what they expect to do in reading. In order to resolve this, it is necessary to rethink what we understand reading to be, to show that, in the case of testimony, this sort of reading as identification, as comprehension, is deeply problematic.

THE GENRE OF TESTIMONY

This seeming aporia—the epistemological impossibility and ethical probation against identification with a prose narrative, which is textual and mediated, against the ineluctable desire to identify with it, as if it were neither textual nor mediated—is resolved by thinking through the idea of context, best understood here as genre. David Trotter describes the way in which texts demand a 'secret complement' which calls 'on the reader to supply information from his or her own experience'.[87] But genre is not simply 'information' that 'complements' reading: it is a way of describing how reading actually takes place. Peter Middleton and Tim Woods argue that texts and genre are the 'key sites of literariness . . . where literary production is not reducible to algorithms of language and cannot be dissolved into wider historical matrices'.[88] They argue that use of the term as pejorative is mistaken since even

the most innovative writing presupposes many generic reading and distribution practices. Equally, the most production-line generic text may sometimes test the limits of genre and reformulate them tentatively, because genre is remade by every instance of its use. Like language, it exists only as practices, and its codes are no more than partially articulated recognition of its sedimented forms.[89]

Centrally, however, they suggest that genre is

too often treated as a formalism, as if it were no more than a form of prosody that could be copied out of a manual. It is better thought of as a code of practise constantly under negotiation between texts and their readers, listeners,

[87] David Trotter, *The Making of the Reader* (London: Macmillan, 1984), 14.
[88] Peter Middleton and Tim Woods, *Literatures of Memory: History, Time and Space in Postwar Writing* (Manchester: Manchester University Press, 2000), 7.
[89] Ibid. 8.

publishers, academics and reviewers, which advises them how they are expected to respond to the text.[90]

Thus, genre is not just a way of writing: it is a way of reading, too. It is where reading and writing meet. Genre—with all its signs, both textual and extra or meta-textual—forms a horizon of expectations which illuminates (or conversely can cover over) texts. Genre is the context of a work that, as it were, both frames it and makes it comprehensible 'externally' and gives it a shape 'internally'. Works are suffused by context, by genre and there are no texts outside genre. And this is the significance of Wiesel's remark about the Holocaust inventing 'a new literature, that of testimony': not that prior to his generation there were no personal accounts of events, but that Holocaust testimony needs to be understood as a new genre, in a new context, which involves both texts and altered ways of reading, standing in its own right. Texts often precede genres, are untimely, and so are understood in different ways. I suggest that much is 'encoded' in Holocaust testimonies that needs to be recognized in new ways. This idea of a new genre—which is not, as the citation from Wiesel suggests, a new idea—means that it is necessary to think about how our ways of reading tend to assimilate texts. To focus on the meaning of genre in relation to testimony texts is, in this way, to draw into significance the generic context, with its inherent and constantly developing practices, codes, and specific relation to issues of the past, the status of the author as witness, of memory and the writing of history, of the relation of form and content, of ethics and ways of reading, each changing with each particular text. This is a dizzying list, suitable in its breadth to thinking through a new genre: here I discuss only the processes and expectations of identification.

Where fiction utilizes, not exclusively but largely, the process of identification, the genre of testimony both in its texts and—this is a crucial step—in the basis for interpreting and reading those texts rejects identification. When critics write that, for example, the 'human imagination after Auschwitz is simply not the same as before', this is so in no small part because the process of identification in reading has been changed.[91] This is why testimony is not pleasurable to read: it rejects the pleasures of identification. This, too, is a sign of it being a different genre. The difference between testimony and fiction is at this

---

[90] Middleton and Woods, *Literatures of Memory*, 7.
[91] Alvin Rosenfeld, *A Double Dying; Reflections on Holocaust Literature* (Bloomington: Indiana University Press, 1988), 13.

very basic level. The attempt by testimony texts to refuse the very strong and often taken-for-granted power of identification is a key 'nuts and bolts' part of the 'strangeness' of testimony that Felman and Laub highlight.[92] The genre prohibits readings that identify and so consume the testimonies and this generic prohibition is how, following Levi, a 'dyke' is erected against this, even though it is often broken.

Felman and Laub suggest that this 'dyke' is erected in part by the way texts themselves 'perform' testimony: thus the importance of Celan's poetry which by 'disrupting any unity, integrity or continuity of conscious meaning' enacts the 'breakdown'.[93] However, this seems first to limit the work of testimony to texts that are formally avant-garde or self-consciously innovative or estranging in literary terms, like Semprun's and Delbo's modernist testimonies or Alina Bacall-Zwirn and Jared Stark's postmodern testimony. In fact, most testimonies—the most famous, perhaps—are clearly not like this. Most testimonies are conventionally written as realist texts, since survivors 'take their bearings from the realistic style of the nineteenth century, in the belief that this is best suited to what they have to communicate'.[94] Moreover, this position seems to ignore the fact that even the most obscure and avant-garde texts become standards: even Celan's poetry, with enough familiarity, could become 'normalized'. However, the idea of testimony as a genre implies engaging with the significance of each testimony's textuality regardless of its form. It brings with it the harder task of reading the performance of testimony—and continuing to uncover it—in each act of testimony, however 'banal' or realist it appears to be.

[92] Felman and Laub, *Testimony*, 7.

[93] Ibid. 37. On this, see also Walter Benn Michaels, ' "You Who Was Never There": Slavery and the New Historicism—Deconstruction and the Holocaust', in Hilene Flanzbaum (ed.), *The Americanisation of the Holocaust* (London: Johns Hopkins University Press, 1999), 181–97.

[94] Reiter, *Narrating the Holocaust*, 193. However, this view itself may be open to question, as it implies that realism is what its critics claim it to be, a form that writes or claims to write the objective truth. In fact, as recent work on realism has argued, no realist novelists 'were deluded into believing that they were in fact offering an unmediated realit . . .. Despite its appearance of solidity, realism implies a fundamental unease about self, society and art . . .. Realists take upon themselves a special role as mediator, and assume self-consciously a moral burden that takes a special form: their responsibility is to a reality that increasing seems "unnameable".' Indeed, far from a 'solidly self-satisfied vision based in a misguided objectivity and faith in representation . . . [realism is a] as highly self conscious attempt to explore or create a new reality. Its massive self-confidence implied a radical doubt, its strategies of truth telling a profound self-consciousness.' George Levine, *The Realist Imagination: English Fiction from Frankenstein to Lady Chatterly* (Chicago; University of Chicago Press, 1981), 8, 12, 20.

To understand testimony as a genre it is necessary to look at the radical doubt and the self-consciousness of each of these texts, to read them with an eye to gaps, shifts, breaks, and ruptures, which show how they are not, in any simple way, easily consumed. To read these texts as testimonies, to read the genre, is to refuse the identification that Rosen believes in as a 'witness through the imagination' as it refuses to let the text itself disappear in an act of identification.

To understand testimony like this has something in common with Michael Rothberg's concept of 'traumatic realism'—an 'attempt not to reflect the traumatic event mimetically but to produce it as an object of knowledge and to transform its readers so that they acknowledge their relationship to posttraumatic culture'.[95] However, the genre of testimony need not be—as 'traumatic realism' is—a hybrid of realism, modernism, and postmodernism, but, more simply, a genre that stands as it is, with its own questions, problems, and issues. Moreover, it utilizes a widely accepted, if hazily understood, term: 'testimony' is both familiar and unfamiliar, uncanny. Finally, and perhaps most importantly, to see testimony in this way, as a new genre, seems most importantly in this context to bring to the fore and focus—for we who come afterwards— the intuitions of survivors and writers of testimony.

The title of Levi's book, *If This is a Man*, comes from a poem—the epigraph to the book, variously titled 'If this is a man' and 'Shemá'—which asks a question about identification. Do we, 'who live safe | In . . . warm houses', consider that one 'Who dies because of a yes or a no' is a man, is like us? Can we, 'who find, returning in the evening | Hot food and friendly faces', identify one 'without hair and without name | With no more strength to remember' as a woman, like ourselves? Levi does not answer his questions and says only that we should 'Meditate that this came about'. Significantly, he refuses to let an identification take place: a wall is erected—or rather, remains—between those in the camps and those outside. Levi demands that we remember these words, curses us if we fail to 'Carve them' in our hearts. Gillian Banner argues that this 'injunction and command' to remember, 'not as a passive act but as a vigorous engagement with the present', is at the core of Levi's work.[96] It is significant that we should remember the *words*, not the victims: it is a reminder that we cannot identify with, be as one with,

[95] Michael Rothberg, *Traumatic Realism: The Demands of Holocaust Representation* (London: University of Minnesota Press, 2000), 140.
[96] Gillian Banner, *Holocaust Literature: Schulz, Levi, Spiegleman and the Memory of the Offence* (London: Valentine Mitchell, 2000), 126.

the victims. As Raul Hilberg writes, the 'words that are . . . written take the place of the past; these words, rather than the events themselves, will be remembered'. He continues: 'Were this transformation not a necessity, one could call it presumptious, but it is unavoidable.'[97] To understand testimonies as a genre in their own right is to play a part in erecting a dyke against their easy consumption. Specifically, it means denying the possibility of identification. It is this sort of reading and the texts that inspire it that marks out testimony as a genre. In the next chapter, I will look at precisely those aspects of testimonies that refute and complicate identification by looking at gaps, shifts, breaks, and ruptures: at the way in which this genre is already encoded in its texts.

---

[97] Raul Hilberg, *The Politics of Memory* (Chicago: Ivan R. Dee, 1996), 83.

2

Traces of Experience:
The Texts of Testimony

If no story is possible after Auschwitz, there remains, nonetheless, a duty to speak, to speak endlessly for those who could not speak because to the very end they wanted to safeguard true speech against betrayal. To speak in order to bear witness. But how? How can testimony escape the idyllic law of the story? How can one speak of the 'unimaginable' . . . without having recourse to the imaginary. And if, as Robert Antelme says, literary artfulness alone can overcome the inevitable incredulity, is testimony not impaired by the introduction, with fiction, of attraction and seduction, where 'truth' alone ought to speak?[1]

INTRODUCTION

Sarah Kofman suggests that speaking of the 'unimaginable' is an aporia. At the end of the previous chapter, I argued that it may be possible to go beyond this by understanding works of testimony as a new genre. These texts, these representations and mediations of experience, have their own generic rules and raise their own specific questions about issues such as authorship and witness, history, interpretation, and form. Perhaps some of these generic rules stem from the nature of these experiences and are chosen, consciously or unconsciously, by the authors: some, certainly, stem from the cultural milieu in which they are written. One of the most important characteristics of this genre was to do with identification. Many forms of prose writing encourage identification and while testimony cannot but do this, it at the same time aims to prohibit identification, on epistemological grounds

---

[1] Sarah Kofman, *Smothered Words*, tr. Madeleine Dobere (Evanston, Ill.: Northwestern University Press, 1998), 36.

(a reader really cannot become, or become identified, with the narrator of a testimony: any such identification is a illusion) and on ethical grounds (a reader should not become identified with a narrator of a testimony, as it reduces and 'normalizes' or consumes the otherness of narrator's experience and the illusion that such an identification creates is possibly pernicious).

This 'doubleness' is central to the genre of testimony: the texts lead to identification and away from it simultaneously. This stress between centrifugal and centripetal forces is played out, but not resolved, in the texts of testimonies and it is this that characterizes the genre of testimony. It is this understanding of testimony as a genre that answers, in part, Langer's complaint that these prose texts fail to represent the Holocaust because literate 'readers can eventually work their way through the pages of a book, no matter what the theme, because the form and style of the narrative are designed to make us complicit with the text'.[2] It is precisely the generic characteristics of testimony, properly approached, that should prevent readers from becoming 'complicit' with the text.

Although the meta-textual 'conventions'—the status of the author and the 'autobiographical pact' (which itself is only a way of recognizing the genre in the first place), for example—are extremely important, many of the characteristics of the genre are encoded in the textual form and content. The aim of this chapter is to examine those textual, and to a lesser extent meta-textual, characteristics of testimonies that disrupt the process of identification. It looks at those tropes and textual strategies under six headings: the textual use of historical evidence and style, the narrative framing, a focus on moments of horror, the way the texts interrupt or disrupt their own flow, moments of excessive over-identification, and the lack of closure in testimony. These headings are not meant to be final or conclusive, or a complete taxonomy, but rather only to point out some textual signs of the genre of testimony.

USING HISTORY

The genre of testimony clearly has a relationship with the discipline of history. Much work has been done on the ways in which historians

---

[2] Lawrence Langer, *Holocaust Testimonies: The Ruins of Memory* (London: Yale University Press, 1991), 16.

draw on, use, and judge testimonies (although, as I argue below, testimonies are not simply works of history, or resources for historians). In turn, many testimonies use history. While most testimony narratives follow an autobiographical chronology, several have moments where the flow of narrative stops and the text, in its style or content, becomes 'historical', offering descriptive history or reportage. Several use historical documents or sourced evidence.

Style

Despite the 'incredible' events it describes, David Rousset's very early Marxist-influenced testimony *L'Univers concentrationnaire* (1946) is not at all surreal in form as is sometimes claimed. It is a realist 'report' on the 'depths of the camps': a historical overview mixed with personal observations. Chapter 5 (ironically titled 'In my father's house there are many mansions') offers a breakdown of the camp system from a Marxist point of view: 'Buchenwald was a chaotic city . . . by virtue of its proletariat . . . and by reason of its swarming officials, its capitalists, its underworld.'[3] The next chapter offers an analysis of the different nationalities in the camps—Soviets, Poles, Greeks, Dutch, Czechs, French, and so on. Neftali Frankel's *I Survived Hell: The Testimony of a Survivor of the Nazi Extermination Camps (Prisoner Number 161040)* is all written in this dry and impersonal 'historical' style.[4] Frankel's testimony is the account of his life in Tarnow before the war, his imprisonment in Auschwitz, and then his survival of a death march to Bergen Belsen. It concludes with his immigration to the US and finally to Mexico. Kitty Hart interrupts the chronology of her second testimony, *Return to Auschwitz*, with a chapter called 'The Final Solution', which outlines the history and development of the persecution of the Jews and of the Auschwitz camp from the 1920s to the Holocaust.[5] This book, like many others, not only has personal photos of her family, but also documentary photos of Auschwitz. Olga Lengyel also has a documentary section, complete with a table of those 'liquidated'.[6] These moments serve to foreground the historical in the testimonies.

[3] David Rousset, *A World Apart*, tr. Yvonne Mayse and Roger Senhouse (London: Secker & Warburg, 1951), 22–3.
[4] Neftali Frankel with Roman Palazon Bertra, *I Survived Hell: The Testimony of a Survivor of the Nazi Extermination Camps (Prisoner Number 161040)* (New York: Vintage Press, 1991).
[5] Kitty Hart, *Return to Auschwitz* (London: Panther, 1983), 111–27.
[6] Olga Lengyl, *Five Chimneys* (London: Panther, 1959), 82

Historical Documentation

Other testimonies insert other sorts of texts into their narratives. After a reflective epilogue, Rudolph Vrba's testimony has two appendices. The first of these is the sworn affidavit, placed and dated, that he submitted to the Eichmann trial. The common UK edition of Levi's *If This is a Man* ends with letters from German readers to him. The final pages of Judith Magyar Isaacson's *Seed of Sarah: Memoirs of a Survivor* describe Isaacson's visits to Hessen, the work camp she had been taken to after Auschwitz, and her thoughts about forgiveness. It ends with some letters to her family and finally a collection of sources. These 'historical' sections, inserted to tie the text more into wider accounts of the past, also prevent or disrupt simple identification by interrupting the narrative flow and by making clear to the reader that this particular story is part of a huge event.

Grammar

However, these sorts of interruptions do not just occur to offer a broad historical sweep. They occur at much smaller levels and (in English translations) are often shown by a shift in tense from the perfect to the pluperfect, or from a particular event to a general or repeated event. Primo Levi is perhaps the most famous exponent of this. His testimony carries not only the narrative of his time Auschwitz but also various excursuses which describe not events in a narrative sequence, but general events that illustrate his time in Auschwitz. But this also happens in other accounts. For example, describing an SS man, Moll, in charge of the Sonderkommando, Müller shifts from his quite strict chronology to more general comments: 'Intellectuals, a sizable number of whom were members of the Sonderkommando, were among the frequent victims of Moll's perverted tortures . . . Another unusual entertainment in which he would indulge every now and then was called swim-frog . . . yet another game in Moll's repertoire was called brick-bashing.'[7] Again, these grammatical dislocations of narrative flow serve to disconnect the reader from identification.

---

[7] Filip Müller, *Eyewitness Auschwitz: Three Years in the Gas Chamber*, with Helmut Freitag, tr. Susanne Flatouer (Chicago: Ivan R. Dee, 1979), 142.

History in Reverse

These strategies, based on using historical evidence, which aim to depersonalize a testimony and stress that it is not simply an adventure story, have an opposite on which many testimonies rely. In most realist fiction, the readers echo the characters in not knowing what is going to happen: the reader and the character experience the events at the same time. In Holocaust testimonies, of course, the reader knows the events—at least in broad outline—and knows also that the narrator survives them. This leads in many cases to heavy and horrid irony. Olga Lenygel:

We tramped past a charming forest on the outskirts of which stood a red brick building. Great flames belched from the chimney, and the strange sickening sweetish odour which had greeted us upon arrival, attacked us even more powerfully now . . . We asked one of the guides, an old inmate, about this structure. 'It is a camp "bakery" she replied'. We absorbed that without the slightest suspicion. Had she revealed the truth we would not have believed her.[8]

Kitty Hart writes: 'there was a sickly, fatty cloying smell. Mother and I glanced at each other, baffled. Who could be roasting meat, great quantities of it, at this hour of the morning?'[9]

This irony is often heightened in those testimonies that do not begin at the point of arrival in the camps but with the pre-war world. Daniel Schwarz argues that Moshé the Beadle in Wiesel's *Night*, who warns the Jews of Sighet of their fate over a year before they are deported, is a metonymy for Wiesel himself, in his role as survivor who has 'miraculously escaped': 'he is urging us that it is our ethical responsibility not to turn away from the witnessing voice'.[10] This is insightful, but the figure of Moshé also serves as reminder to readers that they know what has happened and that the Jews of Sighet do not, that there is a rubicon of knowledge over which it is impossible to return, a point also made and remade by Charlotte Delbo. In occupied Warsaw, the father of Morris Wyszogrod believed that 'in the worst case, we would get ration cards and have to do forced labour'.[11] 'They expect the worst—not the unthinkable.'[12] Edith Hahn Beer described her life in Vienna in the

---

[8] Lengyl, *Five Chimneys*, 33–4.   [9] Hart, *Return to Auschwitz*, 79.
[10] Daniel Schwarz, *Imagining the Holocaust* (New York: St Martin's Griffin, 1999), 50.
[11] Morris Wyszogrod, *A Brush with Death: An Artist in the Death Camps* (Albany, NY: State University of New York Press, 1999), 31.
[12] Charlotte Delbo, *Auschwitz and After*, tr. Rosette C. Lamont (London: Yale University Press, 1995), 4. This will be abbreviated in the text to *AA*.

1930s and says that 'I cultivated blindness the way my grandmother grew cactus in Stockerau. It was the wrong plant for this climate.'[13] In these cases, the gap between what the narrator and audience knows and what the 'characters' know serves to make identification harder. This means that while the reader is distanced from the 'character'— there is no pleasure of anticipation, for example, and limited involvement—they are drawn to the narrator, their guide: the difficulty is, of course, that the 'narrator' and the 'character' are the same. Thus, again, there is the 'doubleness' of testimony, which both repels and attracts identification. When foreshadowing occurs in fiction Michael André Bernstein calls it 'apocalyptic history': the assumption of a fixed and inevitable historical universe, leading inexorably to the Holocaust. But, he writes, the

> intrusion of foreshadowing, the network of portentous signs that signal the future of the characters and their world, is particularly deceptive because it is based on the shared familiarity of a known outcome . . . . To write about their forms of communal life, knowing that the Jews of Vienna's 'golden age' were doomed, and then to blame them for not having realised it themselves in time to escape, is to attribute a far greater clarity and monologic shrillness to contemporary warning signs than they actually warranted.[14]

However, in the pathos of a testimony account, this 'apocalyptic history' works to distance the reader's ability to 'feel themselves into' the witnesses' testimony.

NARRATIVE FRAMES

Another strategy that serves to distance the reader from the text and prevent or problematize identification is a the choice of narrative frame. Many (often ghost-written) testimonies begin with short 'in medias res' vignettes which plunge the reader into the narrative: Fénelon singing at her liberation at Bergen Belsen, Vrba with Himmler's visit to Auschwitz, Frister with an account of losing both his father and his bread, Beer with an account of being disguised as a nurse in a German hospital. This tactic, of course, grabs the attention and

---

[13] Edith Hahn Beer with Susan Dworkin, *The Nazi Officer's Wife* (London: Perennial, 2000), 26.

[14] Michael André Bernstein, *Forgone Conclusions: Against Apocalyptic History* (London: University of California Press, 1994), 30.

draws the reader into the work. However, in contrast to this, some testimonies help preserve distance by framing the narrative in different ways. These different frames serve to put the author and witness (with or without a ghost writer) clearly 'on the other side' of the testimony. Where some authors in fiction efface themselves from the text or use the authorial persona in the text, the special case of the author function of the witness/author is to guarantee the text by stressing their own relation to it. That is, it is their narrative: not them, but a narrative by and about them.

Described Frames

Judith Magyar Isaacson frames her account, *Seed of Sarah*, with a story about a lecture. This ends with an issue of identification. Towards the end of question-and-answer session, Isaacson is asked by a woman student:

'How old were you in Auschwitz?'
'Nineteen—in 1944' . . .
Swinging back her braids with a shake of her head she shuddered as she said: 'Nineteen, like me . . . Dean Isaacson, were you raped in the camps?'
'Raped?' I blanched, reliving the panic: 'Raped you said? I'll tell you how I escaped it . . .'.[15]

These openings and the meta-textual sources and letter discussed earlier serve to frame Isaacson's testimony *as* Isaacson's testimony, a specific document from a specific time by a specific person. The reader is not free, in this case, to identify with and so 'take over', as it were, from Isaacson: despite the novelistic form (in the citation above, for example, the suspense of the escape), it is clearly not a novel but a mediated, retold testimony, and not a text with which anyone can identify.

Formal Frames

Instead of full narratives, some testimonies—the later texts of Levi and Améry, for example— use the essay. The essay, the reflective form *par excellence*, already admits the incompleteness of its range and the fallibility of its author. Améry's essays in *At the Mind's Limits* combine the personal with the more reflective. Indeed, he begins the first essay with

---

[15] Judith Magyar Isaacson, *Seed of Sarah: Memoirs of a Survivor*, (Chicago; University of Illinois Press, 2nd edn., 1991), p. xi.

a discussion how he is going to mix the discussion of mediation between the facts—'I do not want . . . to give a documentary report'—and the more 'intellectual theme of the confrontation of Auschwitz and the intellect': 'however', he writes, 'I cannot bypass what one calls the horrors'.[16] Another 'doubleness'. The horrors are those things that happened to him in contrast to the intellectual issues that the camps raise. The text moves constantly between the essayistic and reflective 'we' to the narrative or introspective 'I', from the general to the particular and back again. Again, this choice of form works to fix the location of the author/witness as separate from the reader: it impresses a sense of difference and otherness, and prevents Améry's narrative from being comfortably assimilated. With Levi, too, the essay form—and the central sections of *If This a Man* seems more to be a series of essays linked by a narrative—serves to present his testimony as suffused in what Gillian Rose described as 'Olympian serenity'.[17] His readers are impressed by 'the sense that there is a kind of judicious neutrality at work in Levi's indictments'.[18] It is this 'serenity', this judiciousness, that leads readers to rely and to trust Levi, to identify with him. Yet, the essayistic frame and Levi's own careful monitoring of his works, and his own repeated insistence of the gulf between him and those who did not experience or the Holocaust, should prevent such simplistic identifications.

Inserted Tags

Beer achieves a similar result but in a more 'folksy' way. The text of her narrative is full of tropes and shifts of register aiming to give the impression that this is a story orally told, as it might be to a family sitting around her chair: for example 'You must understand . . .'; 'Hold that in your mind as I tell you this story'; 'So, you see, . . .'; 'I tell you . . .'; 'Like lightening. Poof. A flame. Poof. Gone. Werner.'[19] In addition, the text specifically locates its contemporary audience in space and time: for example, she writes that the Jews in the Third Reich 'were not bold free Americans—remember that. And there were no

[16] Jean Améry, *At the Mind's Limits*, tr. Sidney Rosenfled and Stella Rosenfeld (London: Granta Books, 1999), 1.

[17] Gillian Rose, *Mourning Becomes the Law: Philosophy and Representation* (Cambridge: Cambridge University Press, 1996), 50.

[18] Gillian Banner, *Holocaust Literature: Schulz, Levi, Spiegleman and the Memory of the Offence* (London: Valentine Mitchell, 2000), 92–3.

[19] Beer, *Nazi Officer's Wife*, 5, 26, 69, 187, 288.

Israelis then, no soldiers in the desert.'[20] The effect of this is rhetori-
cally to frame the narrator as exactly that, a narrator and a witness,
and not somebody whose experiences can be assimilated to one's own.

Frames of Seeing and Knowing

Charlotte Delbo's narrative frames are central to how her testimony
works. Langer, in the introduction to her *Auschwitz and After*, and
Lamont, in the translator's preface, both stress Delbo's maxim 'Il faut
donner à voir'. Langer translates 'they must be made to see' and suggests that her work 'invites us to "see" the unthinkable as a basis for all
that follows' (*AA*, pp. x, xvii). Indeed, seeing and knowing, experiencing and remembering, dominate her work. But throughout, and especially in the first volume *None of Us Will Return*, seeing and knowing
are posed with each other in different combinations, in which seeing
comes before knowing. Those *who haven't seen and don't know* are
those arriving at Auschwitz: they 'do not know there is no arriving in
this station' (*AA* 4), the intellectuals who 'made use of their imagination to write books, yet nothing they imagined ever came close to what
they see now' (*AA* 6), the mother who hits her child 'and we who know
cannot forgive her for it' (*AA* 7). Delbo continues: 'only those who
enter the camp find out what happened to the others' (*AA* 9). These
become those *who know and have seen*, the witnesses, Delbo herself
and her camp sisters. However, they are, at the same time, paradoxically trying not to see, although they know. The section called 'The
Dummies' begins ' "Look. Look" ' as the women look at huge piles of
dead and dying in the yard. It ends

'Don't stare! Why are you staring?' Yvonne P. pleads, her eyes wide open, riv-
eted to a living corpse.
'Eat your soup' says Cecile. These women no longer need anything.
I look too. I look at this corpse that moves but does not move me. I'm a big girl
now. I can look at naked dummies without being afraid.   (*AA* 19)

Delbo has taught herself that she can know and see and yet not see: not
seeing is vital to survival. In the next section, 'The Men', the camp sisters throw bread from women too sick to eat to a column of men with
'wolves' eyes' : they 'did not even turn their heads in our direction' (*AA*
21) because they too have learnt to know and not to see. Later again, in
'The Orchestra', she writes repeatedly 'Do not look, do not listen' to the

[20] Beer, *Nazi Officer's Wife*, 26.

orchestra who play on stolen instruments while 'naked men' (*AA* 106–7) are reduced to skeletons. Those who know and can see should try not to. 'I no longer look' (*AA* 52). In contrast, those who *know and have not seen* should try to see. For example, she writes

O you who know
did you know that hunger makes the eyes sparkle that thirst dims them
O you who know
did you know that you can see your mother dead and not shed a tear.   (*AA* 11)

and later gives three short images, and ends each one 'Try to look. Just try to see' (*AA* 84, 85, 86). This seems as much a challenge to do the impossible, and so presupposing the impossible, as an exhortation. Indeed, between Auschwitz and the world is an 'abyss' (*AA* 181).

Allegories of Failed Understanding

That it is impossible to 'know and have not seen' is made clear later in *The Measure of Our Days* when the narrator meets Pierre, the husband of her friend Marie-Louise. Pierre has an interest in the experiences of his wife: he has read her notebooks, and read widely about the 'deportations'. His wife says that 'my memories have become his own. So much so I have the distinct impression he was there with me.' Pierre returns with 'Ah, Charlotte! I'm so happy to see you at last. I didn't say "make your acquaintance"; I've know you quite a long time.' Pierre lived in France during the war, sent parcels to his wife with messages hidden on them. He did not suspect that she might have died as 'at the time we didn't know anything about the camps.' After the war Pierre and Marie-Louise visited Birkenau. From his wife's descriptions, he recognizes it all, takes photographs, refined his wife's memory ('She no longer knew whether she was on the right or left side [of the block]'). He says to Charlotte, the narrator, 'I saw more than you did when you were there: the crematoria, the gas chambers, the wall below against which the men were shot.' As these sections are almost all in dialogue, it is only possible to gauge the narrator's feeling by her actions. Instead of staying overnight, she leaves—'I can't stay. Forgive me.' Pierre wishes her well: 'Charlotte, you know that this is your home, here with us, with your comrades.' She writes that 'I felt them there standing on the threshold of their pretty house at the end of a cool, shady walk lined with pine trees' (*AA* 280–8). It is clear here that—however supportive and well-intentioned Pierre was—he has colonized and assimilated

memories that are not his, and assumed a role, through reading, talking, and imagination, that does not reflect his experience, not what he
actually saw. He is not, except in imagination, Charlotte's friend or
comrade, though he may be friendly. Although he may have seen the
crematoria and the gas chambers, this is not to have seen more of the
camp, except in a banal sense. Indeed, their pretty house with its cool,
shady walk of pine seems to be, somehow, a domestication or normalization of the events in Auschwitz–Birkenau—other houses with pines
and cold, dark walks. For Delbo, as Sara Horowitz argues, the 'problem lies not only in the survivors' inability to speak the unspeakable; it
lies also in our inability—as non-participants—to imagine the unimaginable'.[21] Delbo sets up Pierre as an allegory for those who read about
the Holocaust and think that they have seen it: he thinks himself to be
a 'witness though the imagination' and Delbo has nothing but scorn—
and perhaps a feeling of disgust—for him. This account, which is similar to the story Levi tells about the schoolboy, is an allegory of failed
understanding. There is an identification taking place here: the reader
(the reader who is not a survivor) is being identified with Pierre or with
the school boy and is being shown, in the text, how ridiculous or pernicious they (we?) look if they claim to understand what Jorge
Semprun calls 'the essential part of the experience'.[22] Again, this sort of
event occurs in the closing pages of Imre Kertész's novelized account,
Fateless. George, the survivor, meets a journalist eager to write about
the camps. But after some conversation, the journalist 'covered his face
with his hands' and declares that the camp can not be imagined: 'That's
probably why they say "hell" instead' thinks George.[23] This serves to
make identification with the survivor impossible precisely because
there is a position for the reader to occupy: who 'knows and has not
seen', the despairing journalist, and any claims made by a Pierre or
others to know more than the banal details are shown—with a chas-
tening shock, perhaps—to be wrong, clichéd, absurd, or harmful.

   Delbo's discussion of Pierre has another implication. It seems to suggest that his wife, Maire-Louise, can no longer see what she has seen.
She has identified herself with those that know but did not see. As

   [21] Sara Horowitz, 'Voices from the Killing Ground', in Geoffrey Hartman (ed.),
Holocaust Remembrance: The Shapes of Memory (Oxford: Blackwell, 1994), 42–69, 45.
   [22] Jorge Semprun, *Literature or Life*, tr. Linda Coverdale (London: Viking, 1997),
87–8.
   [23] Imre Kertész, *Fateless*, tr. Christopher C. Wilson and Katharina M. Wilson
(Evanston, Ill.: Northwestern University Press, 1992), 182.

Delbo writes in *Days and Memory*, the 'skin enfolding the memory of Auschwitz is tough. Even so, it gives way at times, revealing all it contains.'[24] And this leads to an ambiguity in her use of seeing and knowing as a motif. In the prose poem, cited earlier, 'O you who know', the knowers become not only those who know about and have not seen (experienced) the camp, but those who, like Maire-Louise (and others, in Delbo's account of 'after' Auschwitz), have denied it, or 'domesticated' the experience. In this complex way, Delbo makes it clear how hard it is, even for a survivor, to access or to inhabit what Langer calls 'Deep memory'.

Memory of the Dead

Many testimonies end with specific acts of remembering individuals who were murdered. The main body of Vrba's account ends with his participation in a partisan attack, 'tears of happiness were coursing down my cheeks. I was running forwards not backwards.'[25] However, there is an epilogue and two appendices. The second deals with a transport from his region of Slovakia: the final words are 'In this way did young Mrs Tomasov, old Isaac Rabinowic and Mrs Polanska and all the others on that transport from Slovakia die.'[26] Similarly, Ezra BenGershôm's 'U-boat' narrative *David: Testimony of a Holocaust Survivor* ends with an account of the sufferings and deaths of his family and friends:

My sister Toni, posing as an 'ethnic German' domestic help, had lived through the German occupation to the bitter end—only to experience the horrors of the Russian conquest. Toni survived the war. Leon and Lore, I learned, had fallen into the hands of the Hungarian police in July 1944. Soon afterwards they found themselves in a goods wagon, bound for Auschwitz.[27]

These turn the testimony into, in part, a personal memorial, not open to an easy assimilation.

These gestures, linguistic and formal, are, of course, only tropes that serve to create a mimesis of production. It is possible to find such moments in Holocaust testimony precisely because the act of witnessing is always mediated and because all such moments show that 'in

[24] Charlotte Delbo, *Days and Memory*, tr. Rosette Lamont (Marlboro, Vt.: Marlboro Press, 1990), 3.

[25] Vrba, *I Cannot Forgive*, 261.   [26] Ibid. 278.

[27] Ezra BenGershôm, *David: Testimony of a Holocaust Survivor*, tr. J. A. Underwood (Oxford: Oswald Wolff Books, 1988), 283.

addition to time and place', the writer's 'very language, traditions and world view played crucial roles in the making of their literary witness . . . As raw as they may have been at the moment, the ghetto and camp experiences were immediately refined and organised by witnesses within in terms of their Weltanschauung.'[28]

EPIPHANIES

Another factor—hardly a strategy—that prevents identification is simply that the events of the texts are hardly bearable. This is especially clear at the moments that occur in many testimonies which, in other genres, might be called epiphanies. An epiphany, a term drawn from modernist writing and criticism, is a moment of 'showing' or 'revealing' some truth: an unveiling of something. In testimonies, this trope serves to focus the horror in a specific, revealing, incident. In Wiesel's *Night*, the murder of the babies is this moment of horror: 'A lorry drew up at the pit and delivered its load—Little children. Babies! Yes, I saw it—saw it with my own eyes . . . Never shall I forget the little faces of the children, whose bodies I saw turned into wreaths of smoke beneath a silent blue sky.'[29] In *Fragments of Isabella*, there is a similar moment, titled 'My Potyo, My Sister', when the narrator thinks about the murder of her baby sister.[30] There is a matching emblematic moment in Levi, again very early in the imprisonment:

Driven by thirst, I eyed a fine icicle outside the window, within hand's reach. I opened the window and broke off the icicle but at once a large, heavy guard prowling around outside snatched it way from me. 'Warum?' I asked him in my poor German. 'Hier ist klien warum' ('there is no why here'), he replied, pushing me inside with a shove. The explanation is repugnant but simple: in this place everything is forbidden, not for hidden reasons, but because the camp has been created for that purpose.[31]

For the first two, the epiphany consists of the destruction of babies, the hope and future of a community, more than the symbol of innocence; for Levi, the 'there is no why here' is the inversion of reason, the end of

---

[28] James Young, *Writing and Rewriting the Holocaust: Narrative and the Consequences of Interpretation* (Bloomington: Indiana University Press, 1988), 26.

[29] Elie Wiesel, *Night*, tr. Stella Rodway (London: Penguin, 1981), 43, 45.

[30] Isabella Leitner, *Fragments of Isabella: A Memoir of Auschwitz*, ed. and tr. Irving Leitner (New York: New English Library, 1978), 17. See also Delbo, *Days*, 30.

[31] Primo Levi, *If This is a Man*, tr. Stuart Woolf (London: Abacus, 1979), 35.

the possibility of understanding, the inverse of science, the making central of what is forbidden. Meaning 'you are not allowed to ask why here: you are below human conversation', it shows the division between the murderers and the victims and so the end of community at the deepest level. Meaning 'here, there are no actions that could be explained by answering the question why, which presupposes a shared sense of reason', it shows the end of a certain concept of reason. Meaning 'here everything is forbidden, even asking why' it shows the end of freedom: even the freedom to die in a pre-Holocaust way. The Holocaust changed even death, and 'since Auschwitz, fearing death means fearing worse than death' for Adorno: men 'have lost the illusion that it is commensurable with their lives'.[32] And, of course, it is profoundly ironic: as Michael Burleigh argues, there was a 'why': 'to grind people like him into dust'.[33]

These epiphanic horrors are often contrasted with moments of normality. Isabella's narrative begins with 'Yesterday, what happened yesterday? Did you go to the movies? Did you have a date? What did he say?'[34] The date of her and her families deportation—29 May 1944—is used to contrast her experience with the normality of life in America. American girls 'wear stockings, ride in automobiles, wear wrist watches and necklaces . . . they are healthy. They are living. Incredible!'[35]

In Semprun's *The Long Voyage* too, the 'day I saw the Jewish children die'—the murder of a group of Polish Jewish children by the SS and their dogs—is the central, structuring epiphantic moment. The testimony builds up to this event: the awful story 'has never been told . . . [it has] lain buried in my memory like some mortal treasure preying on it with a sterile suffering'. He tells this under protest by himself, uncertain if he can continue, if he wants to continue, certain he ought to continue:

maybe I shall be able to tell about the death of the Jewish children . . . perhaps it is out of pride that I have never told anyone the story . . . as if I had the right, or even the possibility to keep it to myself any longer. It's true that I had decided to forget. I had forgotten everything, from now on I can remember. . . . I feel compelled to tell it. I have to speak out in the name of things that happened.[36]

[32] Theodor Adorno, *Negative Dialectics*, tr. E. B. Ashton (London: Routledge, 1973), 371, 369.
[33] Michael Burleigh, *The Third Reich: A New History* (London: Macmillian, 2000), 202.
[34] Leitner, *Fragments of Isabella*, 1.   [35] Ibid.
[36] Jorge Semprun, *The Long Voyage*, tr. Richard Seaver (London: Penguin, 1997), 162–3.

Retreating from the East, and emptying camps as they go, the SS discover about fifteen Jewish children surviving in a boxcar. At first uncertain what to do, the SS return later with dogs and make a game of
killing the children. The last two die, ' the older one's right hand clasp-
ing the smaller one's left hand'.[37] Even commenting on this, here, seems
to be questionable. *(Indeed, it is hard to know what to 'comment on' in
this passage: the brutality of the SS, the more than pathos of the two
boys. The vocabulary of literary criticism breaks down, or worse,
becomes complicit with the murders. To write something like 'the
extended sentence structure with the brief clauses both makes the piece
breathless as the victims struggle for breath and reproduces, perhaps a
little simplistically, a hunt' as I did in a draft seems in some way to celebrate the killing and its account.)* The event has an epiphantic and
emblematic power for Semprun and sums up metonymically the horror
of the Holocaust. These moments—it seems—are simply so awful that
identifying with the narrators who describe them is impossible.

INTERRUPTIONS

Testimony texts are also riven with interruptions that break up the
flow of narrative. Very often these are to do with the chronology of
events. Edith Hahn Beer's 'U-boat' narrative regularly marks a distinction between the time of the narrative and the time of the narration and
so, the testimony tells its telling. Kitty Hart writes that 'I was not to
know in 1943 that I would survive to see all this for myself.'[38] Delbo
makes use of this trope quite frequently. After her description of 'living
skeletons that dance', she writes, 'Presently I am writing this story in a
café—it is turning into a story' (AA 26). Delbo also discusses the complexities of remembering the past in the present. Frister's testimony,
The Cap, has an extremely complex time structure, mixing different
periods together freely and easily. For example, one section moves
from post-war Prague to a radio interview forty-two years later to
memories of his grandfather before the war and back to Prague in 1947
and then back to his family's attempt to flee Poland in the late 1930s.[39]
The insertions of 'documentary history' also interrupts narrative time.

---

[37] Semprun, *The Long Voyage*, 166.
[38] Hart, *Return to Auschwitz*, 127.
[39] Roman Frister, *The Cap, or the Price of a Life*, tr. Hillel Halkin (London:
Weidenfeld & Nicolson, 1999), 45–8.

Semprun's work, too, is characterized by a complex time structure, involving leaps forward and backwards in the chronological narrative. There are currently three of Semprun's accounts readily available in English, each from a different decade: *The Long Voyage*, *What a Beautiful Sunday!*, and *Literature of Life* (originally published in 1963, 1980, and 1994, respectively). Each of these works in a similar way: taking a set period of time—the journey to Buchenwald, a Sunday during his time there, the days immediately after liberation—as a narrative frame, they weave an account of this with accounts of events before, during, and after the war. Memories of one moment inevitably invoke other memories, and it is only through the whole contextual mesh of memories that make up a person that the events can be approached. Moreover, the nature of writing and narrating, too, affect what can be told. The style of the books aim to reflect this movement of memory and the problems of writing: they are shifting, uncertain. There are slips in the chronology—conversations in 1944 slide into conversations in the 1950s, for example—that serve to disrupt the text.

Other texts, more conventionally realist than Semprun and Delbo, organize their chronologies in different ways, telling the stories in different orders. These have different effects on the testimony. Fénelon begins her narrative with her liberation, singing—oddly in an echo of *Casablanca*— the 'Marseillaise', the 'Internationale', and 'God Save the King' into a microphone for the BBC, 'galvanised by joy'.[40] Despite the ominous English title—*Playing for Time*—it is clear that she survives victorious, able to sing, and this sets tone for the rest of the narrative. Vrba draws out the significance of Himmler's visit to Auschwitz as a leitmotif for the rest of his account: the evil, power, and brutality of the Final Solution from the high (Himmler) to the low (the block Kapo who beats an incorrectly dressed prisoner to death before Himmler arrives). Hart, again, begins her *Return to Auschwitz* in 1946 with her arrival in England, allowing the camp to take up the centre of the testimony and to stress the need to tell an uninterested world. Lengyel begins with a terrible declaration of guilt: 'I cannot acquit myself of the charge that I am, in part, responsible for the destruction of my own parents and of my two young sons.'[41] She made a decision at a selection that led to their death, and so her testimony, as all do, lingers on the 'grey zone' and her forced complicity: 'the Germans

---

[40] Fania Fénelon with Marcelle Routier, *Playing for Time*, tr. Judith Landry (New York: Syracuse University Press, 1977), 9.

[41] Lengyl, *Five Chimneys*, 13.

wanted to infect us with their own Nazi morals. In most cases they succeeded' and 'perhaps the greatest crime the "supermen" committed was their campaign, often successful, to turn us in to monstrous beasts ourselves'.[42] ' "You, too, have become our tormentors" ' cry the patients from whom she is forced to remove clothing.[43]

However, there are interruptions that are more clearly signified precisely as narrative interruptions. Elie Wiesel's exclamation in *Night*, 'Never shall I forget that night . . . which has turned my life in to one long night', and the repeated use of 'never' interrupt the narrative.[44] In his memoirs, he uses this strategy more often: the memoir is disturbed by descriptions of dreams.[45] In the section called 'Darkness' the text becomes more discursive and much less driven by the narrative which is familiar from *Night*. Questions emerge and are discussed. Why did the free world, including Jewish leaders, not warn them? Why 'did the Jews of the free world act as they did?' Why did the allies not bomb the train lines? '[W]hat was the point of this death factory?'[46] Other accounts and reflections on his own work—on 'Moishele, or Moshe as I call him in my books', for example—are woven into the text.[47] There is a discussion of his commentary on the Eichmann trial and, following from that, an argument with Golda Meir.[48] Wiesel outlines his disagreement with Primo Levi, ventriloquized through Dostoevsky, and with Emmanuel Levinas (who, after the war, was taught by the same Talmudic master, Shoshani).[49] The memoir's chronological chapter structure is even interrupted with a full section on 'God's Suffering'.[50] These interventions are so much part of Wiesel's style that his writing has been described as midrash.[51] But perhaps the most poignant intervention is not a discussion or a question, but simply: 'I reread what I have just written, and my hand trembles. I who rarely weep am in tears. I see the flames again, and the children, and yet again I tell myself that it is not enough to weep.'[52] This serves, again, to mark a distinction between the time of the events and the narration of the events, to interrupt the narrative and so foreground the authorial voice.

---

[42] Lengyl, *Five Chimneys*, 57, 219.   [43] Ibid. 151.   [44] Wiesel, *Night*, 43, 45.
[45] For examples, see Elie Wiesel, *All Rivers Run to the Sea* (London: Harper Collins, 1996), 3, 5, 17, 55, 99.
[46] Ibid. 63, 74, 79.   [47] Ibid. 60, 73.   [48] Ibid. 63–4.   [49] Ibid. 82–3, 87.
[50] Ibid. 103–5.
[51] James E. Young, 'Interpreting Literary Testimony: A Preface to Rereading Holocaust Diaries and Memoirs', *New Literary History*, 18 (1986–7), 403–23, 410.
[52] Wiesel, *All Rivers*, 78.

Some prose texts do more than just disturb their narratives. They are, or consist in, interruption. In this they enact in prose—or in the case of Delbo, a mixture of prose and poetry—what Paul Celan and others enacted in poetry: the 'breakage of the verse enacts the breakage of the world'.[53] *Fragments of Isabella* is exactly that, short, broken fragments, picking up on moments of her experience of the camp, the death march, her escape from the death march, and migration to the US. The narrative is made up of gaps and 'snapshots'; it becomes impossible to identify with Isabella herself as there is little narrative material with which to identify. Similarly, Delbo's work is made up of brief sections of text: some dialogues, some prose, some poetic. Although they make up a narrative, the fragmented form reflects the fragmentation that the experience has induced. The final page of the first volume has only one line, 'None of us was meant to return' (*AA* 114). The blankness of the rest of the page signifies for all those who did not return: the emptiness remains empty, a reminder that, as Levi writes, 'each of us survivors is in more than one way an exception: something that we ourselves, to exorcise the past, tend to forget'.[54]

Much of the 'studied disorder' of Jorge Semprun's *Literature or Life* is a result of the uncertainty of how to tell: it is an allegory of the impossibility of telling, as Delbo's Pierre was an allegory of the impossibility of understanding.[55] *Literature or Life* is a testimony mediated doubly: like all testimonies, mediated by language and by narrative, and then again by a meditation on this very mediation. As the testimony is about telling the story, Semprun tells and retells stories, often with warnings: 'Watch out—I'm fabricating: I wasn't able to see the colour of his eyes at that point' (*LL* 33, see also 223–31). He goes on

I told that story about the German soldier in a short novel called *L'évanouissement*[56] . . . I . . . wanted to correct the first version that wasn't altogether truthful. What I mean is, the story is all true . . . the river is true, the town of Semur-en-Auxois isn't some invention of mine, the German really did sing 'La Paloma' and we did shoot him down. But I was with Julien . . . and not with Hans . . . I'd invented Hans Freiberg in order to have a Jewish friend. I'd had

[53] Shoshona Felman and Dori Laub, *Testimony: Crises of Witnessing in Literature, Psychoanalysis and History* (London: Routledge, 1992), 25.

[54] Primo Levi, *The Drowned and the Saved*, tr. Raymond Rosenthal (London: Abacus, 1988), 82.

[55] Semprun, *Literature or Life*, 16. This will be abbreviated to *LL* in the text.

[56] *L'Évanouissement* is the Ur-text for much of *Literature or Life* and recurs often in the text—see e.g. *LL* 171, 188.

Jewish pals at that time of my life, so I wanted to have one in the novel as well. (*LL* 35–6).

The reason for this was because 'we wanted to liquidate all oppression and because the Jew—even passive, even resigned—was the intolerable embodiment of the oppressed' (*LL* 37). But more than this, the book is full of his attempts to tell what happened: to three officers he meets after his liberation ' "No birds left . . . They say the smoke from the crematory drove them away . . ." They listen closely trying to understand. "The smell of burnt flesh that's what did it!". They wince, glance at one another. In almost palpable distress' (*LL* 5). He tries again later, a more gentle approach:

to placate the god of a credible narration, to soften the harshness of a truthful account, I tried to lead the young officer into the universe of death down a dominical path: a garden path . . . I led him into the hell of radical evil [one of the many references to Kant] . . . through its most banal entrance . . . To initiate the young officer into the mysteries of Sundays in Buchenwald, I evoked the pals and poisonous beauty of Pola Negri in Mazurka. (*LL* 71–2).

But this fails as a strategy: 'He hadn't been able, afterward, to let me take him into the teeming depths of those Sundays, and all because of Pola Negri' (LL 87). His narrative had failed to uncover the experience. Reflecting on this in conversation, he continues:

'There are all sorts of good beginnings . . . one ought to begin with the essential part of the experience . . .' . . . The essential part? I think I know, yes. I'm beginning to understand. The essential thing is to go beyond the clear facts of this horror and get at the root of radical Evil, *das radikal Böse*. Because the horror itself was not the Evil—not its essence, at least. The Horror was only its raiment, its ornament, its ceremonial display. . . . One could have spent hours testifying to the daily horror of the camp without touching upon the essence of this experience. . . . What's essential . . . is the experience of Evil. Of course, you can experience that anywhere . . . You don't need concentration camps to know Evil. But here, this experience will turn out to have been crucial, and massive, invading everywhere, devouring everything . . . It's the experience of radical Evil. (*LL* 87–8)

Semprun does not describe this. Instead, he diverts the argument into a discussion of Levinas and Heidegger. However, this does lead him to attempt another 'telling' strategy: he simply shows visiting French nurses the camp,

the rows of ovens, the half charred corpses they still contained. I barely spoke to them. I simply told them the names of things, without comment. They had to see, to try to imagine [shades of Delbo's refrain here]. Then I led them out of the crematory, into the interior courtyard surrounded by a high fence. There I didn't say anything more, not one thing. I let them look. . . . there was a pile of corpses a good nine feet high. A heap of yellowed, twisted skeletons with terror stricken faces . . . I turned round. They were gone. They'd fled from the sight. And I could understand why. It couldn't have been much fun to come to Buchenwald as a tourist and be brutally presented with a small mountain of unpresentable corpses.   (*LL* 121–2)

Directly after this in the text is an account of a discussion among the French intellectuals in the camp. Semprun, who sounds French, is advised to hide his badge which reveals his Spanish identity. The intellectuals discuss how the horrors will be represented. One, an academic, argues that no documents or eyewitness accounts will be able to 'contain the essential truth': this will only be possible through 'the artifice of the work of art' (*LL* 125). Semprun adds 'what's problematical here is not the description of this horror. Not just that, anyway—not even mostly that. What's at stake here is the exploration of the human soul in the horror of Evil . . . We'll need a Dostoyevsky!' (*LL* 127). In part two of the book, Semprun tells about his decisions to write or not to write—about whether to try to be a Dostoevsky. He begins to write but the

memory was too dense, too pitiless for me to master immediately . . . Whenever I awoke at two in the morning, with the voice of the SS officer in my ear, blinded by the orange flame of the crematory, the subtle and sophisticated harmony of my project shattered in brutal dissonance. Only a cry from the depths of the soul, only a deathly silence could have expressed that suffering.   (*LL* 159).

Not only is this very similar to Levi's account of awakening, and 'the dawn command of Auschwitz . . . Wstawàch' but Semprun refers to this, to awakening and to this particular passage, throughout *Literature or Life*. 'No one could say it better than Levi', he writes, and discusses Levi's suicide at length (*LL* 236).[57] Indeed, it is this revelation—that the work of literature or of life cannot be competed or finished and tided away and will always be interrupted, 'awakened', that seems to let Semprun write. He does not write an account of his life or a work of literature that is finished: instead he writes and rewrites, constantly interrupted by his inability to tell and by his dream-like awakening return, as in the final words of *Literature or Life*,

[57] Levi, *If This is a Man*, 380–1.

to the 'tongues of orange flame' which protrude 'from the mouth of the squat crematory chimney' (*LL* 310).

An exception to these particular strategies that serve to prevent identification and assimilation by creating distance is Simon Wiesenthal's *The Sunflower*. Although the book is a testimony, it can 'easily be seen as a moral fable invented to illustrate a universal dilemma'.[58] The sunflower of the title is a recurring motif: the column of slave workers in which Wiesenthal is marching passes a military cemetery and each grave has a sunflower on it. For Wiesenthal, the sunflowers are both memorials of and almost conduits to the dead: 'the dead were receiving light and messages . . . I envied the dead soldiers. Each had a sunflower to connect him to the living world . . . For me there would be no sunflower. I would be buried in a mass grave . . .'[59] The book, because it is about relating to the dead, then becomes the sunflower of its own leitmotif, the sunflower by which we can talk to the dead. It specifically uses the way in which readers identify with narrative to pose a question of guilt and forgiveness. The narrative is straightforward. Simon Wiesenthal is a prisoner in the extermination camp system. From his column of slave labourers he is summoned, at random, by a nurse to attend a young SS man, dying in great pain. The SS man, Karl, begs Wiesenthal to forgive him for the atrocities he has committed. Wiesenthal leaves without answering. The rest of the book is made up of the conversations he has with others about what he should have done.

The question is in part about the relationship between the perpetrators and the victims, but also about identification. Wiesenthal himself moves between identifying with Karl and feelings of hatred. On the one hand, he says, 'I admit I did feel some pity for the fellow'.[60] On the

---

[58] Lawrence Langer, *Pre-empting the Holocaust* (London: Yale University Press, 1998), 166.

[59] Simon Wiesenthal, *The Sunflower* (New York: Schocken Books, 1997), 14.

[60] Ibid., 83. Interestingly, this conversation with an SS man has a correlation in Delbo's testimony: being transported away from Auschwitz through Silesia, she engages her guards in conversations: 'I was dying to approach them, start a conversation, find out, as little as it was bound to be, what's an SS. Why and how does one become and SS? The others go along with that. I go. They turn out to be Slovenes, forcibly enrolled in the SS. They say they know nothing about Auschwitz—all these smokestacks . . . Otherwise . . . They offer us cigarettes, light them for us. When we stop they go to the railway

other hand, even thinking about forgiving the SS man leaves him feeling ashamed. Through an imagined conversation with a fellow inmate, Arthur, Wiesenthal warns himself: in Arthur's voice he accuses himself 'you can't forget a dying SS man while countless Jews are tortured and killed every hour . . . You are beginning to think the Germans are in some way superior , and that's why you are worrying about your dying SS man' and indeed, when Arthur does, in fact, call Karl 'your SS man', Wiesenthal is very hurt.[61] If Wiesenthal can identify with Karl, Karl can be forgiven: if he can't, Karl won't. To identify with Karl means admitting believing in exactly the sort of universal humanity that Karl, by his actions, has denied. And Wiesenthal the narrator ends by asking the reader, directly, what they would have done: by making the reader identify with the narrator, the book puts the reader in the position of deciding what she or he should do. Again, here there is a 'doubleness' on the demand that the reader assimilate and come to judgement of an aporia.

Each of the editions published in 1969, 1976, and 1997 has a large meta-text, a 'symposium' in which, as the blurb states, fifty-three distinguished men and women give their response. These include Holocaust survivors (Améry, Levi), religious leaders, experts in the field of Holocaust studies, survivors of other genocides and murderous regimes, and even Albert Speer. The answers are all considered. Primo Levi offers a gentle dismantling of the whole scenario. Langer, like many in the symposium, writes 'I have no idea what I might have done'.[62] However he goes on: 'nor do I believe the question is a legitimate one. Role-playing about the Holocaust trivialises the serious issues of judgement and forgiveness that *The Sunflower* raises.'[63] Clearly, Langer's position is not opposed to asking questions about the Holocaust in detail: for him the key issue is why people like Karl joined the SS in the first place. He is acutely aware of the way in which narrative accounts allow the Holocaust to become assimilated into everyday experience and how readers identify ('role-play') with the victim narrators. However, the over-identification this seems to demand could be seen to overwhelm the normal processes of identification. The text asks: 'You, who have just read this sad and tragic episode in my life,

canteen, return with ersatz coffee distributed by Red Cross nurses to the soldiers. We had never seen a look of pity or a human expression in the eyes of an SS. Do they strip off the assassin departing from Auschwitz?' (*AA* 179).

[61] Wiesenthal, *Sunflower*, 62, 69.   [62] Lawrence Lange, ibid. 186.
[63] Langer, ibid. 186.

can mentally change places with me and ask yourself the crucial question, "What would I have done?".'[64] The answer seems often to be that the 'mentally changing place' just cannot really happen.

Primo Levi offers another sort of final disturbance in 'The Awakening' the last chapter of *The Truce*: he dreams he is in the 'Lager once more, and nothing is true outside the Lager . . . a well-known voice resounds: a single word, not imperious, but brief and subdued. It is the dawn command of Auschwitz, a foreign word, feared and expected: get up, "Wstawàch" '.[65] 'The Awakening' is not an awakening from a terrible 'dream' of the camps back into normal life, but the awakening into a tormented post-Holocaust existence in which the camps do not interrupt 'normal life' but, rather, 'normal life' interrupts the unceasing experience of the camps. The reason that these endings are disturbing and prevent identification is because, like the frequent practice of rewriting testimony, they reveal that the end is not the end: only a temporary respite.

Barbara Foley suggests that the 'great majority of Holocaust memoirists fall silent when they have completed their tales'.[66] In fact, the opposite is the case. Once they have told their tales, they tell them again: another characteristic of testimony writing is the lack of closure. In postmodern writing this is usually understood as a disavowal of, in Henry James's words, 'a distribution at the last of prizes, pensions, wives, babies, millions, appended paragraphs and cheerful remarks', in favour of an incomplete, unfinished ending. For testimony writing, the refusal of closure comes in other forms because many actual testimony texts about the Holocaust have a structure that ends with the war or with return or with settling after the war. Filip Müller, exhausted on a rafter, is awoken by shouts of 'We are free! Comrades, we are free!' He crawls out into a wood and falls asleep, and is awoken by a column of tanks and 'I realised that the hideous Nazi terror had ended at last'.[67] This chronology offers a basic narrative structure. However, this is

---

[64] Langer, ibid. 98.   [65] Levi, *If This is a Man*, 380–1.
[66] Barbara Foley, 'Fact, Fiction, Fascism: Testimony and Mimesis in Holocaust Narrative', *Comparative Literature*, 34 (1982), 330–60, 339.
[67] Müller, *Eyewitness Auschwitz*, 171.

often disturbed or disrupted by the inability to escape the events: Levi's terrible 'Wstawàch'.[68] Delbo, too, describes this return:

Over dreams the conscious will has no power. And in these dreams I see myself, yes, my own self such as I know I was: hardly able to stand on my feet, my throat tight, my heart beating wildly, frozen to the marrow, filthy, skin and bones. . . . Luckily in my agony I cry out. My cry wakes me and I emerge from the nightmare, drained. It takes days from everything to get back to normal, for everything to get shoved back inside memory, for the skin of memory to mend again.[69]

But the lack of closure also occurs in—or more accurately, *as*—the œuvre of a writer: survivors return again and again to write about the Holocaust. As Wiesel writes, the 'truth is I could spend the rest of my days recounting the weeks, months and eternities I lived in Auschwitz'.[70] Talking with Carlos Fuentes about rewriting in Spanish *Le Grand Voyage*—in rather the same way Wiesel produced *Night* by translating and editing, with Jérôme Lindon, the Yiddish original, *And the World Remained Silent*—Semprun recounts Fuentes's joke: 'And so . . . you will have realised every writer's dream: to spend your life writing a single book, endlessly renewed' (*LL* 275–6).[71] For Fuentes this is a light-hearted remark: for Semprun—with the black humour of the inmate that Levi discussed—it is both a savage commentary and a reaffirmation that others cannot understand the experience. It is not a book that one would choose to rewrite endlessly but the only one possible: as Delbo writes, 'I was in despair at having lost the faculty of dreaming, of harbouring illusions; I was no longer open to imagination. This is the part of me that died in Auschwitz. This is what turned me into a ghost' (*AA* 239). Wiesel writes that, in all his stories, the 'teller of tales still lives in the shadow of the flames that once had illuminated and blinded him'.[72] Semprun's *Literature or Life*, in part a commentary on Levi and on the condition of survivor writing, knows of what closure on the text of this endless book consists: 'only a suicide could put a signature, a voluntary end to this unfinished—this unfinishable—process of mourning' (*AA* 194). And for Semprun, Levi's suicide was exactly this:

---

[68] Levi, *If This is a Man*, 380–1. [69] Delbo, *Days*, 1.
[70] Wiesel, *All Rivers*, 89.
[71] For the account of the development of *Night* see, Wiesel, *All Rivers*, 319.
[72] Ibid. 89.

Why, forty years later, had his recollections ceased to be a rich resource for him? Why had he lost the peace that writing seemed to have restored to him? What cataclysm had occurred in his memory that Saturday? Why did it suddenly become impossible for him to cope with the horrors of remembrance? One last time, with no help for it, anguish had quite simply overwhelmed him. Leaving no hope of any way out. The anguish he described in the last lines of *Le tregua* [*The Truce*]. . . . Nothing was real outside the camp, that's all. The rest was only a brief pause, an illusion of the sense, an uncertain dream. And that's all there is to say. (*LL* 251)

For others, they simply write and rewrite their testimony. For example, Hugo Gryn effectively retold his testimony in a number of times in different fora and media.[73] Kitty Hart's *Return to Auschwitz* was preceded by *I am Alive*, published in 1961 and one of the very earliest, if not the first, testimonies published in the UK, and in a revised edition in 1974.[74] Levi's *The Drowned and the Saved* revisits and expands—if in a slightly different tone—parts of *If This is a Man*.[75]

The reasons for this consistent rewriting and consequent refusal of closure are not simple. Perhaps most importantly, it is a response to the events themselves. The impossibility of closure is simply ineluctable on the part of the survivors. Wiesel goes a bit further: 'I have told the story before and will tell it again, will tell it forever, hoping to find in it some hidden truth, some vague hope of salvation'.[76] But there are other reasons. Writers have shown how the reception history of the Holocaust has developed since the war, how approaches and interest have waned then waxed.[77] Where once even Levi's work was turned down (by 'an important figure in Italian literature, Jewish', as Levi says—it turned out to be Natalie Ginzburg), now many publisher and filmmakers are interested in Holocaust testimonies.[78] This has meant that the opportunity for rewriting, as well as the compulsion to rewrite,

[73] Collated in Hugo Gryn with Naomi Gryn, *Chasing Shadows* (London: Penguin, 2001).

[74] Kitty Hart, *I am Alive* (London: Abelard-Schuman, 1961); rev. edn. (Corgi: London, 1974).

[75] Banner discusses these differences illuminatingly in *Holocaust Literature*, 117–20.

[76] Wiesel, *All Rivers*, 67.

[77] See, e.g., Michael André Bernstein, *Foregone Conclusions: Against Apocalyptic History* (London: University of California Press, 1994), esp. 14–15; Peter Novick, *The Holocaust and Collective Memory* (London: Bloomsbury, 2000); Norman Finkelstein, *The Holocaust Industry* (London: Verso, 2000); Tim Cole, *Images of the Holocaust: The Myth of the 'Shoah Business'* (London: Duckworth, 1999).

[78] Ferdinando Camon, *Conversations with Primo Levi*, tr. John Stepney (Marlboro, Vt.: Marlboro Press, 1989), 50. Her name cited, 51.

has emerged: Kitty Hart's *Return to Auschwitz* was developed in parallel with a Yorkshire TV documentary with the same name. But even then, she ends her book account with rewriting of her own part in the documentary. She writes that she had said 'the experience had been worthwhile'. She continues:

This was not at all what I meant. No such horror and such slaughter of innocents could ever in any sense have been worthwhile. What I was trying to convey, and what I say now, is that if such a terrible thing had to happen . . . then personally I would rather have gone through it than not gone through it. But I would not wish that anyone in the world should ever have to suffer such agonies again.[79]

Hart's second version, too, picks up on issues passed over or ignored in the first: her cool reception in Britain, the lack of interest in or refusal to hear about her experiences in Auschwitz (her uncle, almost as soon as he meets her, says 'there's one thing I must make quite clear. On no account are you to talk about any of the things that have happened to you. Not in my house, I don't want my girls upset. And I don't want to know.').[80] Training to be nurse in Birmingham was 'the nearest I ever came to total despair' she writes.[81] Much of the psychological and social aftermath of the Holocaust, its effect on, for example, her relationship with her mother, are things that have only emerged in texts as the 'epistemological climate' has changed.[82]

Closure, then, for these testimony writers, seems impossible: the compulsion to write, the 'bursting out' of the skin of their memories, and the changing relation of the contemporary world to the events of the Holocaust mean that these texts are never finished. This, too, serves as an interruption to an identification as it disrupts the expectations of closure and comprehension.

CONCLUSION

Here, then, is a taxonomy—partial, particular—of the ways in which testimony texts serve to disrupt identification: in turn, this also serves as suggestions for some of the generic markers of testimony that differentiate it from fiction and from autobiography. These texts sometimes utilize the style of writing more commonly associated with the

---

[79] Hart, *Return to Auschwitz*, 233.   [80] Ibid. 14.   [81] Ibid. 17.
[82] Young, *Writing and Rewriting*, 26.

discipline of history, and use documentary evidence. They set up (and sometimes explore) distinct narrative frames which prevent—or try to prevent—identification. They often use particular moments to focus the horror. They are characterized by interruptions in their narrative and disruptions in their chronology. They can—in the case of *The Sunflower*—attempt to create an over-identification. And they lack closure, both as texts, and as part of each survivor's œuvre.

Of course, texts written at different times, from the end of the war to the current day, also respond to different historical moments and trends: a memoir from 1946 has a different immediate context from one written in 1996. Moreover, the discussion above does not touch on issues of translation or lexical choice. The point of this taxonomy is not to be comprehensive, nor to do what Genette attempted in *Narrative Discourse* in essaying 'laws of narrative', but to bring to the fore illustrative general textual characteristics of this genre. Not every testimony has to have each one, nor are these characteristics criteria for determining what is and is not a testimony: they mark only descriptive 'family resemblances', not prescriptions. That such prescriptions are ineffective is a lesson learnt from the Wilkomirski affair. Moreover, prescriptions might also serve to delimit this still developing genre by, for example, discounting accounts: Anca Vlasopolos describes how her survivor mother felt her voice as a woman was ignored and passed over.[83] Each testimony changes and brings a different focus to the genre. All genres are shifting and developing: this one more than most. In part this is because, as Alvin Rosenfeld writes, Holocaust writing is 'a literature of fragments, or partial and provisional forms, no one of which by itself can suffice to express the Holocaust, but the totality of which begins to accomplish and register a powerful effect . . . Holocaust writing is part of a composite literature, more impressive in the sum of its parts than a separate statements.'[84] No one testimony is the central testimony: testimony works most powerfully as a genre. All this really serves to try to explain why reading testimony is not like reading a novel. These observations only begin to offer a rhetorical and academic apparatus to explain this common feeling, as an attempt to begin to understand the affect of testimonies and how it differs from other genres.

[83] See Anca Vlasopolos, *No Return Address: A Memoir of Displacement* (New York: Columbia University Press, 2000), 78–83.

[84] Alvin Rosenfeld, *A Double Dying: Reflections on Holocaust Literature* (Bloomington: Indiana University Press, 1988), 33, 34.

Why do these texts share these characteristics or strategies? It is not, or is not usually, a consciously planned strategy taken by the author/survivor. While, of course, these texts are constructed and are not immediate—Levi writing furiously, Wiesel editing and editing his Yiddish version, Semprun writing and destroying his manuscripts, Beer persuaded to tell her story, and so on—they were not constructed as part of a movement, as (say) one postmodernist writer imitates another. Cathy Caruth writes that the figures of 'falling' or 'departure'

engender stories that in fact emerge out of the rhetorical potential and literary resonance of these figures, a literary dimension that cannot be reduced to the thematic content of the text or to what the theory encodes, and that, beyond what we can know or theorise about, stubbornly persists in bearing witness to some forgotten wound.[85]

Similarly, the tropes and strategies examined are not a simple reflection in prose of the psychology of trauma. Rather, their tropes and strategies are empowered by their differences to other forms and genres of writing to offer—to be—testimony. This testimony is both personal (Primo Levi writes that one reason to write is to 'free oneself from anguish') and communal (in its bearing witness).[86] These texts draw on cultural resources (ideas about realism and modernism, say, ideas about narrative time lines, the relation between fiction and history) and construct them in a new way. Indeed, it is the cultural resources that are the ground of possibility for these prose testimonies. As James Young writes

if modern responses to catastrophe have included the breakdown and repudiation of traditional forms and archetypes, then one postmodern response might be to recognize that even as we reject the absolute meanings and answers these 'archaic' forms provide, we are still unavoidably beholden to these same forms for both our expression and our understanding of the Holocaust.[87]

But this is not to say that this new or renewed genre is not innovative, but that its innovation consists in its reworking of the 'traditional forms', centrally in such a way that identification is thrown into question.

---

[85] Cathy Caruth, *Unclaimed Experience: Trauma, Narrative and History* (London: John Hopkins University Press, 1996), 5.
[86] Primo Levi, *Other People's Trades*, tr. Raymond Rosenthal (London: Abacus, 1989), 65.
[87] Young, *Writing and Rewriting*, 192.

This also sheds light on the affinity between postmodern novels and testimony. Postmodern novels, too, mix genres, try to defy identification, lack closure, foreground their own textuality. Postmodern texts have found their way to similar textual strategies which have the 'rhetorical potential and literary resonance' which allow them perhaps to reflect a wider collective breakdown in the world, however this is to be understood (whether as a result of the Holocaust or as a shift from cognitive questions to postcognitive questions, incredulity about metanarratives, the death of God, the cultural logic of late capitalism, et cetera). Yet it is postmodern fiction that casts an eye on the tropes of testimony, not vice versa.

However, it is also the case that in testimony, signified by these tropes and strategies, something 'stubbornly persists', a link to a 'forgotten wound' or more accurately to a remembered event. It is these textual signs that bear a trace: the trace, as Derrida makes clear in an interview, which marks 'the limits of the linguistic and the limits of the rhetorical'.[88] The trace is the grounds for that which refuses comprehension (here, through identification): it is the trace of incomprehensible other, the witness.

And it is this, the idea of the trace, which underlies the truth of testimony. There is much debate about the 'historical' truth of testimonies. Many historians, for example, find them very open to question as sources for historical truth: Raul Hilberg suggests that what he sees as reconstructions with literary devices—'tools . . . employed to reach a readership'—form an 'incrustation' which does not 'open windows to this reality'.[89] As I will suggest in detail in Chapter 5, this sort of assessment assumes that there is only one way of understanding truth—as a positivist 'accurate record'. However, there is another way of understanding truth which is not contradictory but complementary: not as 'the agreement or correspondence of a judgement, an assertion or a proposition with its object' but as an existential uncovering or revelation, a showing 'who we are and how things are in the world'. This truth reveals something not quantitatively but qualitatively different from the historical record (yet it does not reveal the 'sublime', outside

[88] Jacques Derrida and Maurizio Ferraris, *A Taste for the Secret*, tr. Giacomo Donis, ed. Giacomo Donis and David Webb (London: Polity, 2001), 76.
[89] Raul Hilberg, *Sources of Holocaust Research* (Chicago: Ivan R. Dee, 2001), 71. Dan Stone summarizes these positions in 'Holocaust Testimony and the Challenge to the Philosophy of History', in Robert Fine and Charles Turner (eds.), *Social Theory after the Holocaust* (Liverpool: Liverpool University Press, 2000), 219–34.

time). While it can be measured as a historical datum, a testimony is not only that. Breaking and remaking the codes of western literature—defying identification, mixing styles, and shifting narrative frames, and so on—are not 'historical facts' but strategies which are affective and revealing. Thus, Delbo's remark 'Today, I am not sure that what I write is true. I am certain it is truthful' (*AA* epigraph) can be taken to mean: 'what I write may not correspond to the genre restrictions of the "historical record"; it certainly reveals in a more profound way what happened in the camps'.

In his influential book *Zakhor*, Yosef Hayim Yerushalmi argued that literature had become the crucible of Jewish memory, not historiography. However, the crucible of Holocaust memory, Jewish or non-Jewish, is not literature understood as fiction, but the genre of testimony. Accounts are not just words that 'signify experiences, but . . . become . . . *traces* of [those] experiences'.[90] A testimony is an encounter with otherness: it is this encounter precisely because identification—a grasping or comprehension which reduces otherness to the same, events outside one's framework reduced to events inside one's framework—cannot (or should not) happen. It is a witness to these events and should not be reduced simply to a historical account or a 'documentary novel' (these are both ways of reducing that otherness to the same): it is part of a genre of its own. And it is this genre—one that is strange not least because it denies the commonly accepted process of identification—that holds best the memory of the Holocaust.

---

[90] Young, *Writing and Rewriting*, 26.

3

'Faithful and Doubtful, Near and Far': Memory, Postmemory, and Identity

For years it lay like an iron box so deep inside me that I was never sure just what it was. I knew I carried slippery, combustible things more secret than sex and more dangerous than any shadow or ghost. Ghosts had shape and name. What lay in my iron box had none. Whatever lived inside was so potent that words crumbled before they could describe. Sometimes I thought I carried a terrible bomb. I had caught glimpses of destruction.[1]

INTRODUCTION

The previous two chapters have argued that testimony texts are a new genre which demands a way of reading which does not consume them through the processes of reading, principally through identification. Yet the link between identifying with a text and our own sense of identity *per se* is complex and unclear. Ian Hacking describes it when he writes that we 'constantly mimic others. Art, from great to tawdry, presents us with a selection of stylised characters from whom we acquire bit of our own ever-evolving personal style—and on whom, selectively, we mould our own character.'[2] It is not only with characters in art that we identify: for example, both Prince Andre Bolkonski in *War and Peace* and Georges Sorel in *The Red and the Black* identify—secretly, perhaps, and early in both books—with Napoleon. The phenomenon of transference, described in psychoanalysis, is a form of identification:

---

[1] Helen Epstein, *Children of the Holocaust: Conversations with Sons and Daughters of Survivors* (London; Penguin, 1988), 1.

[2] Ian Hacking, *Rewriting the Soul: Multiple Personality and the Sciences of Memory* (Princeton: Princeton University Press, 1995), 32.

more important, and again described by psychoanalysis, are the shifting identifications between children and parents. If the testimony texts we read or hear are encounters with otherness—texts that resist identification and cannot be easily comprehended or normalized—this adds a level of difficulty. Perhaps this difficulty—the need for identification, the impossibility of identification—is most acutely felt by the children of survivors. Here, into the mix of identification and identity comes, inevitably, memory—personal and collective—because it plays a major part in identity and in identification. How does the 'post-Holocaust memory' of those who did not live through the events relate to that which it cannot take on board fully? This question is significant not only for the children of survivors, but also—to lesser and different extents—to all of us who come after the Holocaust, and who reflect on it. This chapter begins by exploring the issue of memory and identity, both personal and collective, and then goes on to examine in detail three texts about postmemory to show how these concerns are made manifest in post-Holocaust texts that are centrally concerned with identification.

MEMORY AND IDENTIFICATION

In his book about the Holocaust industry, Norman Finkelstein writes that, although currently 'all the rage in the ivory tower, "memory" is surely the most impoverished concept to come down the academic pike in a long time.'[3] He is right in that certainly the concept of memory in the humanities is receiving a great deal of attention. However, he is wrong when he suggests that it is an impoverished concept: instead, during the 1990s and into the twenty-first century, memory has been and is one of the most fertile, widely ranging, and powerful concepts at work in the arts and humanities and in the sciences. Discussions of memory have begun, stimulated, and revived many important debates. Current debates over memory are not impoverished but, in fact, rather embarrassed by its conceptual riches.

While at first it might seem as if 'we all know what we mean' by memory, serious thought and research on memory reveals how little we understand about it. 'Memory studies'—like consciousness studies—

---

[3] Norman Finkelstein, *The Holocaust Industry: Reflections on the Exploitation of Jewish Suffering* (London: Verso, 2000), 4.

draws in cognitive scientists, biologists, physicists, psychologists, historians, literary critics, psychoanalysts, philosophers, sociologists, archaeologists, and many more. For example, Hacking identifies five areas of memory research in the sciences: the neurological studies, experimental studies of recall, the psychodynamics of memory ('I mean the study of memory in terms of observed or conjectured psychological processes and forces'), work at the level of cell biology, and computer modelling of memory for artificial intelligence.[4] To this list, one could add the studies of memory undertaken in the discipline of history: Kerwin Lee Klein traces the growth of memory as a subject for historians through two key texts (Pierre Nora's *Lieux de mémoire* and Yosef Yerushalmi's *Zakhor*), the establishment of the journal *History and Memory* in 1989, and a series of issues in the study of the Holocaust.[5] In literary studies, Peter Middleton and Tim Woods have also written on the 'cultural poetics of memory.'[6] The relation between memory and the self is one of the most fertile and widely discussed philosophical questions. It is, as Mary Warnock writes, our 'own continuity through time.'[7] It is essentially, deeply, and inextricably involved in 'experience, recognition, consciousness of identify of self through diversity of experience.'[8] A textbook on psychological memory states that 'You would be hard pressed to overstate how important your memory is to you. After all, everything you know about *anything* is stored in your memory.'[9] Indeed, memory and the sciences of memory—all the complex ways it can be understood and approached—evoke nearly everything there is to a person and to a society.

However, though part of 'who we are', memory is not co-terminal with identity. It can change and develop, fail and be reworked. The way in which we remember plays a large role in constructing our identity (personal, social, communal), and in turn our identity shapes in no small way how we remember the past, cope in the present, and hope or expect the future. I suggest that the relation could be thought about in

---

[4] Hacking, *Rewriting the Soul*, 199.

[5] Kerwin Lee Klein, 'On the Emergence of Memory in Historical Discourse', *Representations*, 69 (2000), 127–50, 141.

[6] Peter Middleton and Tim Woods, *Literatures of Memory: History, Time and Space in Postwar Writing* (Manchester: Manchester University Press, 2000), 1.

[7] Mary Warnock, *Memory* (London: Faber & Faber, 1987), 1.

[8] P. F. Strawson, *The Bounds of Sense* (London: Routledge, 1966), 111

[9] Alan Searleman and Douglas Herrman, *Memory from a Broader Perspective* (New York: McGraw Hill, 1994), p. xvii.

this way: *identity without memory is empty, memory without identity is meaningless.*

Many examples of something that tends towards the first part of this, people emptied of internal memory (but clearly identified, externally, as it were, by others), can be found in the psychological literature: most popularly, perhaps, in the accounts of disorientation, confusion, and personal tragedy in works like Oliver Sachs's *The Man who Mistook his Wife for a Hat*. Momik, as a boy in David Grossman's novel *See Under: Love*, is a fictional example of this tragic/comic confusion. His identity is shaped by his parents' memories of 'Over There', of how they survived 'the Nazi beast'. However, they do not tell him anything about it—there is no 'content' to the memories that inhabit him and so his response is to imagine the 'Nazi beast'. Since it can 'come out of any animal if it got the right care and nourishment', he imprisons animals in his cellar to see if he can bring it out and conquer it.[10] An 'empty' identity is soon filled.

The second part can be understood clearly in the Borges story of 'Funes the memorious', the man who remembers every detail of everything, so that this crawling ant is this very particular crawling ant on that bit of floor at this moment, and so on, to the extent that everything becomes particular and can no longer be generalized or schematized (all 'ants' are so particular in shape, time, and space that the term 'ant' is no longer useful and everything—not just ants—becomes meaningless because it overflows with meaning). Unable to maintain recognition through time or schematize his experiences, Funes's identity collapses. However, identity is not only 'personal'. 'Who I think I am' is embedded in various communities and so 'who I think I am' both constructs and is constructed by 'who we think we are'. 'I' and 'we' are circular. Memory stands as a key point of intersection in this process, inextricably involved with the relations between identity, narrative, text, and language.

While it is too strong, perhaps, to claim that 'identity is a matter of telling stories' (some events cannot be narrated, or cannot be easily understood), it is certainly the case the narrative is very important for identity.[11] Storytelling is 'the best analogy to remembering . . . The metaphor for memory is narrative.'[12] These 'memory narratives' take

---

[10] David Grossman, *See Under: Love*, tr. Betsy Rosenberg (New York: Noonday Press, Farrar Strauss Girouz, 1989), 12.

[11] Maureen Whitebrook, *Identity, Narrative and Politics* (London: Routledge, 2001), 4.

[12] Hacking, *Rewriting the Soul*, 250.

place at a number of different levels. As philosophers like Alasdair MacIntyre and Charles Taylor have argued, our self-identity is in no small part a result of the narrative and autobiographical stories we tell ourselves and others about ourselves. These are—or claim to be and should be when in good faith—acts of remembering, of establishing a 'necessary fiction' of ourselves. As Mary Warnock writes, citing Wordsworth and Woolf, the 'concept of re-creation of life' is central to the significance and joys of recollection as well as identity: 'what is re-created is my life.'[13] It is at this point, however, that current discussions expand on more traditional Anglo-American philosophic debates: memory is no longer considered simply a mental phenomenon but as something with much wider ramifications.

Our personal memories relate to our own larger stories—our 'family frames' as Marianne Hirsch names them. And these in turn relate to wider narratives that structure more public life, the narratives that make up our national and international identities, narratives and behaviours that are, as Homi Bhabha argues, both pedagogical and performative, both taught to us and acted out by us.[14] Memory is part of the imagined community, part of the image store (like Seamus Heaney's 'word hoard') that creates and actually is a community: to remember is to bring a communal body (back) together in an act of remembrance. These narratives, told to us as well as told by us, acted out by us and acted out in relation to us, are all interwoven and equiprimordial. We are interpellated, identified by and in a range of different memory narratives. Sometimes, of course, these different circles interpenetrate in a peaceful, constructive way; at other times they are at odds with each other. Their negotiation involves a constant reappraisal of memory and of identity and is a crucial part of the processes of identification. Because of this, contemporary discussions of memory are also precisely discussions of society and how it resolves, or fails to resolve, these negotiations between, for example, different 'memory communities' or between individual and more communal memories, between the private and the public. All this falls under what Hacking names—using the phenomenon of multiple personalities to focus his analysis—memoro-politics.

Memory and memoro-politics are key in all these intersections of personal and communal identity. Memory is a part of everyday

---

[13] Warnock, *Memory*, 142.
[14] Homi Bhabha, *The Location of Culture* (London: Routledge, 1994), 145.

existence, not simply a space for backward-looking reverie. We are the subjects of its sometimes unpredictable effects as, voluntarily or involuntarily, we remember. As we are rooted in time, so part of ourselves is the experience of pastness, and the content of that pastness itself is the memory of specific or general events. In this, memory is textual, as a verbal or written narrative, or invoking material culture (such as costumes, war memorials, tombstones, spaces, archaeological sites, museums, places of worship), ritual (visiting exhibitions, sports events, worshipping, civil functions), and demands different levels of identification and commitment (pride, anger, fear, and so on). Memory is where all these very different forms of text and textual relation meet and so covers the whole range of cultural production: not just 'material culture' but intellectual and social behaviour, habits, positions, practices, and so on. Collective memory is not 'a misleading new name' for 'myth': it is not some spurious spiritual entity like Jung's 'Collective unconscious' but constantly acted out and embodied in collective practices, material, and otherwise.[15] It is, as Nancy Wood writes, 'performative', and covers the whole range of cultural production.[16]

What has allowed memory to expand from the concerns about psychological processes or philosophical discussions—like Elizabeth Anscombe's account of the role of causation in memory—to this current much wider usage is an awareness of the social and linguistic frameworks for memory. Much of this stems from Maurice Halbwachs's insights into memory (Halbwachs's death in Buchenwald is remembered and described by Jorge Semprun).[17] Finding himself 'astonished' that psychological treatises that dealt with memory treated people 'as isolated beings', which makes it appear that to understand memory 'we need to stick to individuals first of all, to divide all the bonds which attach us to the society of their fellows', Halbwachs argued that 'it is in society that people normally acquire their memories. It is also in society that they recall, reorganise and localise their memories.'[18] He argued that memory existed through collective and social frameworks, and that these enabled individual memory to function: 'there is no point in seeing where [memories] are

[15] Noa Gedi and Yigal Elam, 'Collective Memory—What is it?', *History and Memory*, 8/1 (1996), 30–50, 47.

[16] Nancy Wood, *Vectors of Memory* (Oxford: Berg, 1999), 2.

[17] Jorge Semprun, *Literature or Life*, tr. Linda Coverdale (London: Viking, 1997), 41–3.

[18] Maurice Halbwachs, *On Collective Memory*, tr. Lewis A. Caser (London: University of Chicago Press, 1992), 38.

preserved in my brain or in some nook of my mind to which I alone have access: for they are recalled to me externally, and the groups of which I am a part at any time give me the means to reconstruct them.'[19] Memory 'needs continuous feeding from collective sources and is sustained by social and moral props . . . memory needs others.'[20] Following Halbwachs, Jeffrey Prager describes memory as 'embedded': 'Memorial productions are inseparable from the socially and culturally located individual, who is intersubjectively linked to the world of others and to a world defined by interpretative cultural frames that connect each person to the larger cultural whole.'[21] Memory spans personal, communal, and political identities, exists in different forms of text, and is related to language.

One consequence of this is that memory is not motionless, and adapts and evolves as the present changes, as identity changes. It is not the case that 'for most people, their memories are among their most cherished possessions', as memory is not a static 'possession.'[22] This idea of memory as a posession reflects an imagist view of memory, as if memory is like a mental photograph or representation of an event, recalled to the mind's eye like opening the right page of a photograph album. Advances on this argue that memory is perhaps not a 'picture' but an active system—events are recalled as interactions—and, as a result, they can be distorted, changed, or misremembered, but this still assumes a 'storehouse' that the mind can access. But memory is not like this. As the Canadaian writer Anne Michaels writes:

> We do not descend, but rise from our histories.
> If cut open memory would resemble
> a cross-section of the earth's core
> a table of geological time.[23]

We do not store our memories. Much of what makes us what we are simply is our memories: identity without memory is empty (and even the word 'empty' here shows how strong this 'storehouse' metaphor

[19] Maurice Halbwachs, *On Collective Memory*, tr. Lewis A. Caser (London: University of Chicago Press, 1992), 38.

[20] Ibid. 34.

[21] Jeffrey Prager, *Presenting the Past: Psychoanalysis and the Sociology of Misremembering* (London: Harvard University Press, 1998), 70, 71.

[22] Searleman and Herrman, *Memory from a Broader Perspective*, xvii.

[23] Anne Michaels, 'Lake of Two Rivers', *The Weight of Oranges* (Toronto: Coach House Press, 1985), 14. On this, see Nicola King, *Memory, Narrative, Identity: Remembering the Self* (Edinburgh: Edinburgh University Press, 2000), 144–8, although she does assume memory to be a 'storehouse'.

is). Because human beings are in and of time—are historical—their ontological structure reflects this and they experience time as antici- pation of the future and the experience of pastness. Just as conscious- ness is always consciousness of something, pastness always exists not as an abstract, but as full and, with the exception of sleep and forget- fulness, this fullness is manifested as memory. We do not possess mem- ories: memories possess us, we rise from them.

Memory, then, spans divisions between many different but related spheres: between the public and the private, between how each of us acts and is acted upon, between the gamut of activities from everyday improvisations to ritual observances, between 'historical fact' and 'fiction'. Indeed, it is the site for many of these interactions. It takes in all modes of cultural production. It plays a central role in narrative, cultural, social, and psychological processes. Perhaps most impor- tantly it is involved with the adaptation and development of identities of all sorts and at all levels: personal, social, communal, political. For Charlotte Delbo and for the Canadian writer Anne Michaels, memory is skin: defining who we are, where the inside meets the outside.

It is hardly a surprise that these discussions over memory have engaged with the Holocaust: indeed, it is to some extent to deal with the Holocaust that memory has developed as a subject for academic discourse and it is in this context of contemporary discussions about memory—as both public and private, inextricably involved with identification, embedded and yet not static—that the idea of postmem- ory has developed.

POSTMEMORY AND IDENTIFICATION

Ellen Fine asks: 'How does one "remember" an event not experienced? . . . How does the Holocaust shape the identity of those living in its aftermath—"the self's sense of itself"—and how is the burden of mem- ory then assumed? How does the post-genocide generation respond psychologically and imaginatively to the legacy bequeathed?'[24] In approach to the issues that Fine raises, Marianne Hirsch, discussing the relation of photographs to narrative and family memory, hesitantly

---

[24] Ellen S. Fine, 'Transmission of Memory: The Post-Holocaust Generation in the Diaspora', in Efraim Sicher (ed.), *Breaking Crystal: Writing and Memory of Auschwitz* (Chicago: University of Illinois Press, 1998), 185.

(because 'it could imply that we are beyond memory') coins the term postmemory. Postmemory

is distinguished from memory by generational distance and from history by deep personal connection. Postmemory is a powerful and very particular form of memory precisely because its connection to its object or source is mediated not through recollection but through an imaginative investment and creation. This is not to say that memory itself is unmediated, but that it is more directly connected to the past. Postmemory characterises the experience of those who grow up dominated by narratives that preceded their birth, whose own belated stories are evacuated by the stories of the previous generation shaped by traumatic events that can be neither understood nor recreated.[25]

In a way, postmemory represents the ways memories are passed down generations, forming individual and communal identity, made possible by memory's textualization in myriad different forms and, to a large extent, by its narratives of the past. In this light, it does seems unnecessary to invent a new term: memory is already communal, passed down, and not necessarily immediate. However, the idea of 'postmemory' does try to reflect the special concerns of memory and identity in this post-Holocaust context ('the experience of those who grow up dominated by narratives that preceded their birth'): more than this, it points to 'Memory shot through with holes' (Henri Raczymow) or a 'vicarious memory' (Froma Zeitlin), where the collective memory is full of gaps, blanks, uncertainties.[26] Postmemory represents the unhappy truth of the sins against the parents being visited on the children.

Hirsch, although she believes that this concept of postmemory could usefully describe other postmemories, developed this concept in relation to the children of Holocaust survivors (*FF* 242–3). Ellen Fine suggests that the children of survivors 'continue to "remember" an event not lived through. Haunted by history, they feel obliged to accept the burden of collective memory that has been passed onto them and to assume the task of sustaining it.'[27] Hirsch writes that although nobody

knows the world of their parents . . . the motor of the fictional imagination is fuelled in great part by the desire to know the world as it looked and felt before our birth. How much more ambivalent is this curiosity for children of

[25] Marianne Hirsch, *Family Frames: Photographs, Narrative and Postmemory* (London: Harvard University Press, 1997), 22. This will be abbreviated to *FF* in the text.

[26] Henri Raczymow, 'Memory Shot through with Holes', *Yale French Studies*, 85 (1994), 98–105; Froma I. Zeitlin, 'The Vicarious Witness: Belated Memory and Authorial Presence in Recent Holocaust Literature', *History and Memory*, 10/2 (1998), 5–42, 5.

[27] Fine, 'Transmission', 187.

Holocaust survivors, exiled from a world that has ceased to exist, that has been violently erased. Theirs is a different desire, at once more powerful and more conflicted: the need not just to feel and to know, but also to re-member, to re-build, to re-incarnate to replace and repair. (*FF* 242–3)

This exile or displacement, this estrangement from identity is a 'characteristic aspect of post-memory. It brings its own narrative genres and aesthetic shapes' (*FF* 243). In a parallel discussion to Novick, Hirsch discusses 'absent memory' as the way that 'many Jews have built an identity as Jews precisely through the shared traumatic memory and postmemory of the Shoah': 'In perpetual exile, this/my generation's practice of mourning is as determinate as it is interminable and ultimately impossible.... The aesthetics of postmemory ... is a diasporic aesthetics of temporal and spatial exile that needs simultaneously to rebuild and to mourn' (*FF* 244–6). Searching for an identity, 'those born after' attempt to relocate themselves by forging 'an aesthetics of postmemory' (*FF* 40). Helen Epstein, herself the child of survivors, writes of setting out to find and interview others like her who 'were possessed by a history they had never lived.'[28] Aaron Hass explores this sociologically, using a questionnaire at the basis of his research.[29] However, rather than looking at photographs, surveys, or interviews, I want to look at three examples of texts by the children of survivors which are precisely both about Hirsch's postmemory and are themselves acts of postmemory. There are many of these texts now—their number includes Art Spiegelman's *Maus* in 1986 and its sequel *Maus II* in 1991, George Perec's *W or The Memory of Childhood* (1975), as well as Sarah Kofman's *Rue Ordener Rue Labat* (1994). Paul Auster's *The Invention of Solitude* has something of this too: 'The Book of Memory' has its origins in the writer character 'crying without sound, the tears streaming down his cheeks' in the Anne Frank house.[30]

These texts articulate this complex intersection between identity, the past, memory, and culture and, centrally, they concern the process by which identification takes place and then is developed. What is at stake here is exactly this 'aesthetics of memory.' And—not least since aesthetics and identification are so closely linked—this, in turn, is precisely about the relationship between these writers and their identifications.

---

[28] Helen Epstein, *Children of the Holocaust: Conversations with Sons and Daughters of Survivors* (London: Penguin, 1988), 14.

[29] See Aaron Hass, *In the Shadow of the Holocaust: The Second Generation* (Cambridge: Cambridge University Press, 1996).

[30] Paul Auster, *The Invention of Solitude* (London: Faber & Faber, 1989), 82.

JUDAISM FROM WITHOUT: ALAIN FINKIELKRAUT,
THE IMAGINARY JEW

> A family history? If you wish, but only to the extent than this fam-
> ily is neither a homogenous site not an Oedipal battleground, but
> a cultural space traversed by history, built of layers, as Deleuze
> would say, that are not familial at all.[31]

Alain Finkielkraut's engagement with the memory of the Holocaust
and with his Jewishness is the subject of his third book, *The Imaginary
Jew*. He was born in Paris in 1949, his father an Auschwitz survivor, his
mother a 'U-boat' who hid in Germany in the 1930s and in Belgium
during the war with false papers. Like some other survivors they 'chose
not to pass down Jewish traditions to their son, either religious or secular. For them, Yiddish culture had disappeared in Poland, together
with their families and friends.'[32] As a student in Paris at the Lycée
Henry IV, he became involved in the *enlevements* of 1968, and it is with
these events that his reflection on memory and identity begins.
Overwhelmed by Sartre and by the political climate, he felt that he was
'offered a dispensation from every stupidity, exempted from any conformity by a privilege called Judaism':

> With it understood once and for all that the world was divided into torturers
> and victims, I belonged to the camp of the oppressed. I had no need of con-
> sciousness raising: from Spartacus to Black Power, an instinctive and uncondi-
> tional solidarity united me with all the earth's damned. Was I not myself the
> living reproach that suffering humanity aimed at its executioners?   (*IJ* 9)

The reference to the damned—the 'wretched'—reveals, as much of his
later work does, Finkielkraut's debt to Frantz Fanon. Yet, from
'Judaism I drew neither religion nor a way of life, but the certainty of
superior sensitivity' (*IJ* 9). He understood this in a Sartrean manner: 'I
was an authentic Jew . . . courage, even heroism were required for me
to claim so loudly and so strongly my ties to a people in disgrace' (*IJ* 9).
This philosophical image of the 'authentic Jew', the 'living reproach' to
inhumanity filled the gap between 'what I imagined myself to be and

[31] Alain Finklielkraut, *The Imaginary Jew*, tr. Kevin O'Neill and David Suckoff
(London: University of Nebraska Press, 1994), 173–4. This will be abbreviated in the text
to *IJ*.
[32] Judith Friedlander, *Vilna on the Seine: Jewish Intellectuals in France since 1968*
(London: Yale University Press, 1990), 92.

the existence I actually led' (*IJ* 9). The Holocaust was, clearly, central to this. Responding to the stories and memories of survivors, 'I would cry in anguish and anger' (*IJ* 11). Yet the 'terror left no traces . . . I didn't carry the burden of mourning my exterminated family, but I did carry its banner' (*IJ* 11). More than this, he recounted these stories, his family's stories, to eager audiences and 'harvested all the moral advantage . . . for them utter abandonment and death, for their spokesperson, sympathy and honour' (*IJ* 11). Although he did not intend for this to happen, to take on and take over this identity in this way, he did let it: lineage 'made me genocide's huckster' (*IJ* 11) he writes of himself. He had become the 'imaginary Jew' of his title: neither religious nor taking on board the ethical imperatives of Judaism, these characters— and he is least sparing of himself—are 'armchair Jews, since, after the Catastrophe, Judaism cannot offer them any content but suffering, and they themselves do not suffer' (IJ 11). He had created for himself an identification with the Jews murdered in the Holocaust which was politically and socially useful for him in that particular Parisian context and time.

What began his questioning of this untroubled identification with a 'post-Holocaust' identity was his resentment at the famous 1968 slogan 'We are all German Jews', which arose as a protest at the authorities refusal to readmit Daniel Cohn-Bendit to France: it 'despoiled me and sullied my treasure . . . "Hands off", I felt like saying. "You can't become a Jew or a dago just like that. You need certification, references . . . You haven't paid your dues" ' (*IJ* 18). Yet, in resenting this usurpation, he realized that he, too, was a usurper: 'I hadn't suffered either, nor paid my dues . . . Their disguise was temporary . . . for me, every day was a costume party. I was a Jew, and frankly, I never had to take off my disguise' (*IJ* 18). This self-awareness about the inauthenticity of his sense of identity began a development and changed his relation to memory. Finkielkraut writes—against himself—that the 'Holocaust has no heirs. No one can cloak himself in such an experience, incommunicable, if not the survivors' (*IJ* 34). He explored different possibilities that made up his 'jewishness'—psychoanalysis, Zionism, and so on. He describes his growth to the awareness that his parents, keen to protect him by making him 'the perfect little Frenchman', have created a 'mutant' (*IJ* 112) whose experience of his proclaimed identity is one of lack. This lack is complex: it is a lack of his own 'cultural affinity', the 'thousand things we don't have in common that I'll never have a chance to acquire', things that are part of 'a Judaism that flows from the source', and, more ominously, things that make up the 'experience of Nazism as lived' (*IJ* 112–13). He does not have these and is left with a sense of emptiness, lack, and exile. He goes on:

I am not Jewish, in short, because of the Eternal One, the Zionist ideal, the spirit of revolt or an Oedipal symptom are present within me. What makes me a Jew is the acute consciousness of a lack, of a continuous absence: my exile from a civilisation, which for my own good my parents didn't wish me to keep in trust. (*IJ* 113)

This postmemory, here, is the experience of a lack of a specifically Jewish memory.

Yet, this absence and loss—a result of the Holocaust—is not the end of the story of memory for Finkielkraut, nor is it to be understood in a simple way, suggesting that he has been deprived. In fact, it reveals to Finkielkraut—'raised on the debates between Corneille and Racine, not on those between Hillel and Shammai'—a more authentic Judaism.[33] Despite Finkielkraut's account of his own development, Sartre is not too far away in *The Imaginary Jew*. The imaginary Jew is the 'armchair Jew', the inauthentic Jew. In fact, the authentic Jew is the one who experiences Judaism as a lack, as a going out. In Levinas's metaphor—Finkielkraut is very influenced by Levinas—Judaism is not like Ulysses returning home to Ithaca, an identity supported by power and tradition, but Abraham wandering homeless in the desert, 'a movement of the same unto the other which never returns to the same.'[34] Not only does this mean that there is no final victory of a 'real I' over the disguise, it also means that, for Finkielkraut, Judaism 'is not simply a matter of expression or of person sincerity . . . it's to be found outside of myself and it resists any definition in the first person singular: it is received 'from without . . . it brings me more than I contain within' (*IJ* 172, 176). His self undone, 'Judaism, for me, is no longer a kind of identity as much as a kind of transcendence' (*IJ* 176). Being Jewish—an identity worn like a suit that precluded learning about Judaism—has been replaced with a more humble and nomadic becoming-Jewish: 'I learned loyalty and began the imperfect construction of a memory that would retain and transmit as much as possible about those beings who taught me that Judaism was something to love' (*IJ* 179). The memory

---

[33] Friedlander, *Vilna on the Seine*, 104.

[34] Emmanuel Levinas, 'The Trace of the Other', tr. Alphonso Lingis, in *Deconstruction in Context*, ed. Mark. C. Taylor (London: University of Chicago Press, 1986), 345–59 (p. 348). For this influence, see Friedlander, *Vilna on the Seine*, 80–106.

of the Holocaust, this sense of Jewish community and heritage is no longer owned and proclaimed by Finkielkraut (except when he slips into this language, as he admits he does) but instead he inhabits and develops this other, for him, more authentic Judaism. He has developed an understanding of his Judaic heritage that allows him to evolve a leftist ethical, if not religious, Judaism (the term is Judith Friedländer's). The lack he feels—although it comes from the destruction of European Jewry and a feeling of exile—is precisely what turns him back to Judaism, not to fill this lack but as an awareness of transcendence, of the fragility of his own identity under the 'gaze of the other' (*IJ* 15).

His reaction to postmemory is a dynamic one that has led to a new understanding of Judaism for him. The book is primarily in a confessional, philosophical register. Monologues and internal conversations appear, as he develops his own position. Little actual family or community appear. He also discusses relevant events, sometimes implicitly (the book was written at the time of the Faurisson affair, on which Finkielkraut wrote).[35] His position—that cultural and personal identity is not fixed to be proclaimed, but is fluid and evolving—influences his other work. In his book, *The Undoing of Thought*, for example, he argues against transmutation 'of culture into *my* culture': while he agrees that 'we all know that everything is cultural' not racial, he is equally concerned to point out that 'the modern fanatics of cultural identity consign individuals to their backgrounds.'[36] These people, he argues, simply repeat with culture what racists had done with race. In contrast, for him, multicultural means 'well stocked'.[37] His experience of his own postmemory identity and its exiled, nomadic nature leads him to suspect that we are all exiles. To say that there are no heirs to the Holocaust is to say that, in a way, we all are.

---

[35] Alain Finkielkraut, *L'Avenir d'une négation: Réflexion sur la question du genocide* (Paris: Seuil, 1982). See also Pierre Vidal-Naquet, *Les Assassins de Mémoire* (Paris: Éditions de la Découverte, 1987). For some comments on Finkielkraut's role, see the foreword of the English translation by Jeffrey Mehlman, *Assassins of Memory*, tr. Jefrey Mehlman (New York: Columbia University Press, 1993).

[36] Alain Finkielkraut, *The Undoing of Thought*, tr. Dennis O'Keeffe (London: Claridge, 1988), 11, 76, 77.

[37] Ibid. 112.

PSYCHIC COLD: ANNE KARPF, *THE WAR AFTER*

> I began to sob in a way which made me feel uncomfortable. I was
> crying so personally over something which hadn't happened to
> me. It seemed then as if I hadn't lived the central experience of my
> life—at its heart, at mine, was an absence.[38]

In contrast to the more philosophical *The Imaginary Jew*, Anne
Karpf's *The War After* is a much more personal and psychological
account of the effects and the phenomenon of postmemory. The major
part of the book describes her childhood and adult life in relation to the
psychological crisis brought about to some degree by being a child of
survivors. Karpf is frank in admitting that this is not set in stone: 'You
don't need to be the child of survivors or even Jewish to have an ongoing sense of exclusion' she writes, yet her account and experiences do
share a great deal with the children of other survivors and reflect issues
of postmemory (*WA* 142). In different registers—the personal memoir,
the diary, academic accounts, transcribed tapes—it weaves together
her accounts of her own experiences, the testimony of her parents, a
wider and more formal history of British Jewry and a psychologically
informed discussion of what it is like to be a child of survivors.

The narrative of her own crisis is very revealing and quite coura-
geous. She begins the book with a leitmotif: her parents' obsession with
keeping her warm outside the home. It dawns on her that 'cold wasn't
just a meteorological fact but also a psychic state. My parents experienced the post-war world as cold, both in their bodies and minds' (*WA*
4). She and her sister grew up in an atmosphere suffused by the memory of the war: the 'Holocaust was our fairy-tale' (*WA* 94), it was
'enmeshed in our parents' personal subjectivity and was part of the
family tissue' (*WA* 96). The 'war was the yardstick by which all other
bad experiences were judged and thereby found to be relatively good'
(*WA* 38). One of her responses to this was to retell her mother's story
just as Finkielkraut performed his family stories. For Karpf, this gave
her a 'kind of reflected martyrdom', but through 'constant recounting'
the story began to take on a 'life of its own, detached from the original
events to which it referred' (*WA* 95) and she became wedded to what

---

[38] Anne Karpf, *The War After* (London: Minerva, 1996), 146. This will be abbreviated
to *WA* in the text.

she calls its 'storyness' (WA 95), leaving her the version of the story she heard as a child. More than this, she writes that she and her sister had an 'unstated mission' to 'assuage' the impact of the Holocaust: 'we were somehow charged with their redemption' (WA 95). She is aware that her parent's lives were 'bisected': 'but whereas they always seemed to accept the bisection and fully inhabit the second half, I was in some way always trying to recover the former half, for which I felt an enormous sense of loss' (WA 139). Perhaps her parents were so adaptable and resilient that they did not feel their own loss, or perhaps had to shake it off to preserve themselves. Or perhaps, she suggests, 'I felt their loss for them' (WA 139). She did not feel 'a proper person': 'What are not visible in survivors are their anaesthetised parts, their necessary autism. I came to feel that my sense, as a child and young adult, of not being a proper person was somehow connected with this, with a whole school of emotions being out of bounds' (WA 249).

The issues of postmemory begin to be revealed by an identity crisis that starts when she becomes involved with P., a non-Jewish man, which brings to the foreground her relationship to her parents (and so their memory) and their Jewishness. Her body itself become the locus of the conflict, braking out in eczema rashes and causing her to scratch and scratch to the point of self-harm. Her condition worsens and despite her professional success she falls prey to a dark, maddening depression. Her relationship ends and confirms, for her, 'what, viscerally, I'd always supposed that I wasn't allowed to have' (WA 125). This depression reveals what is perhaps the core of her experience of postmemory:

I'd always envied my parents their suffering. This was obviously so shocking that I couldn't have admitted it, had I even been conscious of it. It didn't mean that I underestimated the horror of the war or that I masochistically sought out pain, only that their terrible experiences seemed to diminish—even to taunt—anything bad that happened to us. In its drama, enormity and significance, their war could never be matched. We would always be children in a playpen of misery. But I also envied their suffering because it was so excluding and unshareable. It had originated before we were born, wasn't caused by us and, however much we tried, we would never be able to take it away. I wanted to force an entry into their close world of grief. My whole life had been an act of solidarity—an attempt never to have more pleasure, fun or success than they had had (while at the same time needing to be extravagantly happy and successful to keep them buoyant—no wonder I was confused). It was as if I had been running in some perverse relay race and had gladly grasped the baton of unhappiness. (WA 125–6)

However, through her own desire, through therapy, and her increasing understanding of her own—and so her parents'—experiences, she begins to change her relationships. She resumes her attachment to P., is more assertive, especially about her Jewishness. Her parents accept P., and she faces her feelings of loss more head on. This story is interwoven with interviews with her mother and father, which detail their experience. He father managed to escape to Russia, her mother—a very talented pianist—was moved through a number of camps, including Auschwitz, ending up in Czechoslovakia. After the war, her father was posted to London and asked for asylum rather than return to Poland when he was recalled. In this way, her own account (as postmemory) offsets her parents' memory.

The book then changes genres, as if reflecting the narrator's improving health. There is a section on British Jews before and after the war, and their unwillingness to help European Jews.[39] There is also a discussion on the psychological effects of 'second generation syndrome': the traumatic and damage done by postmemory. These are many and multiple: they include difficulties in individuation, over-identification with the parents, bad reactions to parental overvigilance, and high expectations. Again, the detachment and understanding represented by Karpf the narrator to discuss these—her own symptoms—and the sympathy she shows for survivor parents illustrate that the trauma of postmemory has developed into something else. The form of the book is an analogy for the form of her reaction to postmemory.

The final section represents a coming to terms with memory, community, and identity in three different ways: through motherhood, mourning, and a visit to Poland. Again, like Finkielkraut, these are not a completion but part of the continuing negotiation. She has a daughter, B., which in turn draws her into a closer familiar and communal identity: she writes that 'B's birth completed the healing process between my parents, P., and me' (*WA* 260). She recounts a Seder meal in 1992, a large and successful family occasion. It is the last Seder because, the following year, her father declined and died. Karpf recounts this in a diary form. Again, this serves to unify her with her family through the experience of death and mourning. Symbolically, she inherits her father's desk. From her mother, she inherits the

---

[39] On this, and for a wider historical perspective, see Tony Kushner, *The Holocaust and the Liberal Imagination* (Oxford: Blackwell, 1994).

'Elijah's cup, the special plate, and the cloth to cover the matzos. It was as if she'd passed me the baton of Jewishness: I felt unfamiliarly adult' (*WA* 286). She also goes to Poland, visits sites relevant to her parents' memory. Again, these passages are in the present tense, as in a diary. She is deeply moved, cries 'as if I may be crying for ever' (*WA* 298), but, again, the experience joins her to the past.

Although the text of *The War After* concludes, the 'war after' does not. She is not 'a case history' (*WA* 313) and all her problems have not resolved. She is aware too that the book, about Holocaust experiences, will obviously centre on these and their responses—on issues of post-memory rather than simply autobiography. Her sense of family and community also continues: she tells B. to put her coat on: ' "you'll be cold" '. ' "No, mama" she replies "I'm not cold. You are" ' (*WA* 317).

A HARD WORK OF MOURNING: LEON WIESELTIER, *KADDISH*

> In all this wrestling with memory, family, identity, morality, history and divinity, there is a subject with which I am not wrestling, and it is death. But it turns out that mourning in the Jewish traditions is not really about death. The Jews are not interested in extinction, except to oppose it. Still I am interested in extinction, since I expect it. The Jews will not die; but Jews will die, and I am one of them.[40]

Kaddish, as the name indicates, is a work of mourning. It describes the year following the death of the narrator's father, in which Leon Wieseltier, who prior to this had lived 'undevoutly' (*K* 28), says kaddish for his father. Rather like *The Imaginary Jew* and *The War After*, the book is about how the narrator comes to terms with his Jewish heritage and the memory—personal, ritual, religious, cultural, social—that this entails. If Karpf's account highlights her principally psychological concerns, and Finkielkraut's his philosophical ones, Wieseltier's concerns are more specifically religious: he engages with his traditions both intellectually, by unsystematically exploring the development of the mourners kaddish and the debates it engendered, and ritually, by saying kaddish three times a day for his father for the proscribed period (although, through a mistake, Wieseltier says kaddish for too long). These engagements are dynamic in that they chart

[40] Leon Wieseltier, *Kaddish* (London: Picador, 2000), 198. This will be abbreviated to *K* in the text.

changes in his relation to personal, intellectual, communal, social, and ritual memory.

It is not only his study that is unsystematic. Though held together by the schema of the year saying kaddish, and divided into (nearly) monthly sections, the text of the book is made of fragments of writing that seem to be of different genres: readings of Judaic scholarship, the narrative of ritual and social life and the growing significance of the shul for him, the narrative of his mourning, little fragmentary aphorisms, religious, cultural, and literary thoughts, and passages of philosophy. The fragmentary nature of the book, its refusal of a strict genre, also represents at a level of form his own fragmentation and the different roles that he enacts. Yet, even this wrestling with tradition is part of the tradition: 'I must be faithful *and* I must be doubtful. I must be near *and* I must be far' (*K* 564). It is aphoristic and fragmentary and unified and whole: a midrash on his experience in his year of mourning.

Some strands can be drawn out. If, for Anne Karpf, the handing down of the ceremonial Seder items is a symbol of her taking up her role as Jewish, Wieseltier's detailed engagement with the traditions of Jewish scholarship and ritual make up his: in mourning for his father, he writes 'I don't know what to do. No, I know what to do. I will open a book' (*K* 6) and turns to Nahmanides: 'It is also Jewish. Anyway, it is what I know how to do' (*K* 172). (In an illuminating contrast, Auster turns both to historical archives, philosophers, and to an elegiac immersion in literary style in his mourning book, *The Invention of Solitude*.) Wieseltier's discussion of his exploration of the sages of Judaism are fraught with wonder: debates over the role of women, or the significance of eggs or lentils for mourning. These things that are discoveries for him both matter in themselves but also matter because they are that which makes up the tradition: they are the words of the language of tradition. For Wieseltier, it is not enough simply to declare his 'jewishness': in Finkielkraut's terms this would be the act of an 'armchair Jew'. It needs to be enacted, lived. He writes (after Kirkegaard) that

I have read of people whose lives are transfigured in an instant. I do not believe that such a transfiguration can happen to me. For what changed those people was not only the instant, but also their subsequent fidelity to the instant. This is the paradox of revelation. It disrupts the order of things and then depends upon it. (*K* 61)

He represents how he lives his Judaism intellectually, through these debates and discoveries, through the exploration of his tradition.

His immersion in Jewish learning affects his relation to other areas of intellectual life. He find himself more and more opposed to materialist and reductionist accounts of the world. This is most frequently expressed in little aphorisms. He also locates his own thought in relation not just to his tradition but in relation to other thinkers, sometimes explicitly (Heidegger, Levinas), sometimes less so (Plato, Kirkegaard) (*K* 421). This, too, reflects a dynamic: a creation of identity and the location of an intellectual in relation to a wider tradition.

In terms of memory and identity, the growing ritual life of the narrator, and his evolving relation to it are central to the book. 'Years ago', he writes, 'when I stopped praying, the disappearance of religious structure seemed to bring with it the promise of possibility . . . the adventure of self creation . . . I did not create myself. I merely accepted platitudes and other habits' (*K* 17). Yet, as he begins to undertake his commitment seriously, the shul loses its 'strangeness' (*K* 19). Gradually he becomes more involved: he is given a key ('Today, I became Washington insider' (*K* 162)), he tidies up the outside of the shul. He feels himself a 'member of the congregation' (*K* 218), is involved in 'friendly banter' (*K* 273). In New York, at his father's shul, he takes his father's seat and has 'a physical sensation of inheritance' (K 218); other members of this congregation shake his hand, offering in one gesture 'condolences' and congratulations' (*K* 218). That this is gendered (fathers, sons) is part of its significance: perhaps sometimes tradition can only be countered in tradition. No little part of *Kaddish* is taken up by a discussion of the role of women mourners. Wieseltier is aware of the burden and the enervating effects, sometimes, of saying kaddish three times a day. But the acceptance of the ritual memory shapes and alters his identity. He not only becomes part of the community spatially, but also chronologically: 'I saw some workmen laying a long cable in the street. They, too, were hard at work on the transmission of energy.—A cable running through time, not space' (*K* 401).

The book is in part—for lack of a better term—a spiritual memoir. Not only do the words of the kaddish, especially 'magnified and sanctified', run through the text like a fugue, but the narrative also describes how his 'prayer life' develops. One reason he stopped attending shul is that his experience of prayer was a 'failure' (*K* 19): he found it a 'desolating and debasing form of utterance' (*K* 20). However, the text represents his slowly growing feelings of his authentic experience of prayer. He realizes that it does not 'work' (*K* 247): he is startled by the congregation's response, 'I know what happened. They are believers and I said the right thing' (*K* 400). Yet, as he continues to say the mourner's kaddish, he finds himself coming to a different understanding of the point of prayer. Finally, he says kaddish by the graveside of his father and with 'my own eyes, I saw magnificence' (*K* 585).

The book is also about coming to terms with the death of his father, but not so much in the conventional sense of mourning, although he does discuss his deep hurt and loss: he sits and cries in Dupont Circle, for example (*K* 368). More than 'only personal' mourning, the death of his father is the catalyst for his intentional rediscovery and taking on of the whole burden of being Jewish, which he discovers to be an act of kaddish. He writes

I have been hearing the moaning of wood. It is not like a human moan. It is not a moan of pain, it is a moan of adjustment—the whisper produced by a shift in pressure, by a strain that is ending, by an accommodation with the forces that are pushing and pulling. One day I would like to moan like wood. (*K* 283)

This moaning is, in a sense, the kaddish, the coming to terms with tradition, with the forces that push and pull. And of those forces, in *Kaddish*, one of the strongest is the postmemory of the Holocaust.

If the book is about coming to terms with memory, and so learning to inhabit and so renew it, then for Wieseltier the Holocaust is a constant pressure, something that weighs heavily on the book. The memory of the events reappear again and again: in discussions of catastrophe and extinction (*K* 73), about the afterlife (*K* 236), in his gnomic sayings (*K* 430), in an angry discussion of Semprun and Chagall Christianizing Jewish suffering (*K* 468–9), in the work of Talmudists murdered in 1942 (*K* 57), and the *Responsa from Out of the Depths* of Rabbi Ephraim Oshry in the Kovno ghetto (*K* 537), books saved from Europe (*K* 505). In Maimonides, there are codes for mourning many of one's family at once: 'there are many ways to lose a lot of loved ones at the same time, but . . . only one way comes to mind' (*K* 66).

His grandparents, aunts, and uncles were murdered in Galicia at Bronica: elsewhere he writes that for years he thought a ravine was a place where people went to get killed (*K* 543). He reflects that when his parents' world ended, the rest of the world did not (*K* 77). His parents began sentences 'At home, we used to . . .' (*K* 506). On their tombstones are and will be engraved the names of their relations who were murdered so 'that the family stone, too, should bear a scar' (*K* 25) and the names are revealed at the end of the book (*K* 584). He recalls the responses of US Jewry to his parents and other survivors (*K* 233). But this 'gulf' (*K* 25) is still potent. He writes that for his mother

this is a wound that has not healed . . . With an unspoken bitterness, my parents watched their friends and their neighbours journey to the cemeteries of Long Island in the weeks leading up to Rosh Hashanah, in the natural rhythm of the generations. It is no wonder, I guess, that my mother's mourning for my father became a kind of super-mourning, an encompassing sorrow, in which she could at last perform the duties of a mourner not only for her husband, but also for her father and her mother and her brother. The great bereavement was no longer deferred.

And this, too, is what Wieseltier is doing: coming to terms and—more than this—taking on a broken and murdered tradition through mourning his father. A constant theme that runs throughout the book is that the 'son acquits the father' (*K* 170): the burden and unavoidable necessity of tradition. He writes that he had tried to persuade his father to tape his memories, yet he never did, but his 'memory endures in my memory, his version of him in my version of him' (*K* 564).

Yet his parents were not simply survivors: just as Karpf worries that the positive side of survivors' lives are played down in debates over their children's relation to the memory of the past, Wieseltier is clear that simply survival is not enough. In his most explicit discussion of one of the roots of *Kaddish*, Fackenheim's '614th' commandment forbidding a posthumous victory to Hitler, he writes that, even 'in extremity, there was no such thing as survival for survival's sake. There is no survival without meaning, and there is no meaning without survival. My parents understood this. I am the son of survivors who were not survivalists' (*K* 515). *Kaddish* is exactly this interplay between meaning and surviving. Fackenheim's work, understood in this way, is present in the whole work, as the mourner's kaddish is (at the risk of reducing it far too much) an act of mourning and an act of communal and personal affirmation. Wieseltier argues that the 'preservation of custom is . . . a moral imperative' (*K* 507). He hears his young nephew recite the 'prayer before bedtime. These are my nephew's first Hebrew words. "What do you think?" my sister asks. "I think that Hitler lost", I reply' (*K* 344). However, of course, while politics may not make up the core of his memory, his memory does have a 'memoro-politics'. The conservative Judaism he inhabits is in contrast to, say, Finkielkraut's, despite its deeper similarities, and, of course, uses its tradition in particular ways, specific to its time and place.[41] However, the central theme here has been the negotiation with a tradition *per se*: how the cable is laid rather than what it carries.

Kaddish, then, represents a detailed representation of the working and taking up of Jewish tradition, identity, and postmemory: a close look at the actual mechanics, as it were. The text is where personal and communal memory, ritual memory, religious memory, and Hirsch's postmemory all come together and are discussed and evaluated. The text reflects not a coherent and resolved world view or persona. Wieseltier writes of the kaddish he says by his father's grave, that what 'is happening to me now is nothing like what Americans call "closure" . . . the past soaks the present like the past of a distant star. Things that are over do not end. They come inside us . . . And there they live on, in the consciousness of individuals and communities' (*K* 576). Rather, the text is an engagement with 'memory, family, identity, morality, history and divinity' (*K* 198), and with mourning. By discovering about the mourner's kaddish, by performing it, becoming part of the community, he changes his identity, and the text reflects this. It is concerned with re-establishing a community, within a tradition.

But for Wieseltier, the nature of this tradition is not straightforward. He has (at least) three key conclusions. He argues that tradition 'is never acquired, it is always being acquired' (*K* 259). The point is made again and again that the mourner's kaddish is not, in any straightforward way, said for the dead father: it ties the mourner into memory, into the community, into the movement of tradition, into becoming Jewish. This means, in turn, that 'genetics', against which he writes, or ethnicity matter less than an authentic engagement with the tradition: 'what I wish to accomplish in my study of the kaddish, . . . is to diminish the prestige of blood, to lessen the role of heredity in the articulation of identity' (*K* 254). And, as with Finkielkraut, this reveals something more for Wieseltier, which he articulates after a visit to a dance studio. The dancers, practising their movements, seek to absorb the movements into their body, so that, after reflection and creation, they can be recombined into dance. This metaphor reveals that 'tradition must be an absorption for creation to occur . . . thinking of tradition is not the same as doing something with tradition. The highest

---

[41] On this, see, *inter alia*, Jonathan Boyarin, *Storm from Paradise: The Politics of Jewish Memory* (Minneapolis: University of Minnesota Press, 1992). Jacob Neusner, *Stranger at Home: The Holocaust, Zionism and American Judaism* (Chicago: University of Chicago Press, 1981).

object of study is not study. The highest object of movement is not movement. The highest object of Judaism is not Judaism' (*K* 370). Finkeilkraut argues that the authentic understanding of Judaism is found outside of the self and 'brings me more than I contain within' as a 'a kind of transcendence' (*IJ* 176); in parallel, Wieseltier finds that, through embracing tradition, tradition itself reveals what is higher than itself.

CONCLUSION

Although they come from different contexts—France, the UK, the USA, two by men, one by a women—these texts share profound similarities. They are personal, but not autobiographical, perhaps, because they deal so centrally with one aspect of the writer's lives. They are all by highly educated intellectual diaspora Jews who live in the West. Most significantly, here, they are all accounts by people who have a parent or parents who survived the Holocaust: they are accounts of postmemory, texts that engage with the wide and diffuse category of the memory of the Holocaust. Hirsch suggests that works of postmemory share a number of different characteristics. Postmemory describes the experiences of people with an intense relationship to the traumatic memory of the past. Stemming from this 'deep personal connection', postmemory is 'a powerful and very particular form of memory' because this connection is mediated 'through an imaginative investment and creation' (*FF* 22). Postmemory texts reveal exile, displacement, estrangement, absence: 'a diasporic aesthetics of temporal and spatial exile' (*FF* 245–6). As an act of mourning, properly understood, postmemory is both a sense of loss and the desire to 're-member, to rebuild . . . to replace and repair' (FF 242–3).

Mourning does play a central role in these texts, both actually and metonymically. Karpf discusses her father's death, Wieseltier's book takes as more than a leitmotif the mourner's kaddish. But, as Wieseltier writes of his mother, this mourning serves as 'a kind of super-mourning, an encompassing sorrow' by which to mourn a whole generation of Jews murdered in Europe. In the mourning of one parent, a way of remembering a whole tradition comes about. Wieseltier writes of his own experience—and it stands in part for all—that his experience of mourning, 'a duty I refused to shirk' (*K* 497), brought him to the centre of his tradition, of his communal memory. As an 'ironic consequence', he writes, 'I cannot experience mourning as marginality, as it is supposed to be experienced. For me, it has the aspect of a home coming' (*K* 497). This 'ironic consequence' underlies all these texts: it is through mourning that tradition and memory come to be taken up.

But this mourning that comes from communal memory is not a static process. Young writes that memorials turn 'plaint memory to stone. . . . And it is this finish that repels our attention, that makes a monument invisible' and Hirsch's work focuses on immobile photographs.[42] In contrast to monuments and images, these written representations of mourning, however, suggest that it is a dynamic process, an idea that Hirsch's account of postmemory seems to play down: while involved with absence and loss, they are engaged with the present and the future, both personal and communal, and represent a process. Barbara Foley suggested that Holocaust testimonies reflect or make up a sort of anti-*Bildungsroman*. Instead of growing from ignorance to knowledge and from isolation to community, survivors tell how they fall from knowledge of the world to the 'anti-knowledge' of the camps, and how their communities are destroyed, leaving them alone. These postmemory texts make up a sort of middle position between the traditional and this inverted *Bildungsroman*. The children of the survivors write about their lives overshadowed by the memory of the Holocaust: the symptoms of this include absence and feelings of envy, anger, exclusion, of a desire for solidarity, a turning in of misery and what Finkielkraut describes as an inauthentic 'harvesting all the moral advantage' and Karpf calls a 'kind of reflected martyrdom'. All these and more feelings combine as part of what Karpf called 'some perverse relay race' (*WA* 125–6). Yet these texts display growth and change, a coming to terms with the memory. The narrators learn to take on the burden of memory and of tradition in different and more authentic ways. They also come to terms with the communities—spatial, temporal—in which they live through a process of renegotiation and rejoining: they take on the duties of Judaism, they take on, where they can, the implicit anti-Semitism of their wider societies. These are questions of identification. The result of this movement is not the same as 'closure': all these writers stress the disjunction between their lives and the lives of the narrators of the books. The books have finished: the lives have not. The issues are not resolved, but accommodated. In this

[42] James Young, *The Texture of Memory: Holocaust Memorials and their Meaning* (London: Yale University Press, 1993), p. ix.

regard, postmemory is perhaps better understood as a coming to terms with memory, and all that memory bears with it (tradition, community, a burden), but not an identification with or assimilation of memory, as if it were something else, or if, in itself, it were reducible. This seems to have at least three further consequences.

This ending without closure is exilic and diasporic, but it is also about finding a home in movement. This is not simply a geographical metaphor for existence, but also reflects the epiphanies that underlie the narrator's discussions, that the 'highest object of movement is not movement. . . . The highest object of Judaism is not Judaism' (*K* 370), that Judaism 'is received 'from without . . . it brings me more than I contain within' (*IJ* 176), that home is not at home. These are closures that are not closures.

This also reveals that, in this context at least and opposed to the symptoms that lead to the psychological classification of 'second generation survivors syndrome', postmemory is textual in a wide sense of the word. That these are recollections of despair and misery—of their parents, of themselves—is true: but they are recollections written in (greater, at least) tranquillity. A narrative form—the movement of one state of knowledge to another through mourning the Holocaust—has imposed itself as the representation of memory. Postmemory is representation, mediated by and created in texts: family stories, books, tapes, and so on. These texts are, then, texts on texts, and texts about the effects of texts. They are in part about their own creation. This is not to say that these writings somehow 'float free' of the world or are cut off from it: rather, because of this, they themselves perform what they do. Karpf writes down and passes on her parents' accounts while she describes her struggle with memory and is afraid of their, and other people's, reactions on reading the book; Wieseltier honours his father and his community both by saying kaddish and by his account of it in *Kaddish*; Finkielkraut offered *The Imaginary Jew* to Le Cercle Gaston Crémieux—a group of intellectuals analysing Jewish culture in France—as a leavetaking.[43]

Finally, the lack of resolution reflects the tentative contingency of all the accounts. Indeed, this tentativeness is highlighted by comparing all three, and especially *Kaddish*, to Imre Kertész's prose poem, *Kaddish for a Child Not Born*. Told from the point of view of a survivor addressing his unborn—and never to be born—child, this is bleak and

---

[43] Friedlander, *Vilna on the Seine*, 93.

uncompromising. Where these postmemory texts are about continuity and community, *Kaddish for a Child Not Born* is specifically about the choice of discontinuity and the end of community: where they turn to Judaism, Kertész's book rejects it.

The tension, between the memory the texts are about, between the way in which narrative order is imposed on these events and remembered events, emerges in the form of these texts. Not only do these texts offer tentative ending without closure but they are also fractured and uneven. They are made up of a range of different genres: philosophy, history, sociology, reminiscence, aphorisms, and so on. They have within in them representation of different voices: Finkielkraut uses monologue to talk to himself, Karpf's parents' stories are transcribed, and other psychologists and historians are cited. They use different registers: where Karpf uses the language of psychoanalysis and psychotherapy, Finkielkraut passes beyond it, and Wieseltier rejects it. The texts are, in a way, exiled even from a fixed genre. In a way, they represent an individual's version of the communal Memorial Books: these books are 'compilations of historical essays, memoirs, biographies, chronologies, poems, letters, newspaper articles, photographs, drawings, maps, minutes', and other material, collected together to commemorate communities destroyed by the Nazis.[44] These stress the continuity of the community through destruction, migration, and linguistic change: some of the books, put together in Hebrew and Yiddish, have been translated into English for those in the US Jewish communities who do not speak these languages.

These works also stress that they are not—except in the portions that claim to be, like Karpf's account of Anglo-Jewry's reception of those fleeing Hitler—works of history. Finkielkraut stresses the dangers of assimilating his stories with history. As I have suggested, Karpf becomes wedded to the 'storyness' of her mother's account: it 'was as if I knew, somewhere, that the full account wouldn't support the version we proffered' (*WA* 95). In fact, the account in *The War After* is full of dates and facts, reflecting Karpf's desire to 'pin down what hitherto had always seemed a butterfly of a story' (*WA* 24). This is not to imply for a moment that she doubts the veracity of her mother's story, but rather it reveals a sense of division between memory and history. Whereas history is, rightly, involved with issues of proof, evidence,

[44] Rosemary Horowitz, *Literary and Cultural Transmission in the Reading, Writing and Remembering of Jewish Memorial Books* (London: Austin & Winfield, 1998), 3.

discussion, and debate, memory offers a world and an identity that, although bound into the world offered by historians, is not identical to it. It offers a different form of truth (see Chapter 5), not least because an 'empiricist account of tradition cannot be given' (K 576). Wieseltier writes very clearly that, although his father may have made mistakes in his story, and he in his story of his father, 'I will never mistake my memory of my father for my knowledge of him. I am his heir, not his historian' (K 564). This, in a complex way, reflects the understanding of the existence of two different forms of truth: truth as correspondence (the claim of historical truth) and a sense of an existential, ethical truth, as unveiling and founding a world and our relationships to each other.

Hirsch suggested that postmemory had an aesthetics—exilic, mournful, diasporic. These texts have supported and gone beyond this understanding of postmemory. They are texts of mourning, but this mourning leads to a dynamic, a movement. They are narratives that come after the anti-*Bildingsroman* of the survivors: through their narrative, they lead from isolation to community, from absence to a negotiation between absence and presence. They stress their own textuality, while aware of the role they play in the world (this is not to suggest that the works themselves are therapeutic: they are written in a different time from therapy). The form also reveals this tension, as the texts reject closure, while ending, and are made up of different genres. They have a tense relation to the history of the historians, but are not usually at odds with it.

Memory and postmemory have an aesthetics. Do they also, then, have a philosophy? Could these, in fact, be separated? Questions of identity, identification, and memory, of the personal and the public, of the burden of memory and tradition, are all raised by these texts and answered—implicitly, usually—in similar ways in the text. Specifically, they ask, and offer answers about, how we might come to terms with—mourn for—the Holocaust, and how we might understand it without assimilating it (and so, *pace* Young on memorials, making it invisible). These answers are in the text and, because they represent the dynamic process of mourning, *are* the text, and so are not amenable to easy summary. But the lesson of postmemory seems to be that we are at home not at home, and that what lies at the core of traditions is outside those traditions. Memory and postmemory, homeless but supported by a tradition, however broken, involves inhabiting the demand that, as Wieseltier writes, 'I must be faithful *and* I must be doubtful. I must be near *and* I must be far' (K 564) without bringing the two together. This sort of thought has a very clear parallel in the work of Emmanuel Levinas and Jacques Derrida, as Chapters 9 and 10 will show. As Michael Morgan writes, 'the challenge for those confronting the Holocaust is to grasp both horns of the apparent dilemma of discontinuity and rupture, on the one hand, and continuity and recovery on the other.'[45]

Understanding memory, then, and the postmemory of the Holocaust, in this broader way—experienced in narrative and in other textual forms, in its everyday role in lives, acted out in a range of ways (psychological, ritual, material, in writing), involved in both forming and questioning identity and identification—is a crucial and vital tool in coming to terms with the events. It is memory and the processes of memorialization that are not only an ethical commitment to the past, but a commitment to the future as well.

---

[45] Michael L. Morgan, *Beyond Auschwitz: Post Holocaust Jewish Thought in America* (Oxford: Oxford University Press, 2001), 218.

4

Holocaust Reading: Memory and Identification in Holocaust Fiction, 1990–2003

INTRODUCTION

To take genre not in its more limited and derivative sense, as a pigeon-hole for texts, but as a horizon of understanding where interpretation, text, and readership come together, is to suggest that not only is there Holocaust literature but there is also Holocaust reading: questions, issues, and approaches that typify reading Holocaust literature. The previous three chapters have covered the interlinked issues of identification and memory in relation to the Holocaust: this chapter turns to explore these issues in Holocaust fiction, not only to suggest that they are the central themes in recent, if not all, Holocaust fiction but to argue that they are the key components, the ground, of Holocaust fiction. The idea of genre draws attention to these issues. That is not to say that the different texts deal with these issues in the same way but that that Holocaust literature both leads to and stems from these sorts of question.

WHAT IS 'HOLOCAUST FICTION'?

Debates over whether Holocaust fiction should exist are moot, despite Elie Wiesel's remark that a 'novel about Treblinka is either not a novel or not about Treblinka' and Adorno's despair at the ways in which the 'victims are turned into works of art, tossed out to be gobbled up by the world that did them in'.[1] There are works attributed to this genre,

---

[1] Elie Wiesel, 'The Holocaust as Literary Inspiration', in *Dimensions of the Holocaust* (Evanston, Ill.: Northwestern University Press, 1990), 7. Adorno continues, arguing that the 'so-called artistic rendering of the naked physical pain of those who were beaten down by rifle butts contains, however distantly, the possibility that pleasure can be

books read, reviewed, taught, and so on. Moreover, at first sight, its definition looks very straightforward and driven by content: 'novels, poems and plays (that is—fiction) about the Holocaust'.[2] But both the 'about the Holocaust' and the idea of fiction in this context seem to be quite problematic. First, what does 'about the Holocaust' mean and where does 'being about the Holocaust' start or stop? The Nazi genocide plays a role—often unspoken but significant— in a huge array of post-1945 anglophone and US and UK published fiction, leaving aside works written in Hebrew, German, or other languages.

For example, and unsurprisingly, the Holocaust is central to American-Jewish fiction.[3] Michael André Bernstein—in an argument that Peter Novick's *The Holocaust and American Life* echoes— suggests that the 1960s saw a significant change in Jewish-American literature: early in the decade 'Holocaust delineation was virtually absent . . . by the decade's end it was ever present'.[4] One of the criticisms that has been levied against this position more generally is that a focus on 'public life' and concrete representation of the Holocaust distracts from an awareness of other, more specific, local Holocaust memories: indeed, Novick himself writes that much 'commemorative activity took place within the survivor community, without much effort to involve others'.[5] Just because the events which made up the destruction of European Jews were not amalgamated in the term 'the Holocaust' until the early 1960s does not mean that they did not loom very large in the minds of writers and audiences. Indeed, if 'delineating' the Holocaust meant naming it and writing about it as a 'positive content', then it might be possible to suggest a category of 'negative content': where the events are there, are a 'complement' which calls 'on the

squeezed from it'. Theodor Adorno, 'Commitment', in *Notes to Literature, II*, ed. Rolf Tiedemann, tr. Shierry Weber Nicholson (New York: Columbia University Press, 1993), 88.

[2] See David Patterson, Alan L. Berger, and Sarita Cargas (eds.), *Encyclopaedia of Holocaust Literature* (Westport, Conn.: Oryx Press, 2002), pp. xiii–xviii, for another form of answer to this question.

[3] See, among others: Alan Berger, *Crisis and Covenant* (Albany, NY: State University of New York Press, 1985); S. Lillian Kremer, *Witness through the Imagination* (Detroit: Wayne State University Press, 1989).

[4] Michael André Bernstein, *Foregone Conclusions: Against Apocalyptic History* (London: University of California Press, 1994), 15. Compare 'the Holocaust wasn't talked about very much in the United States through the end of the 1950s': Peter Novick, *The Holocaust and Collective Memory: The American Experience* (London: Bloomsbury, 1999), 127.

[5] Novick, *Holocaust and Collective Memory*, 109.

reader to supply information from his or her own experience', but are not mentioned.[6] Isaac Bachevis Singer's loving and exhaustive recreation of Jewish Poland in the late nineteenth and early twentieth century— published first in Yiddish in the *Jewish Daily Forward* and later in English as *The Manor* and *The Estate*—takes in the whole panoply of Jewish life, 'socialism, and nationalism, Zionism and assimilationism, nihilism and anarchism, suffragetteism, atheism, the weakening of the family bond, free love, and even the beginning of Fascism', and is surely a response to the destruction of all this.[7] Irving Howe began translating Yiddish fiction into English in 1952 in order, as Julian Levinson argues, to recover the Eastern European Jewish literary tradition.[8] That these works, and others, are 'about the Holocaust' and could be 'Holocaust fiction' is clear, even if they lack 'delineation'. Outside the 'Holocaust canon', outside obvious texts like Cynthia Ozick's short story 'The Shawl', the Holocaust plays a major role in Jewish-American fiction: Bernard Malamud 'chose to approach the Holocaust from a safe distance in his novel *The Fixer* (1966) [about] a Jew rotting away in a czarist jail for a murder he did not commit'.[9] Chaim Potok's *My Name is Asher Lev* (1972), for example, is about art and religion, specifically orthodox Jewry, yet the painting that causes the controversy (a crucifixion, Potok's *hommage* to Chagall) and the ensuing debate are in a post-Holocaust context. Issues of Jewish identity after the Holocaust are central not only to Phillip Roth's *The Ghost Writer* (1979), in which Nathan Zuckerman purposefully *imagines* (a point often missed by commentators) that the young woman he meets is Anne Frank, but also to all the 'Zuckerman' novels of this period.

The events that make up the Holocaust play a significant role in a much larger array of fiction. There are works which form a Holocaust literature canon: passing over the impact of recent translations from the German such as Bernhard Schlink's *The Reader* (1997) and W. G. Sebald's *Austerlitz* (2001), these include William Styon's *Sophie's Choice* (1979), D. M. Thomas's *The White Hotel* (1981), Thomas

[6] David Trotter, *The Making of the Reader* (London: Macmillan, 1984), 14.

[7] 'Author's Note', Isaac Bashevis Singer, *The Manor* (London: Penguin, 1975), no page number.

[8] Julian Levinson, 'Transmitting Yiddishkeit: Irving Howe and Jewish American Culture', *Jewish Culture and History*, 2/2 (1999), 42–65.

[9] Andrew Furman, 'Inheriting the Holocaust: Jewish American Fiction and the Double Bind of the Second Generation Survivor', in Hilene Flanzbaum, *The Americanisation of the Holocaust* (London: Johns Hopkins University Press, 1999), 83–101, 84.

Keneally's *Schindler's List* (1986), Martin Amis's *Time's Arrow* (1991), Rachel Seiffert's *The Dark Room* (2001), and Jonathan Safran Foer's *Everything is Illuminated* (2002). However, and importantly, there are many, many more post-war novels which reflect on the Holocaust which are not 'canonical'.

For example, C. S. Forester—the creator of Hornblower—wrote ten stories, collected as *The Nightmare* and published first in 1954, which are Holocaust fiction. The majority of these concern German and SS officers—'perpetrator fiction', perhaps—and are a simple inversion of his usual heroic characters: Hornblower is brave, Untersturmfuehrer Voss is a coward; Hornblower is full of integrity, Schiller, a camp commander is not, and remains unrepentant and uncomprehending at his trial. Some are about the (mythical) 'good German soldier' who serves the Fatherland but hates the Nazis. Two are set in death camps. The final one, very unusually for Forester written in the first person, is about a spectral post-war Hitler, condemned to the earth as a 'wandering gentile'. One, however, is a very odd, mawkish, and perhaps rather questionable 'victim' story called 'Miriam's Miracle', about the arrival at a death camp and subsequent murder of Miriam and her family. Despite being widely reviewed (*The Sunday Times*, *Time and Tide*, *Punch*, *The Statesman*) and being by a major (if not high-brow) author, these stories have sunk without trace. The science fiction writer Philip K. Dick's alternate history, *The Man in the High Castle*, from 1962, is clearly involved with thinking about the Holocaust, and his novel *Do Androids Dream of Electronic Sheep?*—the basis for the film *Bladerunner*—is a direct result of Holocaust research:

given access to prime Gestapo documents in the closed stacks of the University of California at Berkeley, Dick discovered certain diaries scribed by SS men stationed in Poland. One sentence in particular had a profound effect on the author. That sentence read, 'We are kept awake at night by the cries of starving children', Dick explained . . . 'There was obviously something wrong with the man who wrote that. I later realized that, with the Nazis, what we were essentially dealing with was a defective group mind, a mind so emotionally defective that the word "human" could not be applied to them'.[10]

The androids are the perpetrators (which makes the valorization of them in the 'film of the book' *Bladerunner* rather more ambiguous).

---

[10] Paul M. Sammon, *Future Noir: The Making of Blade Runner* (London: Orion, 1996), 16–17. I owe this insight to Adam Roberts.

The Holocaust is often an explicit, present content in literature, as in Thomas Pynchon's novels *The Crying of Lot 49* (1966) and *Gravity's Rainbow* (1973) or Craig Raine's poem *History: The Home Movie* (1994) or Tom Paulin's poem sequence *The Invasion Handbook* (2003). It is central to J. M. Coetzee's novel *Elizabeth Costello* (2003) and to Lawrence Norfolk's *In the Shape of a Boar* (2000). Anthony Rowland convincingly brings to the fore the significance of the Holocaust in the work of the poet Tony Harrison.[11] Sometimes, if not absolutely explicit, it is certainly present: the genocide casts its shadow back over Kazuo Ishiguro's 1989 novel *The Remains of the Day*. This is a novel in part about those who abdicate their responsibility, whether to their master in the name of 'dignity' or to the Nazis in acts of appeasement and anti-Semitism.[12] In Robert Harris's 'alternative history' thriller *Fatherland* (1993), Xavier March turns from a 'Homicide Detective' to a 'genocide detective': he uncovers the secret of the Holocaust as a murder inquiry unravels. In a reversal of the academic trope of 'historian-as-detective', March is 'detective-as-historian' following Hilberg's meticulous documentary trail of train timetables, construction memos, surviving minutes.[13] Patrick Süskind's *Perfume* (1985), a story of a vile murderer who through his perfume enraptures a town so that they not only forgive him but worship him, can easily be read as a Holocaust allegory.

And then there are the huge number of texts where the events are implicit, and make up an 'absent content'. Part of the bleakness of Orwell's *1984* surely stems from the death camps: a 'boot stamping on a human face forever', and the *volk*-ish savagery of William Golding's *Lord of the Flies*, set possibly during another apocalyptic event, harks back to the Holocaust. Adorno, famously, argues that 'Beckett has given us the only fitting reaction to the situation of the concentration camps—a situation he never calls by name, as if it were subject to an image ban'.[14] A full list of 'Holocaust fiction' under this rubric—fiction which refers explicitly or implicitly to the Holocaust—would consist of

[11] Anthony Rowland, *Tony Harrison and the Holocaust* (Liverpool: Liverpool University Press, 2001).

[12] See Gillian Rose, 'Beginnings of the Day—Fascism and Representation', in *Mourning Becomes the Law* (Cambridge: Cambridge University Press, 1996), 41–62.

[13] Hiberg, in his turn, was outraged by *Fatherland's* 'amalgam of fact and fantasy'. Raul Hilberg, *The Politics of Memory* (Chicago: Ivan R. Dee, 1996), 139.

[14] Theodor Adorno, *Negative Dialectics*, tr. E. B. Ashton (London: Routledge, 1996), 380. On this, see also Simon Critchley, *Very Little . . . Almost Nothing* (London: Routledge, 1997), 21–4.

too large a number of works to read in a lifetime. In fact very many works which might at first seem to have nothing to do with the Holocaust, do, in fact, reflect on it. The genre of 'Holocaust fiction' then, begins to spread to take in a significant proportion of post-war writing.[15] One might even be tempted ask the what it means when a novel or poem written after 1945 in Europe or America *did not* engage with the issue.

It seems that a definition driven by content is simply too wide: perhaps, a chronological definition might be more useful. An analogous case to the genre of Holocaust fiction might be seen in the growth of postcolonial fiction. In the 1960s, the genre called 'Commonwealth writing'—which included, for example, Chinua Achebe, Tayeb Salih, and Ngugi wa Thiong'o—was defined geographically as literature in English from the post-imperial countries of the Commonwealth and, rather patronizingly perhaps, in part by content. These were works that reflected on and wrote from the experiences of the collapse of empires and of migration. In turn this became 'new literatures in English' and then 'postcolonial literature' or even 'globalized literature', and now includes many writers in a range of languages. The geographical and content models have dissolved and new approaches and understandings have developed. 'Postcolonial' or 'globalized' now is a temporal term that describes an age, no longer a geographical or content term. That is, 'postcolonial' means not only the experience of an Ibo man of British colonizers (Achebe's *Thing Fall Apart* (1958)), nor only of a Nigerian or Bangladeshi woman migrant to the UK (Buchi Emecheta's *In the Ditch* (1972) and *Second Class Citizen* (1974) and Monica Ali's *Brick Lane* (2003)), but also the experience of that 'central' culture under the effect of decolonization or globalization, the effect of hybridity and migration, as in Zadie Smith's *White Teeth* (2002). In this sense, and bearing in mind the great power inequalities, we are all 'postcolonial', or 'globalized'. The point is that 'postcolo-

---

[15] There are even a few works which uncannily pre-empt—in the more usual sense—the Holocaust: Malamud's short story 'Armistice' written in 1940 about the fall of France as seen and understood by a Jewish American grocer. A survivor of a Russian pogrom, the 'reports of the persecution of the Jews he heard over the radio filled him with dread'. Bernard Malamud, *The Complete Stories* (London: Vintage, 1998), 4. Kressman Taylor wrote an influential and later best-selling epistolary short story called 'Address Unknown', published in *Story* magazine in 1938. She wanted 'to write about what the Nazis were doing and show the American people what happens to real, living people swept up in a warped ideology'. Charles Douglas Taylor, 'Afterword', in Kressmann Taylor, *Address Unknown* (London: Souvenir Press, 2002), no page number. These too, are fiction 'about the Holocaust'.

nial' or 'globalization' establishes one way of naming the culture of an epoch. This understanding of 'postcolonialism' as an age has risks: people can close their eyes to the changes that have occurred and carry on regardless, or, as Spivak argues in *A Critique of Postcolonial Reason*, those in the 'central'—rich, Western—countries can take on the mantle of 'being postcolonial' without being aware of the myriad injustices and imbalances in power and wealth. But the point remains that 'postcolonial' names not only a time but also a way of reading or thinking, a way that brings certain questions and issues to the fore: 'Postcolonial critique focuses on forces of oppression and coercive domination that operate in the contemporary world; the politics of anti-colonialism and neo-colonialism, race, gender, nationalisms, class and ethnicities define its terrain.'[16] Thus, the genre of postcolonial fiction is not simply defined by content but is a way of reading constantly under negotiation, a set of questions that stem from and apply to texts.

There is something akin to this in Holocaust fiction. Holocaust fiction is a temporal, not a content, label, and it names not only texts, but a way of reading: a genre. It is to be read with a specific range of questions, responses, demands, and issues in mind. Without making these larger claims for a Holocaust reading, Sue Vice picks up on some of the issues and characteristics of the genre of Holocaust fiction. Perhaps most importantly, Vice shows that Holocaust fiction is highly intertextual and uses anterior sources much more self-consciously than other genres and in very specific ways, and, as other writers have done, she explores the limits of the fiction in Holocaust fiction. This is a indeterminate zone: it is not—and could not be—clear where fiction stops and the anterior sources start. But this reveals the importance of the historical past as one of the key issues for this genre. Holocaust fiction is, in Edward Said's terms, 'worldly', inescapably tied into the world and the past. Said discusses the interplay of filiation and affiliation. For him, roughly, filiation—the lines of descent—reflects how works influence and descend from each other, how, in T. S. Eliot's terms, the tradition of writing works. Affiliation reflects the text's relation not to the diachronic part of influence, but to the text's location in its own time, context, and culture, a 'phenomenon in the world, located in a network of non-literary, non-canonical and non-traditional

[16] Robert Young, *Postcolonialism: An Historical Introduction* (Oxford: Blackwell, 2001), 11.

affiliations'.[17] For Holocaust fiction, the filiations are more complex than a tradition of great writing: they include personal recollection, the memories of parents and survivors, testimonies, museums, sites, religious traditions, works of history, as well as previous works of art, and part of 'Holocaust criticism' should be to trace and reveal these (as Vice so ably does). There is also, and perhaps more importantly, a 'filiation' to what is absent and unrecoverable—'who could replace my parents, my brother, or the rest of my family, of whom I was the sole survivor?'—a 'negative filiation'.[18] The affiliations, on the other hand, reflect the present and future understandings of the world 'Over There', as the parents of David Grossman's character Momik call the Holocaust. These understandings and their changes over time—ideas about Nazi guilt, for example, or simply an awareness of the enormity of what happened—alter the possibilities of what sort of novel can be written. A character in Prague from Arnost Lustig's *Night and Hope* counts the allies 'on his fingers. And on the last he saw a country so large that he could not imagine her otherwise than as a bear . . . a she-bear determined to protect all her children . . . he had only one wish—that the she-bear should succeed'.[19] Who—after the gulags, Hungary in 1956, Prague in 1968, and so on—could write this sentence in this way about the Soviet Union ('determined to protect all her children')? Not Jorge Semprun, who dedicates much of *What a Beautiful Sunday!* to both mourning and destroying the communist mythology nor Anatoly Kuznetsov, whose *Babi Yar* is as much an attack on the USSR as on the Nazis. The genre of Holocaust reading and writing has a specific relation to both its filiation and its affiliation, and in each case these need to be examined and explored.

Vice also notes that Holocaust literary texts are 'scandalous . . . and provoke controversy'.[20] This reveals that the Holocaust is an issue of considerable significance to people (in a way that, say, the ferocious theological debates of the English Civil War simply are not, for all but a few committed experts). Vice also stresses the unusual way all these novels use time. In part, this reflects the fact that—in Holocaust fiction, even in novels set in 1939—the events are inescapable and that, despite

[17] Bill Ashcroft and Pal Ahluwalia, *Edward Said: The Paradox of Identity* (London: Routledge, 1999), 42.

[18] Filip Müller, *Eyewitness Auschwitz: Three Years in the Gas Chamber*, with Helmut Freitag, tr. Susanne Flatouer (Chicago: Ivan R. Dee, 1979), 111.

[19] Arnost Lustig, *Night and Hope*, tr. George Theiner (Washington, DC: Inscape Publishers, 1976), 203.

[20] Vice, *Holocaust Fiction*, 1.

Bernstein's argument in *Foregone Conclusions*, these do overshadow any writing about this. In *Fatherland*, the only mystery *could* be the genocide of the Jews. Because of this, many texts do something unusual with the passing of fictive time. This is not true only of fictive texts. Gitta Sereny's two texts about the Holocaust, *Into that Darkness* and *Albert Speer: His Battle with Truth*, also work backwards: the past *bildung* of Franz Stangl and Speer is overshadowed by the present. Finally, Vice emphasizes how the Holocaust fiction genre, more than many others, has problems over the relation between the author and the narrator, about the claims to a authority to write about the Holocaust. Again, this reveals its 'worldly-ness'—here not in relation to the past but to the present. As Foucault observed, the ' "author-function" is not universal or constant', and in this genre, as opposed to in others, it has taken on a particular significance to do with the right to speak or write.[21]

All these characteristics (that is, specific movement of filiations, 'worldly-ness', and historicity; the public and political concern shown for these texts; the use of narrative time; and the questions about the authenticity and right of the author to write) and further possible generic characteristics—for example, concerns about race, and about politics and the state—are all involved with or rely upon a more fundamental concern with identification. In the case of the author-function and the public concern, this is clear—'Who is this who uses the lives of the dead?' is a fair question. The use of time reflects the way that identification can be played with, evaded, or encouraged. And the question of filiation refers back in turn to the origins of the question, to the reason why identity, memory, and identification are so central in relation to these texts. It is because the Holocaust has changed what identity, memory, and identification—in this limited context, read-ing—actually are. The reason the issue of identification causes prob-lems is that it is not clear what the human is after the Holocaust: it is not clear how or with whom we can or should identify.

While the issues of memory and identification are at the core of the genre, they do not make up the content of Holocaust fiction: they are not (or not only) the 'events' of a novel or the exclusive concerns of reading. Nor do they necessarily direct its form: Holocaust fiction can be realist, modernist, postmodernist, and so on. However, specific

---

[21] Michel Foucault, *Language, Counter-Memory, Practice*, ed. Donald Bouchard and tr. Donald Bouchard and Sherry Simon (New York: Cornell University Press, 1977), 125.

understandings and characteristics of memory, identity, and identification are the ground of possibility of these novels and can be seen as central to more recent Holocaust fiction. But, as they are the grounds of possibility of these fictions, the bonds that filiate and affiliate them, they do not always work in the same way. I now want to turn to look at the different ways four recent Holocaust fictions—some novels and one bleak, unhappy parody— have negotiated the grounds of their reading.

FICTIONS OF IDENTIFICATION: EMILY PRAGER, *EVE'S TATTOO*

Emily Prager's 1991 novel *Eve's Tattoo* is centrally about acts of identification. Set in 1989, it is the story of Eve, a vain and successful New York columnist. On her fortieth birthday, she feels 'like nothing and no one . . . like I lost my fire'.[22] Reflecting on her life, she remembers her study of the Holocaust during her first job as an assistant to a Broadway director, especially her discoveries that women supported Hitler, that the 'euthanasia programme' preceded the extermination of Jews, and that unmarried non-Jewish women—women like Eve, nominally an Episcopalian—were excluded from the state by the 1935 Citizenship Law. To restore herself, she has the number of an Auschwitz victim—500123—from a photograph she owns tattooed onto her arm. The tattoo, 'she feels, enables and authorises her to identify with the Holocaust victim' and it opens doors 'of identification, doors of terror, doors that led to rooms of questions she had never thought to ask'.[23] 'I haven't done this frivolously', she insists. 'Look, people will ask me about the tattoo and I'm going to tell them tales, based on my reading, tales specially chosen for them, so they can identify, so they can learn' (*ET* 12). Just as Eve has identified herself with the woman with the number ('I call her Eva' (*ET* 11) she says of the woman in the photograph, with no evidence), so others will identify with Eve's (fictional) stories of Eva. This leads to the action of the novel.

In seven different situations, Eve tells seven stories about Eva, each time tailored to her audience to maximize identification: to a dinner

[22] Emily Prager, *Eve's Tattoo* (London: Vintage, 1999), 50. This will be abbreviated in the text as *ET*.
[23] James Berger, *After the End: Representations of the Post-Apocalypse* (London: University of Minnesota Press, 1999), 81; *ET* 31.

party of yuppies, it is the story of Eva Klein, a Jewish yuppie in 1930s Berlin who became a U-boat (a Jew hiding with a false identity) and was betrayed; in the queue at the vet's surgery, it is the story of Eva Beck, who looked after the confiscated pets of Jews and then sold them to the Gestapo, and so on. These stories break the narrative time frame of the novel and are told as short, third-person vignettes, not in reported speech but in free indirect discourse. They have profound effects on their audiences: 'Every one had identified . . . the tattoo had jolted them from the lethe of middle class life and they suddenly looked not sophisticated or cynical . . . just human, exposed, their expressions softened with an empathy they would never have acknowledge that they could feel' (*ET* 29). Even the Smokers Anonymous meeting is impressed: 'well, of course, next to that, this seems like bullshit' (*ET* 47). But all the stories Eve tells are fictions, and the audiences identify with them just as they do with characters in novels: there is none of the tension with identification that occurs when testimonies are read. Both Eve and Emily Prager also have, with some justice, a particular angle: as her name implies ('Eve' as 'Woman') and the epigraph to the book ('For the Women Who resist, and the Women who don't') suggests, *Eve's Tattoo* wants to state a case for the women crushed and murdered in the Holocaust—and after.[24]

---

[24] This is not limited to this book: e.g., in her collection of short stories *A Visit from the Footbinder* (London: Vintage, 1992), one character rightly attacks Jerzy Kosinski, author of the exploitative, misogynistic, and pornographic Holocaust novel *The Painted Bird*. Demanding to know if he really saw a particularly disgusting, degrading and violent scene he describes, she says: 'Cause if you didn't I'm going to kill you. I hate that scene. I hate it so much and it's frightening and painful and ugly. And ever since I unsuspecting read that, it haunts me and comes back when I least suspect it. And if you made that up, then you're a sick guy and I'm going to kill you.' Emily Prager, 'The Alumnae Bulletin', *A Visit from the Footbinder* (London: Vintage, 1992), 157. This is a strong argument not against presenting the worst sexual aspects of the Holocaust, but against its exploitation in fiction. Norman Finkelstein's judgement is spot on in this literary matter when he attacks *The Painted Bird* by citing pre-production readers, who described it as a 'pornography of violence' and 'sadomasochistic'. Norman Finkelstein, *The Holocaust Industry: Reflections on the Exploitation of Jewish Suffering* (London: Verso, 2000), 55. For a discussion of the evidence of the book as 'authentic' and a defence, see Vice, *Holocaust Fiction* and Tom Teicholz (ed.), *Interviews with Jerzy Kosinski* (Jackson, Miss.: University Press of Mississippi, 1993). An interesting counterpoint to *The Painted Bird* are Ka-Tzetnik 135633's remarkable novels *House of Dolls* (tr. Moshe M. Kohn (New York: Simon & Schuster, 1955) about the women forced into prostitution by the Nazis in the camps, and *Atrocity* (New York: Lyle Stuart, 1963; also called *Moni: A Novel of Auschwitz*) about the rise and fall—in the eyes of the Kapos—of a boy homosexual prostitute in Auschwitz: while explicit, neither of these are exploitative. In this context, too, see Arnost Lustig's *Lovely Green Eyes*, tr. Eward Osers (London: Harvill Press, 2001) which concerns a woman forced into prostitution by the Nazis. For

However, Eve's increasing assimilation with Eva ('I need Eva. I need her' (*ET* 76) is the central key act of identification in the novel. Eve goes to a gig, and her relationship with Eva goes 'from remembrance to cohabitation' (*ET* 93). The bass player of the band makes a pass at Eve ' "Go for it", Eva replied' (*ET* 97). That night he asks her about the tattoo:

'Were you in a Nazi camp?' . . . Could it be that he didn't know World War II ended in 1945?
'Yes', she ventured. 'Yes. I was at Auschwitz'. . . .
'Wow . . . the Nazis were really mean, weren't they?'   (*ET* 98)

This Eva, Eva Flick, was sent to Auschwitz for a traffic violation: 'Well, that's how ugly it was, you know' (*ET* 100), says Eve, speaking demotically and using a story about 'the cops' with which even this character would identify.

As Eve merges into Eva, she discovers that her partner, Charles César, although baptized a Catholic at 16 is, in fact, Jewish: his Catholicism is in his 'heart' but his Judaism is in his 'soul' (*ET* 16). Despite repeatedly being compared to a Catholic priest, bishop, or cardinal (the way his clothes move like a cassock, his grace in movement, his eminence in his field), he turns out to be a Jew who hates his Jewishness because he is the son of two French Jews who were 'catchers'—who betrayed Jews in hiding. He leaves Eve. These two tensions—her increasing identification with Eva, her distance from Charles—are resolved in and by a accident: she is hit by a van on a New York street, her arm is shattered. For Elie Wiesel's narrator in *The Accident* the collision is an 'accident-on-purpose', a sort of suicidal epiphany that leads to a new understanding of life. It is so for Eve, too. After telling her Eva story once more (to nuns, nursing her: Eva Hartz is a Catholic charity worker, opposed to the 'euthanasia' programme), her arm is rebuilt and 'the tattoo is gone—in its stead a neat row of suturing stitches' (*ET* 176). This allows her to escape the identification with Eva and to make it up with Charles, who has come to terms with

further discussion of gender issues, germane to Brett, Prager, and Michaels, see, *intra alia*, Marlene E. Heinemann, *Gender and Destiny: Women Writers and the Holocaust* (London: Greenwood, 1986); Dalia Ofer and Lenore J. Weitzman (eds.), *Women in the Holocaust* (London: Yale University Press, 1998); Carol Rittner and John K. Roth (eds.), *Different Voices: Women and the Holocaust* (New York: Paragon House, 1993); Anna Hardman, 'Representations of the Holocaust in Women's Testimony', in Andrew Leak and George Paizis (eds.), *The Holocaust and the Text* (London: Macmillan, 2000), 51–66.

his Jewishness: as they talk, they watch Nelson Mandela being released from gaol on TV. It also allows her to reflect on why Hitler was so successful with German women (they identified him with Christ and Nazism was 'indistinguishable from the structure of Christianity' (*ET* 183)—a simpler version of 'Nazism as political religion' thesis, recently given new weight by the historian Michael Burleigh in *The Third Reich*). There is a final Eva story, a warning of what happens when one identifies too much: from information from the Yiddish Scientific Institute, the 'real' Eva emerges as 'Leni Essen', a Nazi housewife who has an SS lover, sent to Auschwitz because of the action of her anti-Nazi sons.

The novel both revels in identification—the readers with Eve, Eve with Eva, Eve's audiences with 'Eva's' stories—and at the same time is at odds with these identifications. They are disrupted because Eve is shown to be vain, hypocritical, mildly anti-Semitic, confused, and shallow, not least when she meets a survivor, Jacob Schlaren, a transvestite actor, who survived most of the war in hiding disguised—identified—as a girl, and because her audiences are also shown to be shallow, not moved for long by these fictions. Only a life-changing accident can resolves Eve's crisis. As readers, making identifications, we read about Eve's doomed and false identification with Eva and we read about the audiences of Eve's stories making identifications which we know are spurious: in turn, are we not called to question our own identifications? These all rely precisely on the sympathy that the Holocaust questions, on grasping and comprehending the experience—in exactly the way that survivors say is impossible—and so 'normalizing' it. *Eve's Tattoo* is a realist novel which relies on the process of identification, not a testimony which resists this comprehension. The demands of the fictional form run precisely counter to the core of the novel, which leaves the work uncertain: is it 'against identifying' with Holocaust victims ('How can one write about a situation and not identify with all its characters?')?[25] Is it in favour of identification to make us more empathetic? It tries to use the process of identification as a warning against identification: but, like an 'action movie against violence', the contradictions are too strong and the novel is unable to bear this weight. The novel, despite itself, is an allegory about the dangers of making easy and spurious identifications with the victims of the Holocaust.

[25] Elie Wiesel, 'The Holocaust as Literary Inspiration', in *Dimensions of the Holocaust* (Evanston, Ill.: Northwestern Univerity Press, 1990), 7.

FICTIONS OF MEMORY: LILY BRETT, *TOO MANY MEN*

Lily Brett's novel *Too Many Men* is troubled by these questions of identification in a different way. Written in realist style, it is the story of a child of survivors visiting Poland with her father: a postmemory story. Indeed, and bearing in mind the special link between authors and writing that this genre demands, postmemory forms the context nearly all of Lily Brett's work. She was born in a DP (Displaced Persons) camp in 1946, a child of two survivors, and her family migrated to Australia in 1948. The after-effects of the Holocaust are made clear in her early poems, which consist of lines of one or two words only and use a simple and clear vocabulary. They describe first her parent's experiences in Auschwitz and their post-war life in Australia (*The Auschwitz Poems*) and then a trip to Poland (*Poland and Other Poems*) and cover much of the same ground as her later novel *Too Many Men*.

This novel, which is similar in theme to her collection of short stories, *Things Could be Worse*, and other novels *What God Wants* and *Just Like That*, is the story of Ruth Rothwax—a child of survivors— and her pilgrimage to Poland with her father Edek. Like her poems, the journey at the centre of this novel—from New York to Warsaw, Lodz, Kazimierz, and then to the site of the Auschwitz death camp—is a way of seeking out answers and a form of mourning. During the trip, she and her father argue and bicker, visit his former apartment and deal with its residents, and finally uncover a photograph and a story: Ruth's elder brother, a hole in the heart baby born in a DP camp was given away for adoption to increase his chance of living. Many of the themes from her poetry recur in this novel.

One theme that stands out is a fixity of memory and opinion. This is most easily seen in the virulent hatred that both Ruth and the narrator have for the Poles (a hatred not shared by Edek, interestingly). The Poles are presented as anti-Semitic, dirty, corrupt, money-grabbing, hypocritical liars. The cities are unfriendly, even the streets names sound 'militant if not military.'[26] Any attempt to contextualize—or even discuss—the non-Jewish Polish context both before and after the war is dismissed as hypocrisy and self-serving justification (there is no sense either that, for example, the rotting buildings and attitudes are to do with years of communist oppression, or of the weight of the

---

[26] Lily Brett, *Too Many Men* (New York: William Morrow, 2001), 56.

USSR, or just poverty—in *Too Many Men*, the Poles are rotting through an ahistorical moral malaise). Waxing wrath, Ruth declares that the Poles are 'the rudest people on earth. Vulgar, course, bigoted, obscene assholes.'[27] None of the Polish characters has any redeeming features: the woman her father sleeps with, Zofia, is portrayed as an ugly, whorish gold-digger. The inhabitants of her father's former apartment are anti-Semites, obsessed by extorting what they can from Ruth's and Edek's desire to get back some of their stolen property. Even the hotel doorman and the student who aids them are seen in a bad light. Oddly, although a group of Germans make Ruth feel sick on the first page of the novel, the other living Germans are portrayed in a positive way: Ruth has a pleasant evening with one Martina Schmidt who teaches at a Polish film school. Ruth believes that it is 'too hard to go around railing at Germans in general', but has no problems railing at Poles.[28] To condemn this is not to argue that novels should follow a some sort of 'correct agenda'—Ruth Rothwax can scream at who she likes—nor that the Poles were blameless in the Holocaust (Raul Hilberg offers a summary of the Polish experience of the Nazis, their behaviour, and their attitude towards the Jews which 'ranged from tolerance to animosity' and recent research—*Neighbours*—offers a worse picture).[29] However, this attitude is a symptom of the way this text offers a very fixed shape of memory and identity. In the various postmemory texts in the previous chapter, a key feature was a wrangle with memory, an engagement. This has not been a 'working through' or 'resolution' of the events, but a 'coming to terms' with them: in Wieseltier's idiom, a 'becoming like wood'.[30] Ruth's attitude to the Poles is a symptom of the lack of this.

Ruth's fixity is also illustrated by another aspect of this novel: she talks to the spirit of Rudolf Höss, the commandant of Auschwitz. Höss is in 'Zweites Himmel's Lager' a sort of purgatorial camp where he relives his life and death and has lessons in humanity to make him suitable for heaven. He contacts Ruth, who is possibly psychic, to get her to help him. They talk in English, which Höss has learnt after his death. Their conversations—which could be a way to discuss guilt and culpability—are mostly in fact more like comic dialogues with a cartoon Nazi, a familiar figure from post-war television programmes (*Hogan's*

---

[27] Ibid. 444.   [28] Ibid. 326.

[29] Raul Hilberg, *Perpetrators Victims Bystanders: The Jewish Catastrophe 1933–1945* (New York: HarperPerennial, 1992), 203.

[30] Leon Wieseltier, *Kaddish* (London: Picador, 2000), 283.

Heros, Allo! Allo!). Höss is 'amusingly' obtuse and one-dimensional, upset that his reputation is sullied and that he is confused by some with Hess. While he blames all the Germans for the Holocaust, Ruth is prone not to believe him in general, and is keen to point up his own lies and hypocrisy—not hard for the straw figure Brett conjures. This caricature Höss can in no way draw out the evil complexities of Auschwitz. Again, this looks like an evasion of memory, masquerading as a involvement: there is no process or development here but a solid closure.

There are other problematic things in this work: for example, there is much that is contradictory. Ruth, who has studied the Holocaust in no little detail and read 'hundreds of books on the Holocaust' and studies Heidegger ('I've read his books'), is still amazed that there are Jewish Kapos (' "A kapo?" Ruth asked "A Jew?" ').[31] Much of the dialogue is flat and unrewarding, the characters are one-dimensional stereotypes (Max, Ruth's assistant, is 'the single New York Woman', for example). The character of Edek Rothwax is an exception: his habits and linguistic infelicities match Brett's own father's—Brett discusses him in her collection of essays, his love for cars, his appetite, the way he uses 'Don't take your shirt off' for 'keep your shirt on'.[32] But what is odd about this novel, by a child of survivors, is how unlike the other accounts of 'postmemory' it is. Immobile, fixed, unreflective, the characters seem to live in a puppet world. Ruth, unlike Edek, makes herself her own victim. More than this, *Too Many Men* relies on 'secrets from the Holocaust' to motivate, the plot: Edek has a secret (Ruth's missing elder brother) which Ruth desires to discover. The novel feeds the fantasy that there is always more to know, that the missing pieces in postmemory can be found: for the novel, this memory is not an absence, not a 'negative filiation', but a space to be filled. The potential closure offered by the discovery of this next secret offers a questionable redemption, something that fills the holes of memory. It still relies, however, on identification: it is about Ruth's identification with the suffering victims and her attempts to shore up and develop her own identity.

[31] Brett, *Too Many Men*, 46, 116, 53.
[32] Lily Brett, *In Full View* (Sydney: Picador, 1998).

FICTION IN 'STRANGE EPISODIC IMAGES':[33]
ANNE MICHAELS, *FUGITIVE PIECES*

Fugitive Pieces, Anne Michaels's only novel to date, is—as the title suggests—a 'fugue' which brings together memory of surviving the Holocaust, coming to terms with this (but not 'resolving' it or 'working it through'), and postmemory through recurring tropes and themes of paternity, weather, geology, community, love, and music.

Like Lily Brett, Anne Michaels is a poet, and her poetry, too, echoes the context and themes of *Fugitive Pieces*. However, rather than a 'faux naive' imitation minimalism, Michaels takes as her strongest model W. H. Auden (the poem 'Fontanelles' in *Skindivers* takes Auden as an epigraph) and Wallace Stevens. Auden is present not only in the form of the poems—free verse—but is an influence on the thematic and metaphorical content of the poems too. Recognizable Auden tropes— the body, memory, the weather, and geology—and themes—love, suffering, loss—inhabit the poetry. Moreover, as with Stevens and Auden, the poems often have a form of some sort of poetic narrative, considering and exploring problems poetically. This is not to say that Michaels is simply an imitator of these two but it is clear that their work in some part poetically enables hers. For example, the first poem in her collection *The Weight of Oranges* is a statement of identity: she is a 'Lake of two rivers', a pooling of two histories. Natural and geological metaphors abound: 'love wails from womb, caldera, home'.[34] Like the demanding poetry of Stevens, Michaels is concerned with the ways in which experience, memory, and identity are transformed into art and into poetry. This poetic vocabulary also fits the subjects that Michaels wants to address: principally, perhaps, memory.

Memory recurs again and again in her poems, a constant theme, seen in different ways. In 'Words for the Body', 'We decided music is memory | the way a word is the memory of its meaning' and 'Remember' is a leitmotif.[35] In 'Miner's Pond', 'Memory is cumulative selection. | It's an undersea cable connecting one continent | to another'.[36] And in

[33] Anne Michaels, *Fugitive Pieces* (London: Bloomsbury, 1997), 216. This will be abbreviated in the text to *FP*.

[34] Anne Michaels, 'Lake of Two Rivers', *Weight of Oranges* (Toronto: The Coach House Press, 1985), 14.

[35] Anne Michaels, 'Words for the Body', *The Weight of Oranges*, 47.

[36] Anne Michaels, 'Miner's Pond', *Miner's Pond* (Toronto: McClelland & Stewart, 1991), 9.

'Skindivers', 'The moon touches everything' but 'Her sister, memory browses the closet . . . drags possession out on the lawn . . . lifts her head and I nearly | disappear'.[37] Often for Michaels, like Charlotte Delbo, memory is a skin (thus, skin divers). The translation of memory, both personal and communal, is perhaps central to her poem most influenced by Stevens, 'What the Light Teaches', which most clearly prefigures *Fugitive Pieces*. A complex, long poem, it draws on the figure of a widowed father (a figure, too, in the novel), on natural and geological imagery, and on the poetry, the experience of exile, and suffering of Osip Mandelstam, Anna Akhmatova, and Marina Tsvetaeva.

In this poem, the moon, water (rivers, the sea, rain), the fields, and the woods are sites of memory. From there, from 'our river', the memory ghosts from the past—'liquid fossils of light'—come to the present: they are everywhere—indeed we 'float in death'.[38] Yet memory is painful: her father is ghost-like ('I was afraid . . . my hand would go right through him') yet alive and suffering with, or in, or on, memory. And, just as the crust of the earth is crumpled up, and everywhere 'the past juts into the present' these memories are 'pleated': 'one foot | in the spring soil of your farm, | the other in mud where bits of bone and teeth | are still suspended, a white alphabet'. Yet unlike the earth, which slowly turns bones to mud, for living beings the memory ghosts do not go away:

> How can we but feel they're here . . .
> a mother gives birth in the sewer;
> soldiers push sand down a boy's throat.
> There are the voices we hear
> but can't hear.

The memories are preserved in language, 'how ghosts enter the world':

> Language remembers.
> Out of obscurity, a word takes its place
> in history. Even a word so simple
> it's translatable: number. Oven.

Yet, even languages fail: the poets who rescued language 'from the mouths of the dying' in Germany, Poland, and Russia discovered that

---

[37] Anne Michaels, 'Skindivers', *Skindivers* (London: Bloomsbury, 1999), 6.
[38] All quotations from Anne Michaels, 'What the Light Teaches', *Miner's Pond*, 55–65.

they not rescued it but only its alphabet, 'Because language of a victim only reveals | the one who named him'. 'There was no idiom to retreat to'. Revelation can only come through 'outline'

> by circling absence.
> But that's why language
> can remember truth when it's not spoken.

Yet the words, even buried, lead to a regrowth. From a buried testimony come 'orchids and weed': the rain—water again, as an active remembering—make 'one past grow out of another'. This leads to love, and the poem turns to a loved one, 'driving to one who awaits my arrival'. If the exile of memory is out across the fields, beyond the trees, by the river, language is the 'house with lamplight in its windows | visible across fields . . . the house to run to . . . when you've been lost a long time', a place of love and shelter. Yet, shifting and inverting metaphors to dislocate this moment of security, even the 'forest of words' is not safe: the 'only way out' is 'to write myself into a clearing, | which is silence'. (The shades of Heidegger—language as the house of being, the clearings in the forest—are clear here: this thought, either directly or through Wallace Stevens, is also an enabling presence.) Yet, finally,

> your voice in my head reminds me
> what the light teaches.
> Slowly you translate fear into love,
> The way the moon's blood is the sea.

This final metaphor is very hard, and yet sums up the ambiguity of the poem, which offers language both as a safe home and as a risky exile, and offers memory as unbearably precious and painful beyond measure. If the moon is memory, or the site of memory, the blood may be the suffering in and of memory, fear. In turn, as rivers flow to the sea, this becomes translated to love: yet, 'All the rivers run into the sea; yet the sea is not full; unto the place from whence the rivers come, thither they return again' (Ecclesiastes, 1: 7). Here the rivers and sea stand for the process of memory, constantly fluid yet never completed: the translation of fear into love has no end. It is not a trauma to be 'worked through' but a continually moving process to be lived. In the light of her poetry, which foreshadows *Fugitive Pieces*, it is hard to see how, as Nicola King argues, 'Michaels uses language . . . to suspend time, rather than acknowledging the impossibility of fully restoring the past'.[39] Instead, it is in language that time's movement is acknowledged.

Fugitive Pieces takes up these themes and fugue-like weaves them into the story of a survivor, Jacob Beer, like Solomon Memel from Lawrence Norfolk's *In the Shape of a Boar* a poet and an echo of Paul Celan, and Ben, a child of survivors for whom Beer looms large as a wished-for father figure. It is a novel both about 'what the light teaches', and also the power of the night. As with much of her poetry, it is a narrative wrangle with memory, and is best explored in a narrative frame. The first section of the novel is written in the first person, in short, disquieting sections, with a rapidly moving chronology. It is, nominally, the notes for Beer's memoirs, discovered in the second half of the novel. It begins with a section called 'The Drowned City'. The boy Jacob Beer, who has hidden and escaped from a Nazi raid on his family's home in which his mother and father were killed and his sister, Bella, was taken away, digs himself a hiding place every night and walks during the day. Finally, emerging from the soil like a 'bog man', he is seen by Athos who is (among other things) an archaeologist excavating the preserved 2,700-year-old settlement of Biskupin. Often called the 'Polish Pompeii'—which foregrounds associations with Freud, with memory—this settlement, amazing because the wood has been preserved by the action of the silt and water, becomes a motif for the murdered communities of European Jewry, the survival of some of the Jews, and the processes of archaeology-like memory. An old Jewish stevedore tells Athos that the 'great mystery of wood is not that it burns, but that it floats' (*FP* 28): wood is a key metaphor for Wieseltier, too.[40] Athos takes Jacob with him, hiding him until they reach his house on Zakynthos, a Greek island, where Jacob remains hidden during the war. This section, 'The Stone Carriers', mediates on fossils, on the victims carrying stone in Nazi death quarries, on memory. As in 'What the Light Teaches', ghost memories inhabit the earth for Jacob—it is 'no metaphor to feel the influence of the dead in the world, just as it's no metaphor to hear the radiocarbon chronometer' (*FP* 53). The section 'Vertical Time' takes place in immediately post-war Athens and in Canada, where Athos takes a job. Just as, in nature, a huge disruption takes many years to settle down, so after the war Greece remains in turmoil for some years. They settle in Canada, Jacob

[39] Nicola King, *Memory, Narrative, Identity: Remembering the Self* (Edinburgh: Edinburgh University Press, 2000), 148.
[40] Wieseltier, *Kaddish*, 283.

learns English, and Athos dies while working on a book about the Nazis' corrupted archaeology. 'Phosphorous' tells of Jacob's short marriage to Alexandra: like phosphorous this burns very brightly, but quickly, and leaves cinders and confusion in its wake.

It is in this section and the next, 'Terra Nullis', that two things come into focus. The first is Jacob's haunting by his sister, Bella, taken by the Nazis. Because he never saw her body, never found out what happened to her, never saw her face in any of the pictures he eagerly scans, Jacob is especially haunted by her: 'I endlessly follow Bella's path from the front door of my parents' house, in order to give her death a place' (*FP* 139). Memories of her musicianship, her behaviour, come back to him more and more frequently. Second, in this section, Jacob outlines his 'philosophy of history' , the ideas that underlie the whole novel: 'Terra cognita and terra incognita inhabit exactly the same co-ordinates of time and space. The closest we come to knowing the location of what's unknown is when it melts through the map like a watermark, a stain transparent as a drop of rain. On the map of history, perhaps the water stain is memory' (*FP* 137). He goes on: 'History and memory share events; that is, they share time and space. Every moment is two moments' (*FP* 138), a phrase repeated three times later in the novel (*FP* 140, 143, 161). Every moment is both a moment for the discipline of history—that can be written down, recorded, made formal, a event under description—and a moment for memory, outside of history. These two—history and memory—are not opposed in this work: rather, they coexist, but not as equals. Jacob goes on: 'History is amoral; events occurred. But memory is moral; what we consciously remember is what our conscience remembers. History is the Totenbuch, The Book of the Dead, kept by the administrators of the camps. Memory is the Memorbucher, the names of those to be mourned, read aloud in the synagogues' (*FP* 138). This quite harsh division, between the truth of the 'bare facts' and truth of memory, of 'how we are' underlies much in this book (I discuss it in Chapter 5 and 6). Later, his academic biographer writes that the 'search for facts, for places, names, influential events, important conversations and correspondences, political circumstances—all this amounts to nothing if you can't find the assumption your subject lives by' (*FP* 222). What makes Athos so appealing and central is that he bridges these two discourses: he writes 'lyric geology . . . what a splendid anthropomorphist—even down to the generosity of an ionic bond' (*FP* 209) (there is clearly something of the 'Primo Levi as I imagine him' here). Likewise, what makes Bella a great pianist is knowing not the notes, but that 'the best musician learns to play what's not on the page'.[41]

It is the coming together of these two, this realization and the haunting by Bella, that leads to 'what the light teaches' here: 'All the years I felt Bella entreating me, filled with her loneliness, I was mistaken. I have misunderstood her signals. Like other ghosts she whispers; not for me to join her, but so that, when I am close enough, she can push me back into the world' (*FP* 170). Jacob has been studying the histories, scrutinizing the photographs of the camps, to find Bella: yet this is mistaken—this is to abandon oneself to the dead, to leave the world and live with the shades. Paradoxically, to 'remain with the dead is to abandon them' (*FP* 170) because unless life continues its course, unless the river flows, the dead do not assume their proper place, as dead. This is not, as Lawrence Langer might suggest, to 'pre-empt' the Holocaust with some trite resolution: rather it is, for Michaels here, to lay out the dead in their proper place. This does not mean forgetting them, or 'normalizing' them, but bringing them into the fugue with the correct emphasis—playing what's not on the page.

The last section of the first part of the novel, 'The Gradual Instant', echoes the ending of 'What the Light Teaches': Jacob meets, falls in love with, and marries Michaela. They live happily in Greece, and Michela becomes pregnant: their child will be called Bela or Bella. Yet, it is here that the book pushes beyond 'What the Light Teaches' in its poetic thinking, and is at its most fugue-like. The very first page informs us that Beer and his wife were killed in a car accident in Athens in 1993 (another accident), leaving no children. There is no more from Beer, after the discovery of his wife's pregnancy. Yet the novel continues, fugue-like, beginning again with a narrative of Ben, an academic. Again the first section is called 'The Drowned City'.

This drowned city is, again, the Jewish community, but Ben's family in Toronto, drowned in silence about the Holocaust. There is 'no energy of a narrative in our family, not even the fervour of an elegy' (*FP* 204), although, as in other accounts of postmemory, Ben absorbs much. As Helen Epstein writes of her own parents

neither imagined how, over the years, I had stored their remarks, their glances, their silence inside me, how I had deposited then in my iron box like pennies in a piggy bank. They were unconscious of how much a child gleans from the absence of explanation as much as from words, of how much I learned from

---

[41] Anne Michaels, 'Words for the Body', *Weight of Oranges*, 47.

the old photographs hanging on our apartment walls or secreted away in the old yellow envelope below my father's desk.[42]

Some things get through: instead of hearing about 'ogres, trolls, witches, I heard disjointed references to kapos, haftlings, "Ess Ess", dark woods' (*FP* 217). Anne Karpf: the 'Holocaust was our fairy-tale'.[43] Locked in silence, it is Jacob's poems—*Groundwork*, philosophical but tied to the earth—that give him a voice, a way of thinking about the Holocaust. As a boy, like Grossman's Momik, Ben becomes obsessed with things that stand in for the absent Holocaust: bodies preserved in bogs (and, of course, Jacob, the living 'bog boy' will be his subject); what is left behind by tornadoes, by the collapse of industry—'aftermath fascinated me' (*FP* 228). But his parents are silent.

Ben's beautiful wife, Naomi, befriends them and begins to know them better than he does. After their death Ben discovers a photograph of his murdered elder brother and sister, about which he had known nothing: before he can show Naomi, she says 'Its so sad, it's terrible' (*FP* 252). She had broken through the silence. She also reveals also that he is called 'Ben' not for Benjamin, but simply from 'Ben', Hebrew for 'Son'. Unable to cope with this, he leaves her—and goes to seek out Jacob Beer's journal. This section, again 'Vertical Time', describes Ben's time in the Beer's house—Athos's family house— in Greece. By living there, slowly he comes to identify more with Jacob and Jacob's responses to his experiences. In 'Phosphorous', Ben finds a lover, Petra: like Jacob's marriage to Alexandra it is short-lived, explosive, and illuminating. It is Petra who finds the notebooks for which he has been looking, and the note which reveals that Michaela was pregnant. Again, it is in this section that Ben comes to terms with his parents, his postmemory, and his marriage: 'My parent's past is mine molecularly' (*FP* 280). But more than this, Jacob's words to Naomi come back to him: 'there's a moment when love makes us believe in death for the first time. You recognise the one whose loss, even contemplated, you'll carry forever, like a sleeping child. All grief, anyone's grief, you said, is the weight of a sleeping child' (*FP* 280–1). Love and death are intertwined inextricably. The final section, again 'The Way Station', is Ben's return to Canada and to his wife, just as the poem 'What the Light Teaches' ends with a journey to a loved one. He has come to

---

[42] Helen Epstein, *Children of the Holocaust: Conversations with Sons and Daughters of Survivors* (London: Penguin, 1988), 335.

[43] Anne Karpf, *The War After* (London: Minerva, 1996), 94.

terms with his memories and postmemory—not resolved them, but at 'last my unhappiness is my own . . . I see that I must give what I most need' (*FP* 292, 294). Just as Jacob identifies with the dead, is 'inhabited' by his dead sister, and then learns to pass beyond, so Ben identifies with Jacob, and comes to terms with his parents. *Fugitive Pieces* does not offer an easy resolution. Unlike *Eve's Tattoo* it eschews identifications—the story is too disrupted, too intense, too fugue-like and fugitive. Unlike *Too Many Men,* its flow of memory is a process, even if it reaches no conclusion. It seems to offer a novelized version of the diasporic and exiled identity and memory so common in post-Holocaust literature. Even though it concerns an engagement with childhood memory, it stands in stark contrast to a Holocaust text that makes a very strong, but fraudulent, claim for identity, 'Binjamin Wilkomirski's' *Fragments.*

PARODY, LIES, AND FALSE IDENTIFICATIONS: BINJAMIN WILKOMIRSKI'S FRAGMENTS

Much has been written, both academically and journalistically, about this fraudulent memoir.[44] Frauds and lies are nothing new and judging whether Binjamin Wilkomirski/Bruno Grosjean/Bruno Dössekker is bad or mad is not within my remit. Here, I only want to consider what the book and the controversy reveals about Holocaust testimonies and Holocaust fiction—about Holocaust reading. In my discussion so far, I have concentrated on the internal markers and effects of genre, at the level of reading, identification, and memory. However, part of the genre conventions for both testimony and Holocaust fiction/reading are involved in the wider extra- and meta-textual world. Part of the generic context for testimony invokes the status of the author as wit-ness—often thought of as the 'autobiographical pact'. Part of the generic context for fiction invokes both the possibility of scandal—in the media, for example—and the particular claims for authority to write on the Holocaust. Like the Demidenko affair in Australia, *Fragments*—as a book that has moved from the genre of testimony to

---

[44] See, principally: Philip Gourevitch, 'The Memory Thief', *The New Yorker* (14th June 1999), 48–68; Elena Lappin, 'The Man with Two Heads', *Granta,* 66 (1999), 7–65; Blake Eskin, *A Life in Pieces: The Making and Unmaking of Binjamin Wilkomirski* (New York: W. W. Norton, 2002); Stefan Maechler, *The Wilkomirski Affair: A Study in Biographical Truth,* tr. John E. Woods (London: Picador, 2001).

the genre of Holocaust fiction—reveals a great deal, not about the text itself (*Fragments* has changed without a word being altered) but about identification and about genres and generic rules.

First, as the Maechler report makes clear, the book is the result of an immense act of identification on the part of the author. Maechler suggests that, as a response to the trauma and difficulties of his own life, Wilkomirski slowly began to identify, through his victimization fantasies, with the victims of the Holocaust: in 'his fantasises Wilkomirski took narcissistic possession of that remembrance [of the Holocaust] and with the grace of a sleepwalker exploited the collective ritual of remembering'.[45] As I suggested earlier, *identity without memory is empty, memory without identity is meaningless*: the author had to create a memory to establish an identity.

As a victim who could not have been more innocent and more ill-treated he was met with world-wide solidarity and boundless sympathy. As a person who never felt he belonged, he now found entry into a community of victims . . . The most important gain . . . was that he had found a meaningful story for an inexplicable and inaccessible past.[46]

Finkielkraut described himself as 'genocide's huckster' when he 'harvested all the moral advantage' of belonging to 'the camp of the oppressed'.[47] This is more fairly applied to Wilkomirski. But this is not a function of the text *per se*, but of the meta-text.

Frank Kermode cites John Searle arguing that there 'is no textual property . . . that will identify a stretch of discourse as a work of fiction'.[48] Likewise, James Young points out that 'there may be nothing in the text to discriminate between autobiographical and fictional narrative'.[49] *Fragments* has no single textual property that proves it is fiction, rather than what it claims to be, half-remembered testimony (although Maechler records that both Raul Hilberg and Lawrence Langer were suspicious of the fraud before it was uncovered).[50] Kermode argues that fiction is usually labelled so 'metatextually: most

[45] Maechler, *Wilkomirski Affair*, 302. The 'sleepwalker' metaphor is an allusion to Hitler's 'blind assurance of a sleepwalker'.

[46] Ibid. 272.

[47] Alain Finkielkraut, *The Imaginary Jew*, tr. Kevin O'Neill and David Suckoff (London: University of Nebraska Press, 1994), 11, 9.

[48] Frank Kermode, *The Genesis of Secrecy: On the Interpretation of Narrative* (London: Harvard University Press, 1979), 116.

[49] James Young, *Writing and Rewriting the Holocaust: Narrative and the Consequences of Interpretation* (Bloomington: Indiana University Press, 1990), 84.

[50] Maechler, *Wilkomirski Affair*, 117.

novels find ways of assuring the reader that they are fictions, or what Searle calls "non-deceptive pseudo-performances", thereby ensuring the suspension of the conventions by which we normally judge the felicitousness of other kinds of discourse'.[51] What Kermode is pointing out is that the issue of 'fictionality' does not lie in the text, but in the 'meta-text', the context in which the book is read which controls and effects how it is read: in its genre, in fact. Indeed, what is at issue here is not the textual properties of *Fragments*, but the contextual properties in the light of which *Fragments*, in these terms, was crucially (and intentionally) mislabelled. It was a 'deceptive pseudo-performance', a fraud, supported by, as Maechler argues, public sympathy and goodwill, the connivance of the publishing houses until the last minute, the specific Swiss circumstances (the treatment of 'dormant' Jewish accounts in Swiss banks), and the Manichaean tendencies of the media and others involved.

The book certainly does have some of the textual conventions of testimony. Although it does not employ any historical disclosure or documents, it does establish its narrative frame—the memories of a child-survivor—both at the start and in the afterword. It has a number of epiphanies (too many, perhaps, in retrospect) and is constructed of interruptions, slips in narrative time—fragments, in fact. However, it does offer a closure (twice, in fact: 'He understood what I was really saying' at the end of the novel, and the reassurance of 'They should know that they are not alone' at the end of the afterword). It even offers a powerful version of what I called earlier an 'allegory of failed understanding'. In the orphanage, the child Binjamin misunderstands a picture of William Tell: he mistakes Tell for an SS man killing children. He, the putative survivor, is misunderstood by the teacher, the non-survivor, and told he is speaking 'drivel'.[52] Where, in the examples from Delbo or Levi, the non-survivor (the schoolboy, Pierre the survivor's husband) is shown only to be uncomprehending, here the non-survivor is positively angry and unsympathetic, and cannot be identified with (as we know better than she does), forcing the reader to identify with the little boy. The very fact that these conventions—if implicitly understood—can be used implies there is a culturally encoded genre for testimony: the texts 'never happen in social vacuum'.[53] However, as is well established, *Fragments* lacks the 'autobiographical pact'.

[51] Kermode, *Genesis of Secrecy*, 116.   [52] Maechler, *Wilkomirski Affair*, 477.

[53] Gadi BenEzer, 'Trauma Signals in Life Stories', in Kamly Rogers *et al.* (eds.), *Trauma and Life Stories* (London: Routledge, 1999), 30.

Fragments also has some of the characteristics of a Holocaust novel that Vice claims it to be.[54] It is clearly to be read in a 'worldly' way: its filiations are with the Holocaust—even if this turns out to be a complex metaphor for the author's own traumatized life. Its affiliations are, as Maechler points out, all involved with how we understand the past. It certainly has been scandalous: far more so that Kosinski's *The Painted Bird* (1978) or Helen Demidenko/Darville's *The Hand That Signed the Paper* (1994). The novel plays with narrative time, jumping back and forth from the camps to the orphanage, to later in his life. The 'right to speak' has been explored in more detail in this case than in others: indeed, the scandal consists, in no small part, not because of the text but because Wilkomirski has asserted this right to speak as a survivor.

What the book reveals is that there are enough testimonies for their conventions to be successfully copied. In turn this means that—just as *Northanger Abbey* is parody of the gothic novel—so *Fragments* is a parody—if not an amusing one—of a testimony or a novel. A parody works by playing on its audience's expectations, in this case, the readership's expectations of a Holocaust testimony. Once the 'truth of the fiction' was revealed the readership looked like dupes: the parody had been at their expense. This unhappy Holocaust parody, then, is a supplement to both genres. It is clearly parasitic on them: there could be no *Fragments* without Levi, Wiesel, and other testimony, nor without the possibility of Holocaust fiction. But its falsity—and the discovery of this—reveals not only the conventions and tropes of the two genres (that exist enough to be imitated) but also shows that the internal conventions are not enough and that both these genres of writing and reading have spread from the textual to the worldly—they are meta-textual as well as literary. It is their meta-textual side that also draws powerfully on the ideas of identification—not least on audiences' horizons or comprehension and expectations.

The audiences are the target of Maechler's book. He considers them both the most culpable ('Without an audience, there would be no Wilkomirski') and the most deceived, the most gullible as well as the most sympathetic.[55] But Maechler—and all readers after the 'unmasking'—have an advantage: they are no longer reading the book in the same genre. Maechler, very properly, read the book and the context 'as a historian'—and implies that we should all read Holocaust texts in this way—and so came with different questions and different

[54] Vice, *Holocaust Fiction*, 164.   [55] Maechler, *Wilkomirski Affair*, 273.

approaches.[56] But what he draws from the scandal is that 'the Wilkomirski phenomenon, from the origins of his memories to their reception and exposure, is a litmus test revealing how we all—depending on the nature of our involvement—deal with [the Holocaust's] aftermath . . . this fictive "autobiography" of an alleged victim of the death camps reflects the very core structures of the Shoah itself'.[57] He means that, as with an array of other aspects, the Holocaust takes us back to the very basic questions of our own self-understanding, as a culture and as individuals. What is a human being? With whom can I or do I identify? The shifting nature of identification and sympathy that *Fragments* evokes—both as 'words on the page' and as the 'Wilkomirski phenomenon'—reveals this.

ILLUMINATING A GREY ZONE: JONATHAN SAFRAN FOER, *EVERYTHING IS ILLUMINATED*

> Jews have six senses. Touch taste, sight, smell, hearing . . . memory . . . When a Jew encounters a pin, he asks: What does it remember like?[58]

Jonathan Safran Foer's *Everything is Illuminated* is about identification and about memory, but it offers a complex approach to these issues. The novel is, in fact, three interrelated strands with two different authors, all of which focus on the moment of 'illumination'. The book itself is the coming together of at least two literary forms: *pace* Linda Hutcheon, with its emphasis on mimesis of process (on the writing itself) rather than mimesis of product (the world represented), it is a postmodern novel. As it concerns the grandchildren of survivors and bystanders, and although it began with the intention of being a factual 'Holocaust Travel book' like Martin Gilbert's *Holocaust Journey*, it is a third-generation survivor novel: indeed, it is precisely the distance from the events that leads to its choice of novelistic style.

The first strand, chronologically, is the story of the shtetl on the Ukranian–Polish border that comes to be called Trachimbrod. The ostensible author of these sections is 'Jonathan Safran Foer', who has come to the Ukraine from the USA to find the community, or the

---

[56] Maechler, *Wilkomirski Affair*, p. vii.   [57] Ibid. 307–8.
[58] Jonathan Safran Foer, *Everything is Illuminated* (London: Penguin, 2002), 198–9. This will be abbreviated to *EiI* in the text.

remains of it, from which his grandfather escaped. This story begins 18 March 1791, with the accidental drowning of Trachim, and ends 18 March 1942 with the murder of '1204 Trachimbroders, Killed at the Hand of German Fascism' (*Ell* 189). This story is written like a Bachevis Singer novel, rewritten by Borges or by Rushdie, and is comparable to magical realism. It mixes narrative with comedy, satire, and tragedy. Different forms of writing are mixed together: third-person narration, dialogue in imitation of *Ulysses's* 'Circe' chapter, excerpts from books written by the Trachimbroders, dreams. There are also some technical experimental uses of text: a flow chart (*Ell* 259), a page and a half which repeats the phrase 'We are writing . . .' (*Ell* 212–13), and, in place of a description of the bombing of the shtetl, simply two pages of ellipses with the occasional phrase (*Ell* 279–81). This story is told with very conscious foreshadowing: not the implicit type over which Bernstein troubles but with the foreknowledge clearly and reflectively marked out. The dates on which events take place stress this, as do remarks like 'For the next one hundred and fifty years . . .' (*Ell* 14), or 'she thought about it seven years later, on June 18, 1941, as the first German war blasts shook her wooden house' (*Ell* 168). Towards the end of this narrative, as the front sweeps closer, the authorial voice starts to interrupt like a fictional, postmodern Moshe the Beadle: 'GO AWAY! RUN WHILE YOU CAN, FOOLS, RUN FOR YOUR LIVES!' (*Ell* 269) and, more fearfully: '(Here is impossible to go on, because we know what happens, and wonder why they don't. Or it's impossible because we fear they do)' (*Ell* 270).

The significance of this is, on the one hand, to create a sense of community and continuity over time, lost because of the Holocaust, between 'Jonathan Safran Foer' (the character) and the Jewish shtetl. The central characters are his ancestors, and the narrator occasionally uses 'we' to describe them, and the community at large ('We were to be in good hands' (*Ell* 22). However, where Singer, for example, used the realist form to do this, Foer uses a more postmodern style. Instead of focusing on the narrative, for example, he picks up on dreams, and odd, marginal moments. Instead of a consistent focus, he offers an inconsistent style that playfully chops and changes. It is a novelistic equivalent to the deconstructive histories discussed at the end of Chapter 6, which mix Rankean rigour with memory, with that which is outside the reach of the discipline of history. The significance of this choice of style is an admission that, after their massacre by the Wehrmacht, such construction is simply not possible. This explains the anachronistic lack of historical difference in the representation of the community. The shtetl can only be reconstructed, and that only in the light of what 'Jonathan Safran Foer' knows, in the light of his own unavoidable epistemological commitments. That is, this strand of the story creates a community which stresses the impossibility of recreating the community, and, indeed, this lies at the heart of part of the satire of the second part of the novel, which concerns the trip of 'Jonathan Safran Foer' to the Ukraine with 'Heritage Touring'.

This strand of the novel is told by Alexander Perchov, the son of the tour agent: these sections are written in his poor but meaningful English, and just as the first works forwards in time towards the Holocaust, this describes a movement backwards, as the events of Trachimbrod's destruction are uncovered. In a contrast to Lily Brett's work, and despite the comic errors in Alex's writing, Eastern Europe or the former Soviet Union are not patronized here. In fact, the novel is very clear about the passage of time since the war and of the complexities of the region: for example, Alex at one stage explains the delicate distinctions between and reciprocal prejudices of those who speak a fusion of Russian and Ukrainian, and those who speak only Ukrainian (*EII* 112). The novel is at least as much about the memory and identity of Alex and the Ukraine as it is about the American 'Foer'. Alex, who starts off boastful, becomes more honest and profound as the novel continues. The story of 'Foer's' visit is Alex's narrative. Alex and his grandfather drive 'Foer' around the Ukraine, looking for Trachimbrod. They do not find it, but an elderly woman, who, when pressed, says 'You are here. I am it' (*EII* 118). She lives in a house full of boxes of remains from the town. She is a living memorial, and a survivor of an atrocity. To the grandfather, she brings up his memories of the war, and to 'Foer' she gives a ring: this ring 'does not exist for you', she says, 'You exist for the ring' (*EII* 192) and, though it does not fit, it cuts his finger. It is the symbol of a community. It is in this strand of the novel that the 'illumination' occurs, which is the grandfather's involvement in the massacre of Trachimbrod. A non-Jew, he is forced to point out, to betray, his Jewish best friend to the Germans, who is shot. This is the illumination: but it is the illumination of a grey zone, where neither history nor moral judgements are simple.[59]

---

[59] On this sort of event, see Rab Bennett, *Under the Shadow of the Swastika: The moral Dilemmas of Resistance and Collaboration in Hitler's Europe* (London: Macmillan, 1999).

Both these strands are included as part of one half of an epistolary novel. Monthly letters from Alex to Jonathan enclose both Alex's story and Jonathan's, and offer a commentary on both. Here, their friendship deepens and then stops. But it is also clear that the two stories are 'the same story . . . I am Alex and I am you and I am you and you are me? Do you not comprehend that we can bring each other safety and peace?' (*EIl* 214). This is complex: within the narrative, it is the case that the stories of the two families, the victims and the bystanders, have become intertwined, and it seems as if—though it never occurs—there may be some possibility of forgiveness between the two. Outside the narrative, it seems to stress an awareness of the seamless web of human relations, and that a novel about the Holocaust is also a novel about all the others less or more involved. Indeed, in a crucial moment (*EIl* 160), 'Foer' lets Alex read a section of the novel which is yet to occur, and Alex realizes that he is both bound into fiction, and not. Alex is both part of 'Foer' and 'Foer's' process of identification. Alex's final letter to 'Foer' on 26 January 1998 declares that he is a coward as he will not let his characters follow their loves and become happy. Of course, this is the author's dilemma, and, also, whatever 'Foer' does with the characters, all but one (his grandfather) will die in the Holocaust. At the same time, Alex has translated his grandfather's suicide note (of 22 January 1998) which describes both how Alex forces his violent father to leave and his own plans for death. Here, it seems that telling the truth is central: '*Try to live so that you can always tell the truth, I said | I will, he said, and I believed in him, and that was enough*'. (*EIl* 275).

Yet, while this may seem trite, in the complexities of this novel it clearly is not, not least because it is unclear exactly what the truth may or may not be. Moreover, it was precisely a demand to 'tell the truth' about 'who is a Jew' that led to the grandfather's crime. Truth here seems to have more than a factual sense, and approach something to do with having a sense of 'who one is' and 'how things are'. It also means, it seems, an awareness of how complicated and interwoven identifications, ethics, and history are.

CONCLUSION

At the conclusion to Chapter 2, I suggested that it was testimony accounts, rather than fiction, that would be 'crucible of memory', and that Holocaust fiction was, in a sense, secondary. Part of the reason for this is that in fiction, unlike testimonies, identification is more easily achieved (it is easy to be seduced by Eve, for example). Moreover, in a novel, the strangeness of the trace of testimony is lost. This means that, extrinsically, the works are comprehended and consumed and become just one novel amongst others. The hard fear of reading a Holocaust testimony can easily become soft sentiment. This is not to impugn the intentions of any of these authors: all—one hopes—offer an engagement with the events in good faith. Rather it is suggested that the reading that fiction requires too often demands the sort of process of identification that 'consumes' the events.

The reason the issue of identity and identification causes problems is that it is not at all clear, after the Holocaust, how or with whom we can or should identify. In the specific context of reading, as well as in other, wider contexts that rely on identification, this is what the idea that 'the unity of the Human race is shattered' means, and this is what 'Holocaust reading' has to bear in mind. To put this another way: the leading Holocaust historian Yehuda Bauer, in a Fackenheimian moment, writes that the Holocaust is a 'warning' and 'adds three commandments to the ten of the Jewish-Christian tradition: Thou shalt not be a perpetrator; thou shalt not be a passive victim; and thou most certainly shalt not be a bystander'.[60] Bauer's just demand leaves open only two subject positions: each of us should become or be, or identify ourselves as, a resisting victim or an active (third party, as it were) combatant against genocide. That this seems to offer a rather simplistic division—which reflects the Second World War, or even perhaps the post-war trials at Nuremberg and later—rather than the current globalized world is not centrally a problem: stands on human suffering have to be taken after all. But, in the context of reading, it does present a problem. In terms of testimony, I have argued that the reader's position is one in which the traces of the Holocaust do indeed call us to responsibility. But in fiction it seems we are precisely being asked to identify with either the victims (in, say, *The Last of the Just* or, at a remove, in *Too Many Men* or in *Fugitive Pieces*), the bystanders (*Eve's Tattoo*), or—through the next generation or their children—the perpetrators (in *The Reader* or, in a more exculpatory way, *The Dark Room*). It is precisely this tension—between the demand of fiction that we identify and the demand of the Holocaust that we cannot and should not—that unbalances even the most subtle of these novels.

[60] Yehuda Bauer, *Rethinking the Holocaust* (London: Yale University Press, 2002), 67.

The best of these texts gesture towards this: as the reader becomes too comfortable with Jacob Beer's life—as he is happy—he and his pregnant wife are killed in a senseless car accident, and the process begins again with Ben; the 'meaning' of illumination is to make readers aware of the terrible complexities of that time and ours. The worst offer facile and easy answers, to which it is easy (and important) to say 'yes, but...'. But they all circle around these questions, or rely on them. Are there answers to these questions? Levi's poem with which I ended Chapter 1 is phrased as a question. Perhaps their form as questions is a boon, not a burden. James Young writes:

> if modern responses to catastrophe have included the breakdown and repudia-
> tion of traditional forms and archetypes, then one postmodern response might
> be to recognize that even as we reject the absolute meanings and answers these
> 'archaic' forms provide, we are still unavoidably beholden to these same forms
> for both our expression and our understanding of the Holocaust. With this in
> mind, critical reading can lead not only to further understanding of sacred and
> modern literary texts, but also to new understanding of the ways our lives and
> these texts are inextricably bound together.[61]

To rephrase this in the terms of genre, which include both form and world, is to suggest that, although traditional genres seem not to be able to deal with the Holocaust—are not, *pace* Wiesel, a new litera-ture—they still attempt it. A response might be to read these in differ-ent ways, asking (with a nuanced 'critical reading') different sorts of questions of the genre, of the texts. The Holocaust and the texts that refer to it call for a 'Holocaust reading', an interpretation of cinders, which develops and bears these questions in mind. It is this—focusing on the idea of identification—that I have tried to undertake here. However, the questions it raises are also central for historical dis-course—the subject of the next section.

---

[61] Young, *Writing and Rewriting*, 192.

II

Holocaust Metahistories

5

Against Historicism:
History, Memory, and Truth

The Holocaust calls into radical question the very character of
what is historical. It cannot be incorporated within the representational confines of a usual research object for historical inquiry.
Rather, in recoil, it exerts a meta-historical impact on the very
way in which the methods and categories are constituted.[1]

The truth of meaning is not the same thing as the meaning of
truth.[2]

INTRODUCTION

The Holocaust poses problems for historians: not only problems raised
by the huge geographical and linguistic range of the enormous and still-
developing archive, not only about causation and positioning, but, as
Jörn Rüsen suggests, it raises problems about the nature of the discipline of history itself—metahistorical problems. Part II approaches
these and is not, therefore, a work of history, but a work of metahistory. Specifically, it is an attempt to get beyond what often seems to
be a rigid series of oppositions in the contemporary philosophy of history, between those characterized as 'empiricists' on the one hand and
'postmodernists' on the other, by turning to an analysis of the idea of
truth. More than this, it aims to show how, in Holocaust history, many
of these issues have already been debated and negotiated in different
ways and in different terms. Indeed, this should not be a surprise, as
many of the metahistorical issues described as postmodern stem from
thinking about the Holocaust.

[1] Jörn Rüsen, 'The Logic of Historicization', tr. William Templer, *History and
Memory*, 9 (1997), 113–44, 116.
[2] Hayden White, 'An Old Question Raised Again: Is Historiography Art or Science?
(Response to Iggers)', *Rethinking History*, 4/3 (2000), 391–406, 395.

The part begins with a chapter outlining my central argument and then explores this in three detailed studies. This chapter addresses ideas about truth and history and shows how they have been at work in two philosophers of history, Isaiah Berlin and Hayden White. The next chapters respond to questions that this argument begs. Chapter 6 uses the work of Saul Friedländer as an extended example of how these concepts of truth have already been used, looking at the development of historiographical thought and history writing over his career to date. Chapter 7 explores what happens when there are profound meta-historical disagreements, which both stem from and concern the Holocaust, by looking at the *Hitler's Willing Executioners/Ordinary Men* debate. While contemporary work on the Holocaust has moved on from this debate, and in terms of specifically historical work much has already been said, there is a great deal that a study of this one debate, from a particular time and place, can reveal about wider metahistoriographical issues. Chapter 8 deals with the question of what can be said and written historically. Many people claim that post-modernism is a friend of Holocaust denial: by examining one recent case of Holocaust denial in detail, the Irving/Lipstadt libel trial of 2000, I argue that this is far from the case and that these metahistorical questions in fact offer very strong tools against denial.

TRUTH, THE HOLOCAUST, AND HISTORY

If narrative is defined by a claim to establish a certain history, and if history is defined by a claim to explain events through their narrativization, is the mode of operation of these mutual claims (from history to narrative and from narrative to history) itself subject to history? Has contemporary history—with its cataclysm of the Second World War and the Holocaust—left intact the traditional shuttle movement between narrative and history? If not, what is the impact of the Holocaust on the mutual claims of history and narrative and the manner in which they are implicated in each other? Can contemporary narrative historically bear witness, not simply to the impact of the Holocaust, but to the way in which the impact of *history as Holocaust* has modified, affected, shifted the very modes of relationship between narrative and history?[3]

---

[3] Shoshona Felman and Dori Laub, *Testimony: Crises of Witnessing in Literature, Psychoanalysis and History* (London: Routledge, 1992), 94–5.

This complicated set of questions asks, at root, a single metahistorical question: is the Holocaust just an event in the past, written about by historians, or is it an event which changes how history is written and understood? As Dan Stone writes, 'Holocaust historians often begin by stating that the Holocaust signals the downfall of western civilisation and culture, and then go on to write about it with terms, methods, and implied beliefs unquestioningly inherited from that civilisation and culture.'[4] Perhaps the most unquestioned implied belief that historians—and others, of course—take for granted is a belief in truth. However, the discipline of history, and the metahistorical debates over its status, have in general passed over the question of how truth is to be understood, over the meaning of truth. This is problematic because debates about whether history is an art or a science, about the representation of the past, about the relationship between history and memory, are *really debates about the sort of truth to which history aspires*. The key issue here is the way in which our understanding of truth relates to, first, the way in which we construct and narrate our own pasts and so in no small part relate ourselves to others and to the world ('we are all everyday historians in our own case' writes Jonathan Rée) and second, the construction of the discipline of history.[5] It is the understanding of these relationships which is of use for Holocaust historiography.

Bernard Williams, in his book on *Truth and Truthfulness*, identifies two conflicting parties in relation to truth. One is the party of 'postmodern scepticism', who deny 'the possibility of truth altogether'; the other is the 'party of common sense', who assume that truth works quite well in its everyday sense. Williams steers a course between these two: he affirms both the correctness of 'common sense', in that we use and rely on the value of truth all the time, and its flaws:

positivism—in the sense, roughly speaking, of thinking that not much more is needed than to establish the concrete facts and set them down—cannot be seen as a minimalist or default position. Any story is a story, and positivism (which is involved in many contemporary forms of conservatism in the humanities) implies the double falsehood that no interpretation is needed, and that it is not needed because the story the positivist writer tells, such as it is, is obvious.[6]

---

[4] Dan Stone, 'Paul Ricoeur, Hayden White and Holocaust Historiography', in Jorn Stuckrath and Zurg Zbinden, *Metageschichte: Hayden White und Paul Ricoeur* (Baden-Baden: Nomos Verlagsgesellschaft, 1997), 254–74, 270.

[5] Jonathan Rée, *Heidegger: History and Truth in Being and Time* (London: Pheonix, 1998), 47.

[6] Bernard Williams, *Truth and Truthfulness* (Princeton: Princeton University Press, 2002), 12.

He points out that, while the sceptics—or 'deniers' as he calls them—are wrong about their denial of truth itself, they rightly feel that there is 'something to worry about in important areas of our thought and in traditional interpretations of these areas' and 'they sense that it has something to do with truth'.[7] Williams's approach is to turn to accuracy and sincerity, the virtues of truthfulness. While my argument has an analogous starting point and, like Williams, I find both sides open to question, it does not turn to virtues. Following a genealogy of the sort of 'truth' that the 'postmodern' party draws on, which stems from a German hermeneutic tradition, and with an awareness of what the empirical tradition actually relies on, I argue that through ideas about conventions or genre these two understandings of truth continually coexist in a manner that is sometimes constructive and sometimes destructive. The first part of this chapter details briefly with different accounts of the nature of truth. As I wrote in the Introduction, the aim here is to have a rough account of how the idea of truth is used in order to clarify debates in this area. The second part then explores the significance of these two understandings of truth for historiography since 1945.

TWO UNDERSTANDINGS OF TRUTH: CORRESPONDENCE AND BEDROCK

'How am I able to obey a rule?'—if this is not a question about causes, then it is about the justification for my following the rule in the way I do.

If I have exhausted the justifications I have reached bedrock, and my spade is turned. Then I am inclined to say: 'This is simply what I do'.

(Remember that we sometimes demand definitions for the sake not of their content, but of their form. Our requirement is an architectural one: the definition a kind of ornamental coping that supports nothing.)[8]

A significant strand in contemporary philosophy, both analytic and continental, concerns the ways in which truth is to be understood. To

---

[7] Williams, *Truth and Truthfulness*, 5.
[8] Ludwig Wittgenstein, *Philosophical Investigations*, tr. G. E. M. Anscombe (Oxford: Blackwell, 1963), 217, 85e.

simplify: there are two different conceptions, which, especially in historiography, are often considered rivals, although they are not. One is the belief that truth is the agreement or correspondence of a judgement, an assertion, or a proposition with its object. This is the 'common or garden' sense of truth and is often identified with scientific and positivist understandings of the world: Williams's 'party of common sense'. It is assumed to come from Aristotle and also underlies most coherence or consensus theories of truth (roughly, because in these the 'truth' corresponds to what is consistent and what is generally agreed). Assertions made under this way of understanding truth can, given the right circumstances, be proved or disproved. It is this sense that underlies almost all historical work in the Rankean, 'objective' tradition and gives the image and self-image of the discipline of history as a positivist science. For example, Richard Evans writes that 'the idea of objectivity involves a belief in "the reality of the past, and [to] truth as correspondence to that reality" . . . I remain optimistic that objective historical knowledge is both desirable and attainable'.[9]

However, there is a sense of truth which is not like this: a sense of 'who we are and how things are in the world' which is other than correspondence truth, perhaps deeper and more profound: the bedrock of which Wittgenstein writes. A symptom of this is the sense that truth, as fundamental, is not explicable (what more fundamental concept could elucidate it?). Donald Davidson—among others—argues that truth is one of the 'most elementary concepts we have, concepts without which . . . we would have no concepts at all': 'Why then should we expect to be able to reduce these concepts definitionally to other concepts that are simpler, clearer and more basic? We should accept the fact that what makes these concepts so important must also foreclose on the possibility of finding a foundation for them which reaches deeper into bedrock.'[10] Hilary Putnam writes that, about some particular issues, 'I don't know how I know these things: there are cases in which I find that I have to say: "I have reached bedrock and this is where my spade is turned" '.[11] In contrast, then, to truth as correspondence and assertions that can be true or false or easily measured, some thinkers have argued

---

[9] Richard Evans, *In Defence of History* (London: Granta Books, 1997), 252: he is citing Peter Novick, *That Noble Dream: The 'Objectivity Question' and the American Historical Profession* (Cambridge: Cambridge University Press, 1988), 6.

[10] Donald Davidson, 'The Folly of Trying to Define Truth', in Simon Blackburn and Keith Simons (eds.), *Truth* (Oxford: Oxford University Press, 1999), 309.

[11] Hilary Putnam, *The Many Faces of Realism* (LaSalle, Ill.: Open Court, 1987), 85.

for an existential truth that lies outside this realm. Andrew Bowie argues that 'many of the most important philosophical questions lead inevitably to issues connected to art';[12] he links these issues over truth to art 'via the claim that art reveals the world in ways which would not be possible without the existence of art itself—a version of this view can be ascribed to Schlegel, Novalis, Schleiermacher, Heidegger, Benjamin, Adorno and Gadamer . . . Truth here is seen in terms of the capacity of forms of articulation to "disclose" the world.'[13] The reason for discriminating between these two different understandings of truth is that the model of truth as the correspondence of a proposition to its object—which is by far the most widely accepted and dominant model—seems to exclude much that people find of great value: visions of how the world was, is, and ought to be, things that are core for people's personal and communal identity, feelings or judgements that cannot be understood as 'being in correspondence with' something which seems unable to describe the 'bedrock' of what makes us up. To come to terms with these two understandings of truth and the relationship between them in detail would be a study in its own right, and has been part of philosophical debate for a long time. My only aim here is to show how these understandings of truth which underlie the discipline of history are very illuminating for the history of the Holocaust.

Truth as correspondence is well established and is taken for granted, perhaps in an unreflective way, in most work done in history and historiography. The other understanding is less clear, and so I will discuss it and its dangers in some detail. Perhaps both the strongest and clearest discussion of this view (which is prevalent, as Bowie suggests, in the whole German hermeneutic tradition) is laid out by Heidegger, principally in *Being and Time* and 'The Origin of the Work of Art' in his argument over truth as unveiling: and, at the same time, Heidegger is himself the clearest illustration of the worst that this idea can imply, in his career as a Nazi. This discussion is also, perhaps, the most influential for post-war phenomenological, post-phenomenological, and postmodern thinkers like Levinas, Irigaray, and Derrida, as part what Levinas calls the 'debt of every contemporary thinker . . . to Heidegger . . . a debt that he [*sic*] often owes to his regret'.[14]

---

[12] Andrew Bowie, *From Romanticism to Critical Theory* (London: Routledge, 1997), 159.

[13] Ibid. 159.

[14] Emmanuel Levinas, *God, Death and Time*, tr. Bettina Bergo (Stanford, Calif.: Stanford University Press, 2000), 8.

HEIDEGGER'S CONCEPTION OF TRUTH

> From the outset Heidegger runs up against the logical prejudice of conceiving truth primarily as a property of a proposition. This prejudice abets and is abetted by the notion that theory and scientific knowledge, as so many systematic sets of true assertions, form the endgame of philosophy.[15]

Heidegger's argument is well-known and I will summarize it only briefly. In section 44 of *Being and Time* he begins by noting that philosophy has always 'associated truth and Being' and so questions of truth fall within the purview of fundamental ontology, within the analytic of *Dasein*.[16] Heidegger begins his analysis—as he usually does—with the traditional concept of truth: '(1) that the "locus" of truth is assertion (judgement); (2) that the essence of truth lies in the "agreement" of the judgement with its object; (3) that Aristotle . . . not only has assigned truth to judgement as its primordial locus but has set going the definition of "truth" as agreement' (*BT* 214). Heidegger argues that this model of truth, as correspondence between judgement and object, comes from the tradition of Western philosophy from Aristotle, through Parmenides, Isaac Israeli, Avicenna, Aquinas, and to Kant who writes that the 'definition of truth, that is the agreement of knowledge with its object, is assumed as granted'.[17] However, Heidegger asks what else is 'tacitly posited in this relational totality of the *adaequatio intellectus and rei?*' (*BT* 215: agreement of mind and thing).

Every agreement, he argues is a relation, but not every relation is an agreement. For example, a sign points *at* its object: this is clearly a relationship (of pointing at) but this relationship is not an agreement. Likewise, 6 is equal to 16 minus 10: an agreement (6 with 16 minus 10) with relation to—in the context of—the question of 'how much?': 'Equality is one way of agreeing' (*BT* 216) Heidegger writes. So, Heidegger asks, '[W]ith regard to what [in what context] do *intellectus* and *rei* agree?' (*BT* 216). They cannot be equal, because they are different things, nor can they only be similar, since the sort of relation

---

[15] Daniel O. Dahlstrom, *Heidegger's Concept of Truth* (Cambridge: Cambridge University Press, 2001), 17.

[16] Martin Heidegger, *Being and Time*, tr. John Macquarrie and Edward Robinson (Oxford: Blackwell, 1962), 212. This will be abbreviated to *BT* in the text.

[17] Emmanuel Kant, *Critique of Pure Reason*, tr. Norman Kemp Smith (London: Macmillan, 1929), A58/B82.

knowledge claims is that one is 'just as' the other. Thus, Heidegger argues that we must 'go back and inquire into the context of Being which provides the support' (*BT* 216) for *intellectus* and *rei*.

This 'context of Being' is explored by asking what knowledge is. The idea that what 'is true is knowledge . . . But knowledge is judgement' (*BT* 216) presupposes a psychic process (judging), a real object, and the idea of the object (in the judging process). Thus there are three relations—the judgement, the object judged, and real object: and—'in over two thousand years'(*BT* 217)—the link between the ideal and the real (the object judged and real object) has not been clarified. So, what kind of being is knowledge? Knowledge can only be knowledge when it is true. How is its truth shown? Truth is not shown in assertions about or representations of an object, since any assertion about an object already presupposes a relationship with it. The object exists in its 'uncovering', that it might be the object of an assertion or a representation. This uncovering is a bringing-into-relation-with *Dasein*. The confirmation of an assertion (that is, the showing of truth that demonstrates that knowledge is knowledge about it) is based on 'the entity's showing itself' (a picture is only known to be askew if it has already uncovered itself, if it is in a world in which 'straight' and 'askew' make sense): thus knowledge (for example, assertion and confirmation) is only possible as a 'Being towards real entities and a Being that uncovers' (*BT* 218). Truth, then, is fundamentally not correspondence—the likening of one object to another—but an uncovering. Very roughly, things have to *be in relation*, in some way, before they can be judged true (or judged false) in the traditional sense. And it is this 'having to be in relation' that Heidegger calls 'primordial truth'.

Heidegger is not saying that 'truth as agreement' is wrong: his philosophy is 'not at odds with logic'.[18] Rather, he is arguing that the 'traditional' understanding of truth comes from and relies upon the more primordial truth and, in turn, this 'being-true' is possible only 'on the basis of Being-in-the-world' (*BT* 219): 'Dasein is "in the truth" ' (*BT* 221). In the light of his earlier analyses of *Dasein*, this means that to 'Dasein's state of Being, disclosedness in general essentially belongs' (*BT* 221), made explicit through what Heidegger calls care or concern (*sorge*). Investigating the 'world of concern', Dahlstrom argues that

experience is . . . the point of departure for the analysis of the work-world: this world is part of an original and unified structure of being-in-the-world that

[18] Dahlstrom, *Heidegger's Concept of Truth*, 1.

centres, for the respective entity that is-in-the-world, on being itself. *The world of concern is ultimately a way in which the human being is in the world in order to be respectively who he or she is.*[19]

To *Dasein's* Being belongs also 'thrownness [the experience of each of us, finding ourselves already in a definite world] . . . projection [an awareness of our own possibilities] . . . falling' (*BT* 221). Falling—one of Heidegger's more controversial terms—means that a *Dasein* is taken up with 'they' and is dominated by 'the way things are publicly interpreted' (*BT* 222). For Heidegger this is not (primarily) pejorative: indeed, falling belongs primordially to *Dasein*. He writes that it means that 'that which has been uncovered and disclosed stands in a mode in which it has been disguised and closed off by idle talk' (*BT* 222). For example, the amazing discoveries of cosmology about the origins of the universe or about DNA are now part of the everyday vernacular—the big bang and the double helix no longer make us stop and think. We find *Hamlet* is full of quotations. This means that *Dasein* is both 'in the truth' and in the 'untruth'—covering up or passing over the truth—at the same time. Because of this, Heidegger writes, *Dasein* 'should explicitly appropriate what has already been uncovered, defend it against semblance and disguise, and assure itself of its uncoveredness again and again . . . Truth (uncoveredness) is something that must always first be wrested from entities. Entities get snatched out of their hiddenness' (*BT* 222).

This is why, Heidegger argues, to stress this wrestling of truth from the world; the Greeks used an expression that stressed the absence of covering up or hiding: *aletheia*, unforgetting. James Dicenso cites a very illuminating remark by Ortega y Gasset which predates Heidegger but captures his sense well:

Once known, truths acquire a utilitarian crust; they no longer interest us as truths but as useful recipes. That pure, sudden illumination which characterises truth accompanies the latter only at the moment of discovery. Hence its Greek name *aletheia*, which originally meant the same as the word apocalypse later, that is, discovery, revelation, or rather, unveiling, removing a veil of cover.[20]

---

[19] Ibid. 270; italics added.
[20] James DiCenso, *Hermeneutics and the Disclosure of Truth: A Study in the Work of Heidegger, Gadamer and Ricoeur* (Charlottesville: University Press of Virginia, 1990), 67.

Having argued that truth is disclosedness and that *Dasein* is both in the truth and in the untruth, Heidegger goes onto show that truth—when understood as agreement or correspondence—derives from the more primordial disclosedness. Heidegger argues that when we express things in discourse the 'assertion which is expressed is about something, and in what it is about, it contains the uncoveredness of these entities' (*BT* 224). This uncoveredness, in turn, becomes 'ready-to-hand within-the-world' (*BT* 222) like an object. Then it is possible to compare the assertion, at hand, with the object of that assertion, also at hand. In this way truth as disclosedness becomes truth as agreement between two things in the world. Again, this confirms that the most primordial ' "truth" ... is the ontological condition for the possibility that assertions can either be true or false—that they may uncover or cover things up' (*BT* 226).

This means that ' "[T]here is" truth only in so far as Dasein is and so long as Dasein is ... Newton's laws, the principle of contradiction, any truth whatever—these are only true as long as Dasein is' (*BT* 226). This is not to say, of course, that, for example, before Newton 'there were no such entities as have been uncovered and pointed out by those laws' (*BT* 227). Rather, through Newton, 'the laws became true; and with them, entities accessible in themselves to Dasein. Once entities have been uncovered, they show themselves precisely as entities which beforehand already were. Such uncovering is the kind of Being that belongs to "truth" '. (*BT* 227). J. M. Bernstein discusses this in the following way: it is

scientific frameworks—paradigms, research programmes, domains—that at any given time say what any portion of nature is, determine what is scientific and is what not, guide continuing research, provide criteria for theory choice etc. What the concept of a scientific framework invokes with respect to the work of the framework itself is a productive rather than 'reproductive' or 'representational' conception of truth. Scientific frameworks provide the measure of nature rather than being measured against it; the growth of knowledge within a framework is made possible by the framework itself, while the shift from one frame work to another simultaneously reveals the parochialism of past knowing and new possibilities for understanding what nature is and what science is, and hence new possibilities for doing science. Scientific frameworks, in their productive capabilities, provide the conditions in general for both science and its objects.[21]

---

[21] J. M. Bernstein, *The Fate of Art* (London: Polity, 1992), 84.

Julian Thomas sums up this part of the argument, writing that 'if there were no Dasein, no person, there would still be rocks, trees, mountains . . . but no one to recognise them as such or call then those names. . . . Even the "objective" structures of natural science, of ecology and geo-morphology have no meaning without a human presence.'[22]

This is not to open the floodgates to subjectivity, for Heidegger, or for 'subjective discretion'. Indeed, because ' "truth" as uncovering is a kind of Being which belongs to Dasein', *Dasein* cannot choose its pri-mordial truth, in the same way that we cannot choose the year and the society into which we are born. (But this does not mean, of course, that we cannot make false statements.)[23] For Heidegger, then, truth as 'assertion and its structure', what he calls the 'apophantical "as" ', are founded upon 'interpretation and its structure (viz, the hermeneutical "as") and also upon understanding—upon Dasein's disclosedness' (*BT* 223).[24]

The question that arises then is this: what is revealed in this primor-dial revelation of truth? The answer is, in part, in Heidegger's essay 'On the Origin of the Work of Art' . J. M. Bernstein argues that this essay is not only central for understanding Heidegger but is a response to Kant. Very roughly, Bernstein argues that Kant separates the domains of understanding and reason—those that create assertion, truth as correspondence—from the domain of judgement—the faculty that appreciates beauty and art. It is this division that formalizes both the separation of these two forms of knowledge and institutes the first as superior to the second. However, as Bernstein argues and shows in

[22] Julian Thomas, *Time, Culture and Identity* (London: Routledge, 1996), 66.
[23] Dahlstrom, drawing on Heidegger's 1926 *Logic*, goes into the interrelation between these two different forms of truth and discusses how assertions can modify the 'existen-tial truth'. However, their power to modify this relies on their relation to 'existential truth'. See Dahlstrom, *Heidegger's Concept of Truth*, 202–10.
[24] By hermeneutical here, in *Being and Time*, Heidegger means three interrelated things: the way in which the basic structures of being are 'made known to Dasein's understanding of Being' (*BT* 37) through interpretation; the way in which this works out the 'conditions on which the possibility of any ontological investigation depends' (*BT* 37); and, most importantly, it has the meaning of the 'specific sense of an analytic of the existentialty of existence' (*BT* 37). He goes on to argue that as 'far as this hermeneutic works out Dasein's historicality ontologically as the ontical possibility of the possibility of historiology, it contains the roots of what can be called "hermeneutic" only in a deriv-ative sense: the methodology of those humane sciences which are historiological in character' (*BT* 37). That is, this primordial process of interpreting our own being in time is the grounds of possibility for any discipline which interprets works from the past (his-tory, literature): it is only that we understand ourselves to be temporal that disciplines that rely on the passage of time can exist.

Kant, this separation is complicated since judgement is entwined with 'commonality, communication and sensibility' and being 'capable of . . . judgement . . . and being human appear to be consubstantial'.[25] An 'attunement between us and things' is also 'an attunement between persons' and points to, or relies on, our being with others, our 'common' or 'communal sense' (*sensus communis*).[26] Putting the 'traditional' conception of truth as assertion at the summit of philosophy is exactly the gesture Heidegger has been criticizing, as it forgets Being. So, for Bernstein, the question the essay tries to answer is: what was 'art' like before this separation (of 'truth' and 'art') became taken for granted? Only by answering this can we see what the work of art is and does, and so, in turn, what is revealed in *aletheia*.

In 'The Origin of the Work of Art', Heidegger argues that artworks do not simply represent reality as assertions do, although they do this: more importantly and more fundamentally, they open up or unconceal the world. A Greek temple opens a world, an artwork transforms how we are usually tied into the world. Art is able to break 'open an open place, in whose openness everything is other than usual' because of its nature as what Heidegger names 'poetry'.[27] It is 'poetry' because language is the paradigm of how all artworks work, since language 'by naming beings for the first time, first brings beings to word and to appearance. Only this naming nominates beings to their being from out of their Being' (*BW* 185). Thus, for Heidegger, the 'essence of art is poetry. The essence of poetry, in turn, is the founding of truth . . . art lets truth originate' (*BW* 186). An artwork reveals its world, it 'first gives to things their look and men their outlook on themselves' (*BW* 169). It reveals who and how we are, and how things are for us. It does this both by defamiliarizing what we take for granted in the world and so highlighting it but also, and in the same opening, it draws attention from 'the ordinary and particular to that which lets the ordinary and particular have their peculiar shape and meaning'.[28] There is no 'content' in a simple sense: truth reveals a world into which 'content' is put. This world, unveiled in an artwork, will vary from work to work: the world of a Greek temple is not the world of a Van Gogh painting nor the world of *Ulysses*, *Midnight's Children*, or *Fugitive Pieces*. Yet,

---

[25] Bernstein, *Fate of Art*, 54.   [26] Ibid. 55.

[27] Martin Heidegger, 'On the Origin of the Work of Art', in *Basic Writings*, ed. David Farrell Krell (London: Harper & Row, 1977), 143–87, 184. This will be abbreviated to *BW* in the text.

[28] Bernstein, *Fate of Art*, 88.

this understanding of truth as unveiling a world cannot be reduced to truth as correspondence, but opens and shapes a world. As Heidegger wrote later:

Insofar as truth is thought in the traditional 'natural' sense as the correspondence of knowledge with being demonstrated in beings, but also insofar as truth is interpreted as the certainty of the knowledge of Being, *aletheia*, unconcealed in the sense of the opening, may not be equated with truth. Rather, *aletheia*, unconcealment thought as opening, first grants the possibility of truth. For truth itself, just as Being and thinking, can only be what it is in the element of opening.[29]

That is, *aletheia* is the opening of a world on which truth as correspondence rests. First a world is established, opened, then truth claims in that world are made.

HEIDEGGER'S WRECK

Heidegger was a Nazi: correctly, this ground has been gone over and will be gone over many times.[30] In relation to this particular and important discussion of truth, the problem with his account is that it leads to 'a philosophy of origins, in which rationality is surrendered to an original ground that is supposed to be more true than anything which rational discourse can communicate'.[31] The work of art, for Heidegger here, is the sinews of the sense of community and communal identity. To share a world is to share a world revealed by a work of art, or the worlds of works of art, and these worlds are, in a sense, beyond debate and reason. 'Thus, art is history, in the essential sense that it grounds history.' Communities are grounded by sharing the world

[29] Martin Heidegger, *On Time and Being* (New York: Harper, 1972), 69.
[30] See Victor Farias, *Heidegger and Nazism*, ed. Joseph Margolis and Tom Rockmore, tr. Paul Burrell and Gabriel Ricci (Philadelphia: Temple Press, 1989); Hugo Ott, *Martin Heidegger: A Political Life*, tr. Allan Blunden (London: Fontana Press, 1994); Hans Sluga, *Heidegger's Crisis* (London: Harvard University Press, 1993); Richard Wolin, *The Heidegger Controversy: A Critical Reader*, ed. Richard Wolin (Cambridge, Mass.: MIT Press, 1998); Thomas Sheehan, 'Heidegger and the Nazis', *New York Review of Books* (16 June 1988); Alan Milchman and Alan Rosenberg (eds.), *Martin Heidegger and the Holocaust* (Atlantic Highlands, NJ: Humanities Press, 1996); Rüdiger Safranski, *Martin Heidegger: Between Good and Evil*, tr. Ewald Osers (Cambridge, Mass.: Harvard University Press, 1998); Berel Lang, *Heidegger's Silence* (London: Athlone, 1996). Many philosophers in the European tradition have discussed this, some at length.
[31] Bowie, *From Romanticism to Critical Theory*, 178, following Habermas.

opened by artworks: communities are—in this sense—artworks themselves which inaugurate epochs (the age as lived, not as historicizied
into 'the age of Rome' or the 'Elizabethans'). Bernstein argues that, for
Heidegger, 'the polis is the Greek work of great art'.[32] And it is this
contention that 'the political (the City) belongs to a form of plastic art,
formation and information, fiction in the strictest sense' which informs
Lacoue-Labarthe's analysis in *Heidegger, Art and Politics*.[33] This
understanding leads to fears about the Nazi 'aestheticization of politics': a politics understood as a 'truth as unveiling', or following Saul
Friedländer, a 'mystical communion' in place of a rational process of
debate and deliberation.[34] Indeed, this analysis—the totalitarian
regime creating and created by a fiction which places itself above politics as, for example, embodying the voice of the *Volk*—is crucial to
Arendt's *The Origins of Totalitarinaism*. However, one might argue
that this understanding of the 'communal sense' originating as an artwork does not, by itself, lead to fascism: Rorty, for example, imagines
communities as or based around liberal artworks—those by Dickens,
Kundera, and so on.[35] Rather, this is the grounds of possibility of the
being of a community of any sort. Having death camps as the 'founding artwork' of a community is not the result of seeing communities as
works of art, but of the particular development of that community.[36]

[32] Bernstein, *Fate of Art*, 125

[33] Philippe Lacoue-Labarthe, *Heidegger, Art and Politics*, tr. Chris Turner (Oxford:
Blackwell, 1990), 66. Without reference to Heidegger, something like this sense that the
community is a work of culture—not only that works of culture and art underlie and
structure communities, but that the community itself is a shaping and a construction—is
in Benedict Anderson's idea of the community as 'imagined' and held together by e.g. its
war memorials (rather than Greek temples) and in Raymond Williams's idea of culture
as a 'whole way of life'. Neither of these two could be said to be Heideggerians.

[34] Saul Friedländer, *When Memory Comes*, tr. Helen R. Lane (New York: Discus
Books, 1980), 146–7.

[35] See 'Heidegger, Kundera, Dickens', in Richard Rorty, *Essays on Heidegger and
Others* (Cambridge: Cambridge University Press, 1991).

[36] However, for Bernstein, it is precisely this atavism in Heidegger, which understands
how art works by going back to a time before science and truth as correspondence became
dominant, that makes him suspicious: indeed, the 'deep transformation' (*The Fate of Art*,
135) he follows from Heidegger stems from the fact that modern 'art works . . . thrive on
their own essential impossibility, on their failure to be great works of art, to disclose a
world; and they can do no other for that is where art is' (ibid.). From another perspective,
it is the multitude of artworks that disclose worlds that, on the one hand, begins artistic
postmodernism and, on the other, allows a critique of the products of the culture industry—e.g. Hollywood cinema, or 'lad' novels—as works which fail to disclose any other
world. Disclosing multiple worlds leads to the clash of worlds and the impossibility of the
hegemony of one world. On the design of death camps, see Robert Jan van Pelt and
Debórah Dwork, *Auschwitz: 1270 to the Present* (London: Yale University Press, 1996).

As Bowie and others suggest, the understanding of truth as disclosure revealed in art which underlies truth as correspondence in propositions is not unique to Heidegger: indeed his 'concerns, which are often presented as a total novum, map onto the dominant concerns of Romantic philosophy and the history of Kantian and post-Kantian philosophy'.[37] However, if it is in his work that this idea of truth receives its clearest treatment, it is also in his work, his life, and his context that the most awful consequences are displayed. Robert Bernasconi writes:

> Here is an end of philosophy, of philosophy's self conception. It was not the same end of philosophy that Heidegger had envisaged in his works. Nor was it bought about in his works alone. He enacted it in his life and works by showing what for too long had gone unsuspected, that great thoughts, under the mask of nobility, can lead us astray. The task of thinking his end, the task of ploughing through the wreckage, not just to track down the diabolical, but to see what can be salvaged, has barely begun.[38]

The wreckage of Heidegger's thought is more than just the wreckage of one man's thought: this is why his 'case' is so significant. 'We cannot understand' says Derrida, 'what Europe is and has been during this [twentieth] century, what Nazism has been, without integrating what made Heidegger's discourse possible . . . all the questions he was dealing with had to do with Nazism, with the history of Western culture, with Marxism, with capitalism, with technology'.[39]

If we are 'still living on philosophical ground'—dealing with Nazism, Western culture, Marxism, capitalism, technology, and so on—and 'we cannot just go and live somewhere else'—then swimming through this wreck seems unavoidable.[40] Levinas, opposed to Heidegger in many ways, writes in 1947 of the 'profound need to leave the climate' of Heidegger's philosophy and with the 'conviction that we cannot leave it for a philosophy that would be pre-Heideggerian'.[41] In a 1981 interview he said that 'I think that one cannot seriously philosophise today without traversing the Heideggerian path in some form or other'.[42] This is

---

[37] Bowie, *From Romanticism to Critical Theory*, 163.

[38] Robert Bernasconi, *Heidegger in Question* (Atlantic Highlands, NJ: Humanities Press, 1993), 73.

[39] Jacques Derrida, 'On Reading Heidegger: An Outline of Remarks to the Essex Colloquium', *Research in Phenomenology*, 17 (1987), 171–85, 178–9.

[40] Lacoue-Labarthe, *Heidegger, Art and Politics*, 3.

[41] Emmanuel Levinas, *Existence and Existents*, tr. Alphonso Lingis (London: Kluwer Academic Publishers, 1978), 19.

[42] Richard Kearney, *Dialogues with Contemporary Continental Thinkers: The Phenomenological Heritage* (Manchester: Manchester University Press, 1984), 51. This

because, however flawed Heidegger's work is, it offers not only a view into European philosophical life but also salvaged tools for questions for the future. Derrida again: 'I can find help in Heidegger for questioning all the discourses which are today dominating the scene . . . he has a deconstructing strength which is very useful for so many discourses which possess some authority today in our Western culture.'[43] Jonathan Rée—in a speculative mode—suggests that the 'greatest adventures of twentieth century thought . . . may be little more than an incomplete series of footnotes to Heidegger's *Being and Time*' because of the way in which Heidegger asked old questions anew.[44]

Bearing in mind the huge differences between Benjamin, Adorno, and Heidegger, I suggest that Heidegger can be understood in way which parallels how Adorno saw Benjamin's work (and by proxy, his own).[45] Adorno wrote that Benjamin's

> writings are an attempt in ever new ways to make philosophically fruitful what has not yet been foreclosed by great intentions. The task he bequeathed was not to abandon such an attempt to the estranging enigmas of thought alone, but to bring the intentionless within the realm of concepts: the obligation to think at the same time dialectally and undialectally.[46]

Heidegger's work is an attempt—perhaps the most rigorous, and one of the most flawed—to bring into the 'realm of concepts' (philosophy) that which stands outside it: to think rationally about that which cannot be rationally thought, to think, as it were, the bedrock. Indeed, perhaps the point is that, for Heidegger, philosophy was a particular way of thinking, and not the only way of thinking. This attempt, to think, as it were, in the algebra of philosophy that which is not algebra (an attempt undertaken often, of course, by artists and by demagogues) underlies his work and is the motivation for all those who, without endorsing his path, use his idiom, carry on from the clearing he thought he had made. Yet Heidegger's own life, his membership of the Nazi party, and his near silence about the death camps are the starkest warning about the attempt to bring into philosophy that which stands

remark is similar to one by Fackenheim, who writes that, as 'for *Being and Time* itself, it has altered the philosophical landscape—permanently, as far as one can tell'. Emil Fackenheim, *To Mend the World* (Bloomington: Indiana University Press, 1994), 152.

[43] Derrida, 'On Reading Heidegger', 179.   [44] Rée, *Heidegger,* 51

[45] On this relationship in the context of the Holocaust and *Germania*, see Alexander Garcia Düttmann, *The Memory of Thought*, tr. Nicolas Walker (London: Continuum, 2002).

[46] Theodor Adorno, *Minima Moralia*, tr. E. F. N. Jephcott (London: Verso, 1978), 151–2.

outside it, though they are also and at the same time a sign of the need to do this: to think about the death camps. Heidegger's method and his discussion of truth as unveiling is one part of this wreckage of Western thought that thinkers have tried to salvage in different ways in order to address exactly this.

LEVINAS'S CONCEPTION OF TRUTH

Levinas is one of Heidegger's harshest critics. His work—itself a response to the Holocaust—is, in many ways and for several reasons, set against Heidegger's. He outlines the importance of Heidegger's thought for his own in a short piece 'As if Consenting to Horror'. Heidegger, he argues, 'makes the unsaid of the highest discourses of our culture resonate'.[47] Traditionally, thought had aimed at 'what is, arriving at being', yet Heidegger ended this tradition by pointing out that this thought begins in being, and this ontology lies 'beyond any objective knowledge of quiddities'.[48] Yet, unsurprisingly, Levinas was stupefied and disappointed by Heidegger's active Nazism in 1933 (Levinas wrote against 'Hitlerism' in 1934), and continued utterly to despise him and his Nazi sympathies, including his silence on the Holocaust: his remark which equates the death camps to the mechanized food industry as an evil of technology is, Levinas writes, 'beyond commentary'.[49] This leads Levinas to ask of *Being and Time*: 'can we be assured, however, that there was never any Echo of Evil in it? . . . The diabolical is endowed with intelligence and enters where it will. To reject it, it is first necessary to refute it. Intellectual effort is needed to recognise it.'[50] It could be argued that it is this thought of the evil in *Being and Time* that motivates no small part of Levinas's thought.

However, Levinas's thought echoes or salvages parts of Heidegger's work. In terms of how to do philosophy, Levinas takes much from Heidegger. For Heidegger in *Being and Time*, the issue is the question of the meaning of Being and how, using that as a clue ('leitfaden' or guiding thread), Being is to be understood. All philosophy is, first,

[47] Emmanuel Levinas, 'As if Consenting to Horror', tr. Paula Wissing, *Critical Inquiry* 15 (1988), 485–8, 485.

[48] Ibid. 486.

[49] Ibid. 486, 487. For Levinas on Hitler, see 'Reflection on the Philosophy of Hitlerism', tr. Seàn Hand, *Critical Inquiry*, 17 (1990), 62–71.

[50] Levinas, 'As if Consenting to Horror', 488.

'universal phenomenological ontology [which] . . . takes its departure
from the hermeneutic of Dasein' (*BT* 28 and 436). For Levinas, in parallel, the issue is the question of ethics, and he aims to show how ethics are
to be understood: 'his task is to find the sense of ethics and not to construct an ethics'.[51] At the root of philosophy, as 'first philosophy', is not
ontology but ethics, the relation with the other, which is not one of
equality but of responsibility for or, more dramatically, persecution by
the other. The 'ethical relation is not grafted on to an antecedent relation
of cognition: it is a foundation and not a superstructure . . . it is more
cognitive than cognition itself and all objectivity must participate in it'.[52]
In this light, Levinas writes that Heidegger's ontology 'as first philosophy is a philosophy of power': it partakes of evil.[53] For Levinas,
Heidegger's belief that technology is the source of tyranny is only in part
correct: this urge in turn lies in the 'pagan "moods", in the enrootedness
of the earth, in the adoration that enslaved men can devote to their mas-
ters' (*TI* 47). Levinas writes that Heidegger's philosophy is one in which
' "I think" comes down to "I can"—to an appropriation of what is, to an
exploitation of reality . . . Heidegger, with the whole of western history,
takes the relation with the other as enacted in the destiny of sedentary
peoples, the possessor and builders of the earth' (*TI* 46). The 'sedentary
peoples' clearly has an echo of an opposition between a *volkish* culture
and the diaspora of the Jewish people. Heidegger's is a philosophy that
forgets ethics, that passes over it.[54] His thought—and Western
thought—does this by reducing the other to the same: that is, the same,
the ego, only allows the other to appear on the terms that the same, the
ego, has set up, and so denies it any otherness. These terms Levinas calls
'middle and neutral': echoing Nietzsche on Socratic method, Levinas
writes that it 'knows only itself' and receives 'nothing of the other but
what is in me' (*TI* 43). In declaring itself self-sufficient, Socratic reason
assesses everything else in its own terms and thus admits no otherness.
Other examples of this 'middle and neutral term' are 'Hegel's universal,
Durkheim's social, the statistical laws that govern our freedom, Freud's
unconscious', and, of course, Heideggerian 'Being' (*TI* 272).

[51] Robert Bernasconi, 'The Ethics of Suspicion', *Research in Phenomenology*, 20
(1990), 3–18, 9.
[52] Emmanuel Levinas, 'Philosophy and the Idea of Infinity', in *Collected Philosophical
Papers*, tr. Alphonso Lingis (Dordrecht: Kluwer Academic Publishers, 1987), 47–59, 56.
[53] Emmanuel Levinas, *Totality and Infinity*, tr. Alphonso Lingis (London: Kluwer
Academic Publishers, 1991), 46. This will be abbreviated in the text as *TI*.
[54] For a counter-argument to this that seeks to show how Heidegger's thought is ethical, see Joanna Hodge, *Heidegger and Ethics* (London: Routledge, 1995).

In relation to the issue of truth, too, while opposing Heidegger's conclusion, Levinas further reveals his affinity with a Heideggerian way of
arguing: this is 'salvaged'. This is why, for example, Heidegger and
Levinas are described as 'separated by infinity and yet indistinguishable'.[55] Levinas writes that, for Heidegger, truth 'which should recon-
cile persons, here exists anonymously' (*TI* 46). More than this, to
understand 'truth to be disclosure is to refer it to the horizon of him
who discloses' (*TI* 64). He suggests that Heidegger's truth is, in the end,
solipsistic, self-enclosed. For Levinas, truth does not arise from being-
in-the-world, from one's own self: a 'philosopher seeks, and expresses,
truth. Truth, before characterising a statement or a judgement, consists
in the exhibition of being. But what shows itself, in truth, under the
name of being? And who looks?'[56] The core of Levinas's argument in
Totality and Infinity is that the 'primacy of the ethical, that is, of the
relationship of man to man is an irreducible structure upon which all
other structures rest' (*TI* 79). This relation—referred to in many different ways, as the face-to-face, for example, or as justice, or as revelation—is what 'animates the movement unto truth' (*TI* 47). Truth as
correspondence, or knowledge, relies in turn on the relation with the
other, or, more simply 'truth presupposes justice' (*TI* 90). The revelation of the other, then, is that upon which truth as correspondence
rests: the 'absolute experience is not disclosure but revelation' (*TI*
65–6). Here, Levinas, like Heidegger, rejects the idea that the correspondence theory of truth is the most important. Truth is first the revelation of the other and the consequent call to responsibility, and truth
as correspondence (which Levinas sometimes calls knowledge) relies
on this. Or, as he puts it later, paraphrasing Kirkegaard, a 'light is
needed to see the light' (*TI* 192).[57] It is the light of the other that allows
the light of truth to appear. 'Morality thus presides over the work of
truth' (*TI* 304). It is because of this that Levinas's work can be seen as
prophecy, speaking from 'outside'.

Even when the origin of 'primordial' truth is contested, here in the
name of ethics, the structure of 'existential ethical truth', as revelation
(for Levinas) or disclosure (for Heidegger) or as cinders (for Derrida),

[55] Committee of Public Safety, ' "My Place in the Sun": Reflections on the Thought of
Emmanuel Levinas', *Diacritics*, 26/1 (1996), 3–10, 10.

[56] Emmanuel Levinas, *Otherwise than Being: or, Beyond Essence*, tr. Alphonso Lingis
(The Hague: Martinus Nijhoff, 1981), 23.

[57] 'You always need one more light positively to identify another': Soren Kirkegaard,
Papers and Journals, tr. Alastair Hannay (London: Penguin Books, 1996), 9.

underlies truth as correspondence. This is part of the attempt to bring into thought that which is outside it: how a truth prior to the truth of propositions can be exposed. The question remains as to how this sense of truth can play a role in understanding the discipline and work of history.

TRUTH AS HISTORY

In his later work, *Otherwise than Being*, Levinas suggests that truth as correspondence, understood as the production of the logos and located in the propositions of what he calls the Said, loses its power: the 'exceptional words . . . become terms . . . and are put at the disposition of philologists, instead of confounding philosophical language. Their very explosions are recounted.'[58] What relies on the ethical relation comes to cover it up as knowledge, the result of cognition, not as prior to cognition. One example of this is the way in which history—thought of as aspiring to truth as correspondence—covers up the ethical relation.[59]

'History' that aspires to truth as correspondence is, for Levinas, also a 'middle and neutral term' which aims to reduce the other to the same.[60] The 'history of the historiographers' (as opposed to the universal history of, for example, Hegel), Levinas argues, 'rests on the affirmation and conviction that the chronological order of the history of the historians outlines the plot of being itself' (*TI* 55). However, he writes that if 'I am reduced to my role in history I remain unrecognised' (*TI* 252). History, if it only worked within truth as correspondence, could never get near to the existential ethical truth. Historiographers recount 'the way survivors appropriate the works of dead wills to themselves' (*TI* 228). This reduction leads not just to the cliché that the victors write history but to the idea that the writing and discipline of

---

[58] Levinas, *Otherwise than Being*, 169.

[59] For an argument over the same terrain, but with a different slant, see Michael Dintenfass, 'Truth's Other: The History of the Holocaust and Historiographical Theory after the Linguistic Turn', *History and Theory*, 39 (2000), 1–20.

[60] On Levinas and history, see also Keith Jenkins, 'Why Bother with the Past?', *Rethinking History*, 1 (1997), 56–66; James Hatley, 'The Sincerity of Apology: Levinas's Resistance to the Judgement of History', in Lenore Langsdorf and Stephen Watson with E. Matya Bower (eds.), *Phenomenology, Interpretation, and Community* (Albany, NY: State University of New York Press, 1996), 195–206; Robert Young, *White Mythologies* (London: Routledge, 1990).

history itself takes over the (dead) lives of others. History which aims at truth as correspondence destroys others as lives and reincarnates them as things, as historical events. History 'recounts enslavement, forgetting the life that struggles against slavery' and historians 'interpret, that is, utilise the works of the dead' (*TI* 228). It is for these reasons that Levinas writes that the 'virile judgement of history . . . is cruel' (*TI* 243). Levinas is not opposed to history, but rather the way in which the discipline of history understands truth. He writes that 'judgement of history is set forth in the visible. Historical events are the visible par excellence; their truth is produced in evidence. The visible forms, or tends to form, a totality . . . The invisible must manifest itself if history is to lose its right to the last word, necessarily unjust . . . inevitably cruel' (*TI* 243).

For Levinas, the visible and connected ideas of evidence (evidence, that brought to sight or to visibility) will always tend towards a totality which will destroy otherness through the construction of a 'neutral and middle term'. The only way to prevent this is through the paradoxical manifestation of what he calls the 'invisible': a phrase he often turns to describe the ethical relation (ethics are to die 'for the invisible' (*TI* 243), for example). However, 'the manifestation of the invisible [i.e., the ethical relation] cannot mean the passage of the invisible to the status of the visible; it does not lead back to evidence' (*TI* 243). The invisible cannot be new evidence, as this would simply reproduce the same visible counters of the game of history. The invisible is made manifest in the following way: simply, the correspondence truth of history is understood to rely on the more primordial sense of truth as 'ethics' for Levinas, which in turn is developed along similar lines to, or salvaged from, Heidegger's *aletheia*. This means not that these two understandings of truth are opposed, nor that (impossibly, perhaps) a radically new historiography should be developed which could solely reflect the existential ethical truth, but rather that the discipline of history relies first not on 'scientific truth' but upon the 'invisible' revelation of the truth of the ethical relation which is, for Levinas, 'how things are for us'.[61]

---

[61] Kelley Oliver, in an argument that parallels mine but uses 'witnessing' as its central term, writes: 'What the process of witnessing adds to a set of historical facts is a commitment to the truth of subjectivity as addressibility and responsibility. Witnessing is addressed to another and to a community; and witnessing—in both senses, as addressing and responding, testifying and listening—is a commitment to embrace the responsibility of constitution of communities, the responsibility inherent in subjectivity itself, In this sense, witnessing always bears witness to the necessity of the process of witnessing and

This is what I take Edith Wyschogord's 'heterological historian' to be. In a Levinasian idiom, Wyschogord writes that the 'heterological historian' 'assumes liability for the other, feels the pressure of an ethics that is prior to historical judgement, an Ethics of ethics that is a designing prior to her construal of the historical object'.[62] One of the ways in which 'truth as revelation' appears is as memory, which is neither only personal nor only communal but first both. Memory reveals a world and, in so doing, reveals the other. Memory is not reducible to an understanding of history as correspondence because it underlies the idea of history, since it manifests the 'ethical relationship'. Of course, specific memories and accounts also function as 'counters' or evidence in traditional history: but they are not only this—they open up a world that is not ours. It is not a simple opposition, as the fictional poet Jacob Beer suggests, between amoral history 'the Totenbuch, The Book of the Dead, kept by the administrators of the camps' and moral memory 'the Memorbucher, the names of those to be mourned'.[63] Rather, the two have a complex relationship. This relationship means that the discipline of history has to be aware of the 'covering up' power of its own 'historicism'. It also means that the discipline of history should be more amenable to 'evidence' that is not, *per se*, 'evidence' (not open to proof or disproof). More than this, it has to be very sensitive to the appearance of the truth as revelation in the many different ways in which it appears. Yerushalmi is right when he argues that '[M]emory and modern historiography stand, by their very nature, in radically different relations to the past'.[64] Both aspire to different notions of truth. However, he is wrong in his assumption that they are so separate: history relies on memory, because it relies on that

---

to the impossibility of the eyewitness. An ethics of history requires vigilance in witnessing to that which cannot be seen, in witnessing to the process of witnessing itself.'
Kelley Oliver, 'Witnessing Otherness in History', in Howard Marchitello (ed.), *What Happens to History: The Renewal of Ethics in Contemporary Thought* (London: Routledge, 2001), 41–66, 64–5. See also my 'The "Fine Risk" of History: Poststructuralism, the Past and the Work of Emmanuel Levinas', *Rethinking History: 'The Good of History'*, 2/3 (1998), 313–20.

[62] Edith Wyschogord, *An Ethics of Remembering: History, Heterology and the Nameless Others* (London: Chicago University Press, 1998), 3.

[63] Anne Michaels, *Fugitive Pieces* (London: Bloomsbury, 1997), 138.

[64] Yosef Hayim Yerushalmi, *Zakhor: Jewish History and Jewish Memory* (London: University of Washington Press, 1983), 94.

for which memory is a symptom, the existential ethical truth. There is a truth that underlies the correspondence theory of truth.[65]

The discipline of history has been overcome by or confused with historicism, understood either as Rankean 'science' or as the attempt to discover the 'laws of history'. 'Historicism' as a term 'has been much used and misused' and the 'semantic range is very wide'.[66] It ranges from Friedrich Meinecke's definition—'the substitution of an individualising observation for a generalising view of human forces'—to the opposite of this in the ideas of Croce and Popper.[67] For LaCapra, 'to historicise means to contextualize'.[68] Howard Marchitello suggests a 'post-historicism' which arises 'out of the wake of historicism'.[69] However, I am going to use the term in the following sense: 'scientism' describes the creep of methodologies, and the assumptions from which those methodologies stem, from the strictly material to fields in which they are not applicable (science cannot tell us how to live the 'good life', for example), and 'historicism' is the application of scientific methodologies (or something which claims, positivistically, to imitate them) and, more importantly, the assumptions from which those methodologies stem (chiefly, the idea that that 'truth as correspondence' is the only truth that exists, matters, or counts) to the discipline of history. While historical rigour, which is not scientific but stems from the genre or discourse rules of the discipline of history itself, is important, as the next chapters will illustrate, this relies upon the existential ethical sense of truth and not a pseudo-scientific claim to objectivity.

TRUTH AND HISTORY WITHOUT HISTORICISM

The aim, then, is to clarify major debates in historiography since the 1950s by seeing them in the light of these different forms of truth.

---

[65] This is a different claim from, e.g., C. Bethan McCullagh's project in *The Truth of History* (London: Routledge, 1998), which seeks to explore and resolve the problems that the discipline of history has with 'truth as correspondence'.

[66] Donald R. Kelley, *Faces of History* (London: Yale University Press, 1998), 267.

[67] Ibid. 266. See, also, for an illuminating discussion of these confusions, Robert Burns and Hugh Rayment-Pickard, *Philosophies of History: From Enlightenment to Postmodernism* (Oxford: Blackwell, 2000), 57–71. Thanks to Robert Burns for help in this discussion.

[68] Dominck LaCapra, *Representing the Holocaust* (London: Cornell University Press, 1994), 69.

[69] Howard Marchitello, 'Heterology and Post-Historicism Ethics', in Marchitello (ed.), *What Happens to History*, 123–48, 124.

Discussions of the discipline of history in relation to the so-called 'two cultures' (is history an art or a science?) and over postmodern history (meaning mainly, post-Hayden White) are in fact discussions over the sort of truth to which history aspires. Again, this is not dismiss 'historical rigour' but to put it into a context. It is also to argue that the 'artistic' part of historical works are not simply flourishes or incrustations on the 'facts', but are the signs of a much more significant relation to the nature of truth.

In the 1950s, attacks by thinkers like Karl Popper and Isaiah Berlin on the idea that the discipline of history was a science, and so aimed at truth as correspondence, were aimed intentionally at two schools of thought. First, it was aimed at Marxists and fascists who believed that history and the development of the human species were governed by laws. The dedication to Popper's *The Poverty of Historicism* is to the 'memory of the countless men, women and children of all nations or creeds or races who fell victims to the fascist and communist belief in the Inexorable Laws of Historical Destiny'.[70] Those who argue that 'historical prediction' is the principle aim of the social sciences and assume that 'that this aim is attainable by discovering the "rhythms" or the "patterns", the "laws" or the "trends" that underlie the evolution of history' misunderstand the 'methods of physics' as well as misapplying these understandings.[71] 'Historical Inevitability', what his biographer calls Berlin's 'impressive statement of his most fundamental beliefs', is aimed at those who would offer a 'vast, amoral, impersonal monolithic whole'—Marxist, fascist—into which believers can escape from their responsibilities.[72] These positions want to argue that they have a method which produces truth as correspondence about history and that this, in turn, reveals the 'laws of history', analogous to natural phenomena. Berlin and Popper deny the existence of 'laws of history', and so a methodology which aims to uncover them is impossible.

While these liberal attacks clearly reflect Berlin, Popper, and the world's recent past and are influenced by the cold war climate, they also quite clearly target more straightforward positivist history: the idea that history could be 'how it actually was'. Eugene Golob suggests

---

[70] Karl Popper, *The Poverty of Historicism* (London: Routledge, 1986).

[71] Ibid. 3.

[72] Michael Ignatieff, *Isaiah Berlin: A Life* (London: Chatto & Windus, 1998), 205; Isaiah Berlin, 'Historical Inevitability', in Henry Hardy and Roger Hausheer (eds.), *The Proper Study of Mankind* (London: Pimlico, 1998), 189. This will be abbreviated to *PSM* in the text.

that the key debate in historiography for twenty-five years or so after
the war was between 'positivists such as Hempel and idealists such as
Collingwood'.[73] Positivists maintained that 'there is one and only one
scientific method (best exemplified in physics) and genuine historical or
any other kind of knowledge has to be founded upon this method . . .
however they express their findings, historians do, in fact, presuppose
. . . laws or statements'.[74] Golob argues that idealists, to the contrary,
believe that events 'arise out of human thinking, willing and deserting,
and that the mind is capable of re-enacting human thought and that it
is the job of history to study these concrete acts of thought'.[75]
Oppositions like this often hide more than they reveal. Both of these
positions presuppose truth as correspondence. The positivist assumes
that the event is recounted 'as it actually was'. The idealist does not
presuppose any law, save that the people in the past are like him or herself, and that their thought can be re-enacted: that our thought in the
present can correspond to theirs.[76] Both Isaiah Berlin and Hayden
White set out to counter this historicism.

AGAINST HISTORICISM (1): ISAIAH BERLIN

> . . . and anyway, who can say that the history of human events
> obeys rigorous logic, patterns. It is not said that each turn follows
> from a single why: simplifications are proper only for textbooks,
> the whys can be many, entangled with one another or unknow-
> able, if not actually non-existent. No historian or epistemologist
> has yet proved that human history is a deterministic process.[77]

Isaiah Berlin argued this case in most detail and most fervently in a
range of influential essays, unpopular with those who would defend
historicism in any of its forms. He wrote that those

who, without mystical undertones, insist on the importance of common sense,
or knowledge of life, or width of experience, or breadth of sympathy, or natural wisdom, or 'depth' of insight—all normal and empirical attributes—are

---

[73] Eugene Golob, 'The Irony of Nihilism', *History and Theory*, 19/4 (1980), 55–65.
[74] Ibid.　　　　　　　　　　　　　　[75] Ibid.
[76] For a critique of this position and of Collingwood, see Paul Ricoeur, *Time and Narrative*, iii, tr. Kathleen McLaughlin and David Pellauer (London: University of Chicago Press, 1988), 142–56.
[77] Primo Levi, *The Drowned and the Saved*, tr. Raymond Rosenthal (London: Abacus, 1989), 122.

suspected of seeming to smuggle in some kind of illicit, metaphysical faculty only because the exercise of these gifts has relatively little value for those who deal with inanimate matter, for physicists and geologists.   (*PSM* 49)

Berlin's liberalism sets him very clearly against politically or ideologically determined sciences of history: those accounts of the past, as he says in his lecture on 'Historical Inevitability' from 1953, 'for whom history is "more" than past events, namely a theodicy' (*PSM* 126).[78] The 'scientific method' in history, understood as 'setting forth armed with a metaphysical or empirical system, from such islands of certain, or virtually certain, knowledge of the facts' (*PSM* 121), is highly dubious, despite what Berlin calls its deep roots in our 'infatuation with the natural sciences' (*PSM* 129) and 'teleological outlook' (*PSM* 129). While a historical account is 'not identical with imaginative literature . . . it is certainly not free from what, in a natural science, would rightly be condemned as unwarrantably subjective and even . . . intuitive' (*PSM* 165). For Raul Hilberg, for example, the sense of history writing as partaking of both these senses of truth is especially clear. He is acutely aware, for example, that his *magnum opus*, *The Destruction of the European Jews*, was 'appropriating, transcribing, arranging something' and resembled 'not a work of literature but a body of music'.[79] Inspired by Beethoven, who unlike Mozart had to 'build his music like an edifice, draft after draft slowly, painfully', Hilberg writes of his need to 'control my work, to dominate it as Beethoven had dominated his music'.[80] His twelve chapters aim at a symmetry that he found in Beethoven, and his terse style suggests his objectivity as an observer. It is this, as much as the 'facts', that made the work so significant. Berlin's aim, here, is to rule out accounts based on universal laws of history. He does this by denying that they are scientific.

The truth of the past lies, then, not in a seeming 'scientific' correspondence of historical accounts with the past (even if this were possible) but with how we find ourselves in the present. Indeed, constructing history, that is, researching the past and writing about it, turns out to be, for Berlin, deeply and inescapably interwoven with current everyday human concerns and categories: with who we find ourselves to be, in fact. In regard to morality, for example, 'historians

---

[78] Interestingly, and significantly in this context, Berlin suggests that Ranke, too, has a theodicy, that 'All cultures are equal in the sight of God, each in it time and place. Ranke said precisely this' (*PSM* 431).

[79] Raul Hilberg, *The Politics of Memory* (Chicago: Ivan R. Dee, 1996), 84.

[80] Ibid. 85.

need not—are not obliged to—moralise: but neither can they avoid the use of normal language with all its associations and "built in" moral categories. To seek to avoid this is to adopt another moral outlook, not none at all' (*PSM* 188). To write history, for Berlin, is to engage not only with the past, but also with the experience—untestable, too multifarious for any contemporary scientific theory to fully comprehend—of being human in the present. He returned to this theme in his 1960 essay in *History and Theory* entitled 'The Concept of Scientific History'. Here again, while

[a]ny given generalisation may be capable of being tested or refined by inductive or other scientific texts; . . . we accept the total texture, compounded as it is out of literally countless strands . . . without the possibility, even in principle, of any test for it in its totality. For the total texture is what we begin and end with. (*PSM* 29)

Indeed, Berlin goes on to argue that it is this 'sense of the general texture of experience . . . that constitutes the foundation of knowledge, that is itself not open to inductive or deductive reasoning' and it is to this that historians, more than scientists, 'are bound' (*PSM* 29). This means that history 'and other accounts of human life are at times spoken of as being akin to art' (*PSM* 47), akin to the 'untestable' foundation of knowledge.

Although Berlin writes that, without sufficient knowledge of facts, a work of history is only a 'work of romantic imagination' (*PSM* 49), central to it and vital for it is exactly this kind of truth which arises out of our experience of the world. This sort of knowledge is neither 'knowing that' or 'knowing how' (following Ryle) but 'akin to the "I know" of "I know what it is to be hungry and poor" ' (*PSM* 52): a revealed truth. This sort of texture, this sort of truth cannot be tested by the correspondence of an account to its object (or, in the case of a historical account, to documents, other accounts and evidence, and so on) since it arises from the truth of the world of the historian. History, for Berlin, then relies of course upon checkable facts but, more fundamentally, upon a form of knowledge that cannot be reduced to the correspondence between account and the object of that account (here mediated through evidence). This is why, he suggests, if

we ask ourselves which historians have commanded the most lasting admiration, we shall, I think, find that they are neither the most ingenious, nor the most precise, nor even the discoverers of new facts or unsuspected casual connections, but those who (like imaginative writers) present men or societies or situations in many dimensions, at many intersecting levels simultaneously, writers in whose accounts human lives, and their relations both to each other and to the external world are what (at our most lucid and imaginative) we know that they can be. (*PSM* 57)

Berlin is often criticized—as liberals are—for an assumption that his position is a 'neutral' one, blind to its own presuppositions about thinking and society. In the context of discussion of history, at least, it seems that these criticisms are unfair: his liberalism in this context stems from his belief in a intellectual institution called 'history' with its own practices that he—as a historian of ideas—has to clarify and, perhaps, correct. Both of these aspects of his thought are clear from his celebrated account of Tolstoy's view of history from *War and Peace*. For Berlin, Tolstoy was oppressed not only by the impossibility of developing scientific laws for history but also by its opposite: the 'apparently arbitrary selection of material, and the no less arbitrary distribution of evidence to which all historical writing seemed to be doomed' (*PSM* 447). Berlin describes how Tolstoy's intelligence rips through every available approach to the understanding of history— including the liberal one—leaving him with nearly nothing save his negative convictions. Berlin writes that Tolstoy denied not just that history was a natural science, but that 'it was a science at all, an activity with its own proper concepts and generalisations' (*PSM* 461).

For Berlin, Tolstoy has two main ideas here. The first is the idea that a work of history can never, could never, approach with sufficient clarity and depth 'the most real, the most immediate experience of human beings' (*PSM* 447) and, lacking this explanation, the most profound for Tolstoy, a work of history can never be what it claims, an explanation of events. This problem, which appears at first to be one of degree (how can historians write more and more detailed histories?), is in fact an ontological one: there is clearly a point where it is impossible to check or do more than speculate about the inner workings of the mind. A work that follows this prescription soon ceases to be history—ceases to follow the genre requirements of a history that demands a verifiable correspondence between assertion and object. But, for Tolstoy, this is exactly the sort of work that is more true, more revealing, than a work of history, which, at best, can only be true in terms of correspondence, with what others can verify: when 'Tolstoy contrasts . . . the actual everyday, "life" experience of individuals . . . with the panoramic view conjured up by historians, it is clear to him which is real and which is a coherent, sometimes elegantly contrived, but always fictitious construction' (*PSM* 450). The second target is the idea that a work of history would be able to offer, implicitly or explicitly, a world view. Any world view, for Tolstoy, could never be correct, but only an weak imposition upon the multitudinous facts of the world. From this results both inaccuracy and untruth: for example, Tolstoy argues that historians pay attention to orders given by commanders that now seem crucial but at the time were simply some orders amongst others.

Indeed, Berlin's Tolstoy (but not Berlin) is a postmodernist *avant la lettre*: there were no systems of thought or hedgehog visions that would unify his foxlike awareness of the 'manifold objects and situations on earth in their full multiplicity' (*PSM* 463). The 'increasing awareness at the back of his mind that no final solution was ever, in principle, to be found, caused Tolstoy to attack . . . bogus solutions all the more savagely for the false comfort they offered' (*PSM* 464).[81] He was, *pace* Lyotard, not merely incredulous about grand narratives but angry and intellectually scandalized by the idea that intelligent people could believe in them. Yet, Berlin argues that he desperately sought out a unity of moral vision but was unable to make this compatible with his 'sense of reality' (*PSM* 498). Postmodern thinkers contrast thought as bricolage, as a sort of mending, specifically located and related to times and places, with total systems and unified visions, and opt for the former. Berlin's Tolstoy, having reached this position, was unable to accept either alternative, and was thrown into despair at his predicament, 'self blinded at Colonus' (*PSM* 498). That Berlin can see—and can write with such empathy about—the destruction of all points of view and conceptual schema seems to suggest that he was clearly aware that his position, defending the institution of history as a 'liberal art' relying principally not on a slavish following of facts but rather on a sense of 'texture', of 'how the world is', was neither neutral nor without presuppositions. Indeed, based on his belief in human freedom and liberal Enlightenment values, his was an ethical position. But he takes from or shares with Tolstoy a sense that the core of history could not be anything like a scientific truth and a belief that it is projected from the present onto the past.

---

[81] Berlin adds in a footnote that in 'our day French existentialists for similar psychological reasons have struck out against all explanations as such because they are a mere drug to still serious questions, short-lived palliatives for wounds which are unbearable but must be borne, above all not denied or explained; for all explaining is explaining away, and that is a denial of the given—the existent—the brute facts' (*PSM* 464).

Berlin accepted the importance of 'truth as correspondence' and its strictest version—in science—but that he argued that this is not enough, and, for history, he argued that it corresponds to something else ('forms of life') that could not be tested but arises from or is revealed by our experience of the world. He argued that, although history has its own disciplinary and genre conventions, it shares more with what we generally consider to be art works, arising from a primordial and untestable foundation of knowledge of how we are in the world.

AGAINST HISTORICISM (2): HAYDEN WHITE

Hayden White's work reflects these divisions in the understanding of the nature of truth, too. In his groundbreaking essay from 1966, 'The Burden of History', which set the agenda for his later work, he argued that historians have 'for better than a century' defended their discipline: to those who think it is not rigorous enough, historians argued that history is closer to an art and relies on intuition and judgement; to those who think that it fails to present a fuller, deeper picture of the past, they argued that it was more like a science and was not free to manipulate data.[82] And with this, he suggests, history— 'perhaps the conservative discipline par excellence' (*BH* 112)—declined to speculate about itself any further. However, the grounds on which this distinction between science and art is made, White suggests, no longer holds because 'contemporary thinkers do not concur . . . that art and science are essentially different ways of comprehending the world' (*BH* 112): instead, both have 'common constructivist' (*BH* 112) characteristics (in science, White is presumably reflecting on Kuhn's paradigm-based approach as well as Popper's denial of induction as a principle for science). He suggests that, in de Certeau's words, history is 'fed by a philosophy it no longer admits'.[83]

White then goes on to suggest that scientists consider history to be— at best—a third-rate science (if it is a science at all), whereas artists seek

---

[82] Hayden White, 'The Burden of History', *History and Theory*, 5 (1966), 111–34, 111. This will be abbreviated to *BH* in the text. On White in general and this essay in particular, see also Michael S. Roth, *The Ironist's Cage: Memory, Trauma and the Construction of History* (New York: Columbia University Press, 1995).

[83] Michael de Certeau, *The Writing of History*, tr. Tom Conley (New York: Columbia University Press, 1988), 342.

to escape the burden of history. By this White seems to mean that, in novels and plays, historians take the role of 'the enemy within the walls' (*BH* 115) who seeks to capture the living and subvert their freedom. Mr Casaubon's learning and the research of Hedda Gabler's husband, George Tesman, are exactly the opposite of the creative artistic spirit. For many thinkers, the First World War also revealed that history taught nothing and was empty of meaning, and this idea was carried on by mid-century intellectuals. There is a distinction to be made here, however, between the past, which weighed heavily on a range of artists and writers (Joyce, for example), and history, the discourse about that past which seemed so deadening. History, writes White, is not only the burden placed on the present by the 'outmoded institutions, ideas and values, but also the way of looking at the world'. He continues: 'to a significant segment of the artistic community the historian appears as the carrier of a disease which was at once the motive force and the nemesis of nineteenth century civilisation' (*BH* 123).

In the face of this, argues White, the only thing to do is to remake history, to hold that an 'explanation need not be assigned unilaterally to the category of the literally truthful on the one hand [as "science"] and or the purely imaginary on the other [as "art"]' (*BH* 130). Indeed, history should become 'a way of providing perspectives on the present that contribute to the solutions of problems peculiar to our own time . . . to come to terms with the techniques of analysis and representation which modern science and modern art have offered for understanding the operations of consciousness and social process' (*BH* 130) This means to jettison, or at least question, the form of writing—it 'is almost as if the historian believed that the sole possible form of historical narration was that used in the English novel as it had been developed by the late nineteenth century' (*BH* 127)—and to explore other genres of representation. It also means that historians have to get rid of the 'outmoded conceptions of objectivity' (*BH* 127) that characterize their thinking and writing.

It is from this, from a Kuhnian idea that the paradigm governs the research project (which in turn is an echo of the Heideggerian idea that it is *Dasein* that uncovers the laws and not that the laws are written in adamant to be discovered), that White is led to suggest that the 'governing metaphor of an historical account could be treated as a heuristic rule which self-consciously eliminates certain kinds of data from consideration as evidence' (*BH* 130). The work of a historian, then, is like that of the artist or a scientist which 'does not pretend to exhaust description or analysis of all the data in the entire phenomenal field but rather offers itself as one way among many of disclosing certain aspects of the field' (*BH* 130). This does not become a relativism because 'we do not ask if he sees what we would see in the same general phenomenal field, but whether or not he has introduced into his representation of it anything that could be considered false information for anyone who is capable of understanding the system of notation used' (*BH* 130). The 'system of notation' refers here to both the genre and subgenres of the discipline of history. White goes on to suggest that 'we should no longer naively expect that statements about a given epoch or complex of events "correspond" to some pre-existent body of "raw facts" . . . what constitutes the facts themselves is the problem that the historian, like the artist, has tried to solve in the choice of the metaphor by which he orders his world, past, present and future' (*BH* 131). He does suggest that when this metaphor 'begins to show itself unable to accommodate certain kinds of data' it should be abandoned in favour of a 'richer, and more inclusive metaphor . . . in the same way a scientist abandons a hypothesis when its use is exhausted' (*BH* 131). This idea laid the groundwork for his magisterial study *Metahistory* which broadens the concept of 'metaphor' into something more like 'world view'—'inflated from a figure of speech into a figure of thought'.[84] White suggests that the way the historian orders her or his thought breaks down into modes of emplotment (romantic, tragic, comic, satirical), modes of argument (formist, mechanicist, organicist, contextualist), and modes of ideological implication (anarchist, radical, conservative, liberal). These illustrate the way—to adapt a later title of White's—that the form of history has content. This is not to say that history is 'only textual' nor to say that there are no 'facts': it is to say that the truth of history lies not, at first, in the correspondence of its judgement with the object (the work of the historian with its the object, the past), but rather with the world view of the historian, and the language and modes that he or she uses. The archive and truth as corre-

[84] Hans Kellner, 'A Bedrock of Order: Hayden White's Linguistic Humanism', *History and Theory*, 19 (1980), 1–29, 11. In a sense, this is only to follow the current of contemporary thought: as Agamben pithily puts it, 'we are the first human beings who have become completely conscious of language . . . contemporary thought has finally recognised the inevitability, for the fly, of the glass in which it is imprisoned . . . For the fly, the glass is not a thing, but rather that through which it sees things'. Giorgio Agamben, *Potentialities*, tr. Daniel Heller-Roazen (Stanford, Calif.: Stanford University Press, 1999), 45–6.

spondence are vital, but making 'sense of it on a larger scale will be a matter of interpretation, and interpretation is up to us. The past will not make sense unless we make sense of it.'[85]

If there are different versions of the past and different approaches to writing history, then

I cannot claim that one of the conceptions of historical knowledge is more 'realistic' than the others, for it is precisely over the matter of what constitutes an adequate criterion of realism that they disagree. Nor can I claim that one conception of historical knowledge is more 'scientific' than another without prejudging what a specifically historical or social science ought to be.[86]

There are, however, grounds for deciding what histories to follow, or to write. These are not amenable to decision by 'truth as correspondence': the 'grounds for preferring' one vision of history over another 'are moral or aesthetic ones'.[87] That is, the choice relies not at first on the correspondence between the object and the judgement, but on the moral or aesthetic choices of the reader or writing historian. This does not mean that others, who 'understand the system of notation used' (that is, follow the metaphor, the idiom, who understand the world view even if they do not agree with it), cannot judge if information is true or false within that system, nor does it imply that data generated but not accommodated by that metaphor should be ignored. It means only that, before it invokes truth as correspondence, history cannot but invoke truth as disclosure or revelation: existential ethical truth.

Dan Stone, along with other commentators, suggests that White dilutes his position when he discusses the Holocaust in particular.[88] Stone suggests that, against the flow of his earlier work which suggests that 'no historical event is intrinsically tragic' or intrinsically anything (unless historiography makes it so), White argues that he does 'not think the Holocaust . . . is any more unrepresentable than any other event' but that its 'representation, whether in history or in fiction,

---

[85] Williams, *Truth and Truthfulness*, 244.
[86] Hayden White, *Metahistory* (London: Johns Hopkins University Press, 1973), 26.
[87] Ibid. 433.
[88] Stone, 'Paul Ricoeur, Hayden White and Holocaust Historiography', 262. This seems to be a general consensus: see, e.g., Martin Jay's 'Of Plots, Witnesses and Judgements', discussion in Saul Friedländer (ed.), *Probing the Limits of Representation* (London: Harvard University Press, 1992); Richard Evans's *In Defence of History* (London: Granta, 1997), 125–8; Dominick LaCapra's *Writing History, Writing Trauma*, (London: Johns Hopkins University Press, 2001), 17–20.

requires the kind of style, the modernist style, that was developed in order to represent the kind of experiences which social modernism made possible'.[89] Stone suggests that this implies that White thinks this style has a 'special access to the recent past which other forms of historical representation do not have'.[90] However, in the light of this discussion of the nature of truth, in contrast, it seems that White is suggesting this style as more appropriate to representing the Holocaust not because it offers a greater correspondence to the events of the past, but because it is more revealing about us: it is less a rejection of realism and more 'an anticipation of a new form of historical reality . . . that included Hitlerism, the Final Solution, total war, nuclear contamination, mass starvation, and ecological suicide; a profound sense of the incapacity of our science to explain, let alone control or contain these'.[91] This style is more appropriate because it expresses us as post-Holocaust, because it reveals that the events of the past are not limited to their understanding through the discipline of history, but form the cultural horizon of our age, so deeply ingrained is the Holocaust into our reflection.[92] This style, then, is part of a wider sense of genre that reflects on 'how the world is for us, now'. The Holocaust is not just true 'historically' (that is, it is not just true according to the genre rules of history). It is also true in a deeper sense, existentially: it is part of who we are, part of the identity of (at least) the West.

CONCLUSION

The aim here has not been to reduce Berlin and White to simple positions, but rather to show that within their lines of thought lies a similarity in ideas about truth which provides a useful way of discussing issues in the historiography of the Holocaust. General debates in historiography are illuminated by seeing them in relation to questions of how truth is to be understood. Both Berlin and White, in different ways and for different reasons, are opposed to a historicism that sees the only aim and method of history as to produce truth as correspondence.

---

[89] Hayden White, 'Historical Employment and the Problem of Truth', in Friedländer (ed.), *Probing*, 52.

[90] Stone, 'Paul Ricoeur, Hayden White and Holocaust Historiography', 264.

[91] White, 'Historical Employment', 52.

[92] White writes, in a later article, 'I did not say the facts precluded the emplotment of the Holocaust as farce; I said that it would be tasteless and offensive to most audiences to so emplot it': White, 'An Old Question Raised Again', 402.

History, while necessarily involved with truth as correspondence, has more primordial and different obligations to a more primordial form of truth.

This view of truth as *aletheia*, a revelation of the other, runs very deep in Western thought. In a way, all of the work of Michel Foucault is an exploration of it, as it explores, genealogically, precisely how, and with what contradictions and paradoxes, 'truth as correspondence' stems from 'how the word is for us', truth as revealed. It also underlies ideas about communal, communicative reason. To change one's world view, the truth as revealed to you, as you, is a *conversion*: that is why these moments are considered so important. It is a change that happens for many reasons—the experience of war or of religion are common sources: those who champion reason argue that reason, too, can be central in these conversions. It also highlights why art can be important: Proust writes that the

original painter or the original writer proceeds on the lines of the oculist. The course of treatment they give us by their painting or by their prose is not always pleasant. When it is at an end the practitioner says to us: 'Now look!'. And, lo and behold, the world around us (which was not created once and for all, but is created afresh as often as an original artist is born) appears to us entirely different from the old world but perfectly clear.[93]

Art, for Proust at least, here, can reveal a new world.

The aim of this chapter has been to outline two different forms of truth which belong to the deep structure of the discipline of history. To be against historicism is not the same as 'not believing in the past': it is a way of rejecting the claims of the discipline of history to mastery of that past as if it were a science. The other understanding of truth comes from the ethical relation, for Levinas, and the conception of truth as correspondence relies on this. As I will suggest, it comes to be understood, in one context and series of debates, as memory. Existential ethical truths are more shocking: they bring us up more precisely because they cannot be assimilated or reduced by the process of thinking of truth as only correspondence. They are an exposure to the other and so to the world of the other.

However, these two understandings of truth have a complex relation to each other and beg a number of questions.

---

[93] Marcel Proust, *Remembrance of Things Past*, 3 vols., tr. C. K.Scott Moncrieff and Terence Kilmartin (Harmondsworth: Penguin, 1983), ii. *The Guermantes Way*, 338.

First, how do these understandings emerge in actual works of history? To answer this, I turn to the historical and historiographical work of Saul Friedländer. Not only is his work very sensitive to these debates, but he also highlights both the benefits and problems of historicism, especially in his account of the historical 'normalization' of the events of the Holocaust.

Second, this position begs the question of what happens when historians have very different existential ethical truths and so offer incompatible histories. This is made more complex in the case of Holocaust historians because, as I have suggested, how the Holocaust is understood (as a 'watershed' in human history, for example) is itself part of 'how the world is revealed for us'. I look at the controversy between Daniel Jonah Goldhagen and Christopher Browning, which is both about the Holocaust and, I argue, more profoundly about responding to the Holocaust. Here, the two senses of truth lead to positions incommensurably at odds.

Third, this position begs the question of what happens when somebody simply chooses to ignore or, in bad faith, deny the Holocaust and its role in our world. This is the case of Holocaust denial, and, by looking at one instance, I argue for the importance of the metahistorical approach to these questions and show how these two senses of truth complement each other.

6

'Are Footnotes Less Barbaric?': History, Memory, and the Truth of the Holocaust in the work of Saul Friedländer

History and memory share events . . . Every moment is two moments.[1]

To articulate the past historically does not mean to recognise it 'the way it really was' (Ranke). It means to seize hold of a memory as it flashes up at a moment of danger.[2]

INTRODUCTION

The previous chapter argued that there are two ways of understanding truth germane to Holocaust history, truth as correspondence and existential ethical truth, and that, while the latter underlies the former, they exist in a complex relationship. This chapter explores and expands on this relationship by looking at the work of Saul Friedländer, which illustrates the interaction between these two different understandings of truth very clearly. Not only is Friedländer one of the most significant historians of the Holocaust, he has also been one of the most significant thinkers about the Holocaust, meditating on issues such as the relationship between memory and history, representation and the Holocaust, and the 'logic' and presentation of Nazism. By looking at how his thinking about the past and his practice of writing history has developed, it is possible to see how these two different forms of truth interact. Indeed, his work and thought embody the interaction between the truth of positivist history—offering one kind of truth—and the disclosing existential ethical power, which he names memory, offering

---

[1] Anne Michaels, *Fugitive Pieces* (London: Bloomsbury, 1997), 138.
[2] Walter Benjamin, 'Theses on the Philosophy of History', *Illuminations*, tr. Harry Zorn (London: Pimlico, 1999 edn.), 247

another. It is the nature of this interaction, and Friedländer's thought on it, that is the focus of this chapter.

HISTORICAL KNOWLEDGE OVER MEMORY:
DOCUMENTS AND MEMOIR

Friedländer's early work as a historian displays a model Rankean rigour. Geoffrey Elton, perhaps the most influential British historian in this dominant tradition, writes 'what matters are the sources' and Friedländer followed this tradition scrupulously.[3] His *Pius XII and the Third Reich* aims 'to adhere, as far as possible, to the documents', because only 'quotation of the document in extension permits the reader to evaluate its scope and real shades of meaning'.[4] In this case, the result is that Friedländer declares himself unable to give definite answers because 'I have only incomplete documents at my disposal': he is only finally able to ask two leading questions about Pius XII and the Nazis.[5] His work on the US and the Third Reich is based on a 'thorough study of the documents' and judges the influence of the US on Hitler's policies 'strictly from the standpoint of political and military logic'.[6] Even his book on Kurt Gerstein, *The Counterfeit Nazi: The Ambiguity of Good*—in some way a response to Arendt on Eichmann—has only a page and a half at the end which could, strictly, be seen as 'speculation' rather than documentary history and even that aims to elucidate why Gerstein's fate was unique.[7]

However, a watershed for his work was the 'necessary undertaking' of his 1978 memoir, *Quand Vient le Souvenir . . .* (the significant ellipsis is missing in the English translation, *When Memory Comes*).[8] This 'incessant confrontation with the past' (*WMC* 182) begins a turn in his work away from 'documentary history' traditionally understood (that

[3] Geoffrey Elton, *The Practice of History* (London: Collins, 1967), 88.

[4] Saul Friedländer, *Pius XII and the Third Reich*, tr. Charles Fullman (London: Chatto & Windus, 1966), p. xv.

[5] Ibid. 236. These are taken up in John Cornwell, *Hitler's Pope* (London: Penguin, 1999).

[6] Saul Friedländer, *Prelude to Downfall: Hitler and the United States*, tr. Aline B. and Alexander Werth (London: Chatto & Windus, 1967), pp. vii, 310.

[7] See the conclusion to Saul Friedlander, *The Counterfeit Nazi: The Ambiguity of Good*, tr. Charles Fullman (London: Weidenfeld & Nicolson, 1969).

[8] Saul Friedländer, *When Memory Comes*, tr. Helen R. Lane (New York: Discus Books, 1980), 182. This will be abbreviated in the text to *WMC*. It is also an ur-text for W. G. Sebald's novel *Austerlitz*.

is, a conception of history as a judgement producing truth as correspondence to the past) to a different understanding of the sort of truth to which writing history aspires, one which comes from or discloses the work of memory, the ethical existential truth.

At the heart of his memoir is the disappearance and murder of his parents. Intellectually, however—(*writing in this way, about ideas which seem abstract, about people's intellectual careers, it can be easy to forget the intensity of suffering from which this material comes. So, to pause—the utterly bleak heart of his memoir is the effect on him of genocide. His mother's last letter, in unclear handwriting, states that 'We can no longer legally exist . . .' and ends 'I beg you to excuse the appearance of this letter. My hands no longer obey me'* (WMC 78). Intellectually, however, the memoir is an engagement between what can be known (proved, verified objectively, true corresponding to an object) and what is remembered (how the world is disclosed), and the effects of this memory in, among other things, the formation of personal and communal identity. Its leitmotif and epigram (in the French edition) is taken from the writer Gustav Meyrink: 'When knowledge comes, memory comes too, little by little. Knowledge and memory are the same thing': however, significantly, for Friedländer, the sequence was inverted: 'when memory comes, knowledge comes too' (WMC 182).

The memoir is the story of his survival during the Holocaust, and the effects that this survival had on his later life (it is also one source for the character of Austerlitz in the W. G. Sebald novel of that name). In a sense, these can be charted from the changes in his name from Pavel (in Prague) to Paul (in France) to Paul-Henri (in hiding) to Shaul (in Israel) and finally to Saul. Coming from a very assimilated German Jewish family in Prague ('everyone in our house felt German' (WMC 4)), his family fled to France, but did not manage to escape the Nazis. At his parents' request, he was hidden at a Catholic school. He was baptized and 'became someone else: Paul-Henri Ferland, an unequivocally Catholic name' (WMC 79). More than this, the 'first ten years of my life, the memories of my childhood' had to disappear, 'for there was no possible synthesis between the person I had been and the person I was to become' (WMC 80). He remained hidden during the war. Like the philosopher Sarah Kofman, who in her memoir *Rue Ordener Rue Labat* describes both how she was hidden in the war and how this led to a spilt in her self-identification between the Christian woman who hid her and her mother, between a Christian French identity and a Jewish one, this experience affected Friedländer deeply. His reclamation of his Jewish identity began after the war. Discussing his possible vocation in the Catholic Church, a priest, Father L., tells him about Auschwitz, which before had remained indistinct to him: 'It is true that I knew nothing of Judaism and was still a Catholic. But something had changed. A tie had been re-established, an identity was emerging . . . in some manner or other I was Jewish—whatever this term meant in my mind' (*WMC* 138). In his memoir, he meditates over what it was that drew him towards this identity. From an assimilated family, he—like Jean Améry—had no deep memories of his Jewishness.[9] 'What secret work was accomplished within me?' he writes, 'What instinct, buried beneath acquired loyalty suddenly caused a profounder loyalty to emerge? An obscure rupture, brought about by the astonishing discovery' (*WMC* 139). This rupture—of memory—began the long journey of his return to Judaism: he writes that it 'took me a long, long time to find the way back to my own past' (*WMC* 102). Ten years later, in 1956, he read the work of Martin Buber while staying with an uncle near Stockholm, and this, too, made an impression on him. He is reintroduced to Judaism, but not without difficulties. For example, at his first Seder, he declines meat—it is Good Friday. Memory is hard: he tries to remember his past—by, for example, drinking a milkshake as he had with his mother—but it avoids him. Yet he presses on, and memory comes slowly, irregularly. Reversing St Paul's gesture, Paul-Henri Ferland changed his name to Saul Friedländer.

The memoir is full of tension between these two forms of truth: one that reveals his identity, 'how things are for him', and develops, and the other that makes up 'verifiable' history. As a rigorous historian he uses many, often heartrending, documentary sources (letters, telegrams), yet these do not and cannot explain the crucial, obscure rupture of memory. Memory, and the way in which it is crucial in our sense of who we are and how the world is, runs deeper than conventional historical discourse and is, for Friedländer, this understanding of truth as disclosure. Memory, in his work, means more than simply remembering. It is not just remembering the 'white socks' (*WMC* 25) of the protesting Sudeten Germans in 1938, nor reflecting on the links between past and present (say, the rather frightening associations caused by smell of the 'leather overcoats' (*WMC* 37) of the Czech border police in 1967). The 'extraordinary mechanism of memory' (*WMC* 79) and what it does are

---

[9] See Jean Améry, *At the Mind's Limits*, tr. Sidney Rosenfled and Stella Rosenfeld (London: Granta Books, 1999), 83.

suggested by the ellipsis at the end of the title. The epigraph suggests that one completes the sentence with 'knowledge comes too', according to Friedländer's adapted leitmotif. Yet the fact that this is absent is stressed by the presence of the ellipses. But knowledge does not come, or does not come necessarily. This leads one to read it as a critique of knowledge which cannot fill or compare with memory: memory underlies both historical knowledge and exceeds it. It also suggests, perhaps, that memory—the effort, here, to remember—is, to use Henri Raczymow's phrase, 'shot through with holes': it is never final or completed.[10] Memory is tied into identity, both personal and collective. Memory is not, or is not only, a way of making clear all those things that do not fit easily into historical accounts—feelings, senses of identity, and so on. It underlies history. Memory is central to our disclosure of ourselves to ourselves, when it comes or when it does not: it cannot easily be subsumed into the discipline of history, which wants facts it can verify by its own criteria, precisely because memory in this sense is that on which the discipline of history relies.

But it is also in this memoir that the counter to this existential ethical understanding of memory emerges. Once this 'unverifiable' truth and its power has been recognized—just as with the criticism of Heiddegger's particular conception of it—its overwhelming and mythic power emerges. One of the many places that this comes to the fore, and these two understandings of truth interact, is in a discussion of Joachim Fest's *Hitler: A Career*. In the text—which like other testimonies leaps around chronologically—Friedländer has just been interviewing a German Grand Admiral, who—framed in a 'narrow halo of light' (*WMC* 146) by the setting sun during their conversation, a poetic image of Christian hypocrisy—denies knowing about the Holocaust (*WMC* 146). He then reflects that for 'anyone who does not know the facts, the power and the glory still remain . . . For anyone who does not know the facts, the mystical communion with the brownshirt revolution and its martyrs still remains. Thus is evidence transformed over the years, thus do memories crumble away' (*WMC* 146–7). This stresses the truth as correspondence version of history—the facts—but at the same time admits the terrible pull of truth as disclosure as a 'mystical disclosure', as an unarguable and so pre-rational world-founding myth. The memoir, and his later work, is caught between two imperatives: first, the recognition of the

[10] Henri Raczymow, 'Memory Shot through with Holes', *Yale French Studies*, 85 (1994), 98–105.

central and founding power of memory beyond 'scientific' proof as that which founds and underlies the discipline of history but is not of it, and second, for the discipline of history—assertions about the past, generated and judged according to certain criteria—to counter, to hold in check, to refine that which has been disclosed by memory. Only if the reasoned discipline of history is understood as a practice arising from the ethical relation can this be resolved. As Levinas suggests, it is not the case that 'reason creates the relations between me and the other', rather 'the other's teaching me creates reason'.[11] In this context, it is not the 'facts of history' that bring the other to the fore, but the relationship with the other that allows the 'facts of history' to emerge: thes relationship is mediated through this discourse.

HISTORICAL KNOWLEDGE AGAINST MEMORY: 'HISTORICIZATION' AND 'NORMALISATION'

The change in Friedländer's stated historiography and historical practice, signalled by his memoir, is clear in his next book *Reflets du Nazism* (1982). Subtitled 'an essay on kitsch and death', Friedländer argues that 'any analysis of Nazism based only on political, economic and social interpretation will not suffice'.[12] He aims to trace the 'latent discourse ruled by a profound logic' (*RN* 15) of the images used by the Nazis and those who write or make films about that period. The book looks at

not so much by what this or that writer or director has intended to say, but what they say unwittingly, even what is said despite them . . . by granting a certain freedom to what is imagined, by accentuating the selection that is exercised in memory, a contemporary reelaboration presents the reality of the past in a way that sometimes reveals previously unsuspected aspects. (*RN* 18).

This is—*pace* the much-cited remark by Benjamin—to seize the past 'as an image which flashes up at the instant when it can be recognised'.[13] These images—from literature, from film—illumine the Nazi past.

---

[11] Daniel O. Dahlstrom, *Heidegger's Concept of Truth* (Cambridge: Cambridge University Press, 2001), 17. Emmanuel Levinas, *Totality and Infinity*, tr. Alphonso Lingis (London: Kluwer Academic Publishers, 1991), 252.

[12] Saul Friedländer, *Reflections on Nazism: An Essay on Kitsch and Death*, tr. Thomas Weyr (Bloomington: Indiana University Press, rev. edn., 1993), 13. This will be abbreviated in the text to *RN*.

[13] Benjamin, 'Theses', 247.

However, they also illuminate the present, and what Friedländer saw as a 'new discourse' on Nazism in which some 'kind of limit has been over-stepped and uneasiness appears' (*RN* 21). This new discourse in artistic representations will find its parallel in historical representation in Friedländer's debate with Martin Brozat and is in part the subject of the introduction to his edited collection *Probing the Limits of Representation*. In both he seeks to preserve the power of memory as a world disclosing truth from forms which would normalize and so reduce it (history) or distort it through inadequate representation (some 'Holocaust' art). In this book, his analyses are not historical nor do they claim to be a 'true judgement'—'I know how imprecise this is' (*RN* 20) he writes—but they still, as literary or film criticism, illumine Nazism and its contemporary understanding. His understanding here of the relation between history and memory has, on the one hand, let history written in the present critique the past and, on the other hand and at the same time, has let the past be disclosed (but not historicized) as memory critiquing the present.

How the present critiques the past is clear enough: despite some avowals of objectivity, the present maintains its inability not to judge the past (part of the present's 'weak messianic power' to judge and to redeem according to Benjamin).[14] The latter, the way the disclosure of the past as memory disrupts history, is less clear. One example Friedländer gives is of the normalization inherent in historical acade-mic language. 'A scholarly text', he writes, makes the reader . . . ask himself [*sic*] questions every scholarly text raises, those dealing with the accuracy of facts and their interconnection . . . Was it really the Lange Special Commando? Would it not instead have been X or Y? And how many Jews were directed toward Riga, how many others to Kovno, how many more to Minsk?' (*RN* 90). And these unavoidable questions are not enough as the 'the real trap of language is unexpect-edly sprung' (*RN* 90). He cites several sentences of the type '(A) The Jews of some transports . . . were not assigned to the local ghettos or camps . . . (B) These Jews were shot upon arrival' (*RN* 90). The point is that an 'unreality springs from an absolute disparity between the two halves of the phrases: The first half implies an ordinary administrative measure, and is put in totally normal speech: the second half accounts for the natural consequences, except that here, suddenly, the second half describes murder' (*RN* 90).

---

[14] Ibid. 246.

He points out that the style does not and cannot change, and so the events of the past, the truth of memory, is neutralized in the face of the language of historical writing which 'places each one of us . . . in a situation not unrelated to the detached position of an administrator of extermination: interest is fixed on an administrative process, an activity of building and transportation, words used for record keeping. And that's all' (*RN* 90). This is not a criticism of any particular historian, but of the very nature of writing history in a tradition that excludes, or denies the founding significance of memory, of the past disclosed: a tradition that writes history as if it were scientific truth. Sarah Kofman describes this phenomena in a similar, but more personal, way. She describes how her father Berek Kofman, a Parisian Rabbi, was 'taken to Drancy on July 16th, 1942 . . . convoy no. 12, dated July 29, 1942' and murdered in Auschwitz, in a 'neutral' voice which she says echoes the Serge Klarsfeld Memorial, which she incorporates into the text. This 'neutral voice' she writes 'leaves you without a voice, makes you doubt your common sense and all sense, makes you suffocate in silence'.[15] Raul Hilberg advances a similar idea, too, noting that the 'flatness' of documentary files is their 'most striking quality': it is this flatness which levels the 'sharp-edged subject matter'.[16] The perpetrators 'laconic mode' and their 'camouflaging words' are echoed in Hilberg's notably laconic and ironic style and by this conscious and informed repetition, Hilberg draws attention to both the flatness and the events that this attempts to cover up.[17] This bleak irony is a double strategy that repeats (that is, gives no new voice to) and exposes the archive and the work of the historian. But despite this, Hilberg is unsatisfied: he cites Adorno's remark on the barbarism of poetry after Auschwitz, and asks: 'Are footnotes less barbaric?'[18] A more recent example of this normalization occurs in Inga Clendinnen's book *Reading the Holocaust*. Discussing Filip Müller's testimony, *Eyewitness Auschwitz*, she writes that 'I suspect the collaborator's hand in the use of the convention of dramatic direct-direct speech reportage from long public speeches by the SS and . . . for the responses by their victims'.[19] More than this, she writes that she would challenge

[15] Sarah Kofman, *Stifled Words*, tr. Madeleine Dobere (Evanston, Ill.: Northwestern University Press, 1998), 10–11.

[16] Raul Hilberg, *Sources of Holocaust Research* (Chicago: Ivan R. Dee, 2001), 73.

[17] Ibid. 79, 114.

[18] Raul Hilberg, *The Politics of Memory* (Chicago: Ivan R. Dee, 1996), 138.

[19] Inga Clendinnen, *Reading the Holocaust* (Cambridge: Cambridge University Press, 1999), 23.

the few stories she finds 'uplifting'—'scenes of defiance and/or faith', such as Müller's telling of the well-known 'dancer' story of the shooting of SS man Schillinger—'on the grounds of implausibility'.[20] For Clenndinnen, the question is 'is it believable?': 'Am I making too much of the possibility that a few harmless fantasies which could bring comfort to thousands might lurk in Müller's text? No, because the critical evaluation of texts (may I accept this? must I reject that?) stands at the heart of the historical enterprise.'[21] She is concerned that it is hard to assess testimony without 'piety'.[22] That is, the 'truth' of the text, of Müller's account, is reduced to only the 'historical truth'. All the rest is passed over, reduced through 'may I accept this? must I reject that?' It seems that, as Friedländer points out, the risk here is not piety, but *impiety* resulting not from any lack of care or concern on Clendinnen's part *per se*, but arising from the discipline of history understood as a science. Yet, as Friedländer makes clear again and again, not to do this is as bad: for 'anyone who does not know the facts, the mystical communion with the brownshirt revolution and its martyrs still remains'.

Friedländer's defence of memory—of the disruptive power of memory on history—lies at the core of his exchange with Martin Brozat, one of the leading German historians of the period of his generation. This debate, while not part of the *Historikerstreit* narrowly defined, became a 'central point of contention'.[23] Recently, fierce new light has been cast on their discussion by Nicolas Berg's discovery that Brozat—who stated that he had been in the Hitler Youth—had applied to join the Nazi Party when he was old enough towards the end of the war (though, some commentators have suggested, he may not have been formally admitted).[24] Arguing that critically examining the Nazi period has been 'taboo', Brozat writes that the 'moral quarantine of the Hitler period' should be ended and a 'long-term view of the arena of Modern German history' which would allow a more nuanced understanding should be developed: the ' "normalization" of our historical consciousness cannot in the long run exclude the Nazi period'.[25]

---

[20] Ibid. 23, 24.   [21] Ibid. 23, 25.   [22] Ibid. 25.

[23] Peter Baldwin, 'The Historikerstreit in Context', in Baldwin (ed.), *Reworking the Past: Hitler, the Holocaust and the Historian's Debate* (Boston: Beacon Press, 1990), 13. See also Charles Maier, *The Unmasterable Past* (London: Harvard University Press, 1988).

[24] See *Der Holocaust und die westdeutschen Historiker* (Göttingen: Wallstein, 2003). I thank Peter Longerich and Rudolf Muhs for bringing this to my attention.

[25] Martin Brozat, 'A Pleas for the Historicization of National Socialism', in Baldwin (ed.), *Reworking the Past*, 77–87, 87.

Friedländer's response covers an array of issues including the development of German historiography and the relevance of Nazism (the 'history of Nazism belongs to everybody').[26] Key, here, however, is Friedlander's argument that the limits of historicization are not due to a taboo, but come from the crimes themselves. A historicization ('normalization') could only be possible if the crimes of the regime were integrated into a historical framework. However, the crimes are precisely what makes such an integrated historical framework impossible. He cites a review from Geoffrey Barraclough from 1972: 'If the answers still elude us, the easiest assumption is that what is necessary is more fact, more information'. This may not be correct, however. 'If the jigsaw does not work out, the reason may not be that some of the pieces are missing but that we have set it up wrongly.'[27] How we understand the place of the crimes—the murder of European Jews —is a question which relies first on how and who we are, and how the world is for us, crucially on memory, and only in a secondary way on a 'normalizing' historical account.[28] It might be suggested that for Brozat, his historiography itself (embarked on in good faith, perhaps, but lacking Friedländer's wider and more philosophical reflection) was a method which helped this 'normalization', immunizing him, to turn back his own metaphor, from the crimes. The affair is an important example of how, for Friedländer, this sort of history works.

Brozat's response to Friedländer is to suggest that memory is mythic and history is scientific: if memory serves history by producing 'productive images and insights' this is to the good, if it coarsens the past, this is less good.[29] Mythical memory is 'precisely a form of remembrance located outside the framework of (German and Jewish) historical science' at best seen 'alongside the mere dry historical reconstruction of facts'.[30] For Brozat, memory, however important, is simply another (unreliable) source of evidence, which may be important for some particular people. Again, in the light of Berg's revelation, this might be seen as an attempt to distance memory, or to quarantine 'history' from 'memory' in the wider sense for which I have argued, both in disciplinary terms and for himself. In contrast to Brozat, Friedländer's position is that it is only by an adequate understanding of memory in the context of issues over truth that an understanding of the problems can be raised. It is not that memory is separate from history.

---

[26] Saul Friedländer, 'Some Reflections about the Historicization of National Socialism', in Baldwin (ed.), *Reworking the Past*, 88–101, 98.
[27] Ibid. 99.   [28] Ibid. 100.   [29] Brozat, 'Reply', 106.   [30] Ibid. 114.

Rather, memory underlies history. However, history often concretes over or ignores memory while trying to bring it to light (as in the case of the sentences about the Lange Special Commando cited above). Moreover in relation to 'normalization', as Friedländer points out, 'normal life with the knowledge of ongoing massive crimes committed by one's nation and one's own society is not so normal after all'.[31] Historical representation, Brozat's historical science, cannot integrate (historicize or normalize) the Holocaust because the phenomenon of the Holocaust, the memory of it, and what that memory leads to are ways in which the world is disclosed, not facts to be assimilated to science.[32] Whether Brozat was covering up his application for membership to the Nazi party, or whether he felt that his historiography ('historical science') made it irrelevant does not really matter here: the issue is that memory—who we are and how the world is for us—is unavoidably involved with the discipline of history. This debate between Friedländer and Brozat is less, then, about how to do history, and more about ethos and about the ethics of history.

In his introduction to *Probing the Limits of Representation*, Friedländer's discussion is broader, but maintains the same thrust. Beginning with the obligation to bear witness, the obligation of memory, Friedländer suggests that there are 'limits to representation which should not be but can easily be transgressed'.[33] In this, postmodernism, understood in three ways as certain kinds of experimental art, as the problem of the relation of language to truth, and as a discourse opposed to any totalizing view of history (a view itself stemming from a reflection on the Holocaust) plays no little role. If his aim in the debate with Brozat was to protect memory from being paved over by history, then here his aim is to defend both history and memory from being paved over with inappropriate representations. This strategy of cherishing both history and memory is central to his work.

In his interested summary of the articles in this collection, he shows how the view has developed—principally from White and LaCapra— that what is required as a response to the Holocaust is a 'new voice': LaCapra suggests here—thought he develops his position in later works—that with conventional techniques, historical accounts can

---

[31] Friedländer, 'Reply', 120.

[32] For another account of this debate, see Dominick LaCapra, *Representing the Holocaust* (London: Cornell University Press, 1994), esp. 43–67.

[33] Saul Friedländer, *Probing the Limits of Representation* (London: Harvard University Press, 1992), 3.

never come to terms with the Holocaust.[34] Yet, Friedländer points out that this depends 'ultimately on the concrete development of new historiographical thinking and on the possibility of achieving a conceptualisation of the new categories called for by events such as the Holocaust'.[35] Demands for a new historiography are all very well, but they need to be realized. More traditional historians rightly ask what this 'new history' might look like. If the analysis of the question of the sort of truth to which history aspires is correct, a 'new voice' is not just a new form of history writing to add to a list that might include, say, micro-history, economic history, cultural history, and so on, not just new pieces for the jigsaw. A 'new voice' would be a sort of history that did not draw on either one, or a mixture, of these two understandings of truth (as memory and world disclosed, as scientific correspondence truth), and this seems strikingly unlikely to happen. In this broader light, there are no brand-new tools available for the writing of history, only different uses of the older tools in writing a history that both is rigorous and explicitly opens up memory. It is to this that Friedländer turns in trying to develop a historical writing that is able to accommodate both knowledge and memory.

HISTORICAL KNOWLEDGE AND MEMORY: 'HISTORICAL CONSCIOUSNESS'

In the introduction to *Memory, History and the Extermination of the Jews of Europe*, Friedländer sets himself against the 'common thesis' of a 'basic opposition between history and memory'.[36] He argues that this opposition is less convincing in the case of representation of the recent past or 'a past considered to be of cardinal relevance for the identity of a given group': by this last phrase, he clearly means the Holocaust, but it surely must apply to the ways in which all communities construct their identities through the way that they represent their pasts (*MHEJ* p. viii). He suggests that there is a continuum between, at one end, dispassionate works of history and, at the other, public-collective

---

[34] Friedländer, *Probing the Limits of Representation*, 10.
[35] Ibid. 11.
[36] Saul Friedländer, *Memory, History and the Extermination of the Jews of Europe* (Bloomington: Indiana University Press, 1993), p. vii. This will be abbreviated as *MHEJ* in the text.

memory. The poles of this continuum can be seen as works of history as 'scientific', offering historical judgements in which the assertions correspond to what is taken to be evidence, and works of memory and identity which disclose existential ethical truth, not primarily verifiable by reference to documents, evidence, and so on. The middle ground between them Friedländer calls 'historical consciousness' which covers especially those eras that have ' "existential" and ideological relevance to the present' (*MHEJ* p. viii). This 'historical consciousness' reflects the constantly renegotiated mixture of all these verifiable and unverifiable beliefs and facts that make up communal identity. Yet, although he does not say this explicitly, it is clear that communal memory and so shared communal identity socio-ontologically comes before or lies beneath works produced according to a rigorous historiography.[37] That is, he is not saying that public-collective memory is a form of bad history, which would simply fail the generic conventions of history by offering incorrect if widely accepted facts; rather, it underlies the possibility of academic history, and 'historical consciousness' is the negotiation between the two. For example, in the case of German historian Hillgruber, whose book, *Two Kinds of Ruin*, was a catalyst for the historian's debate, he argues that having

been a youngster in the Wehrmacht fighting the Russians in eastern Prussia and having had to flee his home town of Konigsberg must have had a bearing on Hillgruber's peculiar identification with the German populations of the east and the retreating units of the Wehrmacht . . . an identification with previous personal experience is repressed for a long time, but unexpected acting out can hardly be avoided.[38]

This is one particular example, Brozat now another, but the thesis applies to all sorts of historians. In terms of Holocaust history, this is made more acute by the intensity of the unavoidable intermingling of the two poles. There are many issues—such as the ' "exceptionality" or comparability' (*MHEJ* p. ix) of the Holocaust, the responses of the *Judenräte*, and the reaction of scholars from different groups to each other (Friedländer suggests that some German scholars think of work

---

[37] Socio-ontology would be the study of the way in which societies and communities are or come into being. Cf 'memory itself becomes not a simple act of recall but a socially constitutive act': Charles Maier, *The Unmasterable Past* (London: Harvard University Press, 1988), 169.

[38] Saul Friedländer, 'Trauma, Transference and "Working through" in Writing the History of the *Shoah*', *History and Memory*, 4 (1992), 39–59, 45. This will be abbreviated to TTW.

by Jewish scholars as commemorative, not as ' "rational-objective" studies', *MHEJ* p. ix)—which cannot be discussed in a neutral way, or which do not already reflect pre-existing existential, identity, philosophical, or historiographical commitments. Moreover, changes in 'collective memory' or how communities see themselves (changes effected by, for example, the unification of Germany or the situation of Israel) in turn effect how history is written.

For Friedländer, these two ends of the spectrum pose an aporia, an unresolvable problem: 'extricating a "rational-historiography" from the overall field of "history *and* memory" of this epoch is an ever-necessary, yet an ever elusive goal' (*MHEJ* p. x). The characteristic postmodern tension is between an awareness of the 'inadequacy of traditional historiographical testimony and the need to establish as reliable a narration as possible' (*MHEJ* p. x), between an awareness that the existential ethical truth cannot be properly or fully explained and the need to establish a judgement of truth as correspondence. Friedländer explores this most closely, perhaps, in his essay 'Trauma, Transference and "Working through" '. Beginning with a discussion of the status of memory and Jewish historiography, Friedländer suggests that, in the manifestations of memory (Lanzmann's *Shoah*, Levi's work) 'no redemptive theme or sign of resolution is evident', which might lead one to question the work of Cathy Caruth, whose work, following Freud, suggests that it is possible to 'work through' historical trauma. (TTW 43). He argues that much German history of the Holocaust has been characterized by 'defences', beginning with massive denial in the 1940s and 1950s. The student revolts of the 1960s, while fighting against 'fascism', understood the Nazi past only in a very indistinct way. Although a new approach began to develop in the 1960s and 1970s and the 'Historian's debate' of the late 1980s foregrounded many of the issues, this forgetting remains very powerful.[39] One defence he names 'splitting off': relegating the Holocaust to the margins of the Third Reich's history, or normalizing the events as part of the work of history. He also finds defences and avoidance on the side of the victims. Although 'silence did not exist within the survivor community . . . It was maintained in relation to the outside world and was often imposed by shame' (TTW 48: this nuance shifts the emphasis of some of Peter Novick's theses in *The Holocaust and Collective*

---

[39] On this, see also Richard Evans, *In Hitler's Shadow: West German Historians and the Attempt to Escape from the Nazi Past* (London: I. B. Tauris & Co., 1989).

Memory). Major Jewish historians did not write histories of the Holocaust and, as he discusses in his autobiography, Raul Hilberg found it difficult to get his groundbreaking history published. Friedländer suggests that current 'historical interpretation by Jewish historians is still caught between hasty ideological closure (such as the "catastrophe and redemption theses") and a paralysis of attempts at global interpretation . . . This evaluation applies also to my own work' (TTW 51). Having discussed the defences against writing a history of the Holocaust, and having argued that historians should be aware of these defences, he turns to the possibility of 'working through'. For Freud, and for 'trauma theorists', this involves a resolution of the trauma through integration, a 'feeling of familiarity, of being known, of communion . . . the survivor who has achieved commonality with others can rest from her labours'.[40] However, in relation to what remains 'indeterminate, elusive and opaque'—the Holocaust—the historian must reject exactly that sense of integration or closure. Paradoxically, working through this material must entail precisely not a working through: 'the imperative of rendering a truthful account as documents and testimonials will allow, without giving in to the temptation of closure' (TTW 52–3). What is needed, he writes, is a 'simultaneous acceptance of two contradictory moves: the search for ever-closer historical linkages and the avoidance of a naïve historical positivism leading to simplistic and self-assured historical narrations'. Again here, the idea that a 'historical-scientific' truth (historical linkages) and a different form of truth, as a disruptive disclosure, emerges.

One way of maintaining this, he suggests, is for the 'voice of the commentator' to be clearly heard. Moreover, this voice should 'disrupt the facile linear progression of the narration, introduce alternative interpretations, question any partial conclusion, withstand the need for closure' and make use of 'recurring refractions of a traumatic past by using any number of different vantage points' (TTW 53). He continues, with reference to his debate with Brozat: the

dimension added by the commentary may allow for an integration of the so-called 'mythic memory' of the victims within the overall representation of this past without its becoming an 'obstacle' to 'rational historiography' . . . whereas the historical narrative may have to stress the ordinary aspects of everyday life during . . . the Nazi epoch, the 'voice over' of the victims' memories may

---

[40] Judith Lewis Herman, *Trauma and Recovery* (London: Pandora, 1992), 236.

puncture such normality, at least at the level of memory . . . The reintroduction
of individual memory into the overall representation of the epoch implies the
use of contemporaries' direct or indirect expressions of their experience.
Working through means confronting the individual voice in a field dominated
by political decisions and administrative decrees which neutralise the con-
creteness of despair and death.   (TTW 53; italics in original)

This might be taken as a programme statement for future history. On
the one hand, it admits the importance of historical 'science' while also
being aware of its limitations. It aims for a work of history to be open
to the non-verifiable power of the works which foreground the world
of the victims. It is to be written contrapuntally, made up of a mixture
of voices, including that of the narrator historian's own, not seeking a
final answer. James Young discusses Friedländer's methods, arguing
that 'his incorporation of these voices into history has not led to an
abandonment of historical standards but to a deepening of them'.[41]
However, he continues to suggest that 'he incorporates the living memory of survivors into historical narrative, not to privilege it but to show
better how events were apprehended (or misapprehended) as they
unfolded'.[42] This seems to imply that Friedländer is simply adding
more pieces to the jigsaw puzzle, more facts for history. Yet, crucially,
his form of history is an attempt to develop a form of history that has
neither abandoned Rankean rigour nor is limited to it, that flows from
memory but is aware of its dangers. It shuttles from memory to historical knowledge to memory again, holding these two apart and also
together. It is already a deconstructive or 'postmodern' history, which
does not mean it is unrigorous. This is not a solution to the problems
of history in general or the 'insoluble historical and theoretical problems' of Holocaust history in particular but it is an attempt to write history in the light of these problems.[43]

    This is very much the method that Friedländer describes and uses in
the first volume of his *Nazi Germany and the Jews*: this is his major
synthetic work and enacts much that he has thought and written. He
writes in the introduction that the book juxtaposes 'different levels of
reality . . . with the aim of creating a sense of estrangement counter-
acting our tendency to "domesticate" that particular past' (5): the

    [41] James Young, 'Between History and Memory: The Uncanny Voices of the
Historian and Survivor', *History and Memory*, 9 (1997), 47–58, 51.
    [42] Ibid.
    [43] Dan Diner, 'Between Aporia and Apology: On the Limits of Historicizing National
Socialism', *History and Memory*, 9 (1997), 145, 144.

' "mythic memory" of the victims has been set against the "rational" understanding of others' (6). Here, archival history and senses of memory work together. This is made manifest in the book's style: for example, the book does not follow a standard chronology but moves about in time, so that, for example, the story of Anneliese Hüttemann is thrown into relief: she was interrogated in 1935 because she had a relationship with Kurt Stern, a Jew. Nine years later, she wanted to marry one SS-Obersturmbannführer Arthur Liebehenschel, and the record of the interrogation papers were passed up to Himmler: 'At this time Liebehenschel was the commander of Auschwitz'.[44] It offers a wide perspective, suggesting that in the Third Reich there was what Friedländer calls a 'redemptive antisemitism' at work, 'born from the fear of racial degeneration and the religious belief in redemption' and a narrow eye for detail: Mozart's librettist Lorenzo Da Ponte was Jewish, so the Italian version could not be performed, but the German version was by the Jewish conductor Hermann Levi so a 'new translation into purer, nonpolluted German had to be hastily prepared'.[45] Moreover, for example, in order bring the complexity of the issues to the fore, and to confront the individual voice, he discusses the dreams of so-called Mischlings ('our Führer does not mind being seen with me in public, despite my grandmother Recha') and others.[46] There are—as in Hilberg—ironic literary flourishes: a description of the newsreel footage of the Führer's birthday is juxtaposed with the review of a performance put on by the Kulturbund of *People at Sea*, a J. B. Priestley play about survivors aboard a disabled ship: Friedländer notes that the 'characters depicted on the stage are saved at the end. Most of the Jews seated in the Charlottenstrasse theatre that night were doomed'.[47]

In addition to his own work, *Nazi Germany and the Jews*, Friedländer's challenge has been taken up in different ways in two testimony accounts, published in 1999 and 2000. *No Common Place* is the testimony of Alina Bacall-Zwirn with Jared Stark. It has many of the trappings of a conventional testimony: photographs, a map, a chronology—it is even a second version of an earlier manuscript written badly by a ghost writer who 'put in his philosophy too much'.[48] However, as

---

[44] Saul Friedländer, *Nazi Germany and the Jews* (London: Weidenfeld and Nicolson, 1997), 197.

[45] Ibid. 87, 134.   [46] Ibid. 170.   [47] Ibid. 333.

[48] Alina Bacall-Zwirn and Jared Stark, *No Common Place* (London: University of Nebraska Press, 1999), p. xi. See Jared Stark, 'The Task of Testimony', *History and Memory*, 11 (1999), 37–61.

a testimony compiled with a researcher, it is very different. The text is made up of direct transcriptions of the conversations between Bacall-Zwirn and Stark, as well as notes of the time and the place of the conversations. There are notes on the side of the page as meta-textual citations. Just as the testimonies discussed in Chapter 2 had different styles (realist for Hart and Levi, modernist for Delbo) this could be described as a postmodern testimony in form, exchanging mimesis of product—a smooth, finished text—for mimesis of process: the testimony reveals its own making, and the ideas that went into its own construction.

Mark Roseman's *The Past in Hiding* offers another approach. This book is two stories woven together. It is the testimony of 'the individual voice' of Marianne Ellenbogen née Strauss and, at the same time, the account of the piecing together, exploring, and verifying of that testimony by the historian Mark Roseman: thus, a testimony and a historical account of how that testimony is turned into a work of history. Ellenbogen survived the Holocaust by hiding, thus the amphibology of the title: her past was in hiding; the past is in hiding to be uncovered by the historian. Roseman interviewed her and, after her death, found both the Gestapo files for members of her family in Germany and, most rewardingly for him, a whole trunk full of documents that Ellenbogen had kept since the war. However, what makes the book unusual and reflects Friedländer's criteria is the way that these two stories—Ellenbogen's hiding and Roseman's uncovering—interweave and disrupt each other. Roseman changes registers—from detailed family history to wider reflections about the place of Jews in the Reich, from personal meditation to established historical convention—as he relates Ellenbogen's story. Most of all, the 'voice of the commentator' is 'heard' throughout. Roseman not only explains how he got the information, but how he felt about it too. For example, he describes a meeting with one Frau Sparraer, who had (according to Ellenbogen) tormented her at school. He confronts her with her apparent denial of this and her more general 'not having known anything'.[49] He feels proud that he was so 'brutally open' (*PH* 67). Yet, on reflection, he is concerned (the 'virile judgement of history . . . is cruel').[50] He realizes

[49] Mark Roseman, *The Past in Hiding* (London: Allen Lane, 2000), 67. Abbreviated to *PH* in the text.

[50] Emmanuel Levinas, *Totality and Infinity*, tr. Alphonso Lingis (London: Kluwer Academic Publishers, 1991), 243.

that Ellenbogen might be wrong, that Sparrer might not be the tormenter, and anyway, 'who was I to be the avenging angel?' 'Guilt followed pride' (*PH 67*). He also describes his own changing thoughts: on her family tree, submitted to an exhibition in 1936, he writes, 'I had made the mistake at first of seeing in it ostentatious pride. Now I saw a conscious act of self assertion at a time when the Nazis were trying to deny German Jews their right to call themselves German' (*PH 18*). He describes his narrative expectations: after Ellenbogen's story has got to the end of the war: 'I wanted to share in the exhilaration of the moment of liberation. But I didn't get the pay off I was expecting' (*PH 393*) as Marianne stayed under cover for some time afterwards. He is honest about blind alleys: the 'school tormenter' and Ellenbogen offer differ-ent stories about 1930s anti-Semitism: 'I was never going to find out' (*PH 92*) the specific historical truth. Without suggesting that Roseman set out to write something modelled on Friedländer's criteria, it is clear that this 'double history'—not lacking in traditional evidence, docu-ments, photographs, and wider reflection—is one way in which Friedländer's 'programme statement' for future histories of the Holocaust comes to fruition.

CONCLUSION: THE DECONSTRUCTIVE HISTORY
OF SAUL FRIEDLÄNDER

Friedländer is keen not to suggest that his work is deconstructive as this would, he argues, 'demand a primacy of the rhetorical dimension in the analysis of the historical text' (*TTW 52*). This is a very 'American lit-erary critical' reading of Derrida's work and is arguably not the case: as Caruth points out following de Man, 'linguistically orientated theo-ries do not necessarily deny reference but rather deny the possibility of modelling the principles of reference on those of natural law, or, we might say, of making reference like perception'.[51] The intellectual tra-jectory of Friedländer's career makes his work closer to Derridian deconstruction than he suggests. Deconstruction concerns the relation-ship between what can be discussed, the text, and the 'exorbitant' which lies outside the text but forms its context. In Friedländer's work, this exorbitant is the 'Final Solution' and the binding memory of it—

---

[51] Cathy Caruth, *Unclaimed Experience: Trauma, Narrative and History* (London: Johns Hopkins University Press, 1996), 74.

the Holocaust's 'life as a ghost' as Zygmunt Bauman has it.[52] He writes that, even if 'new forms of historical narrative were to develop or new modes of representation, and even if literature and art were to probe the past from unexpected vantage points' (TTW 55), its opaqueness would not be dispelled. Yet, the encounter with this exorbitant—the 'Shoah carries an excess' (TTW 54) he writes—is mediated through the instruments of traditional intellectual work. Both are needed.

This is not to say that Friedländer—or any of the other historians who follow the logic of his thought—is a 'deconstructor', latently influenced by Derrida's thought: this is not to 'deconstruct' Friedländer. Rather, it is to suggest perhaps quite the opposite, to 'Friedländerize' deconstruction. Both have a very similar starting point, the particularity of moments and the thought of the Holocaust. Both want to open a space in conventional discourse for the voiceless other, so both share a similar problematic. Deconstruction always occurs in a context, through a tradition.[53] What Derrida 'Friedländerizes' is generally philosophical: what Friedländer 'deconstructs' is historical. Their lines of thought share and converge and both bring us to our responsibilities and explore our relation to truth.

Friedlander writes that the incremental 'knowledge acquired by historical research is usually integrated within the general framework of the prevailing historical consciousness of a group and moulded according to one of its extant frameworks of interpretation' (MHEJ p. viii). Understanding this framework anew, in the light of these two conceptions of truth, does not offer a new historiography, but rather a new understanding of the discipline of history. The two understandings of truth need to be both recognized and held in a productive tension: both are needed to approach the Holocaust and perhaps any event. Positivistic history and its historicism cannot be abandoned, but its processes and its limits must be seen and acknowledged for what they are. In a sense, the awareness of this tension—rather than, perhaps, the language of psychoanalysis—is what lies at the core of what LaCapra,

---

[52] Zygmunt Bauman, 'The Holocaust's Life as a Ghost', in F. C. Decoste and B. Schwartz (eds.), *The Holocaust's Ghost* (Edmonton: University of Alberta Press, 2000), 3–15.

[53] For example, Derrida states that the deconstruction 'does not exist somewhere, pure, proper, self-identical, outside of its inscriptions in conflictual and differentiated contexts: it "is" only what it does and what is done with it, there where it takes place': Jacques Derrida, *Limited Inc.*, tr. Samuel Weber (Evanston, Ill.: Northwestern University Press, 1988), 141.

whose work is influenced by and responds to Friedländer's, calls the 'Non-Pollyanna understanding of working through the past'.[54]

This chapter has looked in detail at the work of one Holocaust historian, to see how two understandings of truth interact: in turn, this has a parallel with Derrida's work. The next chapter turns to examine what happens when metahistorical views, themselves the result of the Holocaust, conflict.

[54] Dominck LaCapra, *Writing History, Writing Trauma* (London: Johns Hopkins University Press, 2001), 218.

7

'What Constitutes a Historical Explanation?': Metahistory and the Limits of Historical Explanation in the Goldhagen/Browning Controversy

. . . either philosophers must become historians, or historians must become philosophers. Since that is beyond hope, I would plead for the closest possible co-operation between the two on this particular subject. Now, what does a historian do . . . First, he [*sic*] establishes facts . . . Beyond establishing facts, the historian also tries to explain them. What does the philosopher do? He [*sic*] reflects on this and asks, What constitutes a historical explanation?[1]

When it is a matter of trying to assess contending representations and interpretations of the meaning of the same event proffered by different historians of roughly equal erudition and wisdom, the facts cannot be invoked to decide the matter. First, because what is at issue in contending representations is not only, what are the facts? but also, what is to count as a fact and what is not. And secondly, because, when it is a matter of contending interpretations, what counts is not the truth of the fact so much as the meaning that is to be ascribed to the events under discussion.[2]

---

[1] Emil Fackenheim and Raphael Jospe (eds.), *Jewish Philosophy and the Academy* (London: Associated University Presses, 1996), 192–3.
[2] Hayden White, 'An Old Question Raised Again: Is Historiography Art or Science? (Response to Iggers)', *Rethinking History*, 4/3 (2000), 391–406, 399.

INTRODUCTION

While Fackenheim is right to ask for the closest possible co-operation between philosophers and historians over the Holocaust, his assignment of duties is too straightforward. The establishment of historical facts and development of interpretations are inextricably intertwined with philosophical issues, just as philosophy is inextricably interwoven with history. However, as I have argued, the Holocaust asks questions of metahistory, questions about the frameworks of interpretation. The aim of this chapter is to illustrate not only the importance of metahistory for understanding the historical accounts of the Holocaust, but also the importance of the Holocaust for metahistory: the ways in which the Holocaust has affected the nature of the discipline of history.

Among the very many debates in Holocaust history, this was particularly bought into focus by the controversy over Daniel Jonah Goldhagen's *Hitler's Willing Executioners: Ordinary Germans and the Holocaust*. While it is true that, as Dominick Lacapra writes, the affair is more or less over and that 'too much attention may already have been paid to it', it is a very significant 'casestudy' of Holocaust metahistory, and reveals a great deal.[3]

Yehuda Bauer wrote that no 'book on the Holocaust has caused the kind of public controversy that Goldhagen's *Hitler's Willing Executioners* has' and, if the book made a wave in the US, it caused a storm in Germany, where it picked up on unresolved tensions in 'Holocaust historiography, Germans political culture, and ethnic, ideological and generational backgrounds'.[4] Yet in the enormous amount of criticism and discussion rarely do any of the commentators explicitly

[3] Dominick LaCapra, *Writing History, Writing Trauma* (London: Johns Hopkins Univerity Press, 2001), 114.

[4] Yehuda Bauer, ' Daniel J. Goldhagen's View of the Holocaust', in Franklin H. Littell (ed.), *Hyping the Holocaust: Scholars Answer Goldhagen* (Philadelphia: Merion Westfield Press International, 1997), 61; Robert Shandley, 'Introduction', in Shandley (ed.), *Unwilling Germans: The Goldhagen Debate*, tr. Jeremiah Riemer (Minneapolis: University of Minnesota Press, 1998), 5. Preceded by discussions in *Die Zeit* and *Der Spiegel*, the book began a controversy wider and more acute than the *historikerstreit* in the 1980s, drawing in almost all the figures researching the history of the Holocaust. Goldhagen went on a tour, discussing the book in public with leading German historians, principally, Hans Mommsen.

discuss Goldhagen's metahistory, or the reasons for his approach.[5] This
is significant because, at its core, the debate was metahistorical, con-

[5] Interestingly, the criticism of the book mirrored its own polemical style: while some
critics remained within a specifically historical discourse, others moved swiftly to make
metahistorical, moral, and stylistic points. Eberhard Jäckel argues that it is 'inadequate,
disappointing . . . full of errors': e.g., Captain Hoffman, with whom the book begins was,
contra Goldhagen, a member of the SS and had been since 1933 (Jäckel, 'Simply Put', in
Littell (ed.), *Hyping the Holocaust*, 161–4). Hubert Locke argues that the book is poorly
researched and Ullrich Herbert suggests, soberly, that Goldhagen severs 'the German
genocide of the Jews from its intimate connection to the German war effort and, in particular, to the brutal extermination policy directed against the Soviet population, as well
as other ethnic and social groups' (Ullrich Herbert, 'Extermination Policy: New Answers
and Questions about the History of the "Holocaust" in German Historiography', in
Herbert (ed.), *National Socialist Extermination Policies: Contemporary German
Perspectives and Controversies* (Oxford: Berghahn Books, 2000), 2). Hans Mommsen
and Norbert Frei point out his reliance on secondary sources. Many historians argued
that he took an overly reductive, narrow, or one-dimensional approach. Bauer concludes
that his argument is Manichaean, ignoring issues such as the varieties of anti-Semitism in
19TH-cent. Germany, the social and economic traumas in the 1920s and 1930s, the role of
the elites, and the comparative histories of other European nations (Yehuda Bauer,
'Daniel J. Goldhagen's View of the Holocaust', *Hyping the Holocaust*, 71). Other critics
are more explicitly concerned with issues of morals. Goldhagen is widely criticized for
suggesting that the 'German hatred of the Jews' is 'historically inherited and an innate
characteristic' (Mommsen), that in his account 'culture' has replaced 'race' and he 'dehu-
manises, vilifies, even demonises the German people' (Smith), that he is 'almost racist'
(Bauer) and talks in terms of 'biological collectivism' (Jäckel, *Hyping the Holocaust*, 37,
55, 70, 164). For Jost Nolte, Goldhagen's 'rage of Old Testament breath' (itself an odd
and rather weighted formulation) means that 'Sisyphus is a German', that Germans are
always and simplistically tarred with this brush, and that his 'speculations about the
murderous German soul are murderous' (Jost Nolte, 'Sisyphus is a German', Shandley
(ed.), *Unwilling Germans*, 52). These are not simply historical objections with an implicit
moral position (if they were, they might be offering more differentiation and explanation). These are explicitly moral statements, feeling disgust at where these critics find
what they take to be racism. Finally, at the far end of the spectrum between historical
discourse and explicitly moral discourse are accounts of Goldhagen's style, which are all
disapproving. Realizing that 'any young writer or publisher could capitalise' on the interest in the Holocaust to make their reputation, Goldhagen is accused of following the
hype and of writing a 'diatribe in a academic format'; he is a 'pamphleteer', adopts an
incautious 'moralising tone', offering a 'superficially powerful evocation of moral truth'
(*Hyping the Holocaust*, p. xi; Shandley (ed.), *Unwilling Germans*, 52; Geoff Eley (ed.),
The 'Goldhagen Effect': History, Memory, Nazism—Facing the German Past (Ann
Arbour: University of Michigan Press, 2000), 225, 158). More than this, his style is 'a
morally satisfying account of German guilt and redemption' (*The 'Goldhagen Effect'*,
159). Many of the critics accuse him of what Mommsen calls 'a certain voyeurism, which
serious research on the Holocaust avoids through restrained portrayal of criminality'; it
is 'pornography' or 'voyeuristic narration' as Goldhagen respected no '*Schamgrenze*
(shame border) in his work' (*Hyping the Holocaust*, 42; Shandley (ed.), *Unwilling
Germans*, 224; Eley (ed.), *The 'Goldhagen Effect'*, 117). Others, like Jurgen Kocka, are
less worried by this, and argue that 'its strength lies above all in the way it unflinchingly
portrays the everyday reality of the killers and articulates murderous deeds on the border of the indescribable' (Shandley (ed.), *Unwilling Germans*, 199). Certainly, 'No
German historian speaks and writes as graphically as Goldhagen. One can evaluate this

cerning the ethics of historical representation and issues of scholarly and national identity: most importantly, it turned over an extra-historical issue—a view of what it is to be human—and over the consequent moral and then historical claims.[6] The aim of this chapter is not to go over the controversy again but, concentrating on issues of metahistory, to pick up on one aspect of the controversy from the anglophone world, the debate between Goldhagen and Christopher Browning in the late 1990s. This was particularly acute, not only because both historians had used some of the same archival sources, but because both have very different metahistories. This means that their differences lie outside the purview of the genre of history and are not resolvable by historical methods. This chapter contrasts the metahistorical positions of Goldhagen and Browning and argues that these, in turn, are a consequence of a decision both have made—before doing the history, as it were—about the relationship between the Holocaust and the human.

   A leitmotif of both the difference between Goldhagen and Browning and their very different metahistories is their divergent interpretation of Primo Levi's central and influential essay 'The Grey Zone'. Goldhagen takes this comment as guiding thread: Levi writes that 'I do know I was a guiltless victim and I was not a murderer. I know that the murderers existed, not only in Germany, and still exist, retired or on active duty, and that to confuse them with their victims is a moral disease or an aesthetic affectation or a sinister sign of complicity.'[7] Keen to avoid moral disease or affectation or complicity, Goldhagen dismisses 'conventional explanations' which posit 'universal human traits', because 'the conventional explanations should hold true for any people who find themselves in the perpetrator's shoes', and for Goldhagen, they do not.[8] In contrast, Browning reads Levi's essay as a

---

positively or negatively' (ibid. 229). Finally, and with almost nothing to do with the past at all, Goldhagen was denounced for denouncing more senior scholars and for lacking humility. Indeed, during the debates, one commentator writes that 'the sound of junior knuckles being rapped by elder statesmen was especially audible and patently offensive to the audience, which rallied to defend the younger man under attack' (*Hyping the Holocaust*, 25, 71; Shandley (ed.), *The 'Goldhagen Effect'*, 154).

   [6] The story of the debate has been told several times and from several points of view: the furore can be seen as moving through three phases: the book and the immediate response, the controversy, the effect. The clearest introduction is perhaps Robert Shandley, 'Introduction', *Unwilling Germans*.

   [7] Primo Levi, *The Drowned and the Saved*, tr. Raymond Rosenthal (London: Abacus, 1988), 32–3.

   [8] Daniel Jonah Goldhagen, *Hitler's Willing Executioners* (London: Abacus, 1997), 389. This will be abbreviated to *HWE* in the text.

warning against easy blame and as an appeal against the simplistic assimilation of the past into a Manichaean history. Browning's Levi describes the 'murky world of mixed motives, conflicting emotions and priorities, reluctant choices and self-serving opportunism and accommodation wedded to self-deception and denial', as well as a reminder that, for we who come afterwards, judging—even if possible—should not be taken lightly.[9] We who come afterwards, too, are 'dazzled by power and prestige' and 'forget our essential fragility'.[10] For Browning, this essay also implies that historians too, are in a sort of 'Grey Zone', not least because their judgements mean that they are guilty of 'a certain arrogance' (*OM* 188). But more than this, he suggests that, for writing 'perpetrator history' not of the Nazi elite, but of the low-level perpetrators—the reserve policemen of Battalion 101, who felt 'sheer horror and physical revulsion at what they had been asked to do'— empathy is both necessary and possible.[11] Both accounts, then, turn on ideas about the category, the limits, and nature of the human.

THE ACTIVE VOICE OF *HITLER'S WILLING EXECUTIONERS*: GOLD- HAGEN'S METAHISTORY

Goldhagen's *Hitler's Willing Executioners* was published in the US in 1996. Based on his award-wining doctoral and post-doctoral research it develops a resolute line of argument.[12] Assuming, as Yehuda Bauer does, that the Holocaust is explicable by historical methods, Goldhagen aims to explain it by answering the question 'what was the structure of beliefs and values that made a genocidal onslaught against the Jews intelligible and sensible to the ordinary Germans who became

---

[9] Daniel J Goldhagen, Christopher Browning, and Leon Wieseltier, *The 'Willing Executioners'/'Ordinary Men' Debate*, introd. by M Berenbaum (Washington, DC: United States Holocaust Research Institute, 1996), 33. Christopher Browning, *Ordinary Men: Reserve Police Battalion 101 and the Final Solution* (London: Harper Collins, 2nd edn., 1998), 186–8: this will be abbreviated to *OM* in the text. See also, for use of part of this essay in a different context, Christpher Browning, *Nazi Policy, Jewish Workers, German Killers* (Cambridge: Cambridge University Press, 2000), 102–15.

[10] Levi, *The Drowned and the Saved*, 50, 51.

[11] Christopher Browning, 'German Memory: Judicial Interrogation, and Historical Reconstruction: Writing Perpetrator History from Postwar Testimony', in Saul Friedländer (ed.), *Probing the Limits of Representation: Nazism and the 'Final Solution'* (London: Harvard University Press, 1992), 22–36, 36.

[12] His thesis had won two awards: one from Harvard and one from the American Political Science Association.

perpetrators?' (*HWE* 24). He 'asked why humans, who most definitely understood themselves as Germans, were motivated to kill other humans, whom they saw only as "Jews". And he did so in a language that demanded answers.'[13] Goldhagen is explicitly interested in the 'ideational causes of social action' (*HWE* 8), the ideas and mindsets that lead to people's actions, rather than more 'structural' reasons for the Holocaust. Although he acknowledges that the 'incentive structure' was important, he believes that this cannot have caused people to act by itself, but only worked 'in conjunction with the cognitive and value structures' (*HWE* 21) already in place in an individual. He argues throughout his book—made up of studies of particular perpetrator police battalions, work camps and death marches, events read 'like retrospectively conducted experiments'[14] (the term 'experiments' will become important)—that Germany, unlike other European countries, had a 'dominant cultural thread' (*HWE* 47) of 'eliminationist anti-Semitism'. Ordinary Germans were familiar with the idea of the utter annihilation of the Jews and so became willing accomplices. 'Something profound must happen to people' he writes, 'before they will become willing perpetrators of enormous mass slaughter . . . The more that the range and character of the German perpetrators' actions become known, the less the notion appears tenable that they were not tuned into the Hitlerian view of the world' (*HWE* 414). This approach is not chosen at random: it comes from two deep-seated metahistorical beliefs evident in Goldhagen's work. The first stems not from what he calls his methodology (by which he generally means, for example, his choice and use of evidence) but from his anthropological philosophy of history. The second is his explicit moral stand.

Goldhagen's book does not merely take on a 'social science methodology' nor, as Geoffrey Eley says scathingly, does it demonstrate 'at best a sub-Geertzian postulate of cultural coherence'.[15] In its presuppositions and style, it is much closer to Geertz's conception of ethnology or even a form of Foucauldian analysis of discourse than its critics have allowed. Foucault writes of ethnology in *The Order of Things* and speculates on the

---

[13] Shandley (ed.), *Unwilling Germans*, 20.
[14] Jürgen Habermas, 'Goldhagen and the Public Use of History', in Shandley (ed.), *Unwilling Germans*, 268. This text will be abbreviated to GPH in the text.
[15] Eley (ed.), *The 'Goldhagen Effect'*, 19.

prestige and importance ethnology could possess if, instead of defining itself
. . . as the study of societies without history, it were deliberately to seek its
object in the area of the unconscious processes that characterise the system of
a given culture; in this way it would bring the relation of historicity, which is
constitutive of all ethnology in general, into play within the dimension in which
psychoanalysis has always been deployed. In so doing . . . it would define as a
system of cultural unconsciouses the totality of formal structures which render
mythical discourse significant, give coherence and necessity to the rules that
regulate needs, and provide the norms of life with a foundation other than that
to be found in nature, or in pure biological functions.[16]

Goldhagen's target is that which renders the Nazi mythical discourse
significant and offered a so-called 'norm' of life in which the destruction of European Jews occurred and made sense to the perpetrators.
Unlike many other historians, Goldhagen applies ethnography to a
'given culture' and aims to 'approach Germany as an anthropologist'
(*HWE* 28). This is valid, he argues, because that society produced

a cataclysm, the Holocaust, which people did not predict, or, with rare exception, ever imagine to have been possible . . . It constituted a set of actions, and
an imaginative orientation that was completely at odds with the intellectual
foundations of modern western civilisation, the Enlightenment, as well as
Christian and secular behavioural norms that had governed western society
. . . the study of the society which produced this then unimagined, and unimaginable, event requires us to question our assumptions about that society's
similarity to our own.   (*HWE* 28)

Goldhagen, perhaps rather optimistically, suggests the difference
between Nazi Germany and contemporary Western society is analogous to the difference between the Western society from which Clifford
Geertz comes and the Balinese society he studies. For Goldhagen, the
Holocaust and its attendant anti-Semitism is both the chief sign of this
difference and its most fundamental element. However, Goldhagen,
unlike an anthropologist, undertakes this 'anthropological revalua-
tion' (*HWE* 28) using historical methods. For Geertz,

the ethnographer is in fact faced with . . . a multiplicity of complex conceptual
structures, many of them superimposed upon or knotted into one another,
which are strange, irregular and inexplicit, and which he [*sic*] must contrive
somehow first to grasp and then to render. And this is true at the most down-
to-earth, jungle field work levels of his activity: interviewing informants,

[16] Michel Foucault, *The Order of Things* (London: Tavistock/Routledge, 2nd edn.,
1989), 379–80

observing rituals, eliciting kin terms, tracing property lines, censusing house-holds . . . writing his journal. Doing ethnography is like trying to read (in the sense of 'construct a reading of') a manuscript—foreign, faded, full of ellipses, incoherencies, suspicious emendations, and tendentious commentaries, but written not in conventionalised graphs of sound but in transient examples of shaped behaviour.[17]

For Goldhagen, reading documents—often incoherent, suspicious, and tendentious—is doing ethnography. The 'shaped behaviour' that is both the starting point and the focus of his interest is the Holocaust and this can only be understood as part of a wider culture: the study of the Holocaust's perpetrators 'thus provides a window through which German society can be viewed and examined' (*HWE* 456).

Most importantly, Goldhagen is implicitly basing his analysis on an understanding of culture and the idea of the human being taken from—or at least similar to—Geertz. Geertz's anthropology does not accept the Enlightenment vision of the human which suggests that there is 'a human nature as regularly organised, as thoroughly invariant, and as marvellously simple as Newton's universe . . . men are men under whatever guise and against whatever backdrop' (*IC* 34). This produces the belief that one can 'strip off the motley forms of culture' from an individual like layers and find the 'structural and functional regularities of social organisation'; beneath these the 'underlying psychological factors and—at the bottom—the 'biological foundations' (*IC* 38). Geertz criticizes this by suggesting that this image may be 'an illusion, that what man is may be so entangled with where he is, who he is and what he believes that it is inseparable from them' (*IC* 35): indeed, modern anthropology asserts that 'men unmodified by the customs of particular places do not in fact exist, have never existed and most important, could not in the very nature of the case exist'. Geertz argues this by showing how attempts to draw links between 'underlying needs'—the urge to reproduce, for example—and the many different so-called cultural strategies to fulfil them—'marriage'—flounder both because of the huge range of very different practices and the inability to 'construct genuine functional interconnections between cultural and non cultural factors': instead, there are 'only more or less persuasive analogies, parallelisms, suggestions and affinities' (*IC* 43). Geertz suggests we replace this layered view of the human being with a 'synthetic

[17] Clifford Geertz, *The Interpretation of Cultures* (London: Fontana Press, 1993), 10. This will be abbreviated to *IC* in the text.

one . . . in which biological, psychological, sociological and cultural
factors can be treated within a unitary system of analysis' (*IC* 44). In
this, culture—traditionally the 'top layer'—is best seen not as 'concrete
behaviour patterns—customs, usages, traditions, habit clusters . . . but
as a set of control mechanisms—plan, recipes, rules, instructions
(. . . "programs")—for the governing of behaviour' (*IC* 44). Even
further, as Homi Bhabha suggests, a coherent cultural identity is not
'simply historical events or parts of a patriotic body politic [but] a complex rhetorical strategy of social reference' that relies both on the past
enculturation and the acting out of that culture in the present.[18] That
is, identity is both pedagogic, taught, and performative, acted out.
Each reinforces the other. This means that, for Goldhagen, the idea of
a universal human being who just happens to be German, or Jewish, or
American, recedes and instead is replaced by a model of the human
bound in inextricably with their culture, its surface, and deeper trends
and vectors, and the actions ('plans, recipes, rules, instructions') carried out by that culture.

This is not abstract theorizing 'above' the 'historical facts'. Instead,
this deeply held position is very significant in generating Goldhagen's
approach, reconceiving the writing of Holocaust history as a form of
ethnography. The previous models of history, which presuppose the
Enlightenment model of the human so bleakly destroyed by the Nazis,
do not have the resources, for Goldhagen, to properly resolve the questions that need answers, the questions put to history by the Holocaust.

The second deep-seated belief Goldhagen exhibits is, more simply, a
desire to be explicit about his moral stance. As discussed in Chapter 6,
Martin Broszat famously made a 'plea for the historicisation of
National Socialism'.[19] For Goldhagen, the whole period is infected and
must be judged so. For him, there exists an unbridgeable gap between
the perpetrators and the victims, and between the perpetrators and
those of us who come afterwards. Because there are no universal
human traits there are no, or no significant, links to this period. Thus,
he cites one perpetrator who describes 'his awakening' from an 'anti-
semitic trance. The truth came to him suddenly, like an epiphany.
"These were not subhumans . . . It was not 'the Jews are our mis-

---

[18] Homi Bhabha, *The Location of Culture* (London: Routledge, 1994), 145.
[19] Martin Broszat, 'A Plea for the Historicisation of National Socialism', in Peter
Baldwin (ed.), *Reworking the Past: Hitler, the Holocaust and the Historian's Debate*
(Boston: Beacon Press, 1990), 77–87, 87. As I have suggested in Ch. 6, recent discoveries
make this look even more contentious

fortune'. It was all a base lie. We ourselves were our misfortune" '.[20] For Goldhagen, the Third Reich was like a state from which one needs to be converted. This approach does not strip the perpetrators of agency, as if they were robots following a programme: rather, precisely because agency is part of human culture, woven into the synthetic human makeup, it restores agency to the perpetrators.

This moral stance in his work, however, stems from his conception of the human as synthetic. Does an anthropologist, in her or his work, condemn what he or she finds immoral in the people they study? Should a historian/ethnographer do likewise? If the human being is 'synthetic' as Geertz and Goldhagen believe, then it is impossible to escape one's own culture and, for example, to write as if one could not condemn would be an evasive rhetorical trope. Goldhagen would be denying his own enculturation if he denied, or covered up his moral responses, as guilty as the many historians he criticizes for claiming—implicitly—an 'objective' or universalizing view. Thus, if he did not condemn the perpetrators, his philosophy of history would be inconsistent, or worse, in his view, he would be tacitly complicit with the genocide.

By using anthropological models of writing and understanding that do not presuppose (or, at least, try to resist presupposing) the Western Enlightenment human being and still maintaining a very strong moral sense, Goldhagen's historiography points towards something like the 'human beyond humanism'. That is, he is responding to a strong ethical demand, but not one that is grounded on the idea of the human that the Enlightenment takes, the idea that argues that we are all the same. Hilary Putnam suggests that the limitations of an enlightenment ethics based on the idea that the 'other is fundamentally the same as you' is flawed because 'the idea that "we are all fundamentally the same" is that a door is opened for the Holocaust. One only has to believe that some people are not "really" the same to destroy all the force of such a grounding.'[21] Goldhagen is responding to human beings, but not to the idea of the human. Goldhagen is developing a way of writing history that he judges capable of dealing with this issue. In this sense, he is a post-Holocaust historian not only in the content of his work, but in its approach too. He is reacting not only to the history of the Holocaust (understood in terms of establishing data: how many

---

[20] Goldhagen *et al.*, *'Willing Executioners'/'Ordinary Men' Debate*, 19.
[21] Hilary Putnam, 'Levinas and Judaism', in Simon Critchley and Robert Bernasconi (eds.), *The Cambridge Companion to Levinas* (Cambridge: Cambridge University Press, 2002), 33–62, 37.

non-shooters in Reserve Police Batallion 101?), but also to the memory of the Holocaust. Goldhagen's work reflects the impact of the Holocaust on the way that he intends to write his history of it.

Thus, these two deep-seated beliefs—the anthropological approach, the moral focus—govern the whole work. For example, echoing the discussion of the issue by Saul Friedländer, Goldhagen's use of grammar is important and stems from his moral position.[22] He uses the active not the passive voice to ensure that the perpetrators 'are not absent from their own deeds (as in "five hundred Jews were killed in city X on date Y")' (*HWE* 6). Goldhagen argues that the 'conscious, half-conscious and unconscious' use of the passive in other accounts, both by perpetrators and by historians, removes the actors from the scene of the 'carnage' and, more importantly, means that the understanding of the Holocaust that comes from these accounts is robbed of 'human agency' (*HWE* 487). (Browning, too, discusses what he calls 'the "anonymous passive"' in which a perpetrator would say that 'all Jews were being shot, but without mentioning in any way his own or even his unit's participation'.)[23] For Goldhagen, this choice is as much a historical one as an ethical one and reflects as much on the perpetrators as on their later historians.[24] Goldhagen is keen to ensure that questions of moral choice, agency, and will are discussed throughout, and are not covered over or ignored. One example from many, from the death march section: the Jews are marched though they can hardly walk, deprived of food, forced to sleep outside with no protection, cudgled. Goldhagen describes all this and then adds:

Even had the Germans not been contravening a binding order not to kill the Jews and treat them humanely, the Germans multifarious cruel and lethal actions can be seen as having been a expression of their own inner desires. . . .

[22] See Saul Friedländer, *Reflections on Nazism: An Essay on Kitsch and Death*, tr. Thomas Weyr (Bloomington: Indiana University Press, revised edn., 1993), 90–4.

[23] Browning, *Nazi Policy*, 153.

[24] In this context it is significant that Hilberg claims that he avoided emotive words ('murder') and exculpatory words ('executions') in part because of his training in the (so-called) 'value-free' social sciences of the 1940s, and also in part because he did not want his personal experiences to be taken into account; despite this, he admits that he did 'yield to some temptations'. Indeed, as he acknowledges, his whole work is marked by 'an irony recognisably suppressed'. See Raul Hilberg, *The Politics of Memory* (Chicago: Ivan R. Dee, 1996), 87–8. Interestingly, for Zygmunt Bauman in the 1980s, it was the inability of the 'value free' social sciences—of which a claim to so-called neutral language use is symptomatic—to engage with the Holocaust that led to his *Modernity and the Holocaust*.

These Germans chose, against orders, authority and all reason to act as they did. They were voluntaristic actions. (*HWE* 357)

To write in this style—making responsibility and agency clear—automatically attaches blame to the perpetrators. Here, because of the grammar, the discourse of history and the discourse of ethics are inextricable: Goldhagen's grammar asserts blame, the passive grammars he attacks seem to evade condemnation.

This is clear throughout and not just through the statements of horror and rhetorical questions. Even the length of the book is a result of this. Goldhagen often repeats the same point over and again to stress the moral outrage that he feels and that he feels we (understood at least as the readers of the book) should be feeling. For example, the quotation from p. 357 above—already edited down to fifty-seven words—could be edited further to twenty-seven words with very little loss of specific meaning: 'The Germans' actions, contravening an order not to kill the Jews, can be seen as having been an expression of their own inner desires and were voluntaristic.' The extra length stresses Goldhagen's horror and outrage.

To foreground the 'synthetic' enculturation of the perpetrators, Goldhagen passes over 'often inappropriate and obfuscating labels, like "Nazi" and "SS men" ' and simply calls the perpetrators 'Germans'. Goldhagen writes that

We do not hesitate to refer to the citizens of the United States who fought in Vietnam to achieve the aims of the government as 'American' and for good reason. The reason is just as good as in the case of the Germans and the Holocaust. The perpetrators were Germans as much as the soldiers in Vietnam were Americans, even if not all people in either country supported their nations' efforts. Customary usage for analogous cases, as well as descriptive accuracy and rectitude, not only permit but also mandate the use of 'Germans' as the term of choice. (HWE 487–8)

In 'non-Holocaust' history it is usual to use national names to describe forces and here 'accuracy' and 'rectitude' 'mandate' this term for Goldhagen. This is to stress the immoral and voluntary nature of the perpetrators actions, what he takes to be the widespread support for these actions and is as much an ethical statement about perpetrators as it is a critique of the post-war histories that Goldhagen finds evasive.

Finally, both the style and the naming come together in what the anthropologist Clifford Geertz calls—after Ryle—'thick descriptions' of the perpetrators' lives and their killing: 'What *exactly* did they do when they were killing?' (*HWE* 7; original italics). Goldhagen attempts to offer a full ethnography of the killers, their backgrounds, their histories, and their everyday actions in order, to use Ryle and Geertz's analogy, to be able to tell a wink from a blink. Again, his focus in not so much on the wider questions, but on the actions and ideational structure of the individuals.

The structure and style of the book, a history of both the enculturation and the agency (and so, morals) of the perpetrators, are not 'added on', not a choice from a range of possibilities open to Goldhagen. They are not simply 'a stylistic tool, generating emotional effects that dim the capacity for sober judgement'.[25] Nor does their 'logic' exist solely to 'induce both negative and positive identification on the part of the reader' to create a split between 'us' and 'them' (although it may have that effect).[26] It is not simply a 'representational strategy' which 'encourages readers to claim this accusatory tone as their own'.[27] It is part of a whole: the style and structure result ineluctably from Goldhagen's ethnographic philosophy of history and from his moral position, from his metahistory. This happens because a philosophy, a philosophy and methodology of history, and a way of writing history are not separate, indivisible layers, built up like the construction of a building (although an analysis of them makes them look like that): they are interwoven throughout.

Because of this, the book is explicitly involved not just with 'descriptive accuracy'—historical 'facts'—but with 'rectitude', values, and ideals as well. Of course, all histories of the Holocaust do this and clearly any history text has implicit or explicit values. However, one of the things that singles out Goldhagen is that this moral commitment is foregrounded: he is writing an *explicitly moral ethnographic history*. And, as a result of this, the criticisms of the book, discussed above, were unclear whether they were speaking explicitly in the discourse of history or in the discourse of morals, or, as was most often the case, both.

[25] Jürgen Habermas, in Shandley (ed.), *Unwilling Germans*, 264.
[26] Eley (ed.), *The 'Goldhagen Effect'*, 160–2. Ullrich Herbert makes a similar point: 'Goldhagen's explanation offers the possibility of identifying with the victim even to Germans striving thus to circumvent the discomforting demands of post-Holocaust society . . . Goldhagen suggests, especially to Germans of the younger generation, a way of satisfying an understandable desire: by applauding his book, they need no longer be lumped with the vilified but can stand on the side of the vilifiers', Herbert, 'Extermination Policy, 3.
[27] Nancy Wood, *Vectors of Memory: Legacies of Trauma in Post-War Europe* (Oxford: Berg, 1999), 102.

'WHAT WOULD I HAVE DONE IN THEIR PLACE?':
BROWNING'S METAHISTORY

What do we mean when we say that we can place ourselves in the shoes of Heinrich Himmler? Naturally, most of us will reject such placement with disgust: we could never act like that. But we protest too loudly. He was human, and so are we.[28]

Very little has been written on the issues of metahistory that divide Goldhagen from Christopher Browning. Indeed, even in their own discussions of each other's work this is passed over: in one example, Browning restates in detail an empirical case, while Goldhagen discusses their differences at the level of empirical evidence, evaluation of sources, and over matters of interpretation, rather than taking on the wider, more philosophical and metahistorical differences between them.[29] Yet the crucial importance of these profound differences is made clear by comparing Goldhagen's approach to the implicit metahistory of Christopher Browning.

Browning—and others—have a number of historical objections to Goldhagen's thesis. As Browning says, in his generous but critical account of Goldhagen, it is, of course, not unusual 'for different scholars to ask different questions of, apply different methodologies to, and derive different interpretations from the same sources' (*OM* 191). While he acknowledges the 'extensive participation of ordinary Germans' and their 'high degree of voluntarism' (*OM* 192), he does not agree with Goldhagen's account of the role of anti-Semitism in Germany nor, as a consequence, with his account of their motivation.[30] He argues that the reasons were not a deeply set ideology of eliminationist anti-Semitism but the result of shorter term considerations. He suggests—supported by research from Ian Kershaw, Otto Dov Kulka, and David Bankier—that anti-Semitism in pre-war Germany was much more differentiated than Goldhagen argues. Browning cites evidence that the number of 'non-shooters' was as high as 20 per cent

[28] Yehuda Bauer, *Rethinking the Holocaust* (London: Yale University Press, 2001), 19.

[29] Christopher Browning, 'Ordinary Germans or Ordinary Men? A Reply to the Critics', and Daniel Jonah Goldhagen, 'Ordinary Men or Ordinary Germans?', both in Michael Berenbaum and Abraham J. Peck (eds.), *The Holocaust and History* (Bloomington: Indiana University Press, 1998), 252–65 and 301–7. See also: Goldhagen *et al. 'Willing Executioners'/'Ordinary Men' Debate.*

[30] Goldhagen *et al., 'Willing Executioners'/'Ordinary Men' Debate,* 21.

(or even 23 per cent), illustrating that not all the Germans were 'elimin-ationist'.[31] John Weiss, too, suggests that the picture was much more differentiated, stressing the differences between elites and masses, lib-erals and conservatives, and different shades of racial politics.[32] However, where Browning finds the 'opting out' of killing or deporta-tion by people significant, Goldhagen argues that the conditions that created the possibility of 'opting out' are the issue: where Goldhagen sees silence as evidence of a lack of pity and sympathy, others like Browning see it as an indifference to Jewish fate and a realistic fear of the power of the dictatorship. The German population was more linked by beliefs about German racial superiority and anti-communism than an overall anti-Semitism (OM 202), although these are not neces-sarily contradictory: pace Adorno and Horkheimer, racial superiority shows itself in anti-Semitism. Browning's account of the Starachowice work camp illustrates a range of German behaviours, which (to be sure) include the sadistically cruel and the corruptible, but illustrate differences that under a single mindset would be impossible. He cites evidence that Germans killed other nationalities (Poles, Greeks, Italians) and mentally and physically handicapped Germans with as much fervour, showing that the eliminationist anti-Semitism is not a prerequisite for mass murder (OM 203). And he also discusses the case of the Luxembourgers assigned to Reserve Police Battalion 101, who, it seems, 'did not behave differently from their German Comrades', which reveals that the motivational factors were not the result of a long-term mindset—Luxembourg had no eliminationist anti-Semitism—but rather stemmed from the shorter term situation.[33] Moreover, and despite his discomfort with such comparisons, Browning points out that many other events of mass murder during and after the Second World War involve terrible cruelty.[34] Browning also offers a more nuanced approach to reading perpetrators' testi-mony: where Goldhagen excludes it all—or claims to—Browning is prepared to make judgements about what to accept or deny. Overall, then, Browning considers that Goldhagen's account is too monolithic and narrowly focused to account for the events. Browning suggests

---

[31] Goldhagen et al., 'Willing Executioners/Ordinary Men' Debate, 24. Browning, Nazi Policy, 167.

[32] John Weiss, 'Daniel Jonah Goldhagen's Hitler's Willing Executioners: An Historian's View', Journal of Genocide Research, 1/2 (1999), 257–72.

[33] Browning, 'Ordinary Germans', 252–65, 263.

[34] Goldhagen et al., 'Willing Executioners/Ordinary Men' Debate, 32.

Goldhagen takes a 'keyhole' approach to history, viewing 'events through a single narrow vantage point that blocks out context and perspective'.[35]

But Browning's objections to Goldhagen are not just historical: that is, they do not just rely on debates on matters of fact or even interpretation. They lie much deeper, not only in methodology but in their different approaches to the task of doing history and their philosophical world view. A simple example of this lies in the significance of brutality. For Browning, Goldhagen suggests, the brutality was part of a 'utilitarian response of sorts to objective difficulties' and not a form of acceptable sadism.[36] However, for Goldhagen, the brutality is wanton and sadistic precisely because it reflects an eliminationist mindset. How could this sort of difference be resolved? Michael Mann makes an interesting attempt, by looking over the biographies of 1,500 perpetrators: despite his findings, this misses the point.[37] This sort of difference is not one that can be resolved by historical methods: for example, how would one decide what sort of brutality was 'enough' and what sort 'excessive'? This issue lies in the explanation, not the number of bruises, broken bones, and deaths. This sort of difference of interpretation comes from the 'world view'—the approach to issues such as ethics, the nature of the human, the nature of the passage of time, and so on—that the historian takes into the work. And, in order to resolve these sorts of debates, historians have to share the same sorts of beliefs about these very fundamental issues: Goldhagen and Browning do not, so no amount of 'factual evidence' will resolve their dispute. Moreover, they do not share these deep beliefs precisely because of their non-historical ideas about what the Holocaust reveals. As Omer Bartov writes, these debates are 'clearly concerned just as much with the abstract as well as the concrete implications of genocide for our understanding of human nature'.[38]

Christopher Browning rarely make his philosophy of history explicit: in this, as in much else, he is in the broad tradition of Western historiography. His aim is to reconstruct and describe the events, and by means of this reconstruction explain what happened. Most of his work, its focus and remit, is inspired by Raul Hilberg's *The*

---

[35] Ibid. 28.   [36] Goldhagen, 'Ordinary Men', 303.

[37] Michael Mann, 'Were the Perpetrators of Genocide "Ordinary Men" or "Real Nazis"? Results from Fifteen-Hundred Biographies', *Holocaust and Genocide Studies,* 14/3 (2000), 331–66.

[38] Eley (ed.), *The 'Goldhagen Effect'*, 78.

Destruction of the European Jews, a book Browning describes rightly as 'incomparable'.[39] Like Hilberg, whose work predates it, Browning avoids or moves beyond the 'functionalist/intentionalist' debate and concentrates on the 'machinery of destruction', the individuals and small groups that played a part in leading to the Final Solution (the role of German Foreign Office, for example) or enacted it (*Fateful Months*, *Ordinary Men*). Typically, he offers patient and detailed accounts: from survivor testimony of the Starachowice work camp, for example, or his famous and anthologized account of the 'moral Rubicon' for Reserve Police Batallion 101 at Józefów.[40] It is unusual to find Browning making larger claims or sweeping statements. Even in his disagreements with Goldhagen, he refers back to his versions of events and to the archives he has examined, rather than offer a more abstract response.

However, apart from the Western tradition of historiography in general—with its concomitant type of claim to truth—and the methodology of Raul Hilberg in particular, there are at least two other influences on Browning's writing and understanding of the past. The first is best summarized in his reading of Primo Levi's essay, 'The Grey Zone'. As I have suggested, for Browning, this essay is a warning about quick and explicit judgement, and about the ease with which historians deal with the past. When he does reflect on his historiography, he is at pains to point out that, not only is there 'no clean distinction between "facts" and "interpretations" ', but also the difficulty of the whole process of researching or writing history.[41] This is also made manifest in his circumspect style: when, for example, he describes the SS man Muhsfeld as 'deservedly hanged' (*OM* 187), the reader starts at 'deservedly', as this explicit judgement—even if it is one that supports a court—is a surprise.

---

[39] Christopher Browning, *The Path to Genocide* (Cambridge: Cambridge University Press, 1992), 125.

[40] The Starachowice work camp is discussed in Browning, *Nazi Policy*. The action at Józefów is discussed, in slightly different terms, in *Path to Genocide* and in *Ordinary Men*. It also appears in *Lesson and Legacies: The Meaning of the Holocaust in a Changing World* (Chicago: Northwestern University Press, 1991) and in Lawrence Langer (ed.), *Art from the Ashes* (Oxford: Oxford University Press, 1995). That it appears so often illustrates its canonical status, its rhetorical strength, and its centrality as a moment of epiphany in Browning's work.

[41] Christopher Browning, 'German Memory: Judicial Interrogation, and Historical Reconstruction: Writing Perpetrator History from Postwar Testimony', in Friedländer (ed.), *Probing the Limits*, 22–36, 29.

Even closer to the surface lies a second influence on his work: the influence of Stanley Milgram's experiments on obedience and the world view these entail. Goldhagen dismisses these: unlike Browning, his explanation of the Holocaust is not 'generated . . . in a laboratory' (*OM* 24). Yet, for Zygmunt Bauman, discussing Milgram, the 'most frightening news brought about by the Holocaust and by what we learned of its perpetrators was not the likelihood that "this" could be done to us, but the idea that we could do it'.[42] Browning writes that on reading *Hitler's Willing Executioners*, '[N]ot once as I read the 600 pages did it ever occur to me to ask the question of the perpetrators: "What would I have done in their place?" '.[43] This remark highlights the central feature of Browning's philosophy of history: its ahistorical Enlightenment humanism, most explicitly understood through his reliance on Milgram's work.

Browning asks, with a strikingly odd temporal inversion: '[W]as the massacre at Józefów a kind of radical Milgram experiment that took place in a Polish forest with real killers and victims rather than in a social psychology laboratory with naïve subject and actor/victims?' (*OM* 174). Milgram's 'obedience to authority' experiments and the claims they make to explain why a 'person who, with inner conviction, loathes stealing, killing and assault may find himself performing these acts with relative ease when commanded by authority' are well known.[44] The subjects, thinking they were taking part in an experiment on memory, urged on by a white-coated authority figure—the 'experimenter'— gave what they took to be electric shocks to an actor pretending to be 'learner' until, in the majority of cases and despite appeals to stop, the learner appeared to suffer a great deal. However, despite the title, the experiments are not about obedience *per se*: they are more about the clash between conflicting obediences. Milgram's aim was to find out why and how people follow orders to do things they would normally think of as being immoral, why one 'obedience' trumps another. They might as well be described as experiments about the power of science over morality.

Milgram explored this, like the psychologists Bettleheim and Frankl and in parallel to Adorno's work on the authoritarian personality,

---

[42] Zygmunt Bauman, *Modernity and the Holocaust* (New York: Cornell University Press, 1991), 152.

[43] Goldhagen *et al.*, '*Willing Executioners/Ordinary Men*' *Debate*, 30.

[44] Stanley Milgram, *Obedience to Authority: An Experimental View* (New York: Harper Row, 1974), p. ix. This will be abbreviated in the text as *OA*.

because he was trying to respond to the Holocaust with 'post-Holocaust psychology'. The first paragraph of his first chapter states that obedience 'is of particular relevance to our time. It has been reliably established that from 1933 to 1945 millions of innocent people were slaughtered on command.' He continues: the 'Nazi extermination of the European Jews is the most extreme instance of abhorrent immoral acts carried out by thousands of people in the name of obedience . . . obedience to authority, long praised as a virtue, takes on a new aspect when it serves a malevolent cause' (*OA* 1–2). Throughout, the Holocaust serves as Milgram's point of comparison and he refers to it often. He argues that he is uncovering something fundamental about human beings and about Nazi Germany as, 'while there are enormous differences of circumstances and scope [between the laboratory experiments and the activities of the genocidal perpetrators], a common psychological process is centrally involved in both' (*OA* 175).

Milgram constructed a model that explained obedience based on 'antecedent conditions of obedience' and 'immediate antecedents of obedience'. The former included family upbringing (he points out that the parental command 'don't hit other children' implies 'obey my command not to hit other children'), institutional setting, assumptions of hierarchy, and reward incentives. The latter included the reception and trust of authority (the 'scientist in the white coat'), entry into the system, following the lead, and an overarching ideology that led to willing obedience. In the case of Milgram's experiments, this was the ideology or 'mystique' of science 'and its acceptance as a legitimate social enterprise' (*OA* 143): nobody cries out ' "I have never heard of science. What do you mean by this?" ' (*OA* 142).[45] The ideological justification is 'vital for obtaining the willing obedience for it permits the person to see his behaviour as serving a desirable end' (*OA* p. ix): here, scientific progress. Milgram writes that an 'authority system, then, consists of a minimum of two persons sharing the expectation that one of them has the right to prescribe behaviour for the other' (*OA* 142–3). These factors led to what Milgram called the 'agentic state', in which the person 'becomes something different from his former self, with new prop-

---

[45] For a discussion of this from the point of view of teaching the Holocaust, see Ann Saltzmann, 'The Role of Obedience Experiments in Holocaust Studies: The Case for Renewed Visibility', in Thomas Bloss (ed.), *Obedience to Authority: Current Perspectives on the Milgram Paradigm* (London: Lawrence Erlbaum Assoc., 2000), 125–43.

erties not easily traced to his usual personality', and in this state all the activities carried out by the subject, including the 'punishment', are 'pervaded by his relationship to the experimenter' (*OA* 143) (that is, the authority figure). The subject becomes 'tuned' to the wishes of the authority figure and begins to regard everything else, including the 'learner', as 'an unpleasant obstacle interfering with the attainment of a satisfying relationship with the experimenter' (*OA* 144) and also comes to accept the 'experimenter's' definitions of the situation. Most seriously, the subject experiences a loss of responsibility as his moral framework comes to depend 'on how adequately he has performed the actions called for by authority' (*OA* 146). Milgram writes that language 'provides numerous terms to pinpoint this type of morality: loyalty, duty, discipline . . . which refer not to the goodness of the person per se but to the adequacy with which a subordinate fulfils his obligations to authority' (*OA* 146). Once a person has entered the 'agentic state', he or she is bound into it. Milgram argues this happens because of 'situational obligations', social forces that maintain the situation and the sequential nature of the action: the

recurrent nature of the action demanded of the subject itself creates binding forces. As the subject delivers more and more painful shocks, he must seek to justify to himself what he has done; one form of justification is to go to the end. For if he breaks off, he must say to himself 'Everything I have done to this point is bad, and I now acknowledge it by breaking off'. (*OA* 149)

Overall, Milgram stresses both the immediate 'situational' factors and the longer term factors within which the obedience to authority occurs.

It is clear how this maps onto Browning's work, at least in the case of Police Battalion 101. The 'antecedent conditions of obedience' are made up of the 'institutional setting'—the police, with its hierarchy and the opportunities for advancement and promotion. The 'immediate antecedents of obedience' are the brutalization of war, especially 'race war', the division of duties, the isolation of the unit in occupied Poland and indoctrination. Conformity to the group, about which Milgram writes little, also played a role (but conformity too is part of a Nazi ideology, stressing in this context manly and collective, *volkish* virtues). The indoctrination by an overarching ideology led to a willing obedience and the 'ordinary men' of Batallion 101 crossed a 'moral Rubicon', entered an 'agentic state' and became killers feeling devoid of personal responsibility (thus the 'anonymous passive' tense discussed above) and generally unable or unwilling to condemn themselves by ceasing.[46] Browning writes that increasingly 'numb and brutalised, they felt more pity for themselves because of the "unpleasant" work they had been assigned than they did for their dehumanised victims. For the most part, they did not think what they were doing was wrong or immoral, because the killing was sanctioned by legitimate authority' (*OM* 215–16).

Even more significant than this explanatory methodology, however, are the ideas underlying both Milgram and Browning that make this sort of explanation possible. For Milgram, to even think that he could learn something about obedience in a laboratory, he must presuppose a universal model of the human psyche, which is stable across time and across culture: that all people are basically similar. For example, discussing the role of the ideology of science, he writes 'if the experiment were carried out in a culture very different from our own—say, among Trobrianders—it would be necessary to find the functional equivalent of science in order to obtain psychologically comparable results' (*OA* 142). This implies that there is, or could be, something 'in the brain' that would be 'comparable' to Western science. The laboratory, too, is not an alien environment, but 'carries to an extreme and very logical conclusion certain trends inherent in the ordinary functioning of the world' (*OA* p. xii). Milgram writes that the 'behaviour revealed in the experiments reported here is normal human behaviour but revealed under conditions that show with particular clarity the danger to human survival inherent in our make up' (*OA* 188). The point of his experiments is to show how deeply ingrained obedience to authority is, and how dangerous it can be in every circumstance, throughout human history. While the Holocaust was 'a unique historical development that will never again be precisely replicated . . . . the essence of obedience, as a psychological process, can be captured by studying the simple situation in which a man is told by a legitimate authority to act against a third individual' (*OA* 177). This is why Milgram ends his book with an epilogue discussing American war atrocities in Vietnam, and comparing them—explicitly in terms of processes of obedience—to the behaviour of the perpetrators in Nazi Germany. For Milgram, because of obedience to authority, anybody could be a perpetrator of the most appalling atrocities. Milgram, as a psychologist, believed in a timeless and universal basic human being: his response to the Holocaust was to

---

[46] There were exceptions to this, of course: Browning discusses Lieutenant Buchmann, who 'opts out' of Jewish actions (*OM* 103).

argue, through his experiments, that there was a timeless and universal capability for genocide in this human being.

Browning thinks something analogous to this. Arguing that the Holocaust was a watershed event in human history, Browning also contends that the 'collective behaviour of Reserve Battalion 101 has deeply disturbing implications'.[47] Societies everywhere have racist traditions, are involved in war or the threat of war. People everywhere are taught to be obedient, to seek success and promotion, and are the subject of peer pressure: if 'the men of Reserve Police Battalion 101 could become killers under such circumstances, what group of men cannot?' (*OM* 189). For Browning, the conditions of the genocide might have been unique, but the processes that transform men into killers are not: this is why *Ordinary Men* has references to My Lai and the Vietnamese War, to the War in the Pacific, and to the Korean War. Indeed, in his specific responses to Goldhagen, he writes that the

ubiquitous cruelty that accompanies mass murder points . . . to the need for adding a wider perspective . . . if ordinary Serbs, Croats, Hutus, Turks, Cambodians, and Chinese can be the perpetrators of mass murder and genocide, implemented with terribly cruelty, then we do indeed need to look at the universal aspects of human nature that transcend the cognition and culture of ordinary Germans.[48]

Omer Bartov makes some very telling criticisms of Milgram. By looking at a number of his subjects and the accounts of their behaviour in detail, Bartov argues that Milgram's views on race, class, and gender (standard, for his time) were imported clearly into his experiment and conclusions about obedience and resistance to authority: 'this objective scientist brings to the experiment a baggage of preconceived notions and ideas that belie his assertion that all people are fundamentally the same and would act similarly under identical conditions'.[49] Bartov

---

[47] Browning, *Nazi Policy*, 32.

[48] Goldhagen *et al.*, '*Willing Executioners/Ordinary Men*' *Debate*, 32. Philip Dick goes further: 'I felt that this was not necessarily a sole German trait. This deficiency had been exported into the world after World War II and could be picked up by people anywhere, at any time. I wrote *[Do Androids Dream of Electronic] Sheep[?]* right in the middle of the Vietnam War and at that time I was revolutionary enough and existential enough to believe that these android personalities were so lethal, so dangerous to human beings, that it ultimately might become necessary to fight them. The problem in this killing then would be, "Could we not become like androids, in our very efforts to wipe them out?" ' Paul M. Sammon, *Future Noir: The Making of Blade Runner* (London: Orion, 1996), 16–17.

[49] Eley (ed.), *The 'Goldhagen Effect'*, 81.

argues that this means that Milgram's conclusion—that a typical perpetrator was working-class, crude, ill-educated, and unintelligent—
fails to match the facts that a Nazi supporter was generally
middle-class and well-educated. Milgram 'got his history wrong . . . the
results of the experiment could not possibly conform to the reality in
Nazi Germany'.[50] But the significance of Bartov's argument goes
further than he takes it. Milgram takes as read, and Browning accepts
and uses, a model of the human that is, in large part, timeless and universal. This is why Browning argues that it 'is precisely because the
experiments were kept *ahistorical* that the insights from them have
validity, and that scholars now know that deference to authority and
role adaptation are powerful factors shaping human behaviour' (*OM*
219; italics added). He goes on to stress that Milgram and those following his lead both affirm that cultural factors make a difference and
that these have been acknowledged (and so overcome) and (where
possible) screened out (*OM* 257 n. 85). For Browning, we all could be
perpetrators: we have in ourselves the possibility of mass murder: 'I
must recognise that in the same situation I could have been a killer or
an evader—both were human—if I want to understand and explain the
behaviour of both the best I can' (*OM* p. xx). The question 'What
would I have done in their place?' underlies all of Browning's work
because he presupposes a universal, ahistorical human nature. People
from the past, when it comes to the 'universal aspects of human
nature', are the same as us in the present. This explains his odd chronology when he suggests that the atrocities at Józefów were a 'kind of
radical Milgram experiment'. Because he presupposes a universal and
ahistorical human being, it does not matter which comes first: both the
Holocaust and the experiments will reveal the same thing, the inbuilt
capacity for mass murder. In this sense, Browning is not a historian
who believes that the past can affect what it is to be human.

CONCLUSION

It sometimes seemed as if the key issue in the debate between
Goldhagen and Browning was what percentage of the Police
Battalion's complement were 'non-shooters'. Goldhagen suggests 10
per cent or less (*HWE* 553 n. 68). Browning argues for between 10 per

---

[50] Eley (ed.), *The 'Goldhagen Effect'*, 87.

cent and roughly 20 per cent.[51] This 'historical datum' is clearly hard to define and to make absolute. The evidence is tendentious. What hangs on this, for Browning at least, is how complete the wish to annihilate the Jews face to face was among German perpetrators. However, establishing this sort of datum, even if there were unquestionable protocols and procedures, would not resolve the issues between Goldhagen and Browning, as their debate is not about dates or numbers, nor even about the interpretation of dates and numbers. In fact it is based upon very different ideas of what it is to be a human being.

Browning's idea—as can be seen from his reliance on Milgram and on his constant (moral, not historical) question 'what would I have done in their place?'—is based on an ahistroical, universal idea of the human, 'stratigraphic' in Geertz's terms, from which situational and sociological factors can be peeled off to discover a general human psychology and biology: human beings 'like us'. Goldhagen offers a 'synthetic' view of the human in which drawing a line between the universal and the particular, between culture and nature, is not only difficult but even to attempt it is 'to falsify the human situation, or at least to misrender it seriously' (*IC* 36). For Goldhagen the human is woven utterly into—and created *by*—their culture. To explain the Holocaust involves understanding this culture then and there, not people 'like us'. Emil Fackenheim writes:

Why did they do it? I once asked Raul Hilberg this core question. He heaved a sigh and said: 'They did it because they wanted to do it'. Of course, Hilberg know very well that this is no answer, because the next question is, Why did they want to do it? And not only that; one doesn't do everything one wants to do. The main point is that somebody decided to do it.[52]

What Goldhagen does is change the emphasis from 'why did they *want to*' (which, like Browning, assumes an invariant they—the same as a 'we') to 'who were *they* that such a wanting makes sense?' or 'what was revealed about *their* cognitive structures, that this could have happened?' (Fackenheim himself actually tends towards this sort of question, if not answer, in discussing the Hitlerian *Weltanschauung* taken up by the German people.)

Browning asks which of the two approaches 'is predicated upon the humanity and individuality of the perpetrators and allows for a moral

[51] Goldhagen *et al.*, 'Willing Executioners/Ordinary Men' Debate, 24; Browning, *Nazi Policy*, 167; *OM* 159.
[52] Fackenheim and Jospe, *Jewish Philosophy*, 195–6.

dimension in the analysis of their choices?' (*OM* 221). On the one hand, if one assumes an Enlightenment model of humanity, constant across time, then clearly Browning is correct. If, however, one assumes that what it is to be human is bound in time and space, then—without compromising agency or morality—one tends towards Goldhagen. Hayden White wrote that every 'historical narrative has as its latent or manifest purpose the desire to moralise the events of which it treats'.[53] If 'moralise' is understood in terms of ethos—in terms of how we see the world and who we are in it—it is clear that both Goldhagen (manifestly) and Browing (latently) offer models of how we should understand the events; they offer ethical systems and views of what it is to be human. That their views differ so completely is a result of this 'moralizing purpose' and cannot be decided by facts or by factual debate. A different world, as it might be, has been revealed to each of them.

Paul Ricoeur offers a useful insight into this sort of distinction. He argues that one general and widely accepted form of doing history is to 'dull the sting of what is at issue, namely, temporal distance'.[54] This involves what he calls, after Collingwood, the 're-enactment' of the past in the present in the mind and the work of the historian. This means, in effect, that the past is seen, and understood, thorugh the mind and schema of the historian and that it becomes the same as the historian. Thus, Browning takes people in the past to be substantially the same as how he takes himself to be. In contrast to this is what Ricoeur calls history 'under the sign of the other': the historian becomes 'the ethnologist of past times'.[55] He writes that this 'strategy of taking one's distance is put in the service of an attempt at mental "decentering" practised by those historians most concerned to repudiate the Western ethnocentrism of traditional history'.[56] For Goldhagen, a way of writing history that is different from the traditional models and draws on anthropology is the best response to the Holocaust.

This explains, then, why they are unable to agree: their differences lie not so much at the level of history, but in their philosophies, principally in their ideas about what constitutes the human, and in their philosophy of history. And these in turn might be seen to lie in their different responses to the Holocaust itself. One response to the Holocaust

---

[53] Hayden White, *The Content of the Form* (Baltimore: Johns Hopkins University Press, 1987), 14.

[54] Paul Ricoeur, *Time and Narrative*, iii, tr. Kathleen McLaughlin and David Pellauer (London: University of Chicago Press, 1988), 144.

[55] Ibid. 148.   [56] Ibid.

is to find the Enlightenment idea of the universal human broken and destroyed: that there is no longer—or never was—Man and Woman, but only men and women in particular times and particular places, and that these categories shift and change. More than this, perhaps, it is the establishment and taking for granted of these categories—understood in terms of race, say, or *volk*—that in fact laid the groundwork for the Holocaust itself. When Adorno writes that 'Auschwitz confirmed the philosopheme of pure identity as death', he can be taken to mean by identity, the identification of a being as human: once that category is established it is possible to find lives super- or subhuman.[57] In contrast, another reaction to the Holocaust would be to consider that the Enlightenment is not over but had not achieved its project, and that 'daring to know' (in Kant's words) would mean not just daring against the state and religious hierarchy but daring to know the depths of the human being, of how we are. This would be the response of Milgram. *Obedience to Authority* is suffused with historical anxiety: the experiments themselves would not have happened in the first place if he had not being trying to respond to, to explain, the Holocaust. They would not have had the urgency had he not been trying to make a point about atrocities in the Vietnam War, which he does in the penultimate pages by drawing an explicit comparison between Vietnam and the Holocaust. The experiments test not obedience but a historically located possibility for atrocity. This is imported to Browning, who repeatedly shows his concern for other genocides and atrocities. It is not that the Enlightenment is finished, but that it continues, and that historical events continue to illuminate and draw attention to aspects of the human.

This metahistorical debate has consequences for historians. First, about the understanding of genocides: Bartov suggests that Browning's version is more threatening as it asserts that 'humanity will always contain within itself the potential to perpetrate mass murder'. In contrast, Goldhagen's version is 'less threatening', since it leaves the Germans pre-1945 in quarantine and so reduces 'what they did or were capable of doing . . . [to] mere historical interest with little relevance for the present'.[58] Perhaps the lesson of *Hitler's Willing Executioners* is not so much about this as about understanding that genocide arises from a

[57] Theodor Adorno, *Negative Dialectics*, tr. E. B. Ashton (London: Routledge, 1973), 362.

[58] Omer Bartov, *Mirrors of Destruction: War, Genocide and Modern Identity* (Oxford: Oxford University Press, 2000), 179.

whole complex culture and that different genocides have arisen at different times in different places. Indeed, perhaps even the term genocide has started to obscure more than clarify. Perhaps there are no axioms for spotting a nascent genocidal situation, as there might be in, say, predicting a super-nova in an observed star. Perhaps predicting or understanding genocide calls for an ethnographical immersion, an understanding of very different worlds.

Second, this metahistorical debate might suggest lines for historical inquiry. While perhaps Goldhagen overstated his case—for him, an 'eliminationist anti-semite' is mostly synonymous with a German—his methodology, stemming from Geertz, seems quite fruitful. Recently, and in no small way following up Hannah Arendt's suggestions in *The Origins of Totalitarianism* where an understanding of ideology is central, historians have been stressing the role of ideology in the Holocaust. John Weiss's celebrated study is called *The Ideology of Death*. The 'motivation was ideological . . . Nazi antisemitism was pure ideology, with a minimal relation to reality' writes Yehuda Bauer.[59] Peter Longerich looks at the 'context and contiuity of Nazi-Anti-Jewish policy' and stresses, for example, how social 'policy became what the Nazis called "volkspflege" ("care of the Nation") . . . in this way racial and anti-Semitic policy penetrated the individual's life style and private sphere and redefined it in a Nazi sense'.[60] The point of his *The Unwritten Order* is not only to stress Hitler's central role, but also to show how this took place in, fostered, and developed an ideological climate of anti-Semitism: it is in this climate that the various Nazi euphemisms ('annihilation', 'extirpation', 'final solution', 'removal', 'resettlement', 'evacuation') are understood to mean the same thing: destruction.

While 'ideology' has been a debated term for a very long time, it is not clearly defined: Terry Eagleton lists sixteen different and sometimes conflicting definitions, for example.[61] However, in a famous passage, Foucault suggests that the

notion of ideology appears to me to be difficult to use for three reasons . . . it is always in virtual opposition to something like the truth . . . it refers, necessarily I believe, to something like a subject . . . Ideology is in a second position in

---

[59] Bauer, *Rethinking the Holocaust*, 266.
[60] Peter Longerich, *Policy of Destruction: Nazi Anti-Jewish Policy and the Genesis of the 'Final Solution'* (Washington, DC: United States Holocaust Research Institute, 1999), 9–10
[61] Terry Eagleton, *Ideology: An Introduction* (London: Verso, 1991), 1–2.

relation to something which must function as the infra-structure or economic or material determinate for it'.[62]

While these historians do clearly mean ideology in this sense, to some extent, as well as in the 'common or garden' sense of a political party's viewpoint, when they ask questions about 'ordinary Germans', or about the 'climate of the times', it seems that they are getting at something similar to Foucault's terms episteme and, later, discourse. What Foucault is trying to explain is how

the epistemological field, the episteme in which knowledge, envisaged apart from all criteria having reference to its rational value or to its objective forms, grounds its positivity and thereby manifests a history which is not that of its growing perfection, but that of its conditions of possibility ... such an enterprise is not so much a history, as an archaeology.'[63]

Foucault is trying to uncover the horizon within which ideology—as well as daily life—exists: the 'ground of thought on which at a particular time some statements—and not others—will count as knowledge'.[64] Though similar this is not the same as a constructed philosophical or political system, not least because it grows up in complex and unpredictable ways. Later—by the time he wrote *The History of Sexuality*—Foucault was happier with the idea of series of discourses: that is, an age does not share one episteme or world view but rather is made up of a series of interlinked and constantly developing discourses, sometimes agreeing, sometimes at odds with each other. But these discourses still underlie the horizon of what is thinkable. Roughly, Foucault is 'trying to show us how every culture lives, thinks, sees, makes love by a set of unconscious guiding assumptions with non-rational determinants'.[65] What might be written, perhaps, after Goldhagen is an archaeology of Nazism: a wider version of Victor Klemperer's *The Language of the Third Reich*.

Finally, this metahistorical debate asks questions of philosophy. Indeed, when Jürgen Habermas spoke at the award of the Blätter für Deutsche und Internationale Politik to Goldhagen in 1997, he

[62] 'Truth and Power: An Interview with Alessandro Fontano and Pasquale Pasquino', in Meaghan Morris and Paul Patton (eds.), *Michael Foucault: Power/Truth/Strategy* (Sydney: Feral Publications, 1979), 29–48, 36.

[63] Michel Foucault, *The Order of Things* (London: Tavistock/Routledge, 2nd edn., 1989), p. xxii.

[64] Diane MacDonnell, *Theories of Discourse* (Oxford: Blackwell, 1986), 87.

[65] Hilary Putnam, *Reason, Truth and History* (Cambridge: Cambridge University Press, 1981), 160.

suggested—perhaps rather quickly—that 'competing interpretative approaches tend to complement rather than contradict one another' (GPH 271) and went on to discuss the philosophical and political ramifications. His speech focused on the effect the Holocaust has on the German polity and on individual Germans today in their 'ethical-political process of self-understanding' (GPH 271) and the search for 'some clarity about the cultural matrix of a burdened inheritance' (GPH 267). It is because of this that Habermas, a 'non historian who has familiarised himself with the range of controversies in the broad field of Nazi research', declares himself 'won over by the clear argumentative strategy' (GPH 271) of Goldhagen's book while expressing doubts about it as a simple historical work.[66] Passing beyond the structuralist/functionalist debate, between those who argue that the 'breakdown of civilisation' was 'a natural event' (GPH 264) and those who 'insist on seeing it as the consequence of the actions of responsible persons—and not just Hitler and his inner circle' (GPH 264), Habermas finds Goldhagen's 'strategy for analysis' (GPH 268) rather than the 'facts' *per se* crucial.[67] Habermas follows a proposal by Klaus

---

[66] Habermas mentions that other historians have 'been helpful in de-dramatizing its reception' (GPH 268), 'serious qualifications are needed' (GPH 270) before one police battalion represents all Germany, the extermination of the Jews was not 'German "national project" ' (GPH 271). Unlike many other critics, he also stresses Goldhagen's provisos and in the end declares that 'it is not for me to offer a professional judgement on these matters' (GPH 271).

[67] But there is an apparent inconsistency in Habermas's argument. He seems to be dividing the events recounted (the 'history') from their retelling (the 'argumentative strategy') and the manner of their retelling (the 'style'). This would seem to imply that the level of historical *accuracy* is irrelevant compared to the *rectitude* or moral sincerity with which Goldhagen narrates these events: indeed, Habermas writes that a 'clear strategy for analysis does not, of course, guarantee the correctness of its results' (GPH 268). Yet, if Goldhagen had simply written a tract condemning Nazis (a novel or a sermon, say, or genuinely a pamphlet) with no claim to historical truth, it seems hard to believe that this would this have had the same weight and created the same level of controversy (novels and plays have, of course, caused controversy before, but perhaps not with this intensity). Moreover, if Goldhagen had been totally inaccurate, then this would have been easy to show: it too would have no claim to historical truth (this is the force of, e.g., Jäckel's criticism about the incorrect assertion that Captain Hoffman was not a member of the SS). If, as Habermas says, Goldhagen 'overextends the credit of his empirical work' (GPH 271), this implies that there is something there to overextend. It is only because the work claims to be historical that its moral elements—the 'urgency, the forcefulness and the moral strength of his presentation'—are deemed to be important. While Habermas implies that the 'strategy' is central and the 'history' peripheral, the book only had an effect because it claimed to be historical. It is the inextricable mixture of the historical presentation and the explicit moral condemnation aimed at individuals—the work as explicit moral history—that gave it the status in the first place and that means that Habermas's attempt to divide the work up into 'strategy' and 'facts' is not convincing. In

Günther, arguing that 'how we decide questions of accountability for crimes depends not only on the facts but on how we view the facts' and it is Goldhagen's way of looking—his moral anthropological history—that adds to the 'search for the proper way' (GPH 271) to come to terms with the Holocaust.

Is there any way to decide between the Browning version and the Goldhagen version, to find a proper way to 'come to terms' with these conflicting approaches and between different models of post-Holocaust humanity? This is a proper aporia: two conflicting understandings that lead to two conflicting approaches to the past, the present, and the future, with no grounds (metaphysical, methodological, evidential) for a rapprochement. Postmodernism—in some senses—would seem to be a way of accepting that this is a genuine aporia, and that there is no way around it: thus, to think both at once. Both interpretations—in Goldhagen's moral rage, in Browning's more traditional humanism—express a belief in ethics. Perhaps thinking both at once is the proper, if difficult, response. The final chapter in this section turns to an area where the question is not so much competing interpretations, but the issue of what counts as historical interpretation and what does not, and what the contrast means.

the case of works of history, 'argumentative strategy' without 'history' is empty; 'history' without 'argumentative strategy' is blind. The concerns, argument, and style are all bound together inextricably. Goldhagen is still a 'reasonable historian'. His book has a meaningful narrative, follows a methodology which in turn relies on a wider philosophy of history, which in turn relies on an implicit or explicit world view. Perhaps his work pushes at the generic convention—the graphic descriptions, the accounts of moral outrage—but there are clear meta-textual references and the argument is not strictly illogical given its premises. Where it escapes strictly adduceable historical proof most clearly, in its assertion of a wide-ranging eliminationist German anti-Semitism from the late 19th century to the Second World War and the deeply rooted effect of this in the cognitive structures of not just the perpetrators but 'most of the rest of their fellow Germans' (HWE 454), it seems hard to see how this could be counter-asserted. For example, citing the numbers of anti-Semitic pamphlets printed or the number and membership of associations cannot absolutely reveal what is taken to be 'common sense'. It is because *Hitler's Willing Executioners* is a history book that it has moral weight, because it was a history book that there was controversy and that there is a 'Goldhagen effect'. This in turn reveals how seriously, and with what respect, history and historians are regarded.

8

The Metahistory of Denial:
The Irving/Lipstadt Libel Case
and Holocaust Denial

Reputable and professional historians do not suppress parts of quotations from documents that go against their own cases but take them into account and if necessary amend their own case accordingly. They do not present as genuine documents those they know to be forged just because these forgeries back up what they are saying. They do not invent ingenious but implausible and utterly unsupported reasons for distrusting genuine documents because these document run counter to their arguments; again, they amend their arguments if this is the case, or abandon them all together. They do not consciously attribute their own conclusion to books and other sources which, in fact, on closer inspection, say the opposite. They do not eagerly seek out the highest figure in a series of statistics, independently of their ability or otherwise, simply because they want for whatever reason to maximise the figure in question . . . They do not knowingly mistranslate sources in foreign languages to make them more serviceable to themselves. They do not wilfully invent words, phrases, quotations, incidents and events for which there is no historical evidence to make their arguments more plausible to the readers. At least, they do not do these things if they wish to retain any kind of reputable status as historians. Irving has done these things from the beginning of his career.[1]

---

[1] Richard Evans, *Lying about Hitler* (London: Basic Books, 2001), 250–1. There is an identical passage on 739–40 of his expert testimony for Davenport Lyons and Mischon de Reya.

INTRODUCTION

Iain Bank's novel *Dead Air,* set in the months following 11 September 2001, is centrally about truth: about truth in the sense I have called existential and ethical, in the sense of truth as correspondence, the relationship between these two, and about the more prosaic fact of lying. One of the central events is an encounter between the allegorically named main character Ken Nott and a Holocaust denier on the set of a talk show.[2] Nott punches the denier before a so-called debate between them begins and this event is filmed and witnessed. Later, hounded by the press and by the police, Nott simply denies the event ever took place. Bank's novel is also about the Zeitgeist of London at that time, and the denier is clearly a version of David Irving who, as a result of a court case, was in the media in the UK and Europe for much of the first part of 2000.[3] This final chapter on metahistory takes the Irving/Lipstadt libel trial as a case study to look at the relationship between history, Holocaust denial, and the postmodern. This is because Holocaust denial is regularly invoked as limit case for or knockdown argument against postmodernism, as if postmodern thinkers were not already engaged with this problem. In fact, Jean-François Lyotard's most developed book, *The Differend* is explicitly about this. Nothing in Lyotard's book contradicts the long passage cited above from the chief expert witness at the Irving/Lipstadt libel case, Richard Evans, who is very opposed to what he takes postmodernism to be: indeed, what Lyotard seeks to do, among other things, is to explain why arguments like Evans's are correct and what the significance of this is for wider debates.

ACCURACY

Concluding his judgment, the Honourable Mr Justice Gray declares that, 'for his own ideological reasons', David Irving 'persistently and deliberately misrepresented and manipulated historical evidence'. He

[2] He is Scottish, and Ken, meaning 'Know' gives his name as 'know not', meaning both ignoramus or, more appropriately here, sceptic. It could also be taken to mean the knots and contradictions that knowing ties us up in.
[3] For a good account, see D. D. Guttenplan, *The Holocaust on Trial* (London: Granta, 2001).

goes on to say that Irving 'is an active Holocaust denier; that he is anti-semitic and racist and that he associates with right wing extremists who promote neo-Nazism' (*Judgement*, 13.167).[4] The trial ran from 11 January until 11 April, with some thrity-two days in court, and the press was full of stories about David Irving and what was known as 'The Irving Trial'. This was an incorrect name. Although trying 'to give the impression he was being sued and was the defendant in the case', David Irving himself had brought libel charges against an American academic, Deborah Lipstadt, who had discussed him in her book *Denying the Holocaust: The Growing Assault on Truth and Memory*.[5] It was Lipstadt and Penguin, her publishers, who were the defendants. Irving argued that Lipstadt had 'vandalised [his] legitimacy as an historian' and ruined his reputation by accusing him of being a Nazi apologist who distorted facts and manipulated documents. For Irving, and for Mr Justice Gray, the accusation that he was a bad historian was the core of the case. In order to come a judgment on this, the court had not only to evaluate Lipstadt's attack on Irving and Holocaust denial but also, in a wider sense, had to examine the role and scope of historians and the works of history they produce.

Many of those who fight the evil and stupidity of Holocaust denial, and many historians in general, find the constellation of ideas loosely described as postmodernism threatening. Some suggest that these sorts of ideas, in fact, lead to Holocaust denial. Some—rightly, and like Emmanuel Levinas and Jacques Derrida—stress the links between much current thought and Martin Heidegger, who was a Nazi. Lipstadt herself, although she acknowledges that postmodernists are not deniers or sympathetic to deniers, argues that

the 'climate' these sort of ideas create is of no less importance than the specific truth they attack . . . It is a climate that fosters deconstructionist history at its worst. No fact, no event, and no aspect of history has any fixed meaning or content. Any truth can be retold. Any fact can be recast. There is no ultimate historical reality . . . Holocaust denial is part of this phenomenon.[6]

---

[4] The *Judgement* refers to that handed down on Tuesday 11 April 2000 by the Hon. Mr. Justice Gray. At the time of writing, it is available at http://www.guardianunlimited.co.uk/irving/ and at http://www.nizkor.org/hweb/ people/i/irving-david/judgment-00-00.html. It is also available as a book, *The Irving Judgement* (London: Penguin, 2000).

[5] Michael Lee, 'A Witness in Court', *Perspective: Journal of the Holocaust Centre*, Beth Shalom, 3/2 (2000), 8–9, 8.

[6] Deborah Lipstadt, *Denying the Holocaust: The Growing Assault on Truth and Memory* (London: Penguin, 1994), 18, 19.

Richard Evans wrote that postmodernist history 'demeans the dead'.[7] He also suggests that

the increase in scope and intensity of the Holocaust deniers activities since the mid-1970s has . . . reflected the postmodern intellectual climate . . . in which scholars have increasingly denied that texts had any fixed meaning, and have argued instead that meaning is supplied by the reader, and in which attacks on the Western rationalist tradition have become fashionable.[8]

Michael Shermer and Alex Grobman argue that postmodernism is a 'seedbed for pseudohistory and Holocaust denial'.[9] As I suggested in Chapter 5, citing Bernard Williams, these positions reflect more a stratified opposition between straw figures: the postmodern sceptic, the empiricist. These accusations are misplaced because postmodernism does not deny this sort of truth: indeed, the questions that postmodernism does ask of history and historians are very strong weapons in the fight against Holocaust denial.

Holocaust denial is the claim that the murder of approximately six million Jews by the Nazis during the Second World War did not happen.[10] Those who study denial attempt to divide them into 'hard' and 'soft' deniers. 'Hard' deniers claim, for example, that the whole genocide is a hoax, concocted after the war. 'Soft' deniers claim, for example, that Jews were imprisoned in camps but died in limited numbers as a result of illness and other wartime deprivations, or that the genocide was not the result of a systematic Nazi policy but the work of extremist Nazi elements, as if the Nazis were not extreme enough. However, these distinctions are rarely fixed, as they would demand too much consistency from the underground world of bigotry and false argument deniers inhabit. Deniers in general find it hard to keep their stories straight and, when challenged, change their approaches, alter their theories, and shift their emphasis. David Irving, for example, changed from a 'soft' denier to a 'hard' denier after reading a totally flawed and denier-motivated report on the gas chambers: the

---

[7] Richard Evans, 'Truth Lost in Vain Views', *Times Higher Education Supplement* (12 September 1997), 18.

[8] Richard Evans, *In Defence of History* (London: Granta, 1997), 241.

[9] Michael Shermer and Alex Grobman, *Denying History* (London: University of California Press, 2002), 27. See also Charles Maier, *The Unmasterable Past* (London: Harvard University Press, 1988), 168–72.

[10] For a more programmatic list of claims, see Pierre Vidal-Naquet and Limar Yagil, *Holocaust Denial in France* (Tel Aviv: Faculty of Humanities, Project for the Study of Anti-Semitism, 1996), 21.

distinguished Holocaust historian Robert Jan Van Pelt dismissed this report during the trial as 'scientific garbage' (see *Judgement*, 7.113–7.117).[11]

However, nearly all the deniers in Europe and North America have a number of attitudes in common. First, they are always anti-Semitic. So much so, in fact, that Holocaust denial can most simply and clearly be understood as a form of anti-Semitism.[12] Second, these deniers almost always support neo-fascist parties or sects. They seem to believe that, if the Holocaust is 'removed' from the equation, if Nazism is acquitted, and if fascism is exonerated of this, then people will be somehow find their ideas and their identifications convincing. Third, European and North American deniers are almost always racist, believing both in racist categories (that is, that people are ontologically defined by a pseudoscientific and ahistorical concept of race) and in the superiority of 'the Aryan race'. Finally, in a way which echoes the Nazis they defend (see Chapter 11), it is very hard to argue with deniers. Like all conspiracy theorists, they always find new ways of explaining away the consensus of historians. For them, denying the Holocaust is not like establishing a historical datum: for these self-selected arch-doubters, the non-existence of the genocide is beyond question.

In the last twenty years or so, deniers have developed new strategies to convey their message. Analysing the history of denial from its roots in pre-war anti-Semitism to the present day, Lipstadt's book, taking its cue from Pierre Vidal-Naquet's *Assassins of Memory*, is particularly acute about these changing strategies. Lipstadt explores in detail several of the different approaches deniers in Europe and the North America have taken. Deniers use tricks to get publicity. One example, not covered by Lipstadt (although she does discuss this particular denier's other approaches), is the denier who claimed that flying saucers were Axis secret weapons. In a telephone conversation with Frank Miele, who was writing a piece on Holocaust denial for *Sceptic* magazine, the denier revealed that this was simply a ruse:

---

11 Van Pelt discusses and easily demolishes some of the changing stories and bizarre theories about the gas chambers at Auschwitz offered by deniers in his short book *The Science of Holocaust Research and the Art of Holocaust Denial* (Waterloo: Department of Geography, University of Waterloo, 1999).

12 Gill Seidel argues this in *The Holocaust Denial: Antisemitism, Racism and the New Right* (Leeds: Beyond the Pale Collective, 1986). Dan Jacobson makes this point, too, in 'The Downfall of David Irving', *Times Literary Supplement* (21 April, 2000), 12–15.

I realised that North Americans were not interested in being educated. They want to be entertained. The book was for fun. With a picture of the Führer on the cover and flying saucers coming out of Antarctica it was a chance to get on radio and TV talk shows. For about 15 minutes of an hour program I'd talk about that esoteric stuff. Then . . . that was my chance to talk about what I wanted to talk about.[13]

The outlandish idea gave him an entry to broadcast his anti-Semitic Holocaust denial on network TV, with the tacit support of network broadcasters who might not give airtime to a more typical, upfront denier.

However, this sort of pretence is minor compared to the real threat Lipstadt analyses. She points out that, in recent years, deniers have tried to make their work look and sound like the work of professional historians engaged in an intellectual debate (this is very different from what she accuses postmodernists of, questioning the ways in which historians construct history). Against people like these, who she considers the main danger, Lipstadt writes that 'above all, it is essential to expose the illusion of reasoned inquiry that conceals their extremist views'.[14] Lipstadt uses two broad 'pincers' to expose this. The first is to point out that the idea of a debate over the existence of the Holocaust is simply a sham. The second is to argue that there is a difference between what historians do and what the 'history' deniers claim they undertake. These two strategies give the book its polemical tone and contentious edge.

On the first page of *Denying the Holocaust*, Lipstadt tells a story that serves as a leitmotif for her whole book.

The producer was incredulous. She found it hard to believe that I was turning down an opportunity to appear on her nationally televised show: 'But you are writing a book on this topic. It will be great publicity'. I repeatedly explained that I would not participate in a debate with a Holocaust denier. The existence of the Holocaust was not a matter of debate . . . I would not appear with them. (To do so would give them a legitimacy and a stature they in no way deserve. . . .) . . . in one last attempt to get me to chance my mind, she asked me a question: 'I certainly don't agree with them, but don't you think our viewers should hear the other side?'.[15]

[13] Frank Miele, 'Giving the Devil his Due: Holocaust Revisionism as a Test Case for Free Speech and the Sceptical Ethic', *Skeptic*, 2/4 (1994), 58–70.

[14] Lipstadt, *Denying the Holocaust*, 28.

[15] Ibid. 1. Ken Nott is typically, more rambunctious: 'I had that classic dilemma thing going where you don't want to give these people a platform, but on the other hand you want to get them in public and grind the grisly fuckers into the dust—and I actually thought I could do it, because I'm a fucking militant liberal, not the wishy-washy sort

The point is that there simply is no debate in any meaningful sense, no 'other side', about the existence of the Holocaust. Reasonable and responsible people do not have this debate, not least because, for the Holocaust, the 'evidence is overwhelming' (*Judgement*, 7.7). As Vidal-Naquet writes, does an astronomer discuss things with an astrologer 'or with a person who claims that the moon is made of green cheese?'.[16] As previous chapters have shown, there are debates about the Holocaust, of course: history is not set in stone.[17] But there is no debate over its existence. Those who assert that there is such a debate, like the Nazi UFOs denier, are doing so to get 'airtime' and make themselves seem more serious. This is why Lipstadt refused to give interviews: talking to them as if they were reasonable people gives credence to deniers. Indeed, perhaps even giving their names, which can easily be googled, spreads their propaganda.

The penultimate chapter of *Denying the Holocaust* is a case study of the 'sham debate' strategy. Entitled 'The Battle for the Campus', it describes how, in the early 1990s, a denier placed advertisements or op-ed pieces denying the Holocaust in a number of US university newspapers. From his point of view, this was a win/win situation. If the pieces went in, his noxious ideas spread and the claim that this was 'the other side' of the story was made, giving credit to this sham debate. If they were refused, the denier would be able to claim that he was being censored and that his constitutional right to free speech was being silenced by sinister 'anti-freedom' elements: an opportunity for more anti-Semitism. In fact, Lipstadt argues that this appeal to the US Constitution is a 'failure to understand the true implications of the First Amendment'.[18] Some papers refused publication: more did not. Some condemned the ads from their editorials. The series of events left Lipstadt pessimistic: students who had read or even heard of the so-called controversy 'may have walked away . . . convinced that there are two sides to this debate: the "revisionists" and the "establishment historians" . . . That is the most frightening aspect of this entire matter'.[19]

---

that would try to understand the bastard or just be appalled—but then I thought, na [*sic*], just give the piece of shit a taste of his own medicine.'

(Banks, *Dead Air* (London: Little, Brown, 2002), 298).

[16] Vidal-Naquet and Yagil, *Holocaust Denial*, 14.

[17] For example, Dan Michman offers useful tables outlining different interpretations of the Holocaust: *Holocaust Historiography: A Jewish Perspective* (London: Valentine Mitchell, 2003), 35, 53–4.

[18] Lipstadt, *Denying the Holocaust*, 207.　　　　　　[19] Ibid. 208.

Significantly, these events coincided with what was called 'the culture wars' on American campuses and in American intellectual life. To sum up a complex series of debates, the culture wars were fought in debates over education that, by extension, were about the whole structure of American society. On one side were more traditional, conservative ideas, described most famously in Allan Bloom's 1987 *The Closing of the American Mind* and echoed by others. On the other was a fissiparous grouping of those with more radical and often leftist ideas about issues such as race, gender, and sexuality. On this side, too, often uneasily, were many postmodern and deconstructive critics and writers. The debates over the mostly meaningless label of 'political correctness' were tied up in this, too. (*Dead Air*'s Ken Nott is, as ever, more outspoken on this: 'Political correctness is what right-wing bigots call what everybody else calls Being polite, or what everybody else calls Not being a right-wing bigot'.[20])

These 'campus deniers' used the culture wars and discussions of 'PC' as a way in. Since the PC position was that the Holocaust had happened, they suggested that to attack this belief was daring, challenging, and radical, just like the risqué US talk show, *Politically Incorrect*, seemed to be. Anti-Semitism and race hatred, 'correctly cast and properly camouflaged' and as part of the conservative anti-PC agenda (not part of any postmodern movement), were trying to claim the pseudo-rebellious kudos of being 'politically incorrect'.[21] Those pilloried for 'being PC' fought these hatreds just as Lipstadt fights them in her book. Peter Novick suggests that Lipstadt saw the success of this denial campaign as 'evidence of the strength of postmodernism and deconstructionism in the universities' and, as a 'front' in the culture war, this was a 'theme picked up by conservative commentators'.[22] In contrast, Novick suggests that the real influences on the student newspaper editors were the much less contentious and contemporary liberal thinkers Thomas Jefferson and John Stuart Mill. The denier trick here was to 'piggy back' in on a real debate. Denial was not and is not a symptom of the intellectual substance of the 'culture wars' or debates over 'PC', despite the fact that the conservative side seemed to think it was. The conservative side also ignored the fact that it might be argued that their more right-wing elements could themselves be seen as seedbed for denial and anti-Semitism. It is important to differentiate, as Lipstadt

[20] Banks, *Dead Air*, 204.   [21] Lipstadt, *Denying the Holocaust*, 208.
[22] Peter Novick, *The Holocaust and Collective Memory: The American Experience* (London: Bloomsbury, 2000), 271.

does, between real debates and sham debates and postmodernism excludes denial as reasonable debate. That said, deniers will use any trick they can to broadcast their views, and presumably enjoy the dissension sown amongst all those people of goodwill opposing them. Posing as conservative historians is one of their strongest tricks.

The false idea of an 'other side of a debate' relies on there seeming to be 'serious people' involved in this debate. This is the second target of Lipstadt's book. Part of the camouflage that deniers use is the appearance of 'reasoned historical inquiry'. One of the most significant examples is 'The Institute of Historical Review' in California. It sounds like a research centre in an established university: it produces a journal, complete with scholarly footnotes and apparatus, holds conferences, and so on. It is, in fact, an organization dedicated to Holocaust denial. David Irving was considered much more significant than this body. He was, as the leading UK Jewish historian David Cesarani pointed out and as the *Guardian* declared, 'the Holocaust deniers' best shot'.[23] Yehuda Bauer described him as 'the mainstay of Holocaust denial in Europe'.[24] Irving began writing in the early 1960s: his books, which were generally published by reputable publishers, cover the events of the Second World War and, in part because he did not talk about Nazi flying saucers, he was seen by many as a serious historian. It was this reputation as a historian that was at the centre of the case. If he was credible as a historian, his findings, however 'controversial', would stand as history to be debated and discussed. If he was not a credible or reasonable historian, his work—and he—would fall.

In 1990, Irving gave a speech to the Institute of Historical Review, called 'Battleship Auschwitz', ending, in the pseudo-heroic rhetoric typical of deniers, with a parody of British and American naval war films: he commanded 'Sink the Auschwitz!'[25] Like the deniers who have had high-profile trials in Canada and Germany, Irving was setting out to encounter his enemies on the seas that suited him best and 'English libel law has notorious draconian features reflecting its origins in the seventeenth–century Court of Star Chamber. It puts the burden on the publisher to prove the truth of his allegations.'[26] English law takes the side of the plaintiff and assumes the libellous allegations to be false

[23] *Guardian* (12 April 2000), 22.

[24] Cited in Guttenplan, *Holocaust on Trial*, 59.

[25] See Van Pelt, *Science of Holocaust Research*, 17.

[26] Lord Lester of Herne Hill, QC, 'Finding a Common Purpose', Observer (23 July 2000), 28.

until substantially justified. Additionally, in contemporary high-profile cases in the UK, judgements had usually gone with the plaintiff. Irving was presumably hoping that a debate in a law court would confirm his standing as a historian and so his 'findings'. By doing this he would validate some of the claims of Holocaust deniers. If it did not, he still had the chance to broadcast his views. This was why he forced a confrontation by suing Lipstadt and Penguin. Penguin was not 'out for Irving's blood', as some suggested, rather distastefully, given the subject matter.[27] Irving wanted to use a court of law as a tool for Holocaust denial. Both Lipstadt and her publishers deserve to be congratulated for standing up to this tactic. Irving lost spectacularly, leaving his reputation in tatters. The court case also serves as an acute case study for the relationship between postmodernism and history.

THE NATURE OF HISTORY

Despite their very great differences, both Irving and Lipstadt share a traditional empiricist view of history, which postmodern metahistorical thought examines. Irving is 'no postmodern prince of our disorder ... If Irving has any critical beliefs, they are far more likely to be in line with his comrade Faurisson's insistence that "every text has only one meaning or it has no meaning at all" '.[28] The discipline of history has a history and is constructed as a particular form of knowledge and approach. Most significantly, because it represents itself as akin to a positivist science, it aims to recreate the past by representing *wie es eigentlich gewesen,* 'what actually happened' (Richard Evans suggests a better translation: 'how it actually was', but the sense remains fairly similar).[29] Second, it demands that the historian must be objective and stand outside his or her location in the world. Third, it demands that the historian follow an empirical method and, passive in the face of the facts, simply marshal the evidence.

The contemporary discussion of this was in no small part started by Hayden White's *Metahistory* and has been well-discussed elsewhere: and I offer only a summary here.[30] The questions put to the more

---

[27] Neal Ascherson discusses (and also dismisses) this view in 'The Battle May Be Over—But the War Goes on', *Observer* (16 April 2000), 19.

[28] Guttenplan, *Holocaust on Trial*, 290.   [29] Evans, *In Defence of History*, 17.

[30] See, *inter alia*, Keith Jenkins, *On 'What is History?'* (London: Routledge, 1995) and Keith Jenkins (ed.), *The Postmodern History Reader* (London: Routledge, 1997); Alun

empiricist history can be placed in three broad categories: questions about epistemology or how we know about the past; questions about who is creating the history; and questions about the nature of language and writing itself. In terms of epistemology, it is clear that no historical account can cover the bulk of the past. Nearly all information is not recorded or is evanescent. Moreover, the past is not an account, but events, responses, and situations that have passed, and it is impossible to judge the accuracy of an account of the past by going back to the events, the way a natural scientist might be able to recreate an experiment: it can only be judged by being compared to other accounts. Further, events happen in one temporality ('forwards') but are learnt about and written about in another. The retrospective nature of history is philosophically significant. David Lowenthal cites an essay from 1964: 'time is foreshortened, details selected and highlighted, action concentrated, relations simplified not to deliberately alter . . . the events but to . . . give them meaning'.[31] History is made up of these events made significant in prose. Of course, not all the historical knowledge a historian has is written down, but the events of the past are always seen, explained, and represented retrospectively. For all these reasons, there is a difference between the past (the events that have now gone, are no longer actually present, however strong our memories of them) and history. History is not the recreation of the past as it actually was but, this transformation: 'history' is the name for a sophisticated and highly developed genre of the narrative told about the past—though certainly, it is very different from, for example, the genre of the historical novel—and works of history are works that stem from this particular genre (though, as with all genres, great works of history can change the genre).[32]

The question of who is writing the history is also significant: there is simply too much of the past to 'simply' recreate it 'as it happened' and historians choose on what to focus. Deep-seated 'extra-historical'

Munslow, *Deconstructing History* (London: Routledge, 1997); F. R. Ankersmit, *Historical Representation* (Stanford, Calif.: Stanford University Press, 2001). For the classic Rankean statement see Geoffrey Elton, *The Practice of History* (London: Fontana, 1969).

[31] David Lowenthal, *The Past is a Different Country* (Cambridge: Cambridge University Press, 1985), 218.

[32] Bernard Williams, e.g., cites the work of Thucydides over Herodotus, as the first historian to write 'non-mythical' history and so invent 'historical time'. Bernard William, *Truth and Truthfulness* (Princeton: Princeton University Press, 2002), 169.

commitments determine much of the basis on which historical work develops. Each historical work evolves from the historian's focus, the historian's methodology or philosophy of history, which is in turn shaped by the historian's ideas, clear or vague, about life and the world: what White calls their 'model of ideological implication'. This is not the same as arguing that 'men write different history from women, white people write different history from black people', and so on. This is not necessarily the case. What is the case is that historians of different nationalities, races, sexes, sexualities, and so on often have different aims and interests that stem from who they are: these different interests will cause them to look at different things in different ways. Predictably, for example, women's history and black history were ignored by mainstream history for much of the twentieth century, as, more or less, white men were interested in the events they took to be centrally important. However, there is nothing in principle to stop a man writing a fascinating and detailed history of women in nineteenth-century America, or a black person writing the history of almost all-white Ireland. Suggesting that the person's identity is the same as their method is a mistake. This is not to say that the location of a historian is not important but it is to say that what is crucial is not, as it were, the historian's genes, but what the historian chooses to focus on, how they choose to do it, and, in turn, what that choice relies on.

Finally, the very nature of language shapes historical work: as Hayden White writes, a historical work is 'a narrative prose discourse that purports to be a model, or icon, of past structures and processes in the interests of explaining what they were by representing them'.[33] This is absolutely not to say that events did not happen or are 'made up' (or made to disappear), but that unlike

the novelist, the historian confronts a veritable chaos of events already constituted, out of which he must choose the elements of the story he would tell. He makes his story by including some events and excluding others, by stressing some and subordinating others. This process . . . is carried out in the interest of constituting a story of a particular kind. That is to say, he 'emplots' his story.[34]

Writing meaningfully about the past is, cannot but be what White calls the 'emplotment' of events of the past. More than just 'emplotted', each history is also constructed as a narrative *for* an audience. Overall, this is to argue that historical works are a genre of writing, and so a genre

[33] Hayden White, *Metahistory* (London: Johns Hopkins University Press, 1973), 2.
[34] Ibid. 6.

of knowledge, and it is this concept of history as genre that was central to the Lipstadt–Irving libel case.

THE RULES OF GENRES

> There are elements of a research paradigm which . . . I (along with the overwhelming majority of historians) find indispensable, including the importance of contextualisation, clarity, objectivity, footnoting and the idea that historiography necessarily involves truth claims based on evidence—or what might be called an irreducible 'aboutness'—not only on the level of directly referential statements about events but on more structural and comprehensive levels such as narration, interpretation and analysis.[35]

Genres of writing and types of knowledge—together as 'research paradigms'—have rules or 'generic conventions'. As I suggested in Chapter 1, this is not a formalism, but is a 'a code of practise constantly under negotiation between texts and their readers, listeners, publishers, academics, and reviewers, which advises them how they are expected to respond to the text'.[36] For the genre of history, the rules are central. The historian Geoffrey Elton, distinctly unpostmodern and pro-Rankean, was aware of this. He argued that the 'conditions of professional competence and integrity' for historical work were only guaranteed by a professional training as a historian.[37] This can be read as arguing that the generic conventions that are central to history are taught implicitly through this arduous professional training, and only once this has taken place—only once the historian knows the rules—is the history any good. Generic conventions or rules are, then, extremely important for history. If 'objectivity' is a myth, these conventions offer the idea of the 'reasonable historian' and a way of understanding what the genre of history is.

Much in UK law depends on assessments of what a 'reasonable person' would expect or think. Exactly what the 'reasonable person' believes is in every case is hard to pin down—only an nearly infinite list would do the concept full justice—but it is part of the reason for trial

---

[35] Dominck LaCapra, *Writing History, Writing Trauma* (London: Johns Hopkins University Press, 2001), 5.

[36] Peter Middleton and Tim Woods, *Literatures of Memory* (Manchester: Manchester University Press, 2000), 7.

[37] Elton, *Practice of History*, 68.

by jury by one's peers. This 'reasonable person' concept plays a crucial part in professional negligence cases. When deciding whether a defendant has met the standard of care in medical negligence cases, UK courts apply the 'Bolam test', named for the *Bolam v Friern Hospital Management Committee* case of 1957: a 'doctor is not guilty of negligence if he has acted in accordance with a practice accepted as proper by a responsible body of medical men skilled in that particular art'. Not all doctors have to agree that the practice in question is the only practice, but only that is it a recognizsed, responsible one. The 'Bolam test', or versions of it, have been accepted outside medical cases in the UK, too: anywhere, in fact, when issues of negligence and the duty of care are issues. Among those who write history, there is the same sort of idea in a more limited spectrum: the idea of a 'reasonable historian'.

The idea of the 'reasonable historian' has two roots. First, it comes from the very nature of historians as a community. Like all communities historians are defined by implicit or explicit adherence to, and construction by, certain conventions or, in this case, genres. Second, the idea of a 'reasonable historian' means that each historian has followed a recognized mode of argument, or at least outlined and defended the way they have chosen to work: thus, 'reasonable' in that they have a reasoned method. Both of these can be seen as ways in which historians define and police the genre of history by a circular definition which relies on generic conventions. A 'reasonable historian' is somebody who writes according to the generic conventions that define history: history is written in the light of the generic conventions that historians, usually implicitly, decide upon. What makes both a 'reasonable historian' and a work generically history is an adherence to the appropriate generic conventions. A 'reasonable historian' is often—and wrongly—thought of as being an 'objective historian': in fact, a reasonable historian is simply a historian who can be reasoned with, even if there could be no final agreement and one who plays the same language game.

This concept of the 'reasonable historian' explains why controversies between historians are rarely about particular facts and are so fierce. A historian seldom attacks another's knowledge of an archive: more often they attack the way they have chosen to approach the past and the writing of history. As I have argued in the previous chapters, controversies are about the way history is done and what is 'reasonable'. Of course, what defines 'reasonable' can change as new ideas and methods sweep across the historical community, just as new genres of writing come into being, or as the community of historians change. But this takes time, happens slowly, and with great debate. Feminist historians had to fight hard, and for a long time, before their different ways of being a 'reasonable historian' became accepted. Despite changes, there are some conventions that have remained fairly stable.

The most significant generic convention for history is the support of argument from evidence. This differentiates history most clearly from fiction. Just as scientists undertake experiments, historians use traces of the past in the present—for example, documents and oral statements—to support their arguments. As Frank Kermode puts it, the genre of history needs 'metatextual announcements, references to sources and authorities, assurance to the credibility of witnesses'.[38] While it is the case that what counts as evidence—the framework in which a piece of material or document is relevant—is also determined, this, too, the framework, is part of the idea of the 'reasonable historian'. People who do not follow the evidence convention—say, by discussing UFOs without evidence—are simply not doing history. But the evidence convention is even stronger: evidence has to be reliable or testable. Basically, when a historian makes 'metatextual reference' by citing a piece of evidence (a letter, say), another historian needs to be able to find it and check it. The trial has an example of this. Studying Himmler's phone log, Irving argued that on 1 December 1941 Himmler telephoned an SS general to tell him that Jews were to 'stay where they are', thus portraying Himmler as saving Jews. Irving read 'Verwaltungsfuhrer der SS haben zu bleiben' (Administrative leaders of the SS have to stay) and took 'haben' for 'Juden' (thus: 'Administrative leaders of the SS. Jews to stay') (*Judgement*, 5.100). He ignored the lack of a full stop and the fact that 'Administrative officers of the SS. Jews to stay' doesn't actually make sense. As the chief defence witness, Richard Evans checked the documents and found Irving's error. Evans argued that it was 'deliberately a perverse misreading', an odd mistake for a man so keen on factual detail to make. Irving now admits that he misread 'haben'. This insistence on 'testability' is a central convention of the genre of history.

Yet, as Hilberg writes, documents 'never stand alone. As fragments they should be interpreted and explained. If they are to become ingredients of a coherent account, they must first be selected, excerpted and ordered.'[39] Thus, another convention linked to this is the use of

[38] Frank Kermode, *The Genesis of Secrecy* (London: Harvard University Press, 1979), 116.

[39] Raul Hilberg, *The Politics of Memory* (Chicago: Ivan R. Dee, 1996), 87.

sources. An example: Irving wanted to claim that Hitler did not know about the extermination of the Jews in Eastern Europe (a typical 'soft' denier claim). In his accounts, he cites a particular passage from Goebbels's diary: the 'Jews must get out of Europe. If need be, we must resort to the most brutal methods.' However, in addition to ignoring an array of other sources and documents, Irving has edited out a great deal of the passage. Crucial, according to Evans, is Irving's omission of Goebbels's description of Hitler as 'the persistent pioneer and spokesman of a radical solution' which, Evans argued, 'must indicate that Hitler was aware what was going on in the extermination camps in the East' (*Judgement*, 5.174, 5.175). The issue here is more complicated because it is obviously impossible for any historian to cite every source completely, and because each historian uses sources in the light of their own methodology and world view. However, relying on the testability of evidence and the idea of the 'reasonable historian', it is possible to see how far the generic conventions have been followed. A 'reasonable historian' does not make unreasonable edits from quotations. Richard Evans' rigorous book, *Lying about Hitler*, is full of these sorts of examples of the ways in which Irving flouted generic conventions, which he summarizes in his impressive list of 'historians do not' cited above. This is basically a list of the conventions Irving failed to follow.

Another part of the evidence convention is the choice over which historians to trust and which not to trust. This in part explains why, as a discipline, history is so conservative. Since the historical record of any given period is so huge and the books and articles written about any period are now also great in number, probably too great for anyone to read in one life time, it happens perforce that certain historians and certain texts emerge as the most trustworthy and the most influential. These are the works that best follow the generic conventions, perhaps: but they are also the works that have the best marketing, are written in the most suitable way, are by more eminent historians, and a host of other contingent factors—overall, factors that apply to other genres.

Style is also part of the genre of history. Traditionally, history is written in the third person in the style favoured by realist novelists. 'The advantages of third person narration', writes Frank Kermode 'is that it is the mode which best produces the illusion of pure reference. But it is an illusion, the effect of a rhetorical device.'[40] That is, the key

---

[40] Kermode, *Genesis of Secrecy*, 117.

feature of this 'realist' style is to give the impression that it is not really a style at all, but a transparent window or reference to the world beyond, in the past or in fiction. Despite this impression, the 'realist style' is one choice from many different styles of writing. An example: Gitta Sereny has written a number of historical books, complete with scholarly apparatus, archival research, and interviews. However, because her books are in the first person and are mostly concerned with what Goldhagen might call 'ideational causes of social action', she is described in Mr Justice Gray's report, and in other places, as a 'journalist' (*Judgement*, 6.104): she uses the wrong style for the generic conventions. Historical writing must also be consistent. Where a novelist, like Norman Mailer in the 'factional' *The Executioner's Song*, can mix evidence with speculation and invented ideas, a work of history must be consistent in the way it follows genre conventions. Where it does not (where more is speculation, for example) this has to be clearly signalled. Simon Schama's *Landscape and Memory* is an example of this: the historical accounts are both framed and interwoven with moments of personal memory and significance, but these are clearly signalled, often by a change in register.

In conclusion, then, being a 'reasonable historian' and producing history means following the rules of the genre: I have discussed a handful of these above. These rules can be followed more or less well. Following these rules does not make texts more or less objective but makes them more or less *historical*, more or less of that genre of knowledge and of writing. Holocaust denial does not obey rules of the genre. Therefore, denial is not part of the genre of history, but another genre, the genre of politics or of 'hate-speech'. What Irving was desperate to do was show that he was a valid historian, that he had followed the generic conventions, and that his conclusions were as a consequence part of 'history'. In fact, he showed that he did not follow the conventions and so his work was simply anti-Semitism and propaganda.

POSTMODERNISM, HISTORY, AND THE LIPSTADT/IRVING TRIAL

The issues are 'postmodern' for two main reasons. First, because they are to do with the fact that history (separate from memory) is not the past objectively reconstructed, but texts constituted by generic rules that claim to represent the past, and so the issue of how these discourses are validated is important. Second, and as a consequence, because it is by thinking about and admitting that historical writing evolves from specific methodologies and indeed from ideas about how the world is, and is not 'objective work', that the link between denial and anti-Semitism, fascism, and racism is made utterly explicit. Other sorts of questions might include discussions of completeness of archival research, the reconciliation of data from different archives, and so on: these extremely important questions are explored in, for example, *Lying about Hitler*. As I suggested earlier, postmodernism has been much criticized because it can seem antithetical to history. But postmodernist writers generally seek to open up the processes by which history is done and the claims made for historical work. If the software that underlies the discipline of history has become infected with a virus, it is no good just pressing the same keys that used to make it work: it has to be explored in detail. If objectivity as an idea for history has broken down, it is no good repeatedly stating that history should be objective: the ideas that underlie history must be re-examined. Even Richard Evans argues that it 'is right and proper that postmodernist theories and critics should force historians to rethink the categories and assumptions by which they work, and to justify the manner in which they pursue their discipline', although perhaps he underestimated the extent of this rethinking.[41]

This argument follows Jean-François Lyotard's work. *The Postmodern Condition* argues that the various modes which used to legitimate or justify knowledge—the meta-narratives—no longer serve this function. This might seem to open up knowledge as a sort of free-for-all, the 'climate' that Lipstadt thinks aids Holocaust denial. Lyotard, like Lipstadt, was well aware of this but, rather than passing over it, and because he thought deeply about the Holocaust, he approached this matter head on in *The Differend: Phrases in Dispute*, which begins with an account of Holocaust denial and aims to repudiate any links between denial and postmodernism. The book draws on the history of philosophy, law, ethics, epistemology, and history and one key part of the argument deals with precisely how, in postmodernity, facts and events in the past can be found to be truly represented.

Lyotard writes that reality ' is not "given" . . . it is the state of the referent (that about which one speaks) which results from the effectuation of establishment procedures defined by a unanimously agreed upon protocol, and from the possibility offered to anyone to recommence

---

[41] Evans, *In Defence of History*, 252.

this effectuation as often as he or she wants'.[42] He spends much of the book working out in detail how to establish reality. He argues that we work in 'phrases': by this he means something like 'language-games', ways of talking and understanding, or, significantly, genres. Each type of phrase has different 'rules' and blind spots. For example, the phrase of naming gives a relationship to other phrases ('Paris' is in 'France', 'Hamlet' is 'Claudius's nephew') but no actual location or solidity. (Where are they both? There was and is no 'actual' Hamlet.) He argues that reality is established only when three sorts of phrases, three sorts of definition, coincide: when reality is 'able to be signified, to be shown and to be named'.[43] With any item, to be signified is to be given a context in which it makes sense; to be shown is literally to be shown it; to be named is to be given a designation and identity that fixes it. To give an example: 'an agricultural implement, here, a spade' (signified, shown, named). Or 'a telephone log entry relevant to the murder of Jews, here is the text, made by Himmler' (signified, shown, named). None of these phrases can validate itself by itself: just being shown an object you really could not identify several times would not help you know what it is. Just being shown the diary entry is not enough: it needs naming, context, and meaning—a framework—to become a 'historical fact'. All this means that, in order to establish the sort of 'historical reality' that Lipstadt wants, it is vitally important to know what sort of phrases or genre are being used. Holocaust deniers, Lyotard argues, do not have a stake in establishing reality, do not 'accept the rules for forming and validating' statements: 'his [*sic*] goal is not to convince. The historian need not convince [a denier] if [the denier] is "playing" another genre of discourse, one in which conviction, or, obtaining a consensus over a defined reality is not at stake. Should the historian persist along this path, he will end up in the position of victim.'[44] Lipstadt was, indeed, the defendant in Irving's charge.

Richard Evans argued, and showed in detail both in his report to the court and in his *Lying about Hitler,* that Irving did not 'play' the genre of history but was an 'ideologue'.[45] Irving failed the generic conventions of history in many ways and the court found the following long list of accusations substantially justified: Irving

---

[42] Jean-François Lyotard, *The Differend: Phrases in Dispute*, tr. Georges Van Den Abbeele (Manchester: Manchester University Press, 1988), 4.
[43] Ibid. 50.   [44] Ibid. 19 (tr. slightly modified).
[45] Evans, *Lying about Hitler*, 251.

distorts accurate historical evidence and information; misstates; misconstrues; misquotes; falsifies statistics; falsely attributes conclusions to reliable sources; manipulates documents; wrongfully quotes from books that directly contradict his arguments in such a manner as completely to distort their authors' objectives and while counting on the ignorance or indolence of the majority of readers not to realise this . . . wears blinkers and skews documents and misrepresents data in order to reach historically untenable conclusions specifically those that exonerate Hitler. (Judgement 2.10)

But more than this, his world view was an unreasonable one. He was judged to be a anti-Semite and a racist: these things prevented him doing 'reasonable history'. This is the significance to the case of the poem, much discussed in the press, that he often sang to his daughter— 'I am a Baby Aryan | Not Jewish or Sectarian | I have no plans to marry an | Ape or Rastafarian' (*Judgement*, 9.6). The details of his history showed that his methodology was wrong, which in turn showed that his world view was and is profoundly flawed.

This means that, counter-intuitively, the point of all the historical testimony was *not* really simply to prove Irving *wrong*: it was to show that most of the time he was not really a historian at all, he was writing a different genre altogether, an anti-Semitic fascist diatribe to which accounts of historical accuracy or inaccuracy do not apply, or do not apply in the same way (I discuss this in Chapter 11). Holocaust denial is not history that is inaccurate: it is no sort of history at all, and simply cannot be discussed as if it were. Williams writes that a 'historical writer who deliberately or recklessly introduces falsehoods is a liar . . . because he is writing in the mode of history, which is now, and has been for a long time, a mode different from fable, a novel, or a patriotic song': here, mode and genre mean the same thing.[46]

This was the position argued by Richard Rampton, defending Lipstadt and Penguin. He began his speech by arguing 'Mr. Irving calls himself an historian. The truth is, however, that he is not an historian at all.' The defence's winning case rested on providing substantial examples of where Irving had failed the genre requirements of history. The judge, too, was aware of the utmost significance of 'genre' too: throughout the judgment, Mr Justice Gray is at pains to point out that a law court is not the 'court of history'. He states that his job is to 'evaluate the criticisms' of Irving's 'conduct as an historian in the light of the available historical evidence':

---

[46] Williams, *Truth and Truthfulness*, 251.

But it is not for me to form, still less to express, a judgement about what happened. That is a task for historians. It is important that those reading this judgement should bear well in mind the distinction between my judicial role in resolving the issues arising between these parties and the role of the historian seeking to provide an accurate narrative of past events.   (*Judgement*, 1.3)

And again,

The question . . . is whether the Defendants have discharged the burden of establishing the substantial truth of their claim that Irving has falsified the historical record . . . the issue with which I am concerned is Irving's treatment of the available evidence. It is no part of my function to attempt to make findings as to what actually happened during the Nazi regime. The distinction may be a fine one but it is important to bear it in mind.   (*Judgement*, 13.3)

The question is whether 'the available evidence, considered in its totality, would convince any objective and reasonable historian' (*Judgement*, 7.5): that is, whether the evidence would be enough to fit the generic conventions. The judgment compares Irving's work to the conventions of history and finds it wanting. Irving was condemned not because of his relation to the past which is, as the judge makes clear, beyond the remit of the courts, but because much of his writing was not history.

Richard Evans writes that, for the trial, the 'distinction between whether the evidence was that the Holocaust had happened, and whether the Holocaust had actually happened in reality, was a real one' but he also argues that the 'distinction proved almost impossible to maintain' and it remains an unresolved tension in his account of the trial.[47] For Evans, a lot hangs on the existence or elision of this distinction. His metahistorical commitments lead him to elide this distinction: history, the discourse about the past, is the past to all intents and purposes. This exemplifies exactly the thrust of White's argument that 'historians have forgotten about this historical reality and mistaken the product of their tropological encodation of the past for the past itself'.[48] Yet, the very reason why Evans is so effective in defending the discourse of history against Irving and, indeed, was able to condemn Irving, lies in the ontological division between the past and the discourse about the past, and about what forms the limits of the 'phrase regimen'—to use Lyotard's words—of history: not whether the Holocaust had happened or not, but how Irving had misused the

---

[47] Evans, *Lying about Hitler*, 37.   [48] Ankersmit, *Historical Representation*, 254.

evidence. Despite himself, and in part because the format of the law court takes him to the edge of the disciplinary area, Evans finds himself practising postmodern history extremely well but from, as it were, the inside, running up against the generic limitations of the discourse not as the result of an abstract schema or theoretical reflection on first principles, but from his (already theory-laden) analysis of the historical record. Evans writes of the need to 'reassert history's primary purpose of explaining and clarifying the past rather than judging it', both legally and morally.[49] Yet the judging, the non-factual, existential ethical part of the historian's work, and the explanation are inextricably interwoven: words describe both facts and values. Both need to be taken into account. Condemning Irving's history because he is an anti-Semite (a moral judgement) and finding anti-Semitism in his historiography, in its aims, misuses, and elisions (a historical one) really are two sides of the same coin and, contra Evans' claims but in line with his practice, cannot be separated.

CONCLUSION

It is the case that that anybody can say more or less anything, and the best training in historical method will not prevent racists and neo-fascists from making their evil claims. However, in Western culture, history is given a great deal of esteem. Whatever the wider reasons for this, the esteem stems, in part, from the respect for the rigorous generic conventions that construct history. It is this esteem that deniers seek for their views and that Irving sought by suing Lipstadt and Penguin. It is this esteem, the credit of being a historian, that Irving was denied. In the light of this trial, and of the discussion of postmodern questions to history, are there hard and fast rules for determining what is history and what is not, what is worthy of trust, and what we should eschew? Christopher Browning asks and answers:

Is there some scientific or positivist methodology that . . . can say here is where bedrock, indisputable fact lies; here is where transparent, politically motivated falsification begins . . . The archetypal cases seem obvious. But if there is a clear cut method to decide the borderline cases, I do not know it . . . the issue of

---

[49] Richard Evans, 'History, Memory and the Law: The Historian as Expert Witness', *History and Theory*, 41 (2002), 326–45, 345.

drawing a border line for an 'invalid' or pseudohistory remains uncomfortably unresolved.[50]

There is not yet, and could not be, an infallible way of deciding what is part of the genre of history and what is not. However, simply asserting that 'history should be objective' without exploring what this means (and discovering, as historians do, that it is impossible) or counting on history to work without understanding the processes by which it works is bad counsel. Deniers, too, claim to be objective. By trying to explore the thinking beneath history, and asking awkward questions, Hayden White and others reveal more about what history is. And the more we know this, the easier and clearer it is to see what is not history, and which arguments are not historical arguments: as Lyotard writes, the 'proof for the reality of gas chambers cannot be adduced if the rules adducing the proof are not respected'.[51] If deniers believed in being reasonable, of course, they would not be fascists or deniers. The lack of indisputable answers does not mean that we can give up maintaining the rules by which these accounts are written and, perhaps more importantly, constantly checking that those rules themselves still work, and, if necessary, renegotiating them. Indeed, this constant renegotiation, Lyotard's 'possibility offered to anyone to recommence this effectuation as often as he or she wants', is how the discipline of history can change.[52]

[50] Christopher Browning, 'German Memory: Judicial Interrogation, and Historical Reconstruction: Writing Perpetrator History from Postwar Testimony', in Saul Friedländer (ed), *Probing the Limits of Representation* (London: Harvard University Press, 1992), 22–36, 33–5.

[51] Lyotard, *The Differend*, 16.   [52] Ibid. 4.

III

The Trace of the Holocaust

9

Inexhaustible Meaning, Inextinguishable Voices: Levinas and the Holocaust

INTRODUCTION

Adorno finds a line in Sartre's *Morts sans sépulture* immensely significant: it

is said by a young resistance fighter who is subjected to torture, who asks whether one should live in a world in which one is beaten until one's bones are smashed. Since it concerns the possibility of the affirmation of life, this question cannot be evaded. And I would think that any thought which is not measured by this standard, which does not assimilate it theoretically, simply pushes aside at the outset that which thought should address—so that it cannot really be called thought at all.[1]

This final section turns to thinking about the Holocaust in specific strands of post-war philosophy which attempt to be measured by this extra-philosophical standard. This is not supposed to suggest that these represent the solution of problems raised elsewhere, but is rather a response to these events in another form, signified by another necessary exceeding of generic rules. The first two chapters of this section trace the often-overlooked significance of the event of the Holocaust for Emmanuel Levinas and Jacques Derrida, and suggests that this provides a very important context in which to read their work and that, as a consequence, work influenced by them is, perhaps without knowing it, responding to the Holocaust. The final two look at ideas about how far the Holocaust can or cannot be understood, and about what we might take the human to be in its aftermath.

[1] Theodor Adorno, *Metaphysics: Concepts and Problems*, ed. Rolf Tiedemann, tr. Edmund Jephcott (Cambridge: Polity, 2000), 111.

Emmanuel Levinas writes that 'for me . . . the Holocaust is an event of still inexhaustible meaning'.[2] This chapter will not only show how Levinas's thought is saturated with the thought of the Holocaust, but also that it is the trace of the Holocaust that gives Levinas's thought its peculiar characteristics, its span of the prophetic and the philosophical, and in turn what makes it so significant for the thinkers and traditions that he influenced. What does it mean to philosophize about something that has 'inexhaustible' meaning or about the 'inextinguishable' voices of the victims?

THE SIGNIFICANCE OF LEVINAS

At the beginning of the twenty-first century, the significance of Levinas's work is becoming widely recognized: as Simon Critchley writes, one 'might speculate about the possibility of writing a history of French philosophy in the twentieth century as a philosophical biography of Emmanuel Levinas . . . indeed, it now looks as if Levinas were the hidden king of twentieth century French philosophy'.[3] Levinas's influence in the constellation of ideas of the late twentieth and early twenty-first century in general is wide-ranging and profound. His work is a major and acknowledged influence on those often described as 'postmodern' thinkers—Derrida, Lyotard, Irigaray, and others—and Levinas's thought certainly underlies much work on ethics in this post-phenomenological tradition. Moreover, and although they can easily become empty rhetoric, Levinas is often invoked in wider discussions of 'otherness'. Even those whose thought has developed from other traditions (for example, Deleuze, Badiou, Putnam) seem to feel a need to engage with his work. Badiou, for example, writes that it is to Levinas that 'we owe, long before current fashions, a kind of ethical radicalism'.[4]

It is also becoming more and more common to understand Levinas's work in relation to the Holocaust. Tina Chanter is not alone when she argues that Levinas 'gave his life, devoted his work, to thinking the Shoah, to a mourning of philosophy: a mourning of what philosophy

---

[2] Emmanuel Levinas, *Alterity and Transcendence*, tr. Michel B. Smith (London: Athlone Press, 1999), 161.

[3] Simon Critchley and Robert Bernasconi (eds.), *The Cambridge Companion to Levinas* (Cambridge: Cambridge University Press, 2002), 1, 5.

[4] Alain Badiou, *Ethics*, tr. Peter Hallward (London: Verso, 2001), 18.

had become in allowing itself to flee the Shoah'.[5] So, to locate Levinas
as central to significant strands in contemporary thought, and to locate
the Holocaust as central for understanding Levinas's work, is to find
the Holocaust at the centre of three generations of thinkers.
'Postmodern philosophy' did not, as Max Silverman suggests, appropriate ' "Auschwitz" for the purpose of challenging Western philosophy' following Adorno.[6] Rather, 'postmodern philosophy' in the
West—in as much as this often unhappily used term designates serious
attempts to think about the contemporary—comes precisely from
thinking about the Holocaust. It is the Holocaust that leads to the 'doublenesses' and aporias characteristic of 'postmodern thought', which
are themselves prefigured in the work of Levinas.

LEVINAS AND THE HOLOCAUST

Emil Fackenheim, one of the most respected thinkers about the
Holocaust, writes of Leo Strauss and of Levinas that both 'are post-
Holocaust in having lived through and beyond the years 1933–1945.
Neither is a Holocaust philosopher whose work is focussed on those
years.'[7] Fackenheim argues that Levinas's philosophical horizons were
formed before the war by Husserl and Heidegger, and so he cannot
reflect adequately on the Holocaust. Indeed, it is striking how rarely
Levinas mentions the Holocaust explicitly in comparison to a number
of post-war thinkers like Fackenheim himself or those from the next
generation like Arthur Cohen and Richard Rubenstein. Even his near-
contemporaries Hannah Arendt and Hans Jonas discuss it more.

The reasons for this seem complex. Perhaps most simply, as one
interviewer puts its, 'Je sais que vous n'aimez pas étendre les détails

---

[5] Tina Chanter, *Time, Death and the Feminine* (Stanford, Calif.: Stanford University
Press, 2001), 221. See also Leonard Grob, e.g., who argues that 'the whole of Levinas's
philosophical and religious corpus . . . implicitly honours the memory of the six million
murdered Jews and others who suffered their own forms of persecution at the hand of
the Nazis', in John Roth (ed.), *Ethics after the Holocaust* (St John, Minn.: Paragon
House, 1999), 43. Richard Bernstein makes a similar point in *Radical Evil* (Cambridge:
Polity, 2002), 167. See also Daniel Epstein, 'Leçon', in Jean Halpérin and Nelly Hasson
(eds.), *Difficile Justice: Dans la trace d' Emmanuel Levinas* (Paris: Albin Michel, 1998),
79–100.

[6] Max Silverman, *Facing Postmodernity: Contemporary French Thought on Culture
and Society* (London: Routledge, 1999), 14.

[7] Emil Fackenheim and Raphael Jospe (eds.), *Jewish Philosophy and the Academy*
(London: Associated University Presses, 1996), 44.

biographiques' ('I know that you don't like to dwell on biographical details').[8] Levinas does not like discussing the Holocaust generally: in 1967, Levinas complained that the 'acuity of the apocalyptic experience lived between 1933 and 1945 is dulled in memory . . . There have been too many novels, too much suffering transformed on paper, too many sociological explanations and too many new worries.'[9] But Levinas's refusal to address the Holocaust directly also echoes the larger historical context of 'Holocaust memory'. In the US, as Peter Novik suggests, the Holocaust played little role in public discourse in the 1940s and 1950s, and although this is complicated not a little by the experience of collaboration, the Vichy republic, by the role of the French Communist Party and other aspects of the French context, this has a parallel in France.[10] Yet—to sketch briefly a history—the late 1950s and early 1960s marked a change in public discourse about the Holocaust. Internationally, the Anne Frank phenomenon and the Eichmann trial in 1961, and in France the resistance to Algerian War as well as a beginning of the process of coming to terms with Vichy led to an environment where the subject was less taboo in public. Both causes and symptoms of this were the reissue and critical praise heaped on Robert Antelme's *L'Espèce humaine* in 1957 and the success of André Schwartz-Bart's *Le Dernier des Justes*, which was published in 1959 and won the Prix Goncourt that year. The Six Day War in 1967 further broke down the barriers against discussing the Holocaust: even Emil Fackenheim, in Canada, wrote that it was not until the Six Day War that he confronted the Holocaust as a philosopher. And, according to Alain Finkielkraut—a disciple of Levinas's—the events of 1968 opened up discussion of the Holocaust in France, too: 'We are all German Jews' they chanted in May 1968 as Daniel Cohn-Bendit was denied permission to return to France.[11] Levinas's work seems to reflect this. Where he does mention the Holocaust explicitly before the late 1960s it is in pieces for the French-Jewish or Catholic-influenced media. For

---

[8] Salomon Malka, *Lire Levinas* (Paris: Les Editions du Cerf, 1984), 103.

[9] Levinas, *Alterity and Transcendence*, 84.

[10] See, on French memory and the Holocaust, Lawrence Kritzman (ed.), *Auschwitz and After: Race, Culture and 'the Jewish Question' in France* (London: Routledge, 1995); Nancy Wood, *Vectors of Memory: Legacies of Trauma in Postwar Europe* (Oxford: Berg, 1999). On Levinas's life, Marie-Anne Lescourret, *Emmanuel Levinas* (Paris: Flammarion, 1994).

[11] Emmanuel Levinas referred to this in Mar. 1969 in 'Judaism and Revolution', in *Nine Talmudic Readings,* tr. Annette Aronowicz (Bloomington: Indiana University Press, 1990), 94–119, 113.

example, 'To Love the Torah More than God', which addresses this issue directly, was first given as a talk on a Jewish-interest radio pro-gramme, *Ecoute Israël*. [12] Moreover, one suspects that the date of this talk, 29 April, 1955—close to the tenth anniversary of end of the war in Europe—is highly significant, especially as the talk focuses on a near-despairing story set during the Warsaw ghetto uprising and not, say, a celebratory story of liberation: a reminder of loss at a time for more generally happy memories, perhaps. [13] During the 1960s, he discusses the genocide of the Jews more often: for example, in his essay 'Space is Not One Dimensional' from 1968 and in his 1969 essay on Claudel, 'Poetry and the Impossible'. [14] In this sense, Levinas's explicit discus-sions of the genocide very much reflect the development of Holocaust memory since the war. It would be possible to trace this, too, in the changing terms he uses when he does name it. He shifts over time from 'Hitlerism' to using the word 'Horrors' to the phrase 'Nazi persecution' to naming 'Hitlerian massacres' (1969) to 'Auschwitz' to writing 'the Final Solution, the Holocaust, the Shoah' (1987)'. [15]

However, just as Levinas continues to shift his terms for philosoph-ical ideas to prevent 'thematization' (the setting hard as concrete of an idea), it seems probable that he declined to comment on the Holocaust directly and at length precisely because, if the meaning of the Holocaust is inexhaustible for Levinas, then to name it, to focus on it as a theme, implies that it could be finished with, exhausted: that thought could grasp it and then move on. Thus, for example, his char-acteristic use of multiple terms, as above, 'the Final Solution, the Holocaust, the Shoah', to stem the desire in philosophical language to offer one set term, to reduce something to one piece of algebra in a

[12] For the publishing history of this short story, see Paul Badde's essay in Zvi Kolitz, *Yosl Rakover Talks to God,* tr. Carol Brown Janeway (London; Jonathan Cape, 1999), 27–77.
[13] Compare: 'Later I would hear speeches and read articles hailing the Allies' triumph over Hitler's Germany. For us, Jews, there was a slight nuance. Yes, Hitler lost the war, but we didn't win it. We mourned too many dead to speak of victory'. Elie Wiesel, *All Rivers Run to the Sea* (London: Harper Collins, 1996), 96.
[14] On Levinas's publications, see Howard Caygill, 'Levinas's Political Judgement: The *Esprit* Articles 1934–1983', *Radical Philosophy,* 104 (2000), 6–15; Lescourret, *Levinas,* 126.
[15] See, for examples, 'Poetry and the Impossible', in *Difficult Freedom,* tr. Seàn Hand (London: Athlone, 1990), 127–32, 132; Emmanuel Levinas, 'Damages Due to Fire' (1975), in *Nine Talmudic Readings,* 178–97, 182: Emmanuel Levinas, 'As if Consenting to Horror', tr. Paula Wissing, *Critical Inquiry,* 15 (Winter 1989), 485–8, 487.

philosophical equation—in general, he often 'appears to proceed, indeed to leap, from one synonym to the next'.[16]

But more than all this, Levinas does not need to mention the Holocaust too often explicitly because it is there all the time in his work. He recognizes this in a very obscure sentence near the end of *Otherwise than Being* when he writes that there is 'no need to refer to an event in which the non-site, by becoming a site, would have exceptionally entered human history' (*OBBE* 184). Levinas wrote, in his autobiographical essay 'Signature', that his life including his intellectual biography 'is dominated by the presentiment and the memory of the Nazi horror', a remark he repeats in 1986 in the interrogative (in despair at it? As a genuine question, like so many in his philosophical writing?) as 'Will my life have been spent between the incessant presentiment of Hitlerism and the Hitlerism that refuses any forgetting?'[17] Indeed, anecdotal evidence (if any were needed) suggests that the Holocaust was always at the forefront of his mind.[18] Texts on, or developing from, Levinas's work have, of course, followed this up. Much attention has been focused on his use of two epigraphs at the beginning of *Otherwise than Being*. One is in French which dedicates the text to the victims of the Holocaust and 'millions on millions of all confessions and all nations, victims of the same hatred of the other man, the same antisemitism'. The other is in Hebrew and names his family members murdered in Lithuania. Attention has been given to his use of an epigram from Paul Celan and indeed, Levinas discusses Celan with approbation. While recognizing the force of the genealogies that

[16] Jacques Derrida, *Adieu to Emmanuel Levinas*, tr. Pascale-Anne Brault and Michael Naas (Stanford, Calif.: Stanford University Press, 1999), 22.

[17] Emmanuel Levinas, 'Signature', in *Difficult Freedom*, 291–5, 291. *Is it Righteous to Be? Interviews with Emmanuel Levinas*, ed. Jill Robbins (Stanford, Calif.: Stanford University Press, 2001), 39. 'Presentiment' is the correct word: Levinas wrote an article on the evils of 'Hitlerism' in 1934, an article he later refuted on the grounds that 'Hitlerism' had no right to be considered as a 'philosophy'.

[18] For example he vowed never to set foot in Germany after the war, and did not, even when given the Karl Jaspers Prize in Heidelberg; his son accepted it in his place. See Critchley and Bernasconi (eds.), *Cambridge Companion to Levinas*, p. xxviii. William Richardson relates Levinas's conversation with him after his thesis defence: in response to his claim that 1943 was a 'prolific year' for Heidegger, Levinas unsmilingly remarks that in '1943, my parents were in one concentration camp and I was in another. It was a very prolific year indeed.' William Richardson, 'The Irresponsible Subject', in Adriann T. Peperzak (ed.), *Ethics as First Philosophy* (London: Routledge, 1995), 123–31, 125. Christopher Browning points out that 75–80% of those murdered in the Holocaust were killed between mid-Mar. 1942 and mid-Feb. 1943 in a 'short, intense wave of mass murder'. *Ordinary Men: Reserve Police Battalion 101 and the Final Solution* (London: Harper Collins, 2nd edn., 1998), p. xv.

trace Levinas's thought through 'a continuous critical dialogue with Heidegger' or through Rosenzweig, or through Judaism, the Hebrew scriptures, and the Talmud, and pointing out that these are 'not incompatible', Richard J. Bernstein argues that 'the primary thrust of Levinas's thought is to be understood as his response to the horror of evil that erupted in the twentieth century'.[19] Howard Caygill reads Levinas's politics and finds that what 'quickly emerged was a thinker who engaged with the question of the political horror of the twentieth century with an intensity and a bleakness unrivalled in philosophical writing . . . Levinas's two major philosophical works . . . are both works of mourning for the victims of National Socialism'.[20] Oona Ajzenstat argues that the 'Holocaust defines the space' in which Levinas philosophizes (after Wiesel, she calls it 'nightspace').[21] While these all shed light on Levinas's thought, it seems to me that they do not get to the sense in which the Holocaust, to use Blanchot's phrase, 'traverses . . . the whole of Levinas' philosophy'.[22]

TRACES OF THE HOLOCAUST IN THE TEXT OF LEVINAS'S WORK

Levinas's work is not, or not only, a reflection on or engagement with the Holocaust from outside it or the lived memory of it. It is not an application of a pre-existing ethical philosophy to the events of the Holocaust. Rather, Levinas's philosophy is one of the cinders of the Holocaust. The central importance of the genocide of European Jews is not only clear in certain essays such as 'Useless Suffering' and 'Transcendence and Evil' or in moments of reflection: the whole effort of the work is a response to the Holocaust. Levinas writes that the cries of the victims of the Holocaust 'are inextinguishable: they echo and re-echo across eternity. What we must do is listen to the thought that they contain.'[23] His work, then, is precisely this listening. Levinas is a phenomenologist and works by offering phenomenological descriptions which, wave by wave, thread by thread, reveal his overarching thesis

[19] Bernstein, *Radical Evil*, 166–7.

[20] Howard Caygill, *Levinas and the Political* (London: Routledge, 2002), 1, 5.

[21] Oona Ajzenstat, *Driven Back to the Text* (Pittsburgh: Duquesne University Press, 2001), 306.

[22] Maurice Blanchot, 'Our Clandestine Companion', in Richard A.Cohen (ed.), *Face to Face with Levinas* (Albany, NY: State University of New York Press, 1986), 41–50, 50.

[23] Emmanuel Levinas, 'Loving the Torah More than God', in Kolitz, *Yosl Rakover Talks to God*, 79–88. The essay is also included in *Difficult Freedom*.

that 'ethics is first philosophy' and the Holocaust is in each moment of analysis, in each word or phrase, in the themes he deals with, and in the overall structure of the work and its aims. That is, the Holocaust is part of—almost, is—Levinas's work at the level of its language, its thought, and its intentions. More, the inextricable interwovenness of this event and its impact not so much on philosophical conclusions but on how philosophy is done is also a key part of Levinas's legacy. The examples below, tracing these traces of the Holocaust, show how deeply and in what detail his work is an act of listening.

'Good Soup' and Bread

In a crucial part of the argument of *Totality and Infinity*, Levinas draws a distinction between himself and Heidegger over the use of things: for Heidegger, things—hammers, pens, food even—is mere equipment that *Dasein* uses. For Levinas, the

bare fact of life is never bare . . . Life is love of life, a relation with contents that are not my being but more dear than my being: thinking, eating, sleeping, reading, working, warming oneself in the sun . . . When reduced to a pure and naked existence, like the existence of the shades Ulysses visits in Hades, life dissolves into a shadow. Life is an existence that does not precede its essence.[24]

We are not first 'here' and then involved with food, warming ourselves, tools, and so on: rather eating and warming are what life consists of. 'Bare life' is not hungry or cold: cold and hunger are what make up 'bare life'. This is not an ontical manifestation of Heideggerian care (*sorge*): Levinas writes 'love of life does not resemble the care for being, reducible to the comprehension of Being, or ontology' not least because the 'love of life is neither a representation of life nor a reflection on life' but the 'gnosis of the sensible', the immediate experience (*TI* 145). Levinas calls this 'Vivre de . . .', 'living from . . .' or 'living on . . .' We live, Levinas says, on ' "good soup" ' (*TI* 110). The inverted commas are significant: 'good soup' is the camp staple and its 'goodness' is important. Discussions of camp soup occur in nearly every testimony about camp life. Here is Antelme on good and bad soup:

'It's great today' Rene says, looking at it with terrible longing. The others do not say anything, Neither do I. After a few spoonfuls I stop for a minute. I peer

---

[24] Emmanuel Levinas, *Totality and Infinity: An Essay on Exteriority*, tr. Alphonso Lingis (London: Kluwer Academic Publishers, 1991), 112. Future references to this will be abbreviated in the text to *TI*.

at it; the level's gone down. I've spooned up the most watery part . . . The thick part now . . . First I scrape up the mashed beans stuck to the sides; the bowl is almost empty . . . Then I attack what's left; the spoon scrapes the bottom, I can feel it. Now the bottom appears; its all that's left to see. There is no more soup.

The guy from the Aisne began scraping the bottom of his bowl, trying to make the thick part come up. He put one spoonful in is mouth, then another and another; he scraped the bottom without getting anything. Then as though at the end of his patience, and with the same enraged, emphatic slowness, he said, 'Shit. It's water'.[25]

Towards the end of his testimony, *Night*, Elie Wiesel becomes a Muselmann, one of the walking near-dead: '[A]fter my father's death, nothing could touch me anymore. . . . I spent my days in a state of total idleness. And I had but one desire—to eat. I no longer thought of my father or of my mother. From time to time I would dream of a drop of soup or an extra ration of soup.'[26] The importance of 'good soup' is one example of how the Holocaust shapes and suffuses Levinas's thought.

Bread, too, plays a role in his work. Robert Bernasconi mentions Levinas's 'hyperbole, as when in *Otherwise than Being*, on at least nine occasions, he uses as his image of giving the taking of bread from out of one's mouth to give to another'.[27] Of course, in the camps, this is not hyperbole, but a stunning ethical act: literally, not hyperbolically, 'giving to the other the bread from one's mouth is being able to give up one's soul for another', to 'give oneself in giving it'.[28] The head of the barracks says to the young Elie Wiesel, who has been feeding his dying father: 'Everyone lives and dies for himself alone. I'll give you a piece of sound advice—don't give your ration of bread and soup to your old father . . . you're killing yourself.'[29] The narrator of Imre Kertész's *Kaddish for a Child Not Born*, in perhaps the only positive if incomprehensible moment in that work, tells of how 'total surprise screamed unabashed from my face' when one inmate, the 'Professor', returns his ration to him, a portion that would have 'doubled the "Professor's"

[25] Robert Antelme, *The Human Condition*, tr. Jefrey Haight and Annie Mahler (Marlboro, Vt.: Marlboro Press, 1992), 62, 93.

[26] Elie Wiesel, *Night*, tr. Stella Rodway (London: Penguin, 1981), 124.

[27] Robert Bernasconi, 'The Ethics of Suspicion', *Research in Phenomenology*, 20 (1990), 3–18, 4. They are in *Otherwise than Being*, 56, 64, 67, 72, 74, 77, 79, 138, 142.

[28] Emmanuel Levinas, *Otherwise than Being: or, Beyond Essence*, tr. Alphonso Lingis (The Hague: Martinus Nijhoff, 1981), 79, 72. Future references to this will be abbreviated in the text to *OBBE*.

[29] Wiesel, *Night*, 122.

chance of survival': ' "Well, what did you expect . . . ?"' snarls the 'Professor'.[30] As these and other accounts make clear, to give up a ration is exactly, literally, and not hyperbolically, to give yourself. Levinas writes of metaphysics, in the first pages of the analysis proper: the 'acute experience of the human in the twentieth century teaches that the thoughts of men are borne by needs which explain society and history . . . hunger and fear can prevail over every human resistance and every freedom' (*TI* 35). He goes on, in a way that is similar to other survivors, but in a more philosophical idiom:

> There is no question of doubting that this human misery, this dominion the things and the wicked exercise over man, this animality. But to be a man is to know that this is so . . . But to know or to be conscious is to have time to avoid and forestall the instant of inhumanity. It is this perpetual postponing of the hour of treason—infinitesimal difference between man and non-man—that implies the disinterestedness of goodness . . . the dimension of metaphysics. (*TI* 35)

Here, surely, is the echo of the many, many testimonies from survivors about the ways in which the Nazis degraded them in the camps. What philosopher other than Levinas would discuss subjectivity in terms of the ' "famished stomach that has no ears", capable of killing for a crust of bread' (*TI* 118): Levi writes that the 'Lager is hunger: we ourselves are hunger, living hunger'.[31]

Rhetoric, Hatred, Persecution

The Holocaust emerges as the subtext in many other analyses. For example, language is central to *Totality and Infinity*: to 'approach the Other in conversation is to welcome his expression . . . The relation with the other, or conversation, is a non-allergic relation, and ethical relation' (*TI* 51) and 'language . . . announces the ethical inviolability of the Other' (*TI* 195). The 'essence of discourse is ethical' (*TI* 216), and language is twinned with justice (*TI* 100). Yet Levinas is very aware of what he names rhetoric, especially as 'pedagogy, demagogy, psycagogy' (*TI* 70). 'Absent from no discourse . . . [it] approaches [the] neighbour with ruse' (*TI* 170). It is a trickery: 'pre-eminently a violence, that is, injustice' (*TI* 70). Clearly—in this discussion of 'propaganda,

---

[30] Imre Kertész, *Kaddish for a Child Not Born*, tr. Christopher C. Wilson and Katharina M. Wilson (Evanston, Ill.: Northwestern University Press, 1997), 33.

[31] Primo Levi, *If This is a Man*, tr. Stuart Woolf (London: Abacus, 1979), 80.

flattery and diplomacy' (*TI* 70)—the war is at the back of his mind. Indeed, it is justice that overcomes rhetoric.

In relation to hatred, too, the Holocaust appears in Levinas's work. Primo Levi, among others, writes of the phenomenon of 'useless violence', the suffering inflected on the victims above and beyond any possible sadism or (corrupted) reason: in the 'Third Reich, the best choice, the choice imposed from above, was the one that entailed the greatest amount of affliction, the greatest amount of waste, of physical and moral suffering'.[32] For some, this paradox—why the Nazis expended such hate and suffering on those they wished to destroy anyway—lies at the heart of the Holocaust. To instrumentalist answers (which tend to suggest something along the lines of 'it made the Jews easier to kill if they had been dehumanized') and to those which seem to overestimate German efficiency, Levinas adds another in a brief analysis of hatred and suffering. He writes that the

supreme ordeal of freedom is not death but suffering. This is known very well in hatred, which seeks to grasp the ungraspable, to humiliate . . . through the suffering of the Other. Hatred does not always desire the death of the Other, or at least it desires the death of the Other only in inflicting this death as a supreme suffering. The one who hate seeks to be the cause of a suffering to which the despised being must be witness. To inflict suffering is not to reduce the Other to the rank of object, but on the contrary to maintain him superbly in his subjectivity. In suffering the subject must know his reification, but in order to do so he must precisely remain a subject. Hatred wills both things. Whence the insatiable character of hatred; it is satisfied precisely when it is not satisfied, since the Other satisfies it only by becoming an object, but can never become object enough, since at the same time as his fall, his lucidity and witness are demanded. In this lies the logical absurdity of hatred.   (*TI* 239)

This analysis of the 'doubleness' of hatred, its 'willing both things'— the objectification and ('superb') subjectification of its victim—seems clearly to be a reflection on Nazi anti-Semitism. Most wars, even those colonial wars which are aimed at the expropriation of land and certainly most European wars, are not fought out of hatred: in 1871 the Prussians did not seek the destruction of all the French, but merely victory. The genocide of the European Jews, with its useless violence, was clearly involved with hatred in the sense Levinas discusses. The correlation of this passage with Levinas's analyses of murder are discussed below.

[32] Primo Levi, *The Drowned and the Saved*, tr. Raymond Rosenthal (London: Abacus, 1988), 96.

Famously, in *Totality and Infinity* and elsewhere, Levinas contrasts Greek thought to a thought of the 'outside' by using Ulysses as a metaphor: to 'the myth of Ulysses returning to Ithaca, we wish to oppose the story of Abraham who leaves his fatherland forever, and forbids his servant to even bring back his son to the point of departure'.[33] Yet, even this metaphor, above and beyond the opposition of the Greek (Heidegger) and the Jew (himself), has a trace of the Holocaust: one of the very earliest Holocaust deniers was the French Paul Rassinier who, from the late 1940s, argued that the tales of atrocities and of the gas chambers were exaggerations, tales told by returning 'Ulysses' figures. His 1961 book, summarizing the argument that he made throughout the 1950s with which Levinas was surely familiar, was called *Le Mensonge d'Ulysse*. Here, preserved as a trace or even a nuance in Levinas's metaphor, is the fact that most of the Jewish deportees simply did not return.[34]

The term 'persecution' is central to Levinas's thought. It and its cognate terms stress the violence and traumatic experience of ethics, and so without directly referring to it seem to bare the traces of the Holocaust. The term 'persecuted' has sometimes been misread in Levinas's work: like so many of Levinas's terms it is an amphibology, but a very powerful one that cuts both ways. When Robert Bernasconi, for example, writes that Levinas has 'developed a philosophy that arises from the non-philosophical experience of being persecuted . . . for the millions on millions of all confessions and all nations that are victims' he is right in one sense—Levinas's work is about this, about the more normal sense of persecution—but does not take into account of the other sense of 'persecution' in Levinas's work.[35] Persecution also means this sense of what cannot be avoided, of the obligation to the other, ethics. Michael Eskin usefully summarizes Levinas's uses of the term: '(1) Ethics as a traditional philosophical discipline (2) ethics as his own philosophical discourse on (3) ethics as my originary relation to the other'.[36] Persecution is a synonym for this third, and most impor-

---

[33] Emmanuel Levinas, 'The Trace of the Other', tr. Alphonso Lingis, in *Deconstruction in Context*, ed. Mark. C. Taylor, 345–59 (348).

[34] On Rassinier, see Pierre Vidal-Naquet, *Assassins of Memory: Essays on the Denial of the Holocaust*, tr. Jefrey Mehlman (New York: Columbia University Press, 1993); Deborah Lipstadt, *Denying the Holocaust: The Growing Assault on Truth and Memory* (London: Penguin, 1994).

[35] Robert Bernasconi, ' "Only the Persecuted . . .": Language of the Oppressor, Language of the Oppressed', in Peperzak (ed.), *Ethics as First Philosophy*, 77–86, 85.

[36] Michael Eskin, *Ethics and Dialogue* (Oxford: Oxford University Press, 2000), 24.

tant sense, for Levinas. Thus, when Levinas writes, in a Talmudic commentary, that to 'be responsible despite oneself is to be persecuted. Only the persecuted must answer for everyone, even for his persecutor' he is using both senses at once.[37] The persecuted is both the (actually) persecuted (the Jews by the perpetrators of the Third Reich) and the self in its originary relation to the other.

Art and War

The Holocaust also shapes Levinas's view of issues that are not central to his philosophy: art, for example. Levinas's suspicion of art is well documented.[38] That said, as Jill Robbins argues, his view on this is not 'stable' and in some of his essays and his writing for a more general audience, his position is more sympathetic, which allows some critics to 'recuperate' his philosophy for the aesthetic.[39] In general, however, Levinas finds art a source of concern, and—Robbins again—it is 'possible to argue that Levinas's rejection of art is to some extent a response to the Holocaust'.[40] In his early work, Levinas writes that, in art, the 'world to be built is replaced by the essential contemplation of the shadow. This is not the disinterestedness of contemplation but of irresponsibility. The poet exiles himself from the city . . . There is something wicked and egoist and cowardly in artistic enjoyment. There are times when one can be ashamed of it, as of feasting during a plague'.[41] The problem with art is twofold. First, art can only '*seem* to put us primordially in contact with an impersonal sublimity' (*TI* 79): music, for example, is not transcendent and to think that a cello is 'complaining or exulting in the depth of sounds' is a 'misleading anthropomorphism or animism'. The 'cello *is* a cello . . . the essence of the cello, a modality of *essence*, is temporalised in the work' (*OBBE* 41). To look for the ethical in art is to look in the wrong place. Secondly, and more

[37] Levinas, *Nine Talmudic Readings*, 114–15.

[38] See my *Ethical Criticism: Reading after Levinas* (Edinburgh: Edinburgh University Press, 1997) and Françoise Armengaud, 'Éthique et esthétique: De l'ombre à l'oblitération', in *L'Herne Emmanuel Levinas*, ed, Catherine Chalier and Miguel Abensour (Paris: Éditions de l'Herne, 1991), 499–508.

[39] Jill Robbins, *Altered Reading* (Chicago: Chicago University Press, 1999), 75. See, for an example of this, Steve McCaffery, *Prior to Meaning: Protosemantics and Poetics* (Evanston, Ill.: Northwestern University Press, 2001). See also Eskin, *Ethics and Dialogue*.

[40] Robbins, *Altered Reading*, 133

[41] Emmanuel Levinas, 'Reality and its Shadow', in *Collected Philosophical Papers*, tr. Alphonso Lingis (Dordrecht: Kluwer Academic Publishers, 1987), 1–13, 12.

significantly, poetic activity, 'where influences arise unbeknownst to us out of this nonetheless conscious activity' (*TI* 203), threatens to envelop the ethical relation and 'beguile it as a rhythm' (*TI* 203). This concept 'rhythm' has already appeared in 'Reality and its Shadow' and, like its cognate terms disapprobation and intoxication, it plays a role throughout Levinas's work.[42] The danger of the 'rhythm' of art is its ability to create participation and one 'of the peculiarities of Levinas's discourse on the aesthetics is his consistent tendency to think poetry together with participation'.[43] But this participation is not only the individual drunken, stoned, poetic delirium of, for example, Rimbaud.[44] It is also the same blinding, mass- or mob-intoxicating, effect of, for example, marching or chanting rhythmically in a carefully designed rally, the rhythm of demagogy or of prescribed operas: Speer described his designs for the Nuremberg rallies as 'dramatics'.[45] It is precisely the aestheticization of the political—in the Nazi sense—that lies behind Levinas's fear of the aesthetic. He writes elsewhere that it is impossible to escape 'fraternity'—the relation to the other—without 'the torsion of a complex, without "alienation" or "fault" ' (*OBBE* 87) and then in a note he writes that this is how the 'strange place of illusion, intoxication, artificial paradises' is to be understood: the 'relaxation in intoxication is a semblance of distance and irresponsibility. It is the suppression of fraternity, or the murder of the brother. The possibility of going off measures the distance between dream and wakefulness' (*OBBE* 192). In a parallel to Adorno, the 'art' of the Third Reich—the 'fusion of politics and art, the production of the political as work of art'—lies behind Levinas's distrust.[46] This also explains his preference for art that breaks or disturbs this 'drunken-ness': fracturing modernist art, like Sosno's sculptures. But better than this, it is the ethical relation in language which 'dispels the charm of rhythm' (*TI* 203). Language is 'rupture and commencement, breaking of rhythm which enraptures and transports the interlocutors—prose' opposed to poetry (*TI* 203). Art—feasting during a plague (and surely Camus's Holocaust and Occupation allegory is here too)—is blinding, illusory, and is opposed to the expression of the other, to language.

---

[42] See also Gary Peters, 'The Rhythm of Alterity: Levinas and Aesthetics', *Radical Philosophy*, 82 (1997), 9–16.

[43] Robbins, *Altered Reading*, 79

[44] Levinas alludes to him several times: e.g. *TI* 33, 156; *OBBE* 118.

[45] Gitta Sereny, *Albert Speer: His Battle with Truth* (London: Picador, 1995), 131.

[46] Philippe Lacoue-Labarthe and Jean-Luc Nancy, 'The Nazi Myth', *Critical Inquiry*, 16 (Winter 1990), 291–312, 303.

The very first page of *Totality and Infinity* discusses war, the 'state of war that suspends morality' (*TI* 21). But war, here and elsewhere when he uses the term, is not only war in Hobbes's sense, nor a reflection of the Second World War or cold war struggles, but also the Holocaust. In one of his Talmudic readings Levinas writes of the 'ultimate source' of war, 'which is Auschwitz'.[47] Indeed, in a typical move, he locates 'Auschwitz' as the 'paradigm of gratuitous human suffering, where evil appears in its diabolical horror'.[48] This is a typical move because Levinas might be described as a deeply metonymical thinker. One term regularly stands for a whole array of things: 'the face' for the whole singularity of a 'human being' and the ethical demand of the other; 'the third' for the whole panoply of politics and society, from which social law arises; anti-Semitism, for those of 'all confession and all nations, victims of the same hatred of the other man' as the epigraph to *Otherwise than Being* has it. Most contentious perhaps is 'Judaism', which in places in Levinas's work stands for the ethical burden of what it is to be obligated, to be human beyond humanism.[49]

Overall Narrative

But it might be possible to go further, if only as a suggestion, at least with Levinas's first major work, *Totality and Infinity*. While one does not have to agree fully with Nietzsche when he writes that 'every great philosophy has been . . . the personal confession of its author and a kind of involuntary and unconscious memoir', nor to state so clearly that Levinas's book is his '*Mediations on First Philosophy* and *Phenomenology of Spirit*', as John Llewelyn does, the book can be seen as having a narrative that is, but is not only, a philosophical tale.[50]

The preface of *Totality and Infinity* is about the relationship between morality, war, and peace, and beyond that 'messianic' peace. The first section is about the relation between the same and the other, about how they 'at the same time maintain themselves in relationship and absolve themselves from this relation, remain absolutely separated' (*TI* 102).

---

[47] Levinas, 'Damages Due to Fire', in *Nine Talmudic Readings*, 182.

[48] Emmanuel Levinas, 'Useless Suffering', in Robert Bernasconi and David Wood (eds.), *The Provocation of Levinas* (London: Routledge, 1988), 156–65, 162.

[49] For a critique of this position, see, Gillian Rose, *The Broken Middle* (Oxford: Blackwell, 1992) and *Judaism and Modernity* (Oxford: Blackwell, 1993).

[50] Friedrich Nietzsche, *Beyond Good and Evil*, tr. R. J. Hollingdale (London: Penguin, 1973), 37. John Llewelyn, *The HypoCritical Imagination* (London: Routledge, 2000), 200.

The second section is about what the individual needs, corporeally, to survive, and the metaphysical ramifications of this. 'We live from "good soup", air, light, spectacles, work, ideas, sleep etc' (*TI* 110), Levinas writes. It is in this section that Levinas discusses the metaphysics of housing and shelter. The third section, often taken to be the central one, is about the recognition of the face, of the 'relation with the Other' which 'alone introduces a dimension of transcendence' (*TI* 193). Here reason and speech re-emerge, through a discussion of murder: both rely on the relation with the Other. Finally, in the last section, Levinas analyses the metaphysical significance of paternity and fecundity, erotic love, the family, and the book ends in a paean to peace. Thus, it is a journey through separation, isolation from society and 'the human', a rediscovery and re-evaluation of these, and finally an evocation of the 'marvel of the family' and peace. This peace must not be simply the 'end of combats, the cease for want of combats, by the defeat of some and the victory of others, that is with cemeteries or future universal empires' (*TI* 306), rather, it 'must be my peace, in a relation that starts from an I and goes to the other' (*TI* 306).

Levinas became a French citizen in 1930 and, not least because of his links to German philosophy, kept more than a wary eye on the European situation during the 1930s. Having done military service and specializing as a translator of German and Russian, Levinas was mobilized at the beginning of the war. In 1940, a year he called a black hole in history, he was captured with the French 10th Army at Rennes and transported to Germany, to a camp in Fallinpostel near Magdeburg. Alone and separated from his family and unit—Jewish military prisoners were kept separately from non-Jewish ones—he later wrote that the captors 'who had dealings with us or gave us work or orders or even a smile . . . stripped us of our human skin. We were subhuman, a gang of apes . . . We were beings entrapped in their species; despite all their vocabulary, beings without language.'[51] Survival was hard in the forestry commando he worked in, death was always close, and prisoners of all sorts—not least in the 10,000 or so camps in the Third Reich—talk about the needs for basic necessities. His wife and daughter were hidden in France by friends, including Maurice Blanchot, and then by St Vincent de Paul nuns. The rest of his family, including his parents, parents-in-law, and brothers Boris and Aminadab, were

---

[51] Emmanuel Levinas, 'The Name of a Dog, of Natural Rights', in *Difficult Freedom*, 151–3, 152–3.

murdered in Kovno. After the war ended, he returned to France and he was reunited with his wife and his daughter. In outline, this could be said to be a journey through separation, isolation even from what it is to be 'human', the rediscovery and re-evaluation of these, and the recovery of what Levinas calls the 'marvel of the family'. In a sense, this is only to show how philosophies and lives might be intertwined.

Aims

This saturation of his thought in the Holocaust extends, of course, to the aims of his work. To reduce his complex work to two questions, *Totality and Infinity* aims to discover whether or not we are duped by morality: the 'whole of this work aims to show a relation with the other not only cutting across the logic of contradiction . . . but also across dialectical logic . . . The welcoming of the face is peaceable from the first, for it answers the unquenchable Desire for Infinity. War itself is but a possibility and nowise a condition for it' (*TI* 150). This is, of course, a very recognizable Levinasian idea: this peace is the passivity that underlies activity and passivity, this peace—the welcoming of the face—underlies both the possibility of contingent war and the possibility of contingent peace. Yet, as I cited above, this peace should not be simply a state of 'not being at war', but 'must be my peace, in a relation that starts from an I and goes to the other in desire and goodness, where the I both maintains itself and exists without egoism' (*TI* 306). Yet, as ever with Levinas, war, 'which is Auschwitz', is never far away from his thoughts, even here in an invocation of (messianic) peace: contingent war is not far away.

Later, at the start of *Otherwise than Being*, he asks the related question: if 'transcendence has meaning, it can only signify the fact that the event of being . . . passes over to what is other than being. But what is Being's other?' (*OBBE* 3). The answer leads to—and through— 'signification, the-one-for-the-other, the relationship with alterity' analysed as 'proximity, proximity as responsibility for the other, and responsibility for the other as substitution' (*OBBE* 184—again, repeating different terms for the same phenomena to avoid 'thematization'). The aim is to find 'for man another kinship than that which ties him to being, one that will perhaps enable us to conceive of this difference between me and the other, this inequality, in a sense absolutely opposed to oppression' (*OBBE* 177). One part of this is what Levinas calls the 'true problem for us Westerners': 'not so much to refuse violence as to question ourselves about a struggle against violence which, without blanching in non-resistance to evil, could avoid the institution of violence called out of this very struggle. Does not war perpetuate that which it is called to make disappear?' (*OBBE* 177). That is, are we able to learn to 'war against war', but in such a way that the 'just war waged against war' should 'tremble or shudder at every instant because of this very justice' (*OBBE* 185)? It is this—not an attempt to 'restore any ruined concept' (*OBBE* 185)—that Levinas is undertaking: and it is this which is, in itself, a response to the Holocaust, the ultimate experience of war. As I will argue below, it is precisely the failure to prove this, as one might prove scientific fact, that is its success.

PHILOSOPHY AND PROPHECY: LEVINAS A PHILOSOPHER OF 'AMBIVALENCE'

The Holocaust saturates Levinas's work. This is clear in, for example, the dense and allusive pages that make up the final section of *Otherwise than Being*. Yet, even there where he argues for both the justification of just war and the shudder against just war, it is not clear what, if any, response this offers to the Holocaust. This is an interesting contrast with, for example, Fackenheim's declaration of a 614th commandment or Arthur Cohen's interpretation of *tremendum*.[52] Recent thinkers on Levinas have drawn out from his work a range of ideas, all of which clearly orbit around the aims I have discussed. For Richard Cohen, Levinas argues that in response to the Holocaust that 'Jews must remain Jews . . . Humans must remain Humans'.[53] For Tina Chanter, his 'response is patience. Endurance. Enduring Time. Duration. The time of patience'.[54] For Tamra Wright, concerned explicitly with Jewish philosophy, his response is that after the Holocaust a commitment to Judaism is centrally ethical, even without God.[55] Josh Cohen, in a carefully and painfully chosen phrase, after Levi from the end of *If*

[52] See Arthur Cohen, *The Tremendum: A Theological Interpretation of the Holocaust* (New York: Crossroad, 1988).

[53] Richard Cohen, *Ethics, Exegesis and Philosophy: Interpretation after Levinas* (Cambridge: Cambridge University Press, 2001), 279.

[54] Tina Chanter, *Time, Death and the Feminine* (Stanford, Calif.: Stanford University Press, 2001), 222.

[55] Tamra Wright, *The Twilight of Jewish Philosophy* (London: Harwood Academic Publishers, 1999), 97–139.

This is a Man, argues that for Levinas the 'measureless task of religion after Auschwitz' is 'perpetual awakening' to 'one degree more'.[56] And Howard Caygill argues that for Levinas, for a certain Levinas, the response to the Holocaust can be seen in the founding of Israel. But there could be further interpretations, stemming from, for example, Levinas's appeal to the intellectuals on the penultimate page of *Otherwise than Being*. Here he argues that the 'modern world is above all an order, or a disorder in which the elites can no longer leave peoples to their customs, their wretchedness and their illusions nor even to their redemptive systems, which, abandoned to theory own logic, are implacably inverted. These elites are sometimes called "intellectuals" ' (*OBBE* 184). This might seem also to be both a message and interpretation which echoes the work by historians: John Weiss argues in his *Ideology of Death* that the 'nazification' of the German elites was central to the Holocaust.

However, Levinas himself rarely gives answers or reaches conclusions, and this is in no small part a symptomatic enactment of the 'point' of his philosophy. Sometimes this seems bizarre: he concludes his 1987 account of Heidegger and the possible evil of *Being and Time* with the banality that evil offers 'food for thought'.[57] But overall, he believes that 'philosophical research . . . does not answer questions like an interview, oracle or wisdom' (*TI* 29). Indeed, his work is full of questions: not, as Robbins suggests, 'mock rhetorical questions' but real questions.[58] These aim to perform the interruption in consciousness that Levinas feels philosophy should be: something that invokes the other and is 'never a wisdom, for the interlocutor whom it has just encompassed has already escaped it' (*TI* 295). Part of the reason for this is that Levinas is a philosopher of two sides, constantly in internal dialogue. Indeed, Levinas is a philosopher of 'doubleness' or uncertainty, and resolutely one: philosophy 'is called upon to conceive ambivalence, to conceive it in several times' (*OBBE* 162). This 'doubleness', this ambivalence which is characteristic of Levinas's work both stems from and is a response to the Holocaust.

It may sound strange to describe a philosopher so connected with the belief that 'ethics is first philosophy' as a 'philosopher of ambivalence', but Levinas's work is full of 'doublenesses'. Derrida's influential essay 'Violence and Metaphysics' explores the contrast between the 'Greek'

---

[56] Josh Cohen, *Interrupting Auschwitz* (London: Continuum, 2003), 105
[57] Levinas, 'As if Consenting to Horror', 488.
[58] Robbins, *Altered Reading*, 138.

and the 'non-Greek' and, for those who see Levinas's thought as translating Hebrew wisdom into Greek, there is a 'doubleness' since
Levinas, at the same time, is also translating Greek wisdom into
Hebrew. [59] He is constantly moving between the religious and the
rational: he writes that he was concerned about joining Judaeo-
Christian Amity of Paris—a group devoted to Jewish–Christian dialogue—not for religious reasons but because he 'feared that adherence
to an association created with a view to bringing Jews and Christians
closer together might express ingratitude towards the lay spirit, which,
by other means, has united so many human groups separated by a vari-
ety of beliefs and philosophies into one republic'.[60] But there are many
more 'doublenesses' on both the small and big scales in his work. It
occurs in Levinas's analysis of the West: an 'essentially hypocritical
civilisation . . . attached to both to the True and to the Good, henceforth antagonistic. It is perhaps time to see in hypocrisy not only a base
contingent defect of man, but the underlying rending of a world
attached to both the philosophers and the prophets' (*TI* 24). This is one
of the ways that Levinas discusses the two forms of truth outlined in
Chapter 5: in this specific context, the 'Greek' truth of reason (truth as
correspondence) and the other, existential ethical truth. In *Otherwise
than Being*, the idea of the amphibology of the saying and the said is
another 'doubleness', as is the very trope of amphibology, a 'sentence
which may be construed in two distinct senses' (*OED*). As Robert
Bernasconi argues, Levinas has an understanding of the face which is
both 'empirical' and a 'transcendental'.[61] The idea of the trace, too, is
a 'doubleness': a trace is both a material sign and that from which the
other 'shines', 'a disturbance imprinting itself'.[62] Levinas's work grows
from both philosophy—his 'analyses claim to be in the spirit of
Husserlian philosophy . . . It remains faithful to intentional analysis'
(*OBBE* 183)—and prophecy. Prophecy is 'in my "here I am" ' (*OBBE*
149) in the bearing 'witness to the Infinite' (*OBBE* 149), which is in both
individual action and—as a performative—the action of Levinas's own
thought.

---

[59] Jacques Derrida, 'Violence and Metaphysics', in *Writing and Difference*, tr. Alan
Bass (London: Routledge & Kegan Paul, 1978), 79–153, 133.

[60] Levinas, *Alterity and Transcendence*, 85.

[61] Robert Bernasconi, 'Rereading *Totality and Infinity*', in A. B. Dallery and
C. E. Scott (eds.), *The Question of the Other* (Albany, NY: State University of New York
Press, 1989), 23–34, 34.

[62] Levinas, 'Meaning and Sense', in *Collected Philosophical Papers*, 75–108, 106.

It is in relation to the Holocaust that this 'doubleness', the split between these two forms of truth, is at its clearest and where the two parts of Levinas's thought are most clearly separate and, at the same time, most yoked together. This is at its starkest in Levinas's discussion of murder in *Totality and Infinity*. This discussion is present to answer the following question, raised not only by everyday, banal experiences of murder but by the Holocaust: if the face is the site of our relation to the other, if the face is what summons us to our responsibilities, how is it that so many have been killed when looking at their killers? Levinas's answer is complex. Murder is not like other forms of destruction which aims only at things: murder is 'total negation' (*TI* 198).

Negation [and we can read 'killing' here] by labour and usage [thinking perhaps of labour camps and ghettos, in which Jews were worked to death], like negation by representation [the stripping of the rights of the Jews under the Reich of both political representation and the ways in which they were 'caricatured' by Nazi propaganda], effect a grasp or a comprehension, rest on an aim or affirmation; they can. To kill is not to dominate but to annihilate; it is to renounce comprehension absolutely. Murder exercises a power over what escapes power. (*TI* 198)

Levinas seems to mean that using populations as slaves is still to use them, to exert power over them: but to murder people is not to dominate them by turning them into machines or faceless salves, but to recognize them as Other, as beyond one's power. He writes that the 'Other is the sole being I can wish to kill' (*TI* 198): it seems to make no real sense to speak of 'murdering' rocks or trees, for example.[63] Moreover, the victim who struggles against murder is, for Levinas, a 'quasi-nothing' easily 'obliterated because the sword or bullet has touched the ventricles or auricles of his heart' (*TI* 199). Once in the economy of force, the victim is bound to lose. But deeper than this, the victim opposes the murderer not with force but with the 'very transcendence of his being' (*TI* 199): this 'infinity, stronger than murder, already resists us in his face, is his face, is the primordial expression, is the first word: "you shall not commit murder" . . . the resistance of what has no resistance—the ethical resistance' (*TI* 199). This resistance, the 'epiphany of the face', grounds the 'possibility of gauging the infinity of the temptation to murder' (*TI*

[63] On the continuation of this point, see Roger Gottlieb, 'Levinas, Feminism, Holocaust, Ecocide', in C. C. Gould and R. S. Cohen (eds.), *Artefacts, Representations and Social Practice* (London: Kluwer Academic Publishers, 1994), 365–76; and David Clark, 'On Being "The Last Kantian in Germany"', in Jennifer Ham and Matthew Senior (eds.), *Animal Acts* (London: Routledge, 1997), 165–98. In the next chapter, too, I suggest Derrida has a wider interpretation of this, too.

199) and it is this that reveals that war 'presupposes peace, the antecedent and non-allergic presence of the Other' (*TI* 199). As Robert Bernasconi puts it, violence 'is not the only response to violence. Already in advance of violence the face of the Other resists it ethically.'[64] Levinas, as ever, is describing two levels: 'the plane of ontology' and 'the ethical plane' (*TI* 201). In the first, which is where choice and action take place, where being is realized, murder happens: the victims, despite any physical resistance, are killed. And yet this level, the plane of activity and passivity or war and peace as only cessation of war, both relies upon and reveals the ethical plane, where the relation to the other is peaceful.

There is something complex going on in this very significant passage. It recognizes the special quality of murder: that murder first presupposes a relationship. You can only want to kill the other if first you are in a relationship with the other and it is this relationship that is the peace that precedes war. That is to say, to murder someone is already to have recognized one's ethical relationship to them, and murder is one choice of action in response to this. Levinas makes similar arguments in his essay on 'Transcendence and Evil', where he writes that 'evil strikes me in my horror of evil, and thus reveals—or is already— my association with the Good. The excess of evil by which it is a surplus in the world is also our impossibility of accepting it. The experience of evil would then be also our waiting on the good—the love of God.'[65] Here, evil leads to or reveals good. And again, in 'Useless Suffering', the evil of suffering leads to the need to envisage it in the 'inter-human perspective . . . meaningful in me, useless in the Other'.[66] This in turn means that suffering is that which uncovers the 'non-indifference of one to the other, in a responsibility of one for another', and underlies the 'recourse that people have to one another for help'.[67] Murder, evil, and suffering illuminate the 'ethical place', the asymmetrical relationship of the self responsible for the Other, and do not prescribe behaviour. This leads Colin Davis to highlight the 'pervasive but often occluded knowledge in Levinas's texts that ethical obligation does not regulate moral choice; I am just as likely to respond to the other with violence as with respect'.[68] Even, for example, the

---

[64] Robert Bernasconi, *Heidegger in Question* (Atlantic Highlands, NJ: Humanities Press, 1993), 73.

[65] Levinas, 'Transcendence and Evil', in *Collected Philosophical Papers*, 175–86, 183.

[66] Levinas, 'Useless Suffering', 164.   [67] Ibid. 165.

[68] Colin Davis, *Ethical Issues in Twentieth Century French Fiction: Killing the Other* (London: Macmillan, 2000), 187.

commandment 'Thou shalt not kill' has another signification, which reflects our general and unavoidable ethical responsibility.[69] It seems very odd to say that murder is an example of the ethical relationship, but this is the 'prophetic' moment in Levinas: here 'Levinas appeals to the Other, and not to thinking . . . to challenge the tyranny of norms and conduct'.[70]

Here, at the discussion of murder, with its cognate discussions, it becomes clear that Levinas is, Cohen writes, 'defending ethics ethically . . . herein lies his importance, his genuine postmodernity'.[71] That is, this analysis of murder, evil, and suffering is where Levinas's work is no longer philosophical, no longer defending ethics philosophically: meaning, no longer amenable to rational argument and to proof. If it were, ethics would not be 'first philosophy' but it would be reason which had the power to prove and ground ethics.[72] One cannot prove logically that Good and peace underlies Evil and war, one can only believe it: this is both the strength and weakness of Levinas's work. Thus, if 'Levinas seems distinctly uneasy when it comes to explaining why we should accept responsibility for the Other rather than loyalty to the self, why we should respect the commandment not to kill rather than defending ourselves with violence', it is because it cannot be explained: it is simply there and his phenomenological analyses foreground this.[73] This is what he means when he says that if 'there is an

[69] It 'does not mean that you are not to go around firing a gun all the time. It refers, rather, to the fact that, in the course of your life, in different ways, you kill someone. For example, when we sit down at the table and drink coffee, we kill an Ethiopian who doesn't have any coffee'. Tamra Wright, Peter Hughes, and Alison Ainley, 'The Paradox of Morality: An Interview with Emmanuel Levinas', tr. Andrew Benjamin and Tamra Wright, in Robert Bernasconi and David Wood (eds.), *The Provocation of Levinas* (London: Routledge, 1988), 168–80, 173.

[70] Bernasconi, *Heidegger in Question*, 73.

[71] Cohen, *Ethics, Exegesis and Philosophy*, 6.

[72] This, too, is the answer to one of Derrida's points on his work in 'Violence and Metaphysics': Derrida suggests that it is not ethics but rather Levinas's method of 'uncovering ethics that is fundamental: the 'meaning of the non-theoretical as such (for example, ethics or the metaphysical in Levinas' sense)' is only made clear by 'theoretical knowledge' (122). Yet a simple answer is to say that the 'meaning' of the original relation is made clear in any number of technical or common-or-garden discourses and activities: Levinas is simply trying to describe it here in philosophical—phenomenological—language.

[73] Davis, *Ethical Issues*, 186. On the issue of justification, see Robert Bernasconi, 'The Truth That Accuses', in Gary B, Madison and Marty Fairbairn (eds), *The Ethics of Postmodernity* (Evanston, Ill.: Northwest University Press, 1999), 24–34. Here Bernasconi also points out that Levinas believes that you can defend oneself violently: Bernasconi cites the Talmudic lecture 'Judaism and Revolution' (in *Nine Talmudic Readings*, 109) where Levinas says 'unquestionably, violent action against Evil is necessary'.

explicitly Jewish moment in my thought, it is the reference to Auschwitz, where God let the Nazis do what they wanted'.[74] This marks the point where the 'Greek' language of philosophy, of proof and disproof, can go no further.

Does this mean that Levinas is a mystical or religious thinker? Derrida thinks so, writing 'that Levinas is no longer able to distinguish between the infinite alterity of God and that of every Human. His ethics already a religious one . . . the border between the ethical and the religious become more than problematic.'[75] However, this question may not be so clear cut, and can be seen usefully in the context of Levinas's contested relationship with Heideggerian rather than Husserlian phenomenology. Without forgetting Heidegger's attempt to cover up his debt to Husserl (for example, his excision of his acknowledgement to Husserl in the fifth edition of *Being and Time* in 1941), Dahlstrom analyses the development of Heidegger's thought from Husserl: the

young Heidegger sees something that largely escapes Husserl's intellectual radar, namely that the phenomena constituting religious experience, phenomena at the core of timeliness and historicity of human existence, do not readily admit, if at all, of a scientific comprehension. Just as importantly, he has—or better, comes to have—a conception of philosophy that would be imperilled if it either ignored these phenomena or attempted to secure them in a theory. The religious experience calls human beings back to such existential phenomena as anxiety, irresoluteness, conscience, death, not for the sake of theoretical closure but for the sake of opening human beings up to the disclosure of the original sense of these phenomena. So, too, philosophy, as Heidegger conceives it, must retrieve these phenomena for analogous purposes.[76]

Heidegger wants to bring these 'religious experiences' ('anxiety, irresoluteness, conscience' and especially 'death') into philosophy: this is how, centrally, he 'transfigured' Husserl's thought.[77] Despite their profound differences, there is much Levinas's work shares with Heidegger's in terms of method and orientation. Against Heidegger and with an urgency that stems from the Holocaust, for Levinas the central experience to be analysed is that of ethics, of being obligated, of

    [74] Wright *et al.*, 'Paradox of Morality', 175.
    [75] Jacques Derrida, *The Gift of Death*, tr. David Wills (Chicago: Chicago University Press, 1992), 84.
    [76] Daniel O. Dahlstrom, *Heidegger's Concept of Truth* (Cambridge: Cambridge University Press, 2001), 174.
    [77] Levinas, *Is it Righteous to Be?*, 32.

being persecuted, as he writes often. This is the wider significance of the remark of Levinas's that Derrida cites: 'You know, one often speaks of ethics to describe what I do, but what really interests me in the end is not ethics, not ethics alone, but the holy, the holiness of the holy'.[78] Levinas is interested in coming to understand what he takes to be the most fundamental experience, which is given expression in religion but not only in religion, of 'being obligated to the other'. Whereas, for Heidegger, death has mine-only-ness, 'dying . . . is essentially mine in such a way that no one can be my representative' and it is through this angst that *Dasein* comes to its authenticity and individuality, for Levinas what both generates the crucial awareness, the self-understanding, and so is revealed as underlying what it is to be is not death but our obligation to the other, ethics.[79] He writes: ' "Me" is not an inimitable nuance of Jemeiningkeit that would be added on to a being belonging to the genus "soul" or "man" or "individual", and would thus be common to several souls, man and individuals' (*OBBE* 126): that is, one's sense of subjectivity is not a category in a philosophical anthropology, or a defining character of what it is to be 'human'. Rather it is the basis of any such definition in the first place: 'it is I, I and no one else, who am a hostage for the others . . . The self in a being is exactly the not-being-able-to-slip-away-from an assignation' (*OBBE* 126–7). The experience of ethics is that which underlies the self and—just as for Heidegger, death cannot be outstripped—ethics is inescapable. More than this, as it is not solipsistic but is (not just 'comes from', but *is*) the experience of the other or 'proximity' as Levinas calls it, ethics is experienced as 'obsession' (*OBBE* 101), 'responsibility justified by no prior commitment' (*OBBE* 102), being 'summoned as someone irreplaceable' (*OBBE* 114), 'being-in-one's-skin, having-the-other-in-one's skin' (115), the 'unconditionallity of being hostage' (*OBBE* 117), 'an accusation which I cannot answer, but for which I cannot decline responsibility' (*OBBE* 127). Indeed, when 'this relation is really thought through, it signifies the wound that cannot heal over of the self in the ego accused by the other to the point of persecution' (*OBBE* 126). These experiences underlie religion as well as philosophy. Levinas himself said that he always made 'a clear distinction, in what I write, between philosophical and confessional texts' yet

---

[78] Jacques Derrida, *Adieu to Emmanuel Levinas*, tr. Pascale-Anne Brault and Michael Nass (Stanford, Calif.: Stanford University Press, 1999), 4.

[79] Martin Heidegger, *Being and Time*, tr. John Macquarrie and Edward Robinson (Oxford: Blackwell, 1962), 297, 299.

could not 'deny that they ultimately have a common source of inspira-tion'.[80] If philosophy and religion 'happen to be in harmony' in his thought, he says, 'it is probably because every philosophical thought rests on pre-philosophical experiences'.[81]

This position, concerning the limits of philosophy, seems to represent his 'existential ethical truth', his bedrock. It is here that, *pace* Wittgenstein, his spade is turned. Yet, and very significantly, it is precisely the emergence of this, and the thinking through of this 'non-philosophical' site in or as philosophy that makes Levinas's work so powerful and that is his response to the Holocaust.[82] That is, Levinas's response to the Holocaust is enacted in and by his philosophy. If his work is based on what Lyotard calls the 'prescription to place myself in a prescriptive situation', then his response to the Holocaust is precisely this listening to the contradictory, painful, traumatized—'are inextinguish-able: they echo and re-echo across eternity. What we must do is listen to the thought that they contain'.[83] In a sense, while he writes of a need to 'refute' evil, this does no more than stand against it: it does not refute in a traditional philosophical sense except by a total disagreement through the presupposition of 'peace, the antecedent and non-allergic presence of the Other' (*TI* 199).[84] In this, Levinas is utterly opposed—but not only in reasoned argument—to what Hilberg calls the 'most sophisticated' rationalization for genocide. Hilberg cites Oswald Spengler:

[']war is the primeval policy of all living things, and to this extent that in the deepest sense combat and life are identical, for when the will to fight is extin-guished, so is life itself'. Himmler remembered this theory when he addressed the mobile killing personnel at Minsk. He told them to look at nature. Wherever they would look, they would find combat. They would find it among plants and

---

[80] Richard Kearney, *Dialogues with Contemporary Continental Thinkers* (Manchester: Manchester University Press, 1984), 54.

[81] Emmanuel Levinas, *Ethics and Infinity: Conversations with Philippe Nemo*, tr. Richard A. Cohen (Pittsburgh: Duquesne University Press, 1985), 24.

[82] But this, for Levinas, is not a 'broken middle' between the philosophic and the prophetic. He says that the face—which inaugurates and is the ethical relation—is not an object of knowledge. 'There is no evidence with regards to the face; there is, rather, an order, in the sense that the face is a command to value. Consequently you could call it generosity; in other terms, it is the moment of faith. Faith is not a question of the exist-ence or non-existence of God. It is believing that love without reward is valuable' (Wright *et al.*, 'The Paradox of Morality', 176–7). That is, the face, the Good, are not open to proof nor to 'circulation as facts' but are the grounding moment of subjectivity.

[83] Jean-François Lyotard and Jean-Loup Thébaud, *Just Gaming*, tr. Wlad Godzich (Minneapolis: University of Minnesota Press, 1985); 'Loving the Torah More than God', in Kolitz, *Yosl Rakover Talks to God*, 79–88, 81.

[84] Levinas, 'As if Consenting to Horror', 488.

among animals. Whoever tired of the fight went under. From this philosophy Hitler drew strength in moments of meditation. Once, at the dinner table, when he thought about the destruction of the Jews, he remarked with stark simplicity: 'One must not have mercy with people who are determined to perish'.[85]

Levinas seems clearly right, this 'diabolic criminality . . . absolute evil . . . cannot be called "thought" '.[86] And his response to this is not to return to thought, to a 'pure philosophy' or, crucially to a theodicy: explicitly in 'Useless Suffering' and in 'Loving the Torah More than God', and implicitly throughout his work, Levinas, like Hans Jonas, rejects theodicy totally.[87] Instead it is to bring into philosophy that which it has excluded: thus both philosophy and prophecy. Colin Davis suggests that while *Otherwise that Being* is 'movingly dedicated to the victims of the Holocaust . . . the book itself has nothing to say about those victims; in the face of its own tragic knowledge, it can appear at moments like an exercise in wishful thinking' so that Levinas's 'life work on ethics seems reticent or struck dumb when faced with . . . areas of human cruelty'.[88] Yet it is precisely the 'wishful thinking' and the 'being struck dumb'—in the sense of not speaking but listening—for which Levinas is striving. After the Holocaust, Levinas does not think that a rational case can be made for the ethical: while remaining phenomenological (analysing, roughly, physical conditions and then the encounter with the other in *Totality and Infinity*, language in *Otherwise than Being*), he does not set forward a case for ethics or the originary relation, but tries to show it. Reason comes from ethics, but does not underlie it. The originary relation is neither reasonable nor unreasonable but underlies the possibility of either. And it is easily possible to see this as failure of philosophy. However, it is precisely this failure that Levinas sees as the little tremble or shudder in the 'just war waged against war' (*OBBE* 185).[89]

[85] Raul Hilberg, *The Destruction of the European Jews* (London: Holmes & Meier, 1985), 293.

[86] Levinas, 'As if Consenting to Horror', 487.

[87] See 'The Concept of God after Auschwitz: A Jewish Voice', in Hans Jonas, *Mortality and Morality: A Search for the Good after Auschwitz*, ed. Lawrence Vogel (Evanston, Ill.: Northwestern University Press, 1999). As Andrew Taylor suggested to me, much of the argument for Jonas here—if not for Levinas—is a post-Holocaust form of A. N. Whitehead's process theology: indeed, Jonas admires Whitehead greatly.

[88] Davis, *Ethical Issues*, 187, 188.

[89] In thinking about the perpetrators, who he saw as inhuman and android-like, Philip K. Dick asked 'Could we not become like androids, in our very efforts to wipe them out?' Paul M. Sammon, *Future Noir: The Making of Blade Runner* (London: Orion, 1996), 17. This 'little tremble' is, perhaps, the answer to this fear.

CONCLUSION: THE FAILURE OF PHILOSOPHY?

What, then, is the result of all this? There is no one conclusion, no 'answer' or new principle. No 'ruined concept' (*OBBE* 185) is restored. But has Levinas found, or at least found a way to describe, 'another kinship' than that which ties humans to being, another way to speak about being human and to understand and act on ethics after the Holocaust?: 'Can we speak of an absolute commandment after Auschwitz? Can we speak of morality after the failure of morality?'[90]

In a rather charming (and unusual, for Levinas) image, in discussing Jewish–Christian relations (and so, again, the Holocaust, which he mentions), he cites the pilot in *The Little Prince*, who, asked to draw a sheep, cannot draw an appropriate one, so draws a parallelogram in which the sheep is sleeping:

I do not know how to draw the solution to insoluble problems. It is still sleeping in the bottom of a box, but a box over which persons who have drawn close to each other keep watch. I have no idea other than the idea of the idea that one should have. The abstract drawing of a parallelogram—cradle of our hope. I have the idea of a possibility in which the impossible may be sleeping.[91]

This engaging image, sadly, does not tell us anything very new, there is no revelation of, say, the positive qualities of a new, post-Holocaust humanity, no new imperative: yet in its fragility, in its tacit reference to continued community (*The Little Prince* is a book read to children), in its hope, for lack of a better word, there is something. What is important in Levinas's work is that, for all its heritage both Talmudic and phenomenological, it begins to offer a way of doing a different sort of philosophy. It is the inextricable interwovenness of his work with the Holocaust and its orientation on how philosophy is done that is a key part of Levinas's legacy: to summarize this under four headings, this seems to me to be reflected in the failure of philosophy and the meaning of this; the sort of philosophy Levinas sets out to do; the idea of the trace and its implication for thought; and the relationship between philosophy and its 'outside'.

Levinas describes philosophy as a failure, 'betrayed in the said that dominates the saying which states it' (*OBBE* 7). The 'exceptional words . . . One, God—become terms, re-enter the vocabulary and are

---

90 Wright, *et al.*, 'Paradox of Morality', 176.
91 Levinas, *Alterity and Transcendence*, 86.

put at the disposition of philologists, instead of confounding philo-sophical language' (*OBBE* 169). The task of philosophy is to be an 'an endless critique, or scepticism . . . destroying the conjunction into which its saying and said continually enter' (*OBBE* 44). No philosophy can offer a final answer. In a way, this might be a trope that echoes the inability of many writers of testimony to achieve closure, to finish writing: there is always more to say, the story to be told again. But Levinas goes onto explore the meaning of this. The failure of philosophy means that it is constantly renewing itself in a tradition (*OBBE* 169), that its very existence denies a caesura in history. (There is clearly an echo of a continuous tradition of Talmudic scholarship here.) And this, too, ties philosophy into the state, and so highlights the political world in which philosophy operates and to which it is ineluctably tied. Its failure signifies its continuing community.

Levinas's philosophy also states—or more accurately recovers—what it is to do philosophy. It is not, for him, about completing a total system, nor is it 'therapeutic', either in the sense of resolving problems in thought or in the sense of self-development. Indeed, Levinas is the very opposite of a healing, therapeutic philosopher: his aim is to hurt, to wound. Thus, while there may be no answer to questions set by the Holocaust, we are not allowed to escape worrying about it, or about the countless other wrongs that occur in our world, in our time. This, and its wider significance, surfaces in 'Judaism and Revolution'. Drawing out the position offered by Rabbi Eleazar (he summarizes it as 'Man must build the universe: the universe is built through work and study. Everything else is distraction. Distraction is evil'), he analyses the café:

it is a non-place for a non-society, for a society without solidarity, without tomorrow, without commitment . . . without responsibility . . . You relax com-pletely to the point of not being obligated to anyone or anything; and because it is possible to go and relax in a café that one tolerates the horrors and injust-ices of the world without a soul. The world as a game from which everyone can pull out and exist only for himself, a place of forgetfulness—of the forgetful-ness of the other—that is the café.[92]

The café is mundane, but the point is that it is a realization, a symptom, of a form of life. For Levinas, intoxication means forgetting the other. The notorious and widely described drunkenness of the perpetrators of the Holocaust (Browning cites one non-drinking policeman who says

[92] Levinas, 'Judaism and Revolution', 111, 112.

that his 'comrades drank so much because of the many shootings of Jews, for such a life was quite intolerable sober')[93] and the cruel games ('Judenjag'—Jew hunts, the games of sadists like Möll described by Müller) are a similar symptoms: both causes and effects of the 'forgetfulness of the other' which, despite the attempt at such forgetfulness, display the traces of the impossibility of such forgetfulness.

This is part of the significance of the trace, which I discuss in detail in the following chapter. The trace is a way of describing how the infinite, the ethical, is made manifest in the finite in and over time. This idea has been very productive for a number of philosophers, most of all, perhaps, Derrida. And the trace, too, is part of the wider effort of Levinas's thought, and perhaps the most important, to bring into philosophy explicitly that which it had tried to exclude: when he writes that philosophy is 'the wisdom of love at the service of love' (*OBBE* 162) it is a declaration that 'love', outside thought, is bought into it, and consciously and explicitly reflected on. The reason that Levinas does this is not only because he sees that much of the tradition of philosophy that went before him was either blind to its own extra-philosophical commitments, usually Christian or Christian-influenced, but also because he was aware of the terrible consequences of this. The 'identification of will and reason' (*TI* 217), the reduction of the other to the same 'by the interposition of a middle and neutral term that ensures the comprehension of being' (*TI* 43) are all part of the 'philosophy of injustice' (*TI* 46), which ends in the murder of the Holocaust. His philosophy is prepared to measure itself against this.

[93] Christopher Browning, *Ordinary Men: Reserve Police Battalion 101 and the Final Solution* (London: Harper Collins, 2nd edn., 1998), 82.

Cinders of Philosophy, Philosophy of Cinders: Derrida and the Trace of the Holocaust

The thought of the incineration of the holocaust, of cinders, runs through all my texts . . . What is the thought of the trace, in fact, without which there would be no deconstruction? . . . The thought of the trace . . . is a thought about cinders and the advent of an event, a date, a memory. But I have no wish to demonstrate this here, the more so, since, in effect, 'Auschwitz' has obsessed everything that I have ever been able to think, a fact that is not especially original. Least of all does it prove I have ever had anything original or certain to say about it.[1]

We must begin wherever we are and the thought of the trace, which cannot not take the scent into account, has already taught us that it was impossible to justify a point of departure absolutely. Wherever we are: in a text where we already believe ourselves to be.[2]

I do not find in *any* discourse *whatsoever* anything illuminating enough for this period [the twentieth century]. (Original italics)[3]

In the previous chapter I argued that Levinas's work stems from the Holocaust. In this chapter I turn to the work of Jacques Derrida, a philosopher who has been greatly influenced by Levinas, and focus on the idea of the 'trace', which he considers central to his thinking.[4] By

---

[1] Jaques Derrida, 'Canons and Metonymies: An Interview with Jacques Derrida', *in* Richard Rand (ed.), *Logomachia: The Contest of the Faculties* (London: University of Nebraska Press, 1992), 195–218, 211–12.

[2] Jacques Derrida, *Of Grammatology*, tr. Gayatri Chakravorty Spivak (London: Johns Hopkins University Press, 1976), 162. This will be abbreviated in the text as *OG*.

[3] See Jacques Derrida, 'On Reading Heidegger: An Outline of Remarks to the Essex Colloquium', *Research in Phenomenology*, 17 (1987), 171–85, 179; italics in original.

[4] On this, but with a different angle from mine below, see also Pada Marrali-Guénoun, *La Genèse et la trace* (London: Kluwer Academic Publishing, 1990).

looking at this idea, I want to show how the Holocaust is a crucial context for Derrida's thought, and so for those influenced by him: more
than this, his relation to the Holocaust highlights his relation to ethics
and clarifies his reaction to the 'linguistic turn' in twentieth-century
thought. Both these areas have, of course, been targets for his critics. As
with Levinas, because the Holocaust forms the backdrop to his work,
it is not a question of 'deconstructing the Holocaust' or applying his
ideas to the genocide, though one might be able to explore and deconstruct the ideas that underlie, say, a Holocaust memorial museum. I
want to show that the Holocaust is *all-pervasive* in Derrida's work.
That is, deconstruction is not indebted to the Holocaust, nor does it
explain it, but it stems from it: ' "Auschwitz" has obsessed everything
that I have ever been able to think'. So, to write about deconstruction
and the Holocaust is not to write about a relationship between two
utterly separate things. 'One way or another', writes Gideon Ofrat,

the spirit of the Holocaust or a holocaust hovers over Jacques Derrida's writing: the refugees who seek hospitality in his various books; the ghosts that frequent his thoughts; and above all the verdict of 'extermination' that awaits all
redemptive metaphysical light—all prove and assure an intimate relationship
between philosophy and that great trauma of the twentieth century[5]

Derrida's work begins in the Holocaust as a philosophy of the cinder
(that stems from the cinder, that is about the cinder).[6] To follow this
through, it is necessary to look at the aims of Derrida's work and how it
works (the first part of the chapter, 'Cinders of Philosophy') and what
the consequences of this are (the second part, 'Philosophy of Cinders').

CINDERS OF PHILOSOPHY

The Task of Reading

In *Of Grammatology*, in the section called 'The Exorbitant. Question
of Method', Derrida discusses what a critical reading should produce,

[5] Gideon Ofrat, *The Jewish Derrida*, tr. Peretz Kidron (Syracuse, NY: Syracuse
University Press, 2001), 152.
[6] Other specific discussions of this occur in Amanda Grzyb, 'Jacques Derrida and the
Holocaust: Cinders, Deconstruction and Excessive Responsibility', MA thesis,
University of Western Ontario, 1996; James Berger, *After the End: Representations of
Post-Apocalypse* (London: Minnesota University Press, 1999); Elaine Marks, 'Cendres
juives: Jews Writing in French "after Auschwitz" ', in Lawrence D. Kritzman (ed.),
Auschwitz and After (London: Routledge, 1995).

and, in explaining this, he writes that he would have to 'initiate a justification of my principles of reading . . . entirely negative, outlining by exclusion a space of reading that I shall not fill here: a task of reading' (*OG* 158). This 'task of reading' (later to be called deconstruction) cannot be the repetition of a text which is commentary, a text which in a way simply repeats the first text. That said—and a point often missed by Derrida's detractors—this

moment of doubling commentary should no doubt have its place in a critical reading. To recognise and respect all the instruments of its classical exigencies is not easy and requires all the instruments of traditional criticism. Without this recognition and respect, critical production would risk developing in any direction at all and authorise itself to say almost anything. (*OG* 158)

'But' he continues 'this indispensable guardrail has always only protected, it has never opened, a reading' (*OG* 158). 'Opening' has Heideggerian connotations: the way for Heidegger the work of art opens up the Being of beings for example. It has Levinasian overtones, too—opening to the other. What this opening involves, for Derrida, is defined negatively. It is not reading a text in the light of a fixed point (not, for example, in relation to an author's biography) but instead it is 'intrinsic and remain[s] within the text' (*OG* 159). While it does not refer to a fixed point, it does have aims, however. These aims are 'exorbitant'. By 'exorbitant', Derrida and Gayatri Spivak, the translator, do not mean principally 'grossly expensive' but rely on an older sense of the word which derives from the Latin root, 'exitorbitare', 'to go out of the wheel track'. What this means can only be defined in a negative way, by what it is not, and so this 'opening' is the exorbitant, 'the point of a certain exteriority to the totality of the age of logocentrism. Starting from this point of exteriority . . . a certain deconstruction of that totality which is also a traced path . . . might be broached' (*OG* 159). The exorbitant is that which is outside the orbit, the orb (eye), or more prosaically, outside the wheel rut, of Western philosophy. To open a work to the 'exorbitant' is to see it in a way that questions or reframes the framework in which the work appears: to break the old—and perhaps to make new—generic connections.

The question then is *why* one might want—as Derrida says in an interview elsewhere—to find 'a non-site, or a non-philosophical site, from which to question philosophy': why escape the wheel rut?[7] There

---

[7] Richard Kearney, *Dialogues with Contemporary Continental Thinkers: The Phenomenological Heritage* (Manchester: Manchester University Press, 1984), 108.

would seem to be a number of answers to this. To ask what Athens has
to do with Jerusalem (or Rome, or Mecca, or Benares, though using a
city metonymically to stand in for a community or religion shows the
European origin of this metonymy and its presuppositions) is to suggest that certain sorts of fundamental religious beliefs are not totally
commensurable to reason and Western philosophy, and they might
form such a site. Another answer might be to suggest that there may
also be a sort of drunken, destructive creative madness or rage (the urge
to destroy is a creative urge after all—an urge to shape and so to reveal)
which would question philosophy from outside it. Totalitarian states,
which, following Hannah Arendt's ananlysis, work by presuming certain grounds (for example, 'the party cannot be wrong', 'the Führer is
to be obeyed') and then following out the logic of those grounds, would
want to question the sorts of philosophy which take as their aim questioning those grounds: indeed, a philosophy that questioned these
grounds would be an enemy of totalitarianism. However, the answer
Derrida gives right at the beginning of *Of Grammatology* is that this
exorbitant position from which to question philosophy is sought
because of a desire to 'focus attention on the ethnocentrism, which,
always and everywhere had controlled the concept of writing' (*OG* 3).
It is an attempt to expose this ethnocentric exclusion of those other to
Western thought, outside its usual rut. This is an ethical motivation.

   In his essay 'Force of Law: The "Mystical Foundation of
Authority" '—and in response to demands that he discuss explicitly the
ethics of deconstruction—Derrida argues that 'Deconstruction is justice'.[8] That any particular law can be deconstructed, interpreted differently, taken apart and that justice, which includes the call for justice,
cannot creates the gap in which deconstruction occurs. This is the
motivation which underlies his work: 'justice as the possibility of
deconstruction . . . the law, the foundation or the self-authorisation of
the law as the possibility of the exercise of deconstruction' (FL 15). *Of
Grammatology*'s target, ethnocentrism—as a rule—has to be deconstructed because it is against justice. (Why ethnocentrism, in particular? As the epigraph above: '[W]e must begin wherever we are and the
thought of the trace, which cannot not take the scent into account, has
already taught us that it was impossible to justify a point of departure

   [8] Jacques Derrida, 'Force of Law: The "Mystical Foundation of Authority" ', tr. Mary
Quaintance, in Drucilla Cornell, Michael Rosenfeld, David Gray Carlson (eds.),
Deconstruction and the Possibility of Justice, 3–67, 15. This will be abbreviated to FL in
the text.

absolutely': ethnocentrism because it is one form of injustice, and Derrida does analyse others.) What makes Derrida different from those opposed to Western reason discussed above (the religious, the mad, the totalitarian)—and this is a crucial point—is that he aims to ask these questions philosophically, to find the exorbitant within the text of philosophy (here the 'wheel rut' metaphor on which the word is based breaks down). Derrida is not without philosophy, ignoring or censoring philosophy like a totalitarian regime, nor outside philosophy like a madman or a mystic: he does not have an 'anti-philosophical attitude'.[9] While his work has something in common with religious thought (God, after all, is often taken to be exorbitant) he is not a religious or irrational thinker.

This sort of approach to Western thought is not unique to Derrida: indeed, as the work of Robert Bernasconi, Simon Critchley, and others has shown, it owes a great deal to Levinas's analysis of how the relation to the other, of ethics, both underlies and is covered up by philosophy. Adorno, too, thought that the 'system is belly turned mind' which consumed the (exorbitant) otherness which exceeded it.[10] And, of course, this approach clearly echoes Heidegger's argument about how the meaning of the question of Being has been forgotten by philosophy: something outside a structure of thinking that grounds thinking. But where Levinas offers the Other, Heidegger Being, and Adorno the Not-I, Derrida refuses to be pinned down to exactly what the exorbitant is. This is the significance of the 'trace' in his work.

Following the Trace from Levinas . . .

The trace is part of Levinas's response to the Holocaust, and comes to the fore at a key moment in his philosophical development. It is a way of describing how the infinite, the ethical is made manifest in the finite in and over time. It is the question of how it appears that marks the change between his two major works, *Totality and Infinity* in 1961 and *Otherwise than Being* in 1974. In *Totality and Infinity*, the ethical appears in the actual, really present face-to-face relation of one to another. The face is not a metaphor: the moment of facing is the moment of ethics. 'To manifest oneself as face is to impose oneself above and beyond the manifested phenomenal form, to present oneself

---

[9] Kearney, *Dialogues*, 108.
[10] Theodor Adorno, *Negative Dialectics*, tr. E. B. Ashton (London: Routledge, 1973), 23.

in a mode irreducible to manifestation, the very straightforwardness of
the face to face, without the intermediary of any image, in one's
nudity.'[11] For Levinas here, the face is not a representation, even of
itself, but the actual moment in which the infinite responsibility of
ethics appears. In order to stress that the face is *not* a representation,
Levinas is forced to use phrases like 'true representation', 'nudity',
'present oneself in a mode irreducible to manifestation', 'very straightforwardness', 'appealing to me in destitution' (*TI* 200), and so on.
Levinas is trying to suggest that the face, although made manifest like
objects, is beyond manifestation: it represents itself without representing itself, it has access to infinity. Even language—vital for Levinas—
only is truly language if it is guaranteed by presence: the speaker 'never
separates himself from the sign he delivers' (*TI* 97) and 'must present
himself before every sign—present a face' (*TI* 182). Writing is 'a language impeded' and to be expressed by symbols, 'by one's works, is
precisely to decline expression' (*TI* 176). Although Levinas does trust
that 'the interpretation of the symbol can assuredly lead to an intention
divined', this interpretation is a 'burglary' and occurs 'without conjur-
ing the absence' (*TI* 177) of the author.

However, this causes a problem for his ethics: if the ethical moment
is only the moment of facing, with the face actually present, then how
are we responsible for those who are absent, who have no faces? How
does the ethical relation appear in an absence, the absence of the past,
for example? This question, too, with the sense of absence, clearly
bears a trace of the Holocaust. The question for Levinas here is not:
does one have an ethical responsibility to the dead, to the other,
because he would suggest that this is already answered by our very existence, 'in the "pre-history" of the ego posited for itself speaks a responsibility, the self is through and through a hostage, older than the ego,
prior to principles' (*OBBE* 117). The question is: how is this made manifest? The answer to this problem, a major turning point in his thought
and the clue that opens to the ethical discussion of language in
Otherwise than Being, occurs in Levinas's discussion of the trace. This
discussion begins in full in 'The Trace of the Other' from 1963 and he
returns to it in an essay on the ethical significance of culture in general
called 'Meaning and Sense' from 1973.

---

[11] Emmanuel Levinas, *Totality and Infinity: An Essay on Exteriority*, tr. Alphonso
Lingis (London: Kluwer Academic Publishers, 1991), 200.

For Levinas, the trace has a double meaning. The trace 'plays the role of a sign'.[12] It is a mark of the past in the present: the animal's spoor, the clues a detective finds, the 'vestiges left' by an ancient civilization uncovered by the historian or archaeologist.[13] However, it is much more than this: the meaning of the trace as material, as content *per se*, is secondary. More importantly, the trace is a mark of the other. Levinas writes that when 'a stone has scratched a stone, the scratch can, to be sure, be taken as a trace, but in fact without the man who held the stone this scratch is but an effect'.[14] It is in 'the trace of the other that a face shines'.[15] The trace, beyond its material, inaugurates the same ethical relation to the other in the past as the face does to the actually present other: it is a 'proxy' for the face, as Edith Wysgorod has it.[16] *What* a particular trace signifies is not central: *that* it signifies and what this implies is. The trace is to the absent other of the past what the face is to an other person actually here present. While the 'Infinite would be belied in the proof that the finite would like to give of its transcendence' (meaning: the whole system of proof and disproof would betray the infinite), Levinas argues that the way prophecy, the ethical, 'could take on the appearances of information circulated among others' is 'the enigma, the ambiguity but also the order of transcendence, of the infinite': the trace.[17] The trace is both a piece of information, a thing, and also that which is beyond, the other. To offer a sense of this: to hold a coin from an ancient civilization is both to hold a lump of stamped metal and also to be reminded of the people who traded with it, played with it, had lives and loves that involved it, and to feel, in some way, obligated to those people, if only to remember them and wonder about them. It is this idea of the trace—of how the absent other appears—that allows Levinas to develop his understanding of language as Saying and Said in *Otherwise than Being*. It is the trace that allows representation to have an ethics. The trace is how the other appears in representation, and it is a terribly fertile idea for Derrida.

[12] Emmanuel Levinas, 'Meaning and Sense', in *Collected Philosophical Papers*, tr. Alphonso Lingis (Dordrecht: Kluwer Academic Publishers, 1987), 75–108, 104.
[13] Ibid.   [14] Ibid. 106.   [15] Ibid.
[16] Edith Wyschogrod, 'God and "Being's Move", in the Philosophy of Emmanuel Levinas', *Journal of Religion*, 62 (1982), 145–55, 150.
[17] Emmanuel Levinas, *Otherwise than Being: or, Beyond Essence*, tr. Alphonso Lingis (The Hague: Martinus Nijhoff, 1981), 152.

. . . to Derrida

Derrida writes that he relates 'this concept of *trace* to what is at the centre of the latest work of Emmanuel Levinas and his critique of ontology' (*OG* 70). He is keen not to give a particular name to 'the exorbitant' as that would both place it into a system and invoke a specific point or referent which would anchor the text being read. So, where, for Levinas, the trace is the trace of the other (the other absent and present, disrupting presence), for Derrida, the trace 'signifies . . . the undermining of an ontology which, in its innermost course, has determined the meaning of being as presence and the meaning of language as the full continuity of speech' (*OG* 70). The trace is, then, the moment of disruption in thought, it is what exceeds philosophy. It 'is nothing, it is not an entity, it exceeds the question "what is" and contingently makes it possible' (*OG* 75). It is, in fact, 'the absolute origin of sense in general. Which amounts to saying once again that there is no absolute origin of sense in general . . . Articulating the living upon the nonliving in general, origin of all repetition . . . the trace is not more signification than an opaque energy and no concept of metaphysics can describe it' (*OG* 65). What this means emerges in contrast to the thinkers Derrida admires. For Heidegger, *aletheia* is the ground on which truth understood as agreement of judgement with its object appears, most clearly in art, and this is the origin of sense in general: philosophy's job is to think about what that means. For Levinas, it is the relation with the other, that grounds intelligibility and sense: 'truth presupposes justice' (*TI* 90). For Derrida, the trace is at once highly complex and, in a way, very straightforward. It is not one concept or thing because it is outside what concepts can cover or ideas about what 'things' are. Thus, it cannot be named or delimited. It is the disruption of intelligibility (it interrupts systems of thought) and the limit of intelligibility (it cannot be described). Without the trace, deconstruction would be impossible. It marks the infinite appearing in the finite, the ethical in the material. It is 'arche-phenomenon of "memory" ' (*OG* 70), that without which memory would be impossible.

Whatever it is—and even the 'it' and 'is' are clearly already saying too much about it—the trace is clearly not only in language. In an interview which stresses the intellectual context of the 'linguistic turn' in which he was developing these ideas, Derrida says that, 'I take great interest in questions of language and rhetoric, and I think they deserve enormous consideration'. But 'there is a point where the authority of final jurisdiction is neither rhetorical nor linguistic, nor even discursive. The notion of the trace or of the text is introduced to mark the limits of the linguistic turn.'[18] The trace is that which is always outside of language, or systems of thought, and yet on which they rely (for example, the world, the other, truth, temporality: but to name these things is to have subsumed them into language). While Levinas's idea of the trace refers only to the other person, for Derrida, the other manifested in the trace is much wider.

The trace, then, is where what is outside philosophy—the other, however understood or manifested—is made manifest within philosophy: and the task of deconstruction is to reveal—to open—this. In *Positions*, Derrida says that to deconstruct 'philosophy . . . would be to think . . . the structured genealogy of philosophy's concepts, but at the same time to determine—from a certain exterior that is unqualifiable or unnameable by philosophy—what this history has been able to dissimulate or forbid'.[19] The trace is the appearance of the exterior that is unqualifiable or unnameable by philosophy, not describable by metaphysics, the infinite responsibility that arises from the other appearing before (and so outside) reasoned thinking. Derrida's obsession with spectres and 'hauntology' in *Spectres of Marx* and with ghosts, ashes, spirits, and spirit in *Of Spirit* again show the importance of the trace: ghosts are both present and absent, a presence that marks an absence. This is not to say that the trace, and the deconstruction that opens and is opened by it, offers a new philosophy: Derrida argues that 'the passage beyond philosophy does not consist in turning the page of philosophy . . . but in continuing to read philosophy in a certain way'.[20] Derrida, like Levinas, constantly renames his terms to avoid them becoming systematic and in order to fix them in definite responses to certain texts: a reading not a methodology. The trace, the opening of justice, is a constant pressure on thinking and on ways of reading. As is well-known, Derrida's readings are supposed to follow no method, but to be attentive to the text: however, it seems clear that the Derridian terms that emerge from very specific readings—'shibboleth' from reading Paul Celan, 'hymen' in 'The Double Session', 'pharmakon' from Plato, and so on—can all be seen as specific, located versions of

---

[18] Jacques Derrida and Maurizio Ferraria, *A Taste for the Secret*, tr. G. Donis, ed. G. Donis and D. Webb (London: Polity, 2001), 76.

[19] Jacques Derrida, *Positions*, tr. Alan Bass (London: Athlone Press, 1981), 6.

[20] Jacques Derrida, *Writing and Difference*, tr. Alan Bass (London: Routledge & Kegan Paul, 1978), 288.

reading under the pressure of the trace. The opening or unveiling of the trace is what deconstruction does: and, if deconstruction is justice, unveiling the trace in a discourse is justice. (And, of course, all this above is to 'thematize' the term 'trace'.)

Cinders

Derrida writes that '[O]f course, the word trace doesn't mean anything by itself. . . . I would prefer something which is neither present nor absent: I would prefer ashes as the better paradigm for what I call trace: something which erases itself totally, radically, while presenting itself'.[21] The word 'trace' does not mean anything: like 'hymen' or 'pharmakon' it is one word taken from a certain context to describe what 'no concept of metaphysics can describe'. Even the idea of trace as 'imprinting' is to force it too much into a conceptual framework: it appears each time in each context as different. But could this constellation of words around trace or ashes be better understood? Derrida said that the 'thought of the trace, without which there is no deconstruction, is a thought about cinders and the advent of an event, a date, a memory'.[22]

Derrida turns to this in *Cinders*, a very oblique (to say the very least) prose poem, written first to be spoken and then to be read. It concerns an untranslatable phrase that haunts Derrida, 'Il y a là cendre': there are there cinders, cinders there are. It seems to be about the relationship between singular moments, philosophy, writing, and the Holocaust. However, in contrast to his normal habit of offering a new term, specific to the text he is reading, for the trace, Derrida suggests exploring what underlies the trace itself.

The cinder

visible but scarcely readable . . . referring only to itself, no longer makes a trace, unless it traces only by losing the trace it scarcely leaves

—that it just barely remains.

—but that is just what he [Derrida himself? Heidegger? Levinas? the unnamed party being discussed?][23] calls the trace, this effacement. I have the impression now that the best paradigm for the trace, for him, is not, as some have believed,

---

[21] Derrida, 'On Reading Heidegger', 177.   [22] 'Canons and Metonymies', 211.
[23] James Berger suggests unproblematically that this is Derrida: yet the terms used echo both Heidegger and Levinas, and so, perhaps, a whole philosophical tradition. James Berger, *After the End* (Minneapolis: University of Minnesota Press, 1999), 119

and he as well, perhaps, the trail of the hunt, the fraying, the furrow in the sand, the wake of the sea, the love of the step for its imprint, but the cinder (what remains without remaining from the holocaust, from the all-burning . . .).[24]

The 'the trail of the hunt, the fraying, the furrow in the sand, the wake of the sea, the love of the step for its imprint' are all metaphors that imply that what makes the trace is still present chronologically, just over there, just charged through, on the other side of frayed material, the other side of the beach, three paces along. The cinder is temporal: that particular fire and that particular burnt 'thing' can never be recreated, brought back, brought to life. The cinder brings the trace into temporality: and into a specific temporality, of a Europe and North America shadowed (if not overshadowed) by the Holocaust, what remains from the Holocaust. We live in a particular time, we reflect particular moments, dates as Derrida writes on Celan. 'We must begin wherever we are' and the 'writer [Rousseau, Derrida] writes in a language and in a logic whose proper system, laws and life his discourse by definition cannot dominate absolutely' (*OG* 158). Like Celan and others he analyses, Derrida is set in time and makes no claim to a God-like view from outside of time and history. Other writers at other times did not, may not, might not have the same shadows, the same ashes. But for Derrida on Derrida—and this is the significance of the fact that *Cinders,* unlike other texts by Derrida which discuss other writers, is a discussion of a phrase in his own work, a self-reflexive unveiling—for Derrida on Derrida, it is clear that the 'best paradigm' for the trace is the cinder 'what remains without remaining from the holocaust'. The cinder underlies deconstruction and the cinder is the cinder of the Holocaust. This is why Derrida said in interview that the 'thought of the incineration of the Holocaust, of cinders, runs through all my texts'. The trace, for Derrida, for us (who could 'we' be? Perhaps, for me?) is best considered as the cinder.

This is not the only 'haunting' through Derrida's work—although it is perhaps the most significant. The trace is the appearance of an infinite responsibility and Derrida's work has been concerned with deconstructing ethnocentrism, racism, and so on. But, as Derrida has often made a point of claiming, deconstruction grows out of singularities, from specific times, places, and texts. And, for Derrida, that

---

[24] Jacques Derrida, *Cinders,* tr. and ed. Ned Lukacher (London: University of Nebraska Press, 1991), 43.

singularity was the Holocaust, with its continuing echoes.[25] These
echoes include, for Derrida and others, the events of the Algerian war
of independence.[26] What Derrida offers, developing a lacuna in
Levinas's thought, is a philosophy haunted throughout by those events,
a philosophy that can articulate the debt to what it cannot name.
A philosophy of the cinder, and it is in these cinders that Derrida's
deconstruction originates. And, *pace* the interview above, this is to say
nothing 'original or certain' about Derrida or about the Holocaust,
save that it happened, an event, a date, a memory.

'Singular in General'[27]

A consequence of this is that, for Derrida, the Holocaust is both a universal injustice and a singular injustice. This has not been and perhaps
cannot be thought through philosophically. While all events are unique
and singular, it is hard, philosophically, to respond to this. Indeed, the
discourse of Western thought cannot but cover the 'singularity' of
events up by turning them into examples of an abstract category or general cases. (Indeed, after Kant, the ability to do this is what guarantees

[25] This is, of course, to begin to make an argument from biography. For this, see
Geoffrey Bennington and Jacques Derrida, *Jacques Derrida* (London: University of
Chicago Press, 1993), 325–7. But see also Derrida's comments on this when writing on
Paul de Man, where he both satirizes and states the sort of self-justifying biographical
approach that claims 'As for me, no one can suspect me of anything: I am Jewish, I was
persecuted as a child during the war, I have always been known for my leftist opinions',
in Jacques Derrida, 'Like the Sound of the Sea Deep within a Shell: Paul de Man's War',
Critical Inquiry, 14 (1988), 590–652, 648. But then, in contrast, see 'it is no longer possible—for me or for anybody else—to distinguish the biographical from the intellectual,
the non-intellectual from the intellectual biography'. Derrida and Ferraria, *Taste for the
Secret*, 37.
[26] Pierre Vidal-Naquet writes that 'I personally entered the fight against the Algerian
war and specifically against torture . . . with a constant point of reference: the obsessive
memory of our national injustices . . . and of the Nazi crimes of torture and extermination. That reference to Nazism remained in effect throughout the war. For instance, the
day after the Paris pogrom of October 17 (I still regard that term as appropriate), a certain number of intellectuals, at the behest of *Les Temps Modernes*, Jean-Paul Sartre's
journal, signed a manifesto . . . "we refuse to make any distinction between the Algerian
piled up at the Palais de Sports while waiting to be 'dispatched' and the Jews stored at
Drancy before their deportation".' Pierre Vidal-Naquet, *Assassins of Memory*, tr. Jefrey
Mehlman (New York: Columbia University Press, 1993), 127–8. On Derrida and Algeria,
see Robert Young, *Postcolonialism: An Historical Introduction* (Oxford: Blackwell,
2001), 410–28.
[27] This paradoxical phrase occurs in Maurice Blanchot/Jacques Derrida, *The Instant
of my Death/Demeure*, tr. Elizabeth Rottenberg (Stanford, Calif.: Stanford University
Press, 2000), 91.

identity over time.) In historical discourse, this is why 'normalization' happens, and where (*pace* Friedländer) 'the real trap of language is unexpectedly sprung'.[28] And this is the philosophical context that, in no small part, has led to the 'uniqueness debate', however this is formulated. While we may be keen to see each event as particular and unique, our very conceptual system, the very working of language and identity, cannot but turn it into an example of an abstract category, an example of something. The continued insistence on the uniqueness of the Holocaust, taken out of any political significance, is really a complaint about the ways in which our very way of thinking makes it impossible to discuss as particulars as particulars. The Holocaust both differs from and defers to (that is, takes its meaning in contrast to) other events: it was much larger and much more organized than a Russian pogrom, different from the genocide of the Armenians, and so on. Thus, in terms of our abstract understanding, it is clearly linked to these and also separate from them. In this light, it seems important to be clear how and why claims for its uniqueness are made and how and why it is aligned with other events. In contrast, perhaps, testimonies are an attempt if not to think then to enact this very particularity: this is the theme of Derrida's essay on Paul Celan: what his poems, and the poem in general

marks, what enters and incises languages in the form of a date, is that there is a partaking of the shibboleth, a partaking that is at once open and closed. The date (signature, moment, place, gathering of singular marks) always functions as a shibboleth. It shows there is something not shown, that there is ciphered singularity: irreducible to any concept, to any knowledge, even to history or tradition . . . A ciphered singularity which gathers a multiplicity *in eins*, and through whose grid a poem remains readable . . . the poem speaks, even should none of its references be intelligible.[29]

This inability to think the particular without, implicitly, invoking the universal is also why Derrida and others, including Levinas, are forced to make a slippage, to mention in the same breath particular events—'Auschwitz'—and other evil events that are in the same abstract category, not only in relation to the Holocaust ('why this name rather than those of all the other camps and mass exterminations?') but more

[28] Saul Friedländer, *Reflections on Nazism: An Essay on Kitsch and Death*, tr. Thomas Weyr (Bloomington: Indiana University Press, rev. edn., 1993), 90.

[29] Jacques Derrida, 'Shibboleth: For Paul Celan', tr. Joshua Wilner, in *Wordtraces: Reading of Paul Celan*, ed. Aris Fioretos (London: Johns Hopkins University Press, 1994), 3–72, 35.

widely to other horrors—the gulags, Cambodia, Sarajevo, Rwanda.[30] This is also, perhaps, why Derrida almost always refuses to capitalize the word 'holocaust'.

This overall leads to a wider question of justice. 'Deconstruction, while seeming not to address the problem of justice, has done nothing but address it, if only obliquely, unable to do so directly' (FL 112), responding to a universal, ahistorical demand for justice. Deconstruction, while seeming not to address the Holocaust, has done nothing but address it, if only obliquely, unable to do so directly: coming from a particular, historical, located demand for justice. Both these demands—justice, which is unrepresentable 'as the experience of absolute alterity' (FL 27)—and the singularity of the Holocaust are bought together in the figure of the cinder.

PHILOSOPHY OF CINDERS

If deconstruction is the cinders of philosophy, what marks does it bear of this? In what way is this claim not empty rhetoric? It is certainly possible to read books that deconstruct 'the Holocaust' if this is taken to mean to 'deconstruct' how the 'Holocaust' as an event in history is represented, understood, exhibited, and so on. But this is cultural critique, carefully describing and judging, implicitly or explicitly, how this most terrible event is presented and remembered. This is commentary, relying on an external referent, not opening a reading. James Berger, in his illuminating study of post-apocalyptic thinking, asks how deconstruction views the Holocaust. However, this presupposes that deconstruction is a method or a model of thinking, and the Holocaust is one event: as if the deconstruction is a telescope and the Holocaust a remote constellation on which it might be focused. Deconstruction is already the cinders of philosophy. It is always already involved with, a response to the Holocaust. It is also the philosophy of cinders, reflecting on and engaging with the events of the Holocaust: I will illustrate this briefly in relation to the past, the present, and the future.

Cinders Then

What is philosophy about? In contrast to Derrida's tradition, and to choose one voice from many, Michael Dummett argues that only

---

[30] Derrida, 'Canons and Metonymies', 112.

with Frege was the proper object of philosophy finally established: namely, that the goal of philosophy is the analysis of the structure of thought; secondly, that the study of thought is to be sharply distinguished from the study of the psychological process of thinking; and finally, that the only proper method for analysing thought consists in the analysis of language.[31]

This approach—perhaps typical of the analytic school—seems to claim to be ahistorical, and so unable to reflect, philosophically, on the Holocaust. In the case of Dummett, this does not mean that he has no opinions on these matters: with his admirable work in anti-racist activity, it would be surprising if he did not. However, asked if his philosophical views 'impelled' him in the struggle against racism, he says that they did not.[32] In contrast, Derrida's form of philosophy/questioning of philosophy developed in the European philosophical tradition where the 'natural affinities of philosophy have rather been taken to be with literary and artistic culture, and the concerns of the philosophy have centred on moral, literary, spiritual, socio-political and cultural questions rather than on the logic of the sciences'.[33] Indeed, Derrida writes that deconstruction generally takes one of two styles (although its mixes them together): one 'takes on the demonstrative and apparently ahistorical allure of logico-formal paradoxes. The other . . . seems to proceed through readings of texts, meticulous interpretation and genealogies' (FL 21). Both these are profoundly historical against apparent 'ahistoricism', through reading texts, contexts, traditions. This approach to thinking engages with the past and the thinkers finitude and historicity. A philosophy of cinders has already located Derrida (and we who live in Europe, physically, intellectually? we of what Derrida calls the Graeco-European adventure? or those who respond to those events?) in a post-Holocaust world, with no way to escape that world. Cinders are what is left of the events of the past and so are that with which we make history.

Cinders Now

But cinders are also present. In the 'Post-scriptum' to 'Force of Law' Derrida ventures to describe how Walter Benjamin might have

<hr />

[31] Michael Dummett, *Truth and Other Enigmas* (London: Duckworth, 1978), 441, 458.
[32] Michael Dummett, *On Immigration and Refugees* (London: Routledge, 2001), pp. xi, xii.
[33] Eric Matthews, *Twentieth Century French Philosophy* (Oxford: Oxford University Press, 1996), 7.

responded to the Final Solution. There are two different versions. The first, Derrida suggests, corresponds to what might be a commentary on Nazism, on its use of language (evil is a possibility in all languages), on its totalitarian 'logic' of the state and corruption of democratic institutions—especially the police—and on its total, 'mythical', violence: Michael Burleigh's recent history offers an acute historical account of this. But this is to think the Final Solution from the point of view of Nazism, to follow through Nazism's thought.

Derrida also suggests a counter-commentary, based on what the Nazis aimed to exclude: a commentary aiming to analyse the Final Solution from the point of view of Nazism's other, 'that which haunted it at once from without and within' (FL 60). This view is to be thought from the 'possibility of singularity', from the view of the victims of the Final Solution, 'human lives by the millions' and also a more universal 'demand for justice'. In D. M. Thomas's often maligned novel *The White Hotel*, the narrator writes of the 30,000 killed on the first day of the Babi Yar massacres that

their lives and histories were as rich and complex as Lisa Erdman-Berenstein's [the character who has been the subject of the rest of the novel]. If a Sigmund Freud had been listening and taking notes from the time of Adam, he would still not have explored even a single group, even a single person. And this was only the first day.'[34]

The 219 pages of the novel up to this point have been, *pace* Michael André Bernstein's foreshadowing, an exercise in making one of the victims 'singular' but not as a victim. This is one way of understanding singularity. For Derrida, as Benjamin, the 'Final Solution' must be thought of as a 'project of destruction of the name', meaning, the destruction of each singular individual as a singularity and the more general naming that binds and creates communities. ('Name' is not just a metaphor: on 'August 17 another decree prepared by Hans Globke, announced that from January 1, 1939, Jews who did not bear the first names indicated on an appended list were to add the first names Israel or Sara to their names'.[35]) 'From this point of view', he writes, 'Benjamin would have judged vain and without pertinence . . . any juridical trial of Nazism . . . any judgmental apparatus, any historiography still homogenous with the space in which Nazism developed . . . any interpretation drawing on philosophical, moral, sociological,

---

[34] D. M. Thomas, *The White Hotel* (London: Penguin, 1981), 220.
[35] Saul Friedländer, *Nazi Germany and the Jews* (London: Phoenix Giant, 1998), 254.

psychological or psychoanalytic concepts' (FL 60). That is, any concepts that developed in the same forest as Nazism, any trees that grew in the same soil, as Derrida put it in *Of Spirit*, would be 'vain and without pertinence'. The implication is that only that which is truly outside Nazism and the Final Solution could judge it or measure its significance. At this point, Derrida bridles, finding something 'intolerable' in this interpretation. If the Final Solution can only be measured by what is outside all these concepts, then this means that one might say that 'only a God can explain this': the Holocaust is 'an uninterpretable manifestation of divine violence' (FL 61). Derrida writes that one 'is terrified at the idea of an interpretation that would make of the holocaust an expiation and an indecipherable signature of the just and violent anger of God' (FL 62). Derrida is not alone in this, or in seeing how a path might be followed to this conclusion. It was in response to both Christians and Jews suggesting this that led to Richard Rubenstein's response in *After Auschwitz* (at least in the first edition in 1966). This is one of the terrible ideas, terrible in its proper sense, with which Elie Wiesel wrestles, too. It is here—'only a God can explain this'—that Derrida finds Benjamin, and these alternatives, 'too Heideggerian, too messianico-marxist or too archeo-eschatological for me' (FL 62).

Neither of these paths, then, is enough response in the present to the past, or can 'take the measure of the event' (FL 59). One is too complicit, describing the Holocaust through the logic of Nazism (nothing *post*-Holocaust about that, just the Holocaust written); the other—dismissing the first—is too much the opposite, in which no 'anthropology, no humanism, no discourse of man on man, even on human rights' could 'be proportionate' (FL 61) (the Holocaust has consumed everything: *nothing* post-Holocaust here, either). Neither is an opening and both correspond in a way to Nazism, to its false logic and science, and to its appeals to myth beyond reason. For Derrida, this leaves us with the task of thinking about the complicity of the discourses we still have, of rights, of ethics, of identity, or race, with the Holocaust: 'Nazism was not born in the desert . . . it had grown in the shadow of big trees . . . In their bushy taxonomy, they would bear the names of religions, philosophies, political regimes, economic structures, religious or academic institutions. In short, what is just as confusedly called culture, or the world of the spirit.'[36] For Derrida, in this self-conscious

[36] Jacques Derrida, *Of Spirit: Heidegger and the Question*, tr. Geoffrey Bennington and Rachel Bowlby (London: University of Chicago Press, 1987), 109–10.

Heideggerian metaphor, the forest that philosophy inhabits (that is, culture, spirit) is the sign of a continuing and unavoidable contiguity with the Nazi genocide. The task, as we inhabit the forest, is to examine how these are complicit.

Cinders to Come

And it is this that leads to his thinking of the future. Cinders are also future. Could there be a future that grows out of but is no longer contaminated by traces/cinders/ashes/marks? Not complicit with the thinking of violence and oppression in so many contexts, perhaps all with their different logic or perhaps linked by a shared logic, as Arendt suggests? Is there what Derrida calls an 'atheological heritage of the messianic', a future both of and for justice?[37] Derrida has projected several facets of this, and it is possible to show how these, too, stem from cinders.

The first is the idea of the human. At the end of *Night*, what looks back at Elie Wiesel from the mirror after liberation is 'a corpse', not a human being. Derrida, but not a joke: 'How do you recognise a ghost? By the fact it does not recognise itself in a mirror.'[38] Derrida addresses this in detail, and the 'human' is the subject of the final chapter of this book. Yet one current branch of this is the question—one Derrida returns to often—is of the relation between the human and the animal, and, despite his fond memories of Bobby in his essay 'The Name of the Dog', this marks another divergence between Levinas and Derrida. However, this debate too, lies in the cinders of the Holocaust. J. M. Coetzee's 'The Lives of Animals' section of *Elizabeth Costello* illustrates this. In despair and with words 'so outrageous that they are best spoken into a pillow or into hole in the ground, like King Midas', and that echo Heidegger's remarks on mechainized farming, Elizabeth Costello, the anti-carnivore activist and novelist, compares the Holocaust to the slaughter, use, and consumption of animals: 'a crime of stupefying proportions . . . It is as if I were to visit friends and remark about the lamp in their living room, and they were to say, "Yes, its nice isn't it? Polish–Jewish skin it's made of" '.[39] The Holocaust marks the

---

[37] Jacques Derrida, *Spectres of Marx*, tr. Peggy Kamuf (London: Routledge, 1994), 168.

[38] Ibid. 156.

[39] J. M. Coetzee, *Elizabeth Costello* (London: Secker & Warburg, 2003), 114–15. Throughout this section of the novel, a link between eating meat and the Holocaust is made, but the novel also deals with the Holocaust and questions of representation more generally.

horizon of this debate. Derrida suggests in *Politics of Friendship* that what it is to be human, or even what it is to demand justice, is yet to be decided or is yet to come as a process of humanization. It is to be aimed for, not a state from which we begin and this future-facing responsible shaping—'messianic telepoesis'—is the activity we should be under-taking.

The second is the question of the state and of democracy. This ground—the 'democracy to come'—has been very well covered by others. But again, it takes its origin from the Holocaust. Derrida writes that 'deconstructions have always represented . . . the at least necessary conditions for identifying and combating the totalitarian risk'.[40] Bernstein glosses this by arguing that the 'totalitarian risk is the risk of the coming into being of a totalitarian regime as a consequence of prin-cipled metaphysical totalization, even the principle of freedom. On this account no discrimination is made between "good" and "bad" acts of totalization since *qua* acts of totalization all entail the same risk.'[41] In this anti-totalitarian sense, Derrida's work echoes the work of liberals like Isaiah Berlin and Karl Popper for whom the totalitarianism of Nazism and of the Soviet Union was the enemy. But his position goes further than theirs, not only because he is not defending a cold war sta-tus quo but also because he is more than cautious about liberalism itself.[42] Here, in this warning way, deconstruction projects itself into the future, resistant to those discourses that will reduce it or delimit the potential of the polis for justice. It aims for the 'democracy to come'.

Finally, and perhaps delicately, the Holocaust underlies his develop-ing thought on forgiveness. Arguing that we 'are all heirs, at least, to persons or events marked, in an essential, interior, ineffaceable fash-ion, by crimes against humanity', the 'proliferation of scenes of repen-tance, or of asking "forgiveness", signifies, no doubt, a universal urgency of memory: it is necessary to turn towards the past; and it is necessary to take this act of memory . . . beyond the juridical instance'.[43] When forgiveness is used in a calculated fashion as part of the language of politics, then for Derrida these are not acts of 'forgive-ness', really, but acts of economic-political exchange. Forgiveness must

---

[40] Derrida, 'Like the Sound of the Sea', 647.

[41] J. M. Bernstein, *The Fate of Art* (London: Polity, 1992), 183.

[42] On this, see, e.g., *Deconstruction and Pragmatism*, ed. Chantal Mouffe (London: Routledge, 1996).

[43] Jacques Derrida, *On Cosmopolitanism and Forgiveness*, tr. Mark Hughes (London: Routledge, 2001), 29, 28. This will be abbreviated in the text as *OCF*.

be 'exceptional and extraordinary, in the face of the impossible: as if it interrupts the ordinary course of historical temporality' (*OCF* 32). He also makes it clear that forgiveness has an Abrahamic (that is—Judaic, Islamic, and Christian) heritage. But Derrida, in a discussion of the Holocaust—the Shoah he names it here—finds a contradiction in forgiveness. He cites the work of Vladimir Jankélévitch: ' "Forgiveness died in the death camps". Yes. Unless it only becomes possible from the moment that it appears impossible. Its history would begin, on the contrary, with the unforgivable' (*OCF* 37). That is, to forgive something inside the confines of ordinary life, a minor infraction, is simply part of the economics of rubbing along with the rest of the people in the world: forgiveness, in real sense, only begins outside this system of exchanges. Does this mean that Derrida thinks the Holocaust forgivable? Gideon Ofrat cites Derrida in interview:

I would say that in no case there is a right of anyone to argue that one must forgive or that one must not forgive . . . There should not be a duty to forgive or not to forgive . . . Everyone must reach the forgiveness in his own way, to take about it a responsibility without resorting to calculation of the judgement, the punishment, the penalty.[44]

That is, Derrida's task is not to sermonize, but to explore the grounds on which forgiveness is possible and the significance of these grounds. This analysis of forgiveness reveals that it is unclear whether one asks forgiveness for something or of someone, and if of someone, how and who? His example is the church in France who, again in relation to the Holocaust, 'asked forgiveness of God; it did not repent directly or only before people, or before the victims, for example the Jewish community who they took only as a witness, but publicly it is true, of the forgiveness asked in the truth of God' (*OCF* 38). This also reveals that forgiveness is sovereignty, with power which in the very act of forgiving 'confirms its own freedom or assumes for itself the power of forgiving' (*OCF* 58). Indeed, each 'time forgiveness is effectively exercised, it seems to suppose some sovereign power' (59). Derrida concludes this short discussion by naming his dream, that there could be 'forgiveness without power: unconditional but without sovereignty' (*OCF* 59). He goes on, as with the discussion of the human and of democracy, to say that the 'most difficult task, at once necessary and apparently impossible, would be to disassociate unconditionality and sovereignty. Will that be done one day? It is not around the corner, as is said. But since

---

[44] Ofrat, *Jewish Derrida*, 153.

the hypothesis of this unpresentable task announces itself, be it as a dream for thought, this madness is not so mad' (*OCF* 59–60).

All three of these examples demonstrate the same structure: that is, the sense of being interwoven into an existing and not innocent discourse; its problems and contradictions; and a sense of openness towards the future—a hope, if this is not too religious a word—that, in the act of thinking or even just identifying these questions, a change might be begun.

CONCLUSION

In this chapter I have argued that Derrida's work grows out of the Holocaust. Both in how it developed and in what it hopes, deconstruction already *is*, in its origins, about the Holocaust, not least because the cinder, the trace, underlies the time in which Derrida (and 'we', perhaps) think. The idea of the trace, developed from Levinas's work and expanded and explored by Derrida, emerges as the cinder, the both present and absent mark of the Holocaust. In turn, the cinder underlies the ways in which Derrida undertakes philosophy, how he understands the continued unavoidable complicity of thought with the Holocaust, and how, in three examples, Derrida exhibits a structure of deconstructive hope. A hope that is 'a certain emancipatory and messianic affirmation, a certain experience of the promise that one can try to liberate from any dogmatic and even from any metaphysic-religious determination, from any messianism'.[45] Again, this is not to recuperate the Holocaust, not to say that everything is fine and so ignore or reduce the genocide: quite the opposite. It is an attempt to approach the event as a singular event and to find, in its particularity, that which underlies both hope and despair.

In the final two chapters, I am going to explore how this thought illuminates discussion of the limits of reason and about the nature of what it is to be human, two specific issues raised by the Holocaust, and how these, in turn, illuminate this tradition of thought. That this is possible only stresses again how interwoven this thinking is with the Holocaust.

---

[45] Derrida, *Spectres*, 89.

11

The Limits of Understanding: Perpetrator Philosophy and Philosophical Histories

But the destruction of Nazism also leaves a silence after it: one does not dare think out Nazism because it has been beaten down like a mad dog, by a police action, and not in conformity with the rules accepted by its adversaries' genres of discourse (argumentation for liberalism, contradiction for marxism). It has not been refuted.[1]

INTRODUCTION

Primo Levi describes an encounter with Dr Pannwitz, who examines his knowledge of chemistry in Auschwitz: 'that look was not one between two men; and if I had known how completely to explain the nature of that look, which came as if across the glass window of an aquarium between two beings who live in different worlds, I would also have explained the essence of the great insanity of the Third Reich'.[2] A great pressure is felt to explain the 'great insanity' of the Third Reich, to explain Nazism, and so, at the same time, why the Holocaust happened, as these two 'events' are inextricably linked. The sources of this pressure and its results are open to question, but one consequence is what might be called 'perpetrator philosophy'. By this, I do not mean the 'theories of those who sought to cloak the Nazi tyranny in quasi-philosophical garb', like 'Ernst Hüber, Otto

---

[1] Jean-François Lyotard, *The Differend: Phrases in Dispute*, tr. Georges Van Den Abbeele (Manchester: Manchester Univerity Press, 1998), 106.
[2] Primo Levi, *If This is a Man*, tr. Stuart Woolf (London: Abacus, 1979), 111–2. On another encounter with Dr Pannwitz/Pannowitz, see Paul Steinberg, *Speak You Also*, tr. Linda Coverdale with Bill Ford (London: Penguin, 2001), 101.

Koellreuter and Carl Schmitt', and, of course, Martin Heidegger.[3] Rather, following the two previous chapters, I want to explore philosophical thought after the Holocaust which engages with the perpetrators to try to explain what the events mean for us afterwards.

THE POSSIBILITY OF EXPLANATION?

However, this very project seems to have three sorts of problems before one even begins. First, there is a 'meta-debate' over whether any understanding at all is even possible. The two positions might be summarized in the positions of Elie Wiesel and Yehuda Bauer. Wiesel argues that nothing 'justifies Auschwitz. Were the Lord Himself to offer me a justification, I think I would reject it . . . The barbed wire kingdom will forever remain an immense question mark on the scale of both humanity and its creator.' Yehuda Bauer says that the 'murder was committed by humans for reasons whose sources are found in history and which therefore can be rationally analysed'.[4] The former position Gillian Rose calls 'Holocaust piety', a mystification 'of something we dare not understand, because we fear that it may be all too understandable, all to continuous with what we are—human, all too human'.[5] Giorgio Agamben goes further when he argues that those 'who assert the unsayability of Auschwitz should be more cautious in their statement': 'if, joining uniqueness to unsayabilty, they transform Auschwitz into a reality absolutely separated from language, they break the tie between an impossibility and a possibility of speaking that . . . constitutes testimony; then they unconsciously repeat the Nazi's gesture' (*RA* 157).[6] However, the flaw with this opposition to 'Holocaust piety' is that it implies that 'mystification' or 'piety' is the end of the discourse, that—as if by evil fiat—it ends the conversation.

---

[3] Michael Burleigh, *The Third Reich: A New History* (London: Macmillan, 2000), 161. However, in the case of Heidegger, instead of attempting to justifying Nazism, Derrida writes that one 'could say he spiritualises National Socialism' and in part, this—rather than a 'justification'—is the difficulty with his legacy. Jacques Derrida, *Of Spirit*, tr. Geoffrey Bennington and Rachel Bowlby (London: University of Chicago Press, 1989), 39.

[4] Elie Wiesel, *All Rivers Run to the Sea* (London: Harper Collins, 1996), 105; Yehuda Bauer, *Rethinking the Holocaust* (London: Yale University Press, 2001), 7.

[5] Gillian Rose, *Mourning Becomes the Law* (Cambridge: Cambridge University Press, 1996), 43.

[6] On this, see also Zachary Braiterman, 'Against Holocaust-Sublime: Naive Reference and the Generation of Memory', *History and Memory*, 12 (2000), 7–28.

If this were the case—if Holocaust piety were the end of the matter, and all the witnesses remained piously silent and all the historians, theologians, philosophers, and what Rose calls 'Holocaust Ethnographers' did something else—then the opponents of this would be right. However, as I showed in the first and second chapters, not only are survivors unable to name precisely of what the 'unsayability' of the Holocaust consists (they give it different names: 'Night' for Wiesel, 'Radical Evil' for Semprun, 'Wstawàch', for example) but, and in this context more importantly, they continually discuss it, they publish and republish, tell and retell their experiences. This is neither to give up on explanation nor to claim it is possible. That we have to see their work as a different genre is part of the process of approaching the Holocaust; that historiography and so Holocaust history has to change, and has already in part changed, is also part of this process. Yehuda Bauer, with his usual intellectual generosity, makes this point, too: he writes that while Elie Wiesel claims that the

> suffering of the victims and the brutality of the perpetrators . . . can never be
> fully grasped or understood, and that therefore the Holocaust is inexplicable
> . . . he does everything in his power to transmit those experiences and make
> people understand them. His readers see the Holocaust shrouded in irrational-
> ity and mystification. . . . Yet by his great literary work, he actually does the
> opposite of mystifying: he explains.[7]

There is no sense that 'Holocaust piety' necessarily leads to closure or leads to 'myth and sentimentality' (as Rose describes the film *Schindler's List*).[8] Indeed, the idea behind 'Holocaust piety', taken honestly and not where the destruction of the European Jews is being used for cheap affect, seems to be that there could be no total explanation, no closure and that historical and other Holocaust scholarship should avoid (*pace* Friedländer and others) being 'normalized' or 'integrated' by offering such a closure. As Lacoue-Labarthe writes, its 'inexplicablility' means that National Socialism 'never ceases to haunt modern consciousness as a sort of endlessly latent "potentiality", both stored away and yet constantly at hand within our societies'.[9] This does not make any discussion or debate impossible: indeed, part of the task of much twentieth-century philosophy has been to bring into the 'realm of concepts'—philosophy— the inexplicable which stands outside it. And if 'Holocaust piety' means all thinking about the Holocaust throughout

---

[7] Bauer, *Rethinking the Holocaust*, 15.
[8] Rose, *Mourning Becomes the Law*, 47.
[9] Philippe Lacoue-Labarthe, *Heidegger, Art and Politics* (Oxford: Blackwell, 1990), 77.

all thinking, as in Adorno, for example, where 'no word tinged from on high . . . has any right unless it underwent a transformation' and 'All post-Auschwitz culture, including its urgent critique, is garbage', or in Derrida, where ' "Auschwitz" has obsessed everything that I have ever been able to think', then it underlies the work of Rose and Bauer, too.[10]

Second, there is a deep-seated and to some extent healthy cynicism among historians and others about philosophical attempts to engage with the Holocaust. In part, this stems from the historian's disciplinary, generic predisposition to detail, to small-scale facts, 'trails' of documents, and so a distrust of overall schema. Moreover, philosophers do not feel the need to keep up with the cutting-edge historical research, let alone visit the archives, which means many historians think less of them in this context: this creates a time lag between disciplines. However, this disciplinary bias itself is often the result of a blindness to their own and their discipline's theoretical and philosophical basis, not least as facts come to light, come to be facts in a sense, in relation to larger frameworks. More importantly, historians of the Holocaust are deeply aware of both the complexity of the events of the Holocaust and of how much is still opaque. Because of this, any attempt to make a definite judgement about, say, 'what the perpetrators thought' is almost always open to disproof, exceptions, and so on. Raul Hilberg points out that the personalities of the perpetrators 'did not fall into a single mould' and that they had many different reasons for committing the crimes they did: they were 'Zealots, Vulgarians and Bearers of Burdens'.[11] There are philosophers, too, who believe that philosophical work on the Holocaust is foolish. Alain Badiou, amazed by the conceited arrogance of philosophers taking on 'the burden of the century and . . . plead[ing] guilty', argues that if

philosophy is incapable of conceptualising the extermination of the European Jews, it is the fact that it is neither its duty nor within its power to conceptualise it. It is up to an other order of thought to render this thinking actual. For example, the thinking of historicity, that is, of History examined from the stand point of the political'.[12]

[10] Theodor Adorno, *Negative Dialectics*, tr. E. B. Ashton (London: Routledge, 1973), 367. 'Canons and Metonymies: An Interview with Jacques Derrida', in Richard Rand (ed.), *Logomachia: The Contest of the Faculties* (London: University of Nebraska Press, 1992), 195–218, 211–12.

[11] Raul Hilberg, *Perpetrators Victims Bystanders: The Jewish Catastrophe 1933–1945* (London: Harper Perennial, 1992), 51.

[12] Alain Badiou, *Manifesto for Philosophy*, tr. Norman Madarazs (Albany, NY: State University of New York Press, 1999), 30.

In fact, and passing over the point that saying that the Holocaust is beyond explanation by philosophy is itself very revealing and that other 'orders of thought' or genres have 'philosophemes' too, Badiou backtracks immediately: it would be to 'concede a strange victory to Hitler and his henchmen'—and even, he writes, perhaps rather tastelessly—'tantamount to making the Jews die a second time'—if 'thought itself . . . is in effect incapable of taking stock of the force which intended to annihilate it'.[13] For Badiou, as for Levinas and Derrida, in different ways, not only is Evil 'possible only through an encounter with the Good', living (and philosophizing) after the Holocaust is a question of pushing on, taking 'one more step'.[14] The reason that philosophers need to address the Holocaust is made, with a purposefully familiar and domestic metaphor, by Mary Midgley who suggests that philosophy is 'like plumbing' (an English cousin to continental *bricolage*). Both 'activities . . . arise because elaborate cultures like ours have, beneath their surface, a fairly complex system which is usually unnoticed, but which sometimes goes wrong'.[15] The task of the philosopher is to address this 'complex system', and the Holocaust, most clearly, calls for this. Historians and philosophers are bound up with one another: history through its unavoidable 'extra-historical' and philosophical commitments, philosophy—and certainly post-Holocaust philosophy—through both its involvement with the past and its implicit historicity. In this field at least, there may be much that they can teach each other.

Finally, attempts to explain the Holocaust do not suffer from a lack of information, although there is always more history to be written, or from a lack of interpretations: if anything, there are too many explanations of the Holocaust. This itself raises a significant issue: the difficulty lies in 'picking one', in following a historical interpretation or explanation. The same is as true of more 'philosophical' explanations, explaining the events through modernity (Bauman) or the paradoxes of the Enlightenment (Adorno, roughly) or Idealist philosophy (Levinas), as it is of more 'historical' ones. Philosophical accounts of the Holocaust are not immune from the same sorts of 'metahistorical issues' that are implicit in the discipline of history: they, too, are

[13] Badiou, *Manifesto for Philosophy*, 31.
[14] Alain Badiou, *Ethics*, tr. Peter Halliward (London: Verso, 2001), 91; Badiou, *Manifesto for Philosophy*, 32.
[15] Mary Midgley, *Utopias, Dolphins and Computers* (London: Routledge, 1996), 1.

attempts to explain the past by representing it. Just as with more historical accounts, it is in the 'choice' of explanation that the central problem behind this debate is revealed. It is impossible to accept one explanation without revealing or uncovering a truth about ourselves that may not be amenable to rational debate or discussion. Philosophical decisions are, as it were, the result of what is 'pre-philosophical'. The thought of Levinas and Derrida, and those they influence, to some extent, approaches this by discussing how the 'pre-' or 'non-'philosophical emerges in philosophy. Where they differ to many others is that, in the 'pre-' or 'non-'philosophical, they hold the thought, the memory of the Holocaust: as I have argued, it underlies all their work. This does not commit them to a single particular view of it—indeed, it may prevent any single such a view—but it does mean that they will reject both structures of thinking and conclusions that pass over the trace of Holocaust. This is to say, really, that in the West, the event of the Holocaust has already become part of how we identify ourselves, already part of out intellectual and cultural architecture: deciding how to explain the Holocaust (including deciding not to try to explain it) is to decide how to explain ourselves and in attempting to explain ourselves we cannot but try to explain the Holocaust.

'REFUTING' NAZISM?

It is these difficulties that create the context for thinking about the Holocaust philosophically. The inability of philosophy to 'refute' Nazism, the fact that it was 'beaten down like a mad dog', is disturbing and significant not for the Nazis, who could not have cared less, but for the claims of philosophy and culture more generally.[16] This concerns not the question of the political inefficacy of philosophy in this context, but wider questions of what philosophy specifically and culture more generally can do. The main reason that 'refutation' of Nazism was impossible philosophically is clear for historians. There was really no one Nazi ideology: 'Nazism's attraction lay less in any explicit ideology than in the power of emotions, images and

---

[16] Fackenheim, discussing the Holocaust and history, remarks dryly that he thinks 'the wisest man to deal with the Nazis was not a professional historian but an amateur, Winston Churchill'. Emil Fackenheim and Raphael Jospe (eds.), *Jewish Philosophy and the Academy* (London: Associated University Presses, 1996), 193.

phantasms.'[17] Struck by the fact that at Nuremberg none of the prisoners defended Nazi ideology, Mary Midgely commented that this was
because

> there was not really much coherent ideology that could be defended. The only
> part of it which carried real passionate conviction was emotional and destruc-
> tive; it was the hatred of the Jews. This always remained constant, but almost
> every other element varied according to the audience addressed and the polit-
> ical possibilities of the moment. The enemy might be Communism or capital-
> ism, the elite or the rabble, France or Russia or the Weimar government, just
> as interests dictated.[18]

That is, in terms of logical arguments, positions, and so on, there is not
much, in fact, to refute. As histories of the Reich show, Hitler revelled
in the impossibility of arguments against the voice of the *Volk*: moreover, for Arendt, it is precisely the (illusory) elevation by the Nazis of
race and 'Volk' out of national politics—the sphere of factional interests negotiated by argument and elections—that was their most basic
manœuvre and underlay their political success: indeed, this choice
against argument is characteristic of fascists in general.[19] This means
that, for example, analysing the 'logic' behind *Mein Kampf* will not
achieve anything, save to show that the author eschewed logic, a fact
he was happy to proclaim.

The question to be asked, then, is: how might one engage with
Nazism if their framework of understanding is so different? In one of
his odd Holocaust stories from the early 1950s, C. F. Forester tells the
story of the trial of 'Peter Schiller', commandant of the 'Rosenberg
Concentration camp'. In this fiction, told from the Nazi point of view,
Schiller is totally unable even to understand the framework of the legal
system by which he is being tried or why the British officer who
arrested him at the camp was so angry and vicious towards him. He
feels he did not do anything wrong. Finally, he comes to understand his
hanging through recent 'developments in German mythology . . . he
was being sacrificed to the God of the English'.[20] He only understands
what is happening to him through his own (Nazi) framework. Hilary

[17] Saul Friedländer, *Reflections on Nazism: An Essay on Kitsch and Death*, tr.
Thomas Weyr (Bloomington: Indiana University Press, rev. edn., 1993), 14.

[18] Mary Midgley, *Wickedness* (London: Routledge, 1984), 61–2.

[19] An international conference of fascists from thirteen countries, though not Germany,
held in 1934, was unable to agree 'a shared set of doctrinal principles', not least because
they were all committed to 'their own self-assertive form of hyper-nationalism' and not to
argument, Roger Griffin (ed.), *International Fascism* (London: Arnold, 1998), 1.

[20] C. S. Forester, *The Hostage* (London: New English Library, 1970), 111.

Putnam's *Reason, Truth and History* is haunted by Nazis and by the
questions that this short story begs. Putnam, in this book, develops
what he calls an 'internalist' perspective 'because it is characteristic of
this view to hold that *what objects does the world consist of?* is a question that makes sense to ask only *within* a theory or description'. [21] He
goes on

'Truth' in an internalist view, is some sort of (idealized) rational acceptability—some sort of ideal coherence of our beliefs with each other and with our
experiences as those experiences are themselves represented in our belief system . . . There is no God's eye point of view that we can know or usefully imagine; there are only the various points of actual persons reflecting various
interests and purposes that their descriptions and theories subserve. (*RTH*
49–50)

But Putnam is not arguing for a cultural relativism which, monstrously,
would accept the Nazis.[22] Rather, he believes that 'every fact is value
loaded and every one of our values also loads some fact . . . fact (or
truth) and rationality are interdependent . . . A being with no values
would have no facts either' (*RTH* 201). Indeed, 'truth is not the bottom
line: truth itself gets its life from our criteria of rational acceptability'
(*RTH* 132). In science, the criteria of 'rational acceptability' is
'revealed by what theories scientists and ordinary people consider
rational to accept . . . instrumentally efficacious, coherent, comprehensive and functionally simple' because this sort of 'representation system
is part of idea of human cognitive flourishing, and hence part of our
idea of total human flourishing, of Eudaemonia' (*RTH* 134). But science is not the be-all and end-all. Putnam suggests that the standards of
rational acceptability have to be broadened to take in other areas of
human life. The lack of a clear distinction between fact and value
reveals that—in ordinary speech—we make all sorts of ethical and
evaluative comments: for example, 'considerate' and 'inconsiderate'
are not only descriptions but also judgements and in writing historians
describe and judge simultaneously. Our ethical standards—what
people would expect, what they can and cannot defend, and so on—
also fall under the standards of rational acceptability for Putnam:
they can be investigated, discussed, explored, justified, and so on in an

[21] Hilary Putnam, *Reason, Truth and History* (Cambridge: Cambridge University
Press, 1981), 49. This will be abbreviated to *RTH* in the text.
[22] He argues that reducing 'all there is to "rationality" ' to 'what your culture says
. . . that [rationality] is simply defined by the local cultural norms is a scientific theory
inspired by anthropology' (*RTH* 126).

open-ended way, that is, not simply compared to an axiom and judged, but weighed against standards of consensual rationality. This is not to rule out indeterminate cases, or suggest that there are single, unambiguous answers. It is to say that, while

different ideas of human flourishing are appropriate for individuals with different constitutions . . . diversity is part of the ideal. And we see some tragic tension between ideals, and the fulfilment of some ideas always excludes the fulfilment of others. But . . . belief in a pluralistic ideal is not the same thing that belief that every human flourishing is as good as every other.   (*RTH* 148)

Putnam argues that we can and should reject some ideals of human flourishing as 'wrong, as infantile, as sick, as one-sided' (*RTH* 148). The choice of our 'conceptual scheme' both shows and is who we are. From a Levinasian perspective, however, all this falls within the 'said': it does not explain *why* or *how* ethics appears in the first place, only that it does and that is made manifest in different ways.[23] Indeed, Putnam, after Stanley Cavell, calls Levinas a 'moral perfectionist', a philosopher who believes that 'there is a need for something prior to principles or a constitution'.[24]

In the context of arguing that some ideals can—and should—be rejected, Putnam invokes that the 'rational Nazi' as a test case for both relativism and for Benthamiteism, and a real example of a wrong world view. Putnam suggests that if the Nazi has chosen 'Nazi' ends—had chosen or accepted standards of acceptability that were alien—then it is unclear, how he could be argued with: he is a 'rational Nazi'. Later, Putnam returns to this, tentatively, suggesting that this is too quickly to identity the Nazi with his ends. It might be more important to analyse not his final beliefs (in the superiority of the 'Aryan race', for example) but rather the irrationality of his beliefs and arguments—of how he came to believe in those final goals. If the Nazi tries to argue that his beliefs are right and good, this, Putnam says, is 'rubbish', a position for which he has 'no good arguments' since the 'notion of a 'good argument', he writes, is 'internal to ordinary moral discourse' (*RTH* 212). Moreover, if Nazism repudiates moral norms, Putnam argues it devel-

---

[23] Robert Bernasconi writes that Levinas addresses the ethical theories of the Western philosophical tradition 'rarely and never in much detail': this in part explains his lack of work on this area. Robert Bernasconi, 'The Truth that Accuses', in Gary Madison and Marty Fairburn (eds.), *The Ethics of Postmodernity* (Evanston, Ill.: Northwestern University Press, 1999), 24–34, 24.

[24] Simon Critchley and Robert Bernasconi (eds.), *The Cambridge Companion to Levinas* (Cambridge: Cambridge University Press, 2002), 36.

ops into a culture that 'would lose the ability to describe ordinary inter-personal relations, social events and political events adequately and perspicuously *by our present lights* . . . if the different ideology and moral outlook are . . . warped and monstrous, then the result will simply be an inadequate, unperspicuous, repulsive representation of inter-personal and social facts' (*RTH* 212; original italics). Even if the Nazi still maintains a moral vocabulary of sorts (say, believes it is wrong to steal cigarettes from death camp inmates, as Himmler did) then even these terms will no longer work in the same way that normal moral notions work. Michael Burleigh writes that, in the T-4 office in Berlin which administered much of the Holocaust

men and women coldly and calculatingly organised the murder of thousands of people. It is no use describing them as 'desk-bound murderers' . . . since even the secretaries shared their offices with jars of foul-smelling teeth, listening to dictation which enumerated 'bridge with three teeth', 'a single tooth' and so on. To bring this account to the moral level at which these people operated, one should mention that all T-4 employees could avail themselves of cut-price dental work, which utilised gold recycled from the mouths of their victims.[25]

Here, the 'confusion' of morality in the Third Reich emerges. Finally, for Putnam, if the Nazis simply say that they are Nazis because that is how thay feel, without offering an explanation, arbitrarily, then we are right to blame them for unjustified actions and beat them down like mad dogs. But all these seem really to describe ways in which the Nazi is simply not amenable to debate or rational discourse. Putnam's argument, at least in relation to Nazism, concurs with Lyotard's, and with C. S. Forester's short story: that the Nazi is simply beyond the moral world, beyond philosophical discourse, beyond the limits. This, as I suggested above, is no discovery, really, but something the Nazis claimed for themselves. Hilberg takes this further by stressing that it was not the action of a few Nazis, as the machinery was just too huge: the 'German perpetrator was not a special kind of German. What we have to say here about his morality applies not to him specially but to Germany as a whole.'[26]

In addition to the many histories of the Third Reich that detail the rise of Nazism, Hannah Arendt offers a complementary way of under-standing how this world emerges by exploring how the ideology of the

[25] Michael Burleigh, *Death and Deliverance* (London: Pan, 1994), 123.
[26] Hilberg, *The Destruction of the European Jews* (London: Holmes & Meier, 1985), 277.

totalitarian regimes works. Ideology for Arendt here means an '-ism which to the satisfaction of their adherents can explain everything and every occurrence by deducing it from a single premise' and so the 'logic of an idea'.[27] The Nazi ideology—'inadequate, unperspicuous and repulsive'—offered a total explanation of history, of the past, present, and future. This ideological thinking 'becomes independent of all experience'.[28] She continues:

> Ideological thinking orders facts into an absolutely logical procedure which starts from an axiomatically accepted premise, deducing everything else from it. The deduction may proceed logically or dialectically; in either case, it involves a consistent process of argumentation which, because it thinks in terms of a process, is supposed to be able to comprehend the movement of the suprahuman, natural or historical processes . . . Once it has established its premise, its point of departure, experiences no longer interfere with ideological thinking, nor can it be taught by reality.[29]

That is, the incommensurable world of Putnam's Nazi relied upon the foundation of an axiomatically established premiss (the Führer's will or the hatred of the Jews), which in turn created a world radically different from our own. These axioms are not accepted—as one might accept the criteria for an economic model, say, which would imply debate, discussion, and further co-dependent rational criteria—but are simply established by both physical and institutional force, and it is this establishment of these axioms that simply puts the Nazi outside rational discourse. In fact, while accurate on the split between 'experience' and the world, Arendt's analysis is almost too optimistic in its avowal of process: in the Third Reich the central principle was 'the "Führer" principle—what the leader said became law'.[30] The content of this, the Führer's will, could shift and change. What both Putnam and Arendt have drawn attention to is the phenomenon of Orwellian 'Doublethink': the ability to blot out experience and one's own judge-

---

[27] Hannah Arendt, *The Origins of Totalitarianism* (London: Harcourt Brace, 1973), 468.

[28] Ibid. 470.   [29] Ibid. 471.

[30] Burleigh, *The Third Reich*, 165. Kitty Hart tells how, in the days after the camp collapsed, she wandered about Salzwedel, getting food and exploring German houses. In one, she finds, hidden under the bed, 'a large framed portrait of Hitler. The elderly woman of the house . . . let out a cry. "Take anything, but please not the picture of my beloved Führer, please . . ." ': Kitty Hart, *Return to Auschwitz* (Panther: London, 1983), 202. Isabella Leitner describes, on the liner crossing to the USA after the war, how she saw a young German girl secretly kissing stamps with Hitler's face on. *Fragments of Isabella: A Memoir of Auschwitz*, ed. and tr. Irving Leitner (New York: New English Library, 1978).

ment from the world, and it is possible through the historical record to see how these fascist and genocidal 'axioms' became established in Germany.

THE HUMAN AND THE 'HUMAN'

> Only the brother can be betrayed. Fratricide is the general form of temptation, the possibility of radical evil, the evil of evil.[31]

However, from a Levinasian perspective, this wider situation is more complex, not least because, contra Arendt here (though not elsewhere), Levinas always finds the possibility of the experience of the other at the root of his thought. For Levinas, ethics is the originary relation to the other, an experience of persecution, an unavoidable feeling of responsibility. This underlies any system or organization (any 'said') and is made manifest even—especially, in fact—in the act of murder: the 'Other is the sole being I can wish to kill' (*TI* 198). Levinas writes that the 'unnarratable other loses his face as a neighbour in narration' (*OBBE* 166), meaning that the ethical relation, the moment of facing, is often 'concreted over' in the stories we tell and the ideologies we offer. In this context, the 'dehumanization' of the Jews is clear enough. However, while attempts to understand the Nazis through confronting their world view seems bound to show only that it is evil and also very different from ours, Levinas's work—the philosophy of a survivor—throws into disconcerting relief some of their actions.

The constant reawakening to the horror of the Holocaust in recent years often takes the form of sorts of questions like this: how could the murderers have carried out the killings? Did they think of the Jews as simply animals, as Hitler seemed to? Hitler, speaking to Horthy in April 1943, is recorded to have said:

If the Jews there [in Hungary] don't want to work they will be shot. If they can't work they must rot. They are to be treated like a tubercular bacillus that might attack healthy bodies This is not cruel, if one keeps in mind that even innocent natural creatures like rabbits and deer have to be killed to stop them causing damage.[32]

---

[31] Jacques Derrida, *The Politics of Friendship*, tr. George Collins (London: Verso, 1997), 275.

[32] Cited in Peter Longerich, *The Unwritten Order; Hitler's Role in the Final Solution* (Stroud: Tempus Publishing, 2001), 117.

It seems, however, that, in terms of the perpetrators, that there was something more problematic going on. The Nazi killers saw their victims as both human and not human at the same time: that is, in Levinas's terms, not human on the 'ontological plane', their face lost in the narration of and propaganda about the 'Jews', but clearly human on the 'ethical plane' which, as it were, grounds and orients—but does not prescribe behaviour on—the 'ontological plane'.

Hilberg writes of how Hitler had described the destruction process as 'humane' and indeed the ' "humaneness" ' of the destruction was an important factor in its success. It must be emphasised, of course, that this 'humaneness' was evolved not for the benefit of the victims but for the welfare of the perpetrators'.[33] But the very need for 'humaneness'— apart from its so-called efficiency—implies that the action of killing Jews was not like killing lice as the propaganda would have it, but something much, much worse. Vermin control agents do not usually have special alcohol consignments nor other assistance that distances them from the vermin they kill. Two examples from the perpetrators: in *Ordinary Men* Browning makes clear, but rightly without sympathy, the ways in which the killing was psychologically damaging for many of the men involved at the bottom end of the genocidal chain of command. Indeed, 'psychological demoralization' of these men in Reserve Police Battalion 101 led to changes in the killing process, and this form of demoralization was in part one of the reasons for the gas chambers and the creation of the Sonderkommandos.[34] This demoralization happened because, while the killers got better and more ruthless (and drunker), and the anti-Semitic propaganda became even more all-pervasive, they were still on some level (the ethical plane) seeing their victims as human. Again, at the opposite end of the genocidal chain of command, something similar is revealed in Himmler's famous speech at Posen on 4 October 1943:

It's one of those things it is easy to talk about—'The Jewish race is being exterminated', says one party member, 'that's quite clear, it's in our program—elimination of the Jews, and we're doing it, exterminating them'. And then they come, 80 Million worthy Germans, and each one has his decent Jew. Of course, the others are vermin, but this one is an A1 Jew. Not one of all those who talk this way has witnessed it, not one of them has been through it Most of you know what it means when 100 corpses are lying side by side, or 500, or 1000.

---

[33] Hilberg, *Destruction of the European Jews*, 276.
[34] *Ordinary Men: Reserve Police Battalion 101 and the Final Solution* (London: Harper Collins, 2nd edn., 1998), 77.

To have stuck it out and at the same time to have remained decent fellows, that is what has made us hard. This is a page of glory in our history which has never been written and is never to be written, for we know how difficult we should have made it for ourselves if—with the bombing raids, the burdens and the deprecations of war—we still had Jews today in every town as secret saboteurs, agitators and trouble makers.[35]

The distinction between the Jew as other, the phantasmogorical figure of the Jew-as-subhuman-yet-all-powerful of Nazi propaganda ('vermin'), and actual existing Jews that were neighbours and colleagues ('an A1 Jew') reveals that Himmler is aware of dichotomies in German attitudes. But more interesting, he admits that the sight of corpses affects one (in the way that, presumably, dead bacilli do not), and to have faced this and still gone ahead is what has made them 'hard'. The Jews here are both human and they are not. And the final, usual lie—about the Jews as saboteurs—also recognizes Jewish humanity: as 'equals' to whom one can ascribe emotions, actions, and so forth, not simply animals causing damage. One does not bother to deny or hide something that is not a crime.

Another trace of this ambivalence towards the Jews occurs in the language used. Much has been written about what Victor Klemperer called the 'philologically unique' language of the Third Reich, but it is only necessary to look at Hilberg's account to see how the Nazis concealed the process of genocide even from themselves with their own jargon—'special installations', 'special treatment', 'sent to the East', and so on.[36] But more importantly, they tried to conceal the process from their victims: the false station at Treblinka, the lie that the gas chambers were showers. Of course, these existed to try to help prevent Jewish or other rebellion: but this in itself shows that they knew they were dealing with those who might rebel, in a way that rabbits and deer do not. We do not lie to dogs or lice, only to each other.

It is this 'doubleness' of the Nazi view of the Jews—as human, as not human—that Levinas foregrounds: and it is precisely this that reveals the Nazi crime for what it is. It is as if to say that the very mechanization of the genocidal killing process, the isolation of the victims from the murderers wherever possible, the very gas chambers themselves,

---

[35] Office of United States Chief of Counsel for Prosecution of Axis Criminality, *Nazi Conspiracy and Aggression*, iv (Washington, DC: United States Government Printing Office, 1946), 563.

[36] Victor Kemperer, *The Language of the Third Reich*, tr. Martin Brady (London: Continuum, 2000), 11.

are proof of the 'antecedent and non-allergic presence of the Other' (*TI* 199), the 'ethical plane' (*TI* 201). This is to make a distinction between the idea about what it is to be human, that can clearly be changed and shifted, altered through the processes of identification, and some sense of the 'other', the 'human' beyond this that is the basis for any possible identification: a humanism beyond humanism. This is not to recoup or, in Langer's phrase, 'pre-empt' the Holocaust: Levinas is not ignorant of evil which he says 'is infinitely profound, its texture thick and inextricable. Its impregnable fortresses survive at the heart of a refined civilisation and deep in the souls conquered by grace.'[37] But it is to say that, for Levinas, while evil 'claims to be the contemporary, the equal, the twin, of the Good', it is in fact 'neither alongside of nor in front of the Good, but in the second place, beneath, lower than, the Good'.[38] It is to put the crimes in a context: the Nazi murderers knew that they were committing a most terrible crime, and yet the structure of subjectivity allowed them to do so. The various different forms of denial that Stanley Cohen analyses are psychological and political counterparts to this philosophical position: he writes that the 'state of "both knowing and not-knowing" . . . is indispensable for those who deliberately inflict terrible suffering on their fellow human beings'.[39]

CONCLUSION

Chapter 2 cites Levi's epiphanic moment, when an icicle is snatched from him and it is explained to him that 'there is no why here': it is emblematic for attempts to come to terms with the Holocaust. This 'there is no why here'—a chance remark made to and remembered by a prisoner who survived—sums up precisely how, as Adorno puts it, after Auschwitz our 'metaphysical faculty is paralysed because actual events have shattered the basis on which speculative metaphysical thought could be reconciled with experience'.[40] Philosophy of a certain sort can neither argue with the perpetrators nor has the tools to engage with the Holocaust. Indeed, the branches of philosophy that are more

[37] Emmanuel Levinas, 'Poetry and the Impossible', in tr. Seàn Hand (London: Athlone, 1990), *Difficult Freedom*, 127–32, 128.
[38] Emmanuel Levinas, 'Humanism and Anarchy', in *Collected Philosophical Papers*, tr. Alphonso Lingis (Dordrecht: Kluwer Academic Publishers, 1987), 127–40, 137, 136.
[39] Stanley Cohen, *States of Denial* (London: Polity, 2001), 50.
[40] Theodor Adorno, *Negative Dialectics*, tr. E. B. Ashton (London: Routledge, 1973), 362.

concerned with the nature of argument itself (as logic, say) or those that take argument and reason exclusively as a *sine qua non* of philosophy seem bound to be unable to engage with these issues in this way, which, since this is rarely their aim, is perhaps no flaw. But for those branches of philosophy that are ineluctably interwoven with the past, whether they acknowledge this or not, this is a serious matter. Indeed, the Holocaust reveals the limits of certain philosophical approaches: this is not a sign that they are finished or desiccated, but that they need to invoke new methods. And this is not even to raise the complex question of how to relate to contemporary neo-Nazis.

The route taken by Levinas, Derrida, and those influenced by them (as well as by Arendt and Bauman, for example) is to bring into the realm of philosophy that which it had previously done its best to pass over, that which was considered to be a-rational or irrational. With a terrible irony, of course, Heidegger's work is a very significant model for this. It is this influence as well as the seeming embrace of the irrational that leads some commentators to accuse these thinkers, and postmodernist thought in general, of being close to Nazism. If for these thinkers, an embrace of the irrational was all there was—just as for the Putnam's Nazi, the pre-rational embrace of the will of the *Volk* made clear in the Führer law was all there was—then this criticism would have some weight. However, these thinkers, as I have tried to show, are neither overthrowing philosophy or reason nor replacing it with an 'unarguable' truth. Rather in their work, they have admitted the 'irrational' and the historical, centrally, the Holocaust, into philosophical debate while still maintaining a commitment to reason, without letting either dominate. The 'irrational' and the historical question are questioned by the rational, and their work moves between the two constantly.[41] It is in this way that they are able to recognize the events of Nazism, to say more about it than simply acknowledge its evil. The point of philosophical histories is not, perhaps, to offer a complete account of the Holocaust and the Third Reich, nor should they absorb and supplant the generic rules and importance of other disciplines. What they do is to foreground certain issues, the complexities with

---

[41] In interview, Elie Wiesel, a student of Jewish mysticism, describes Levinas—who is often described by philosophers as mystical—as a 'rationalist' (Elie Wiesel; *Conversations*, ed. Robert Franciosi (Jackson, Miss.: University of Mississippi Press, 2002), 151. This is not to say that he is, but that from the point of view of someone committed to Kabbalah and mysticism, Levinas the philosopher—as his roots in the more rationalistic traditions of Lithuanian Judaism might suggest—looks very much a rationalist.

which we are, *pace* Derrida and others, still engaged, and which, if we maintained a strict delineation between what was philosophical and what was not, might not be obvious. Levi, with his terrible and wonderful detachment, writes of wanting to meet Pannwitz again, when he was free, 'not from a spirit of revenge, but merely from a personal curiosity about the human soul'.[42] The approaches suggested in the work of Levinas and Derrida, from more than curiosity, might be illuminating of the 'human soul', even that of Pannwitz.

---

[42] Levi, *If This is a Man*, 111.

12

The Postmodern, the Holocaust, and the Limits of the Human

> Humanism has to be denounced only because it is not sufficiently human.[1]

INTRODUCTION

The preceding chapter was about the impact of the Holocaust on reason and understanding. This chapter is about what the Holocaust means for the idea of the human. In one sense, of course, this is a banal topic, and has been discussed over and over again. However, the postmodern has a great deal to say about the human, and the idea of the human after the Holocaust foregrounds a great deal about postmodern thought.

Discussions of the human characterize postmodern discourse.[2] For example, in her celebrated essay 'A Cyborg Manifesto', Donna Haraway uses the image of the cyborg 'as a fiction mapping our social and bodily reality and as an imaginative resource' because, she suggests, our humanity has changed: 'we are all chimeras, theorised and fabricated hybrids of machine and organism; in short we are cyborgs'.[3] Haraway wants to offer biological change as a way of thinking about a wider moral or cultural change. In the constellation of ideas known as postmodernism much is made of transformations of the body into the inhuman or the posthuman and this celebration of technology is one strand of post-war anti-humanism. More generally, this anti-humanism takes the form of deposing the agency and power of the human subject and suggesting that the human is prey to unavoidable

---

[1] Emmanuel Levinas, *Otherwise than Being: or, Beyond Essence*, tr. Alphonso Lingis (The Hague: Martinus Nijhoff, 1981), 128.

[2] See, e.g., Neil Badmington (ed.) *Posthumanism* (London: Palgrave, 2000).

[3] Donna Haraway, *Simians, Cyborgs, and Women* (London: Free Association Books, 1991), 150.

and 'extra-human' forces: the unconscious, the social, the genetic, the linguistic, the profound structures of being, all with proper names attached (Freud, Marx, Darwin, Saussure, Nietzsche). From a post-Holocaust perspective it is tempting to see the embrace of these as somehow both trying to explain what happened ('how did a whole system go so wrong?') and of being exculpatory and, despite their orientation, oddly theological ('it wasn't us, but some force beyond us' or even 'we were only following orders'). But this perspective itself is open to the criticism that it already presupposes a fixed set of human values, such as agency and moral choice, and it is precisely these values that the Holocaust has put into question.

Within this heterogeneous movement there is another thread, not so much anti-humanistic as about the hypocrisy and failures of humanism. In both a colonial and Second World War context, Fanon—badly wounded in action on 25 November 1944 at the Battle of the River Doubs and awarded the Croix de Guerre—named 'this Europe where they are never done talking of Man, yet murder men everywhere they find them'.[4] Levinas, too, writes of how the horrors of the twentieth century show up the 'basic inability to guarantee the privileges of humanity of which humanism had considered itself the repository'.[5] It is this thread, not the discussion of technological advances, which is most revealing about the human after the Holocaust. The more serious work of those thinkers described as postmodern approaches this issue and, despite what Levinas calls 'the horror of 1933', usually through the phenomenological and post-phenomenological tradition opened up by Heidegger.[6] However, while there are many histories of how the status of 'human' was withdrawn from the victims of the Holocaust, it is hard to explore how this felt and what this meant: here, the personal and subjective works of testimony are of more guidance, describing, while emplotted within the limits of genre, narrative, and form, how this 'becoming inhuman' was experienced.

---

[4] Franz Fanon, *The Wretched of the Earth*, tr. Constance Farrington (Harmondsworth: Penguin, 1990), 251. For his life, see David Macey, *Frantz Fanon* (London: Granta, 2000), 102.

[5] Emmanuel Levinas, *Difficult Freedom*, tr. Seàn Hand (London: Athlone, 1990), 281

[6] *Is it Righteous to Be? Interviews with Emmanuel Levinas*, ed. Jill Robbins (Stanford, Calif.: Stanford University Press, 2001), 33.

HEIDEGGER AND HUMANISM

> You ask . . . 'how can some sense be restored to the word
> "Humanism"?' Your question not only presuppose a desire to
> retain the word 'humanism' but also contains an admission that
> this word has lost its meaning.[7]

In the year after the war, Jean Beaufret wrote to Heidegger:
Heidegger's response is 'Letter on Humanism', which—not least in the
way it analyses and summarizes a tradition of thought—forms a backdrop to later debates over the human.[8] Though Heidegger takes
Sartre's work as his implicit target, the backdrop to the letter is the
Second World War, the destruction of Germany and the Nazis, and the
Holocaust. Though it is some matter for debate how much Germans
knew of the death camps during the war, from 1945 the stories, testimonies, and evidence of the genocide were rapidly becoming public
knowledge, although perhaps in confused and confusing form even for
the International Military Tribunal at Nuremberg: while the 'collection and cataloguing of documentation was a uniquely valuable service
to students of Nazism . . . the overall analyses of the murder of the Jews
by the Allied courts were nowhere near as helpful. Indeed, beyond the
basic outlines of the murder programme . . . the jurists got it wrong
more often than they got it right.'[9] Yet more than the outline of what
had happened was clear, even to Heidegger.

The themes of the 'Letter on Humanism' are what Heidegger calls
the leading forth of Being, the role of language as the house of being,
and the nature of thinking, which he argues is not 'practical' or 'scientific', and yet, in this, not irrational. Heidegger makes a division
between the organic, animal 'homo' and the human 'humanus' (*BW*
200) and stresses that for a humanism 'meditating and caring, that man
be human and not inhumane' (*BW* 200), the human 'really does remain
the concern of such thinking' (*BW* 200). Yet this is not so clear cut: 'if
one understands humanism in general as a concern that man become
free for his humanity and find his worth in it, then humanism differs

---

[7] Martin Heidegger, *Basic Writings*, ed. David Farrell Krell (London: Harper & Row,
1977), 224. This will be abbreviated to *BW* in the text.
[8] Jean Beaufret became a supporter of Robert Faurisson and a Holocaust denier and,
as a denier, attacked 'Emmanuel Levinas in a way that far exceeded a justifiable critique'.
Victor Farias, *Heidegger and Nazism* (Philadelphia: Temple University Press, 1989), 287.
[9] Donald Bloxham, *Genocide on Trial* (Oxford: Oxford University Press, 2001), 2

according to one's conception of the "freedom" and "nature" of man'
(*BW* 201). Indeed, Heidegger offers a history of 'humanism' from
Greece to (predictably) Germany: '*Humanitas*, explicitly so called, was
first considered and striven for in the age of the Roman Republic.
Homo Humanus was opposed to *Homo Barbarus*', writes Heidegger
(*BW* 200). To be a human was to be Roman with a Greek education;
then, in the eighteenth century, to be in the tradition of Goethe and
Schiller (this irony is too simple for Semprun at Buchenwald: 'Goethe
and Eckerman on the Etterberg, their refined, learned conversations on
the very spot where the camp was built . . . No, too easy!' (*LL* 94)).
Because it is historically conditioned, every 'humanism' is already a
'metaphysics': for the Romans, the human was a rational animal; for
Marx, the human is defined in and through society which secures
human needs; for Christianity, in redemption. To recover 'humanitas',
humanism is to be 'opposed because it does not set the humanitas of
man high enough' (BW 210). It is only, for Heidegger, by recovering
Being and the role of 'man' as 'shepherd of Being' (221) that this can be
resolved, and philosophy—metaphysics—gets in the way. In contrast
to philosophy, Heidegger argues that thinking 'does not overcome
metaphysics by climbing still higher, surmounting it, transcending it
somehow or other; thinking overcomes metaphysics by climbing back
down into the nearness of the nearest' (*BW* 231). In this way, in 'climbing down', Heidegger argues that the essence of ethics—already a term
laden with too much metaphysical weight—comes into view, through
Heraclitus's saying *ēthos anthrōpōi daimōn*: in Heidegger's translation,
which is not only linguistic but also 'chronic' (that is, he suggests,
across time), 'Man dwells, in so far as he is man, in the nearness of god'.
Heidegger writes that ' "ethics" ponders the abode of man' (*BW* 235)
and thinking 'the humanitas of homo humanus' is brought 'into the
realm of the upsurgence of the healing' (*BW* 237). This thinking 'that is
to come is no longer a philosophy, because it thinks more originally
than metaphysics' (*BW* 242).

    Of course, there is no mention here of the death camps, and the ref-
erence to healing may have as much to do with the healing of
Germany—the successor of Greece and the heir of Europe for
Heidegger—as with any other healing. However, the idea of the distinction between the 'human animal' and the 'human', and the role of
the metaphysics that shapes how we think of the 'human', offer a crucial and effective insight and one that other thinkers have taken up. The
recent work of Giorgio Agamben on the Holocaust is the clearest

example of this, and illustrates both the strengths and weaknesses of this approach.

AGAMBEN, *ZOE*, AND *BIOS*

Like many others, Agamben believes that that 'almost none of the ethical principles our age believes it could recognise as valid have stood the decisive test, that of an *Ethics more Auschwitz demonstrata*' and aims to analyse what the human might be after the Holocaust.[10] Agamben's work begins in 'biopolitics'. Where Foucault followed through the discourses that constituted subjects—the 'technologies of the self'—and Arendt explored the logic and actions of the totalitarian and imperialistic states of the first half of the twentieth century, Agamben's fertile insight is to bring these two together and explore how these two combined to create the recognizable 'biopolitics' of modernity. The source of much of Agamben's thought—and Arendt's and Foucault's too—is the work of Heidegger.

Agamben responds to Heidegger's terrible silence on the Holocaust and, where Heidegger finds the human 'conditioned by metaphysics', Agamben finds the human 'conditioned by politics' in biopolitics. The 'human' operates precisely as a political formation. Agamben argues that the distinction between the Greek terms *zoe* ('the simple fact of living common to all living beings . . . animals, men or gods') and *bios* ('the form of living proper to an individual or a group') underlies all discourse in the West on what the human is, on sovereignty, and on ethics and that the Holocaust was the most potent manifestation of the problems inherent in this for modernity.[11]

In modernity, the 'modern state does nothing other than bring to light the secret tie uniting power and bare life' (*HS* 6) and the Muselmann is the ultimate figure of biopolitical power. No longer he or she, it

not only shows the efficacy of biopower, but also reveals its secret cipher . . . a survival separated from every possibility of testimony, a kind of absolute biopolitical substance that, in its isolation, allows for the attribution of demographic, ethnic, national and political identity . . . the Muselmann is nothing

---

[10] Giorgio Agamben, *Remnants of Auschwitz*, tr. Daniel Heller-Roazen (New York: Zone Books, 1999), 13: further references will be abbreviated to *RA*.

[11] Giorgio Agamben, *Homo Sacer*, tr. Daniel Heller-Roazen (Stanford, Calif.: Stanford University Press, 1998), 1: further references will be abbreviated *HS* in the text.

other than . . . the space empty of people at the centre of the camp that, in separating all life from itself, marks the point in which the citizen passes in to the
Staatsangehöringe of non-Aryan descent, the non-Aryan into the Jew, the Jew
into the deportee and, finally, the deported Jew beyond himself into the
Muselmann, that is, into a bare, unassignable and unwitnessable life   (*RA*
156–7).

It is because the Muselmann is a 'life that is absolutely indistinguishable from law' (*HS* 185), and because in turn that the camps created the
Muselmann, that the camps are the 'biopolitical paradigm of the modern' (*HS* 117). Every 'attempt to rethink the political space of the West
must begin with the clear awareness that we no longer know anything
of the classical distinction between zoe and bios, between private life
and political existence' (*HS* 187).

There are a number of problems with Agamben's account. First, to
concentrate on the Muslemanner as the 'event' at the heart of the
Holocaust is open to question. Certainly, they serve to illustrate his
thesis better than, for example, the open-air shootings of around
1,300,000 Jews *or* the ghetto clearances *or* the millions more selected
and herded straight to the gas chambers (a 'man would step off a train
in the morning, and in the evening his corpse was burned and his
clothes were packed away for shipment to Germany'[12]) *or* what Primo
Levi, in his essay 'The Grey Zone', called 'National Socialism's most
demonic crime', the organization of the Sonderkommando, *or* (in case
the numbers and events are too numbing) the murder of Yankel Meisel
in Auschwitz on 17 July, 1942 *or* the murder of Potyo, Isabella Leitner's
younger sister, at their arrival at Auschwitz.[13] The Holocaust is all
these events, and more. Moreover, each of them—along with many
other phenomena—reveal much about the issue of the human and
humanism. The point is not that the focus on the Muselmanner is
wrong, but any focus on any event of the Holocaust is already the result
of a theory-laden choice, and will already lead to certain conclusions
and answers. Second, Agamben's argument about how the camps mark
a world different from the past—modernity formed by the 'radical
transformation of politics into the realm of bare life'—also applies to

[12] Raul Hilberg, *The Destruction of the European Jews* (London: Holmes & Meier,
1985), 221.
[13] Primo Levi, *The Drowned and the Saved*, tr. Raymond Rosenthal (London:
Abacus, 1988), 37; Rudolf Vrba and Alan Bestic, *I Cannot Forgive* (London: Didgwick &
Jackson and Anthony Gibbs & Phillips, 1963), 1; Isabella Leitner, *Fragments of Isabella:
A Memoir of Auschwitz*, ed. and tr. Irving Leitner (New York: New English Library,
1978), 17.

the colony and the colonial subject: the 'fact that racism is the main ideological weapon of imperialistic politics is so obvious that it seems as
though many students prefer to avoid the beaten track of truism'.[14]
Indeed, Homi Bhabha argues that for 'the emergence of modernity—as
an ideology of beginning, modernity as the new—the template of this
"non-place" [of modernity] becomes the colonial space'.[15] This is not
to say Agamben is wrong, but only that his definition, if he wants to
limit it to the death camps, is too narrow. Thirdly, and importantly
from a Levinasian perspective, Agamben's bare life is too bare, too
much like Heidegger's abstract *Dasein*. For Levinas, the 'bare fact of
life is never bare'.[16] 'Bare life' is intentional, not simply 'there', even in
the case of the Muselmann. We do not have 'bare life' and then eat or
warm ourselves. Eating and warming are what life consists of. 'Bare
life' is not hungry or cold: cold and hunger are what makes up 'bare
life'. And in the eight testimonies cited in Agamben's *Remnants of
Auschwitz* there are suggestions the Muselmann maintained an interest in food, warmth, and survival ('I used to . . . look for skins in the
trash' (*RA* 166); 'I kept myself warm when the Germans weren't watch-
ing' (*RA* 166); 'I just wanted to survive another day' (*RA* 167); 'They
spoke only about their memories and food' (*RA* 168). This is significant
because it is precisely on the content of 'bare life' and experience that
crucial arguments, discussed below, about the nature of the human
turn. For Levinas, the ethical signifies 'within experience' (*TI* 23). That
is, he argues that ethics—the relation with the other—is grounds of the
possibility of experiencing the world in the first place. Levinas, in this
respect, is a good phenomenologist, and seeks to make his case by
recourse to reflection on experience alone. Beyond or behind all philosophical, political, or theological language, for Levinas, the act of facing is the source of ethics. This arises not from doctrines of humanism
or from education, but from the experience of the other. Ethics relies
not on human life but what is between human lives. This ethics is not
one of reassurance, it does not mobilize a morality but a responsibility.

Finally, neither Heidegger nor Agamben explores fully the processes
that go between 'bare life' and the 'human', from *zoe* to *bios*.
Heidegger argues that 'humanitas' set Romans apart from barbarians,

---

[14] Hannah Arendt, *The Origins of Totalitarianism*, new edn. (New York: Harcourt,
Brace & World, 1966), 160.

[15] Homi Bhabha, *The Location of Culture* (London: Routledge, 1994), 246.

[16] Emmanuel Levinas, *Totality and Infinity: An Essay on Exteriority*, 3rd printing, tr.
Alphonso Lingis (London: Kluwer Academic Publishers, 1991), 112.

and of course, it was precisely this idea of the 'human' that created the idea of the uncultured barbarian, hardly able to speak (thus 'bar-bar-bar'). The Romans

were particularly fond of cutting off people's heads. Obviously there was no particular concentration of severed heads in any one period, as in historical times closer to our own, but rather a constant and recurrent presence of this practice distributed throughout Roman history. Heads severed with great finesse or lopped off clumsily . . . stuck up on pikes or poles in military camps, exposed at the focal point of civil life . . . head of common folk or of the great actors in history.[17]

'Humanitas' seems to have little to do with a 'deep layer of human solidarity' or behaving well in a more modern sense, and more to do with identification as and with a certain group, and it is to this, the process of identification, to which I now return.

IDENTIFICATION

In the first chapter I discussed the process of identification as a literary process: I argued that it was ineliminable and unavoidable, even when, perhaps, it was better not indulged. I also argued that it was hard to understand: indeed, no discourse, even psychoanalysis, seemed to have grasped what happens at its core. And this chapter returns to this central, everyday but enigmatic experience in another, wider way. It is this process of identification that is the interplay between the human animal and the human: identification creates both the humanitas and the homo, the humane and the inhuman. To clarify: we are not first simply organic beings and then, in a sudden moment of self-awareness, become humans. Indeed, it is the very fact of our humanness that gives meaning as said or as narrative to the human animal and, likewise, the human animal gives a site to the human. This is the central idea that underlies Judith Butler's *Gender Trouble*, that the meaning and identity of the body is determined by the culture that it is already within. However, at the same time, the body in its needs and very form serves to give not a meaning to but is that which underlies the human. The idea of the human and the human body define each other. This is the

---

[17] Andrea Giardina (ed.), *The Romans*, tr. Lydia Cochrane (London: Chicago University Press, 1993), 4. See also in this context ch. 12, Paul Veyne, 'Humanitas: Romans and Non-Romans', 342–96.

significance of the face for Levinas: that facing which is there before it has a determinate face. He explains that

One can first of all consider the face, *le visage*, as if it were something seen, although I would then say, in French, it is defaced, *dévisagé*. Defacement occurs as a way of looking, a way of knowing, for example, what colour your eyes are. No, the face is not this. 'Face', as I have always described it, is nakedness, helplessness, perhaps an exposure to death.[18]

The face is not the colour of the eyes but the possibility of eyes having a colour. This shuttling process between the site and the meaning is one of identification. This process is hard to explain clearly not only because of difficulties with psychology and linguistic terms, but because the process is part of what it is to be 'human', the 'content'— how one is identified, what one is identified as—varies so much from time to time and from place to place. Thus literature and, in or after dark times, testimony, especially that which is singular and particular, is the best guide to this.

But identification is not just a literary process, although the literary process is clearly involved with it. Identification names part of what it is to be human. As I suggested in my discussion of memory, our self-identity is in part created within and in part interpellated from without: the process of identification is both internal and external, both voluntary and involuntary, active and passive. Even without self-reflection (and this word is a metaphor that stresses the inextricable interlinking of the animal and the human, the face reflecting the person), identification is 'the psychical mechanism that produces self-recognition'.[19] It is also a central part of the way we build—or have built—the imagined communal identities that shape our personalities. But identifications are not simply chosen nor evolved but often thrust upon people. Jean Améry wrote that

I don't believe in the God of Israel. I know very little of Jewish Culture. I see myself as a boy at Christmas, plodding through a snow covered village to midnight mass; I don't see myself in a synagogue . . . The picture of my fathers . . . did not show me a bearded Jewish sage, but rather a Tyrolean Imperial Rifleman . . . If being a Jew implies having a cultural heritage or religious ties, then I was not one and can never become one.[20]

[18] *Is it Righteous to Be?*, 144–5.
[19] Diana Fuss, *Identification Papers* (London: Routledge, 1995), 2, abbreviated to *IP*.
[20] Jean Améry, *At the Mind's Limits*, tr. Sidney Rosenfeld and Stella Rosenfeld (London: Granta Books, 1999), 83. This will be abbreviated as *AML* in the text.

But he goes on:

> On my left forearm I bear the Auschwitz number; it reads more briefly than the Pentateuch or the Talmud and yet provides more thorough information. It is also much more binding than the basic formulas of Jewish existence. If to myself and to the world, including religious and nationally minded Jews, who do not regard me as one of their own, I say: I am a Jew, then I mean by that those realities and possibilities that are summed up in the Auschwitz number. (*AML* 94)

This contrast between how one feels and how one is interpellated is why Améry calls this essay 'On the Necessity and Impossibility of Being a Jew' and makes clear in the starkest terms that identification is not, or is not only, a personal, 'internal' matter. This is clear, too, from Friedländer's memoir and many, many other Holocaust testimonies.

Diana Fuss suggests that identification 'names the entry of history and culture into the subject, a subject that must bear the traces of each and every encounter with the external world' (*IP* 3). Following Fanon, whom she argues offers the 'critical notion that the psychical operates precisely as a political formation' and 'draws our attention to the historical and social conditions of identification', Fuss writes that 'identification names not only the history of the subject but the subject in history' (*IP* 165). This is why she cites Philippe Lacoue-Labarthe, 'why would the problem of identification not be, in general, the essential problem of the political?' (*IP* 164). It is the process by which we orient ourselves and are constructed by relations to the historical and political contexts in which we live. It is crucially important because, as Lacoue-Labarthe says, while the

> term 'identification' is, however, borrowed from Freud, because it is ultimately the only one we possess to designate what is at stake in the mimetic process and, above all, because once eased out of its aesthetico-psychological context, in which it in fact remains problematical, it can be drawn into the stronger network of the proper (or own: *le propre*) and appropriating, of appropriation and de-propriation or disappropriation etc.[21]

That is, identification and the act of naming that identification is the basis of politics ('*We*, the people . . .') and so involved with art. What is at stake in the mimetic process is identification, which is what makes up the political: thus, the politics of deconstruction, 'an interrogation of the mimetologism and essentialism and hence of the metaphysics of

---

[21] P. Lacoue-Labarthe, *Heidegger, Art and Politics* (Oxford: Blackwell, 1990), 82.

presence'.[22] Clearly the process of identification is part of the revelation of 'how the world is for us' as well as part of the way that representation changes the world. However, as Lacoue-Labarthe makes clear, this process is one of 'appropriation', 'de-propriation', or 'disappropriation'. The outcomes of this process are perhaps at their starkest, in Western history, in the Holocaust.

Indeed, for Jean-Luc Nancy and Lacoue-Labarthe, it is this process that lies at the heart of Nazism. In 'The Nazi Myth' they focus on the Nazi ideology, understood in Hannah Arendt's terms. As I have suggested, for Arendt an ideology is an idea or grounding principle that, for its adherents, can explain everything, and so makes the regime's created world independent of experience. The first premiss of Nazism, Nancy and Lacoue-Labarthe argue, was racism: in fact, it might be more accurate to argue that it was the combination of anti-Semitism and the Führer principle, but the structure of the argument remains the same. The ideological processes taken from a central assertion or axiom not only aimed 'to organise the infinite plurality of human beings as if all humanity were just one individual' but also consumed all otherness into its own system.[23] The logic on which this states relied was omnivorous. Nancy and Lacoue-Labarthe go further, and suggest that this means that there is a 'logic of fascism. This also means that a certain logic is fascist, and this logic is not wholly foreign to the general logic of rationality inherent in the metaphysics of the Subject.'[24] It is this 'logic', which, for them, neither belongs to the philosophical tradition nor is utterly alien to it, that allows them to explain the 'Nazi Myth', or, rather, the grounds of possibility on which this myth arose. Identity was 'bound up in the construction of a myth', an 'identitificatory mechanism' (NM 296). For Plato, they argue, a myth

is a fiction, in the strong, active sense of 'fashioning' or . . . 'plastic art': it is, therefore, a fiction, whose role is to propose, if not to impose, models or types . . . in imitation of which an individual, or a city, or an entire people, can grasp themselves and identify themselves . . . myth, like the work of art that exploits it, is an instrument of identification. It is, in fact, the mimetic instrument par excellence.   (NM 297, 298)

---

[22] J. M. Bernstein, *The Fate of Art* (London: Polity, 1992), 147.

[23] Arendt, *Origins of Totalitarianism*, 438.

[24] Philippe Lacoue-Labarthe and Jean-Luc Nancy, 'The Nazi Myth', *Critical Inquiry*, 16 (Winter 1990), 291–312, 294. This will be abbreviated to NM in the text.

The Nazi state took over the 'appropriation of the means of identification' (NM 299). It was not simply the 'aestheticicisation of politics' (to which 'it would have been sufficient to respond, in a Brechtian manner, with a "politicisation of art", as if totalitarianism were not perfectly able of assimilating that as well'), but the 'fusion of politics and art, the production of the political as work of art' (NM 303). The Nazis did this through myth: this is understood not as 'mythology'—Wotan, the Edda, the Black Sun, and so on—but as 'the power to bring together the fundamental forces and directions of an individual or of a people, the power of a subterranean, invisible, non-empirical identity . . . and exclusive difference, and its affirmation' (NM 305). This identity is not a fact, nor a discourse but is 'given as dreamed. Mythical power is the power of the dream, of the projection of an image with which one identifies' (NM 305). The specifics of the Nazi myth, they suggest, lie in the assertions that the race is 'linked to blood', that the Aryan race are the 'founders of civilisation *par excellence*' (NM 309): it opposes the idea of a *Volk* to the idea of a universal humanity.

The Jews, as well as other minorities to a lesser extent, were involved in this process: to create one *Volk*, others need to be 'depropriated', de-identified, which in turn powered the Nazi identification. Of course, the 'depropiation' can only occur to someone who is already recognized as human: the ways in which the Jews in Germany had their identity as Germans and Jews taken away and as Nazi-defined 'Jews' imposed is a clear case of this. In modern polities, as Hannah Arendt argues, rights accrue to identity: as identity changes or is changed, either internally or externally, though both are of course related, so rights change. Towards the end of the 1930s, a Jew in Nazi Germany, she points out, technically, had more rights if caught committing a crime and so was identified as a criminal than as a Jew.

The question of legal and political identity is only part of a wider question of human identity: Lacoue-Labarthe's and Nancy's argument can be pushed further, from legal and national identity to a sense of identity as 'human', the sense of *humanitas*. The Holocaust is precisely where the process of identification, understood as sympathy or even as a basic 'sense of humanity', broke down. As Geoffrey Hartman writes, 'the limits of human sensibility have become clear . . . There was no greater collective failure of sensibility in a mainly Christian Europe than what happened in the Holocaust. The status of being human was denied the Jews; all pity, all feeling was withdrawn from them, even within their own country.'[25] This is the 'depropriation' of the human already recognized, and can be seen over and over again, in many different ways. David Patterson cites several testimonies to stress the dehumanizing effect of being tattooed and losing one's name:

'I became A-7713, After that I had no other name' (Wiesel) . . .

'Henceforth I would be, merely, KZ prisoner A 8450' (Nyiszli) . . .

'Mine was 55091—my new name from now on' (Zyskind) . . .

'I looked at my number: 7, 115. From that moment I ceased to be a man' (Donat) . . .

'That, indeed, was the last time I used my name . . . for now I was prisoner number 44070' (Vrba) . . .

'A filthy needle . . . erased Nathan Schapelski from the human race and bought into being Haftling 134138' (Schapell) . . .

'I was number 25,403. I still have it on my right arm and shall carry it with me to the grave' (Lengyel) . . .

'We ceased to be human beings with family names . . . In my metamorphosis I was number 124753' (Sandberg) . . .[26]

The tattoos marked a change in status from human to less than human. Levi writes 'I have learnt that I am Haftling; we have been baptised, we will carry the tattoo on our left arm until we die . . . It seems that this is the true initiation.'[27] Lengyel, cited above, writes that a 'tattooed woman felt that her life was finished she was no longer anything but a number'.[28] Another very common point of comparison in testimony is with animals, against whom the victims come off worse. 'On the door a metal plaque gave the number of horses the building would shelter. "Mangy animals to be separated immediately" it read. How fortunate the horses had been! Nobody ever bothers to take any precautions on behalf of the human beings who were kept there.'[29] 'I'm still a calf in a truck'.[30] 'At night we slept on the dirt floor, sitting cross legged or lying on someone else's buttocks. The weak dozed standing up, pushed

---

[25] Geoffrey Hartman, *The Sympathy Paradox: Poetry, Feeling and Modern Cultural Morality* (Austin, Tex.: Harry Ransom Humanity Research Centre, 1996), 17.

[26] David Patterson, *Sun Turned to Darkness* (Syracuse, NY: Syracuse University Press, 1998), 165.

[27] Primo Levi, *If This is a Man and the Trace*, tr. Stuart Woolf (London: Abacus, 1979), 33.

[28] Olga Lengyl, *Five Chimneys* (London: Panther, 1959), 116.   [29] Ibid. 36

[30] Vrba and Bestic, *I Cannot Forgive* 46.

against the walls. (Decades later, I was to recognise similar conditions in a chicken coup.)'[31]

This division—the 'human' from the 'non-human'— has a profound meaning. In discussing 'mimesis, this identification or imitation, or exchange of roles between oppressor and victim', Levi derides Liliana Cavani, a film director, who claims that 'we are all victims or murderers, and we accept these roles voluntarily': Levi writes that he does 'not know, and it does not interest me to know, whether in my depths there lies a murderer, but I do know that I was a guiltless victim and not a murderer'.[32] For Levi, there is a gap between the murders and the victims: their 'humanitas' has been shattered, utterly divided between perpetrator and victim. Améry argues that torture was the 'essence of National Socialism' (*AML* 30): it hated the word 'humanity' like 'the pious man hates sin' (*AML* 31). Being tortured, 'trust in the world breaks down . . . The other person, opposite whom I exist physically in the world and with whom I can exist only as long as he does not touch my skin surface border, forces his own corporeality on me with the first blow' (*AML* 28). The social contract is destroyed and the 'physical destruction by the other then becomes an existential consummation of destruction altogether' (*AML* 28). He writes that torture is 'ineradicably burnt into' the victim 'even when no clinically objective traces can be detected' (*AML* 34). Moreover, there is an impassible gulf between the victim and the torturer, as 'No bridge leads from former to the latter' (*AML* 34) and one's fellow man becomes the 'antiman' (*AML* 40).

The victims of the Nazis were profoundly aware of this, of how their identification as 'humanitas' was being depropriated. The Sonderkommando doctor Miklos Nyiszli had to behave as impressively as possible in front of the SS to convince them of his 'humanity'. Of his first interview with the SS, he writes that the 'scope of our conversation was extremely limited. How was my trip? What was I doing in the KZ? These were questions they could not ask . . .' However, they were 'much impressed by the fact that I spoke their own language better, or at least in a more cultivated manner, than they did'.[33] Sereny wonders why the Sonderkommando at Treblinka chose only to wear the finest (stolen) clothes and wear the best eau-de-cologne, to dress like dandies. The

[31] Judith Magyar Isaacson, *Seed of Sarah* (Chicago: University of Illinois Press, 2nd edn., 1991), 68.

[32] Levi, *The Drowned and the Saved*, 32.

[33] See Miklos Nyiszli, *Auschwitz*, tr. Tibere Kremer and Richard Seaver (London: Grafton, 1963), 42.

answer: because they had seen that the SS and other guards killed more easily those who looked less human, so dressing in a sophisticated style made them look more human and so less easy simply to kill.

Can anything 'human' be salvaged from this? Arendt writes moving of this, using Hobbes as her guide. While containing nothing of modern race theory, Hobbes provided the idea that it was possible to exclude

the idea of humanity . . . Hobbes affords the best possible theoretical foundation for those naturalistic ideologies which hold nations to be tribes, separated from each other by nature . . . unconscious of the solidarity of mankind and having in common only the instinct for self-preservation which man shares with the animal world.

She goes on: 'If the idea of humanity . . . is no longer valid . . . then . . . all together are predestined by nature to war against each other until they have disappeared from the face of the earth.'[34] Thus, if peoples are all set against each other, there is not much hope left for us, for the species, for our past and future, the continuing war that Spengler outlined and from which, as Hilberg suggests, Himmler and others took inspiration.

Yet, it is this point of view with which Levinas begins *Totality and Infinity*, asking if we have been duped by morality. He argues that, below this level, below the actual processes of identification and de-identification, lies the ground for the very possibility for this, and it is this that is the ethical relation to the other. He argues that while, at one level, the level of narration, the said, the other loses their face (*OBBE* 166), can become a 'non-human', at a more profound level, the saying, it cannot: to speak in terms of identification, one can only want to 'depropriate' or 'de-identify' that which can be, is possible to be identified as human. This idea—a humanism without humanism—occur and recurs in different ways.

For example, this resurgence of a reflective humanism underlies the recent work of Paul Gilroy in his postcolonial, post-Holocaust book *Between Camps* where he talks of a 'pragmatic, planetary humanism' which is beyond gender and the 'bonds of all raciology'.[35] For Gilroy, race has been the central form of identification in the modern world. He goes on to suggest that this 'radically nonracial humanism exhibits a primary concern with the forms of human dignity that race-thinking

---

[34] Arendt, *Origins of Totalitarianism*, 157.
[35] Paul Gilroy, *Between Camps* (London Penguin, 2000), 17, 15.

strips away' and its 'signature is provided by a grim determination to make that predicament of fundamentally fragile, corporeal existence into the key to a version of humanism that contradicts the triumphal tones of the anthropological discourses that were enthusiastically supportive of race-thinking in earlier, imperial times'.[36] Gilroy is alive to the problems of this, however: citing Levinas and Martin Luther King together as those who give this idea 'a religious cast' he argues that 'it can be rescued from the worst excesses of idealism if only it is recognised as incorporating a provocative attempt to reactivate political sensibilities so that they flow outside the patterns set for them in a world of fortified nation states and antagonistic ethic groups'.[37] Gilroy is insistent to stress both the 'ethical response' and the political, both to think universally and to think in terms of particulars: again, this demonstrates the postmodern shuttle between these two positions.[38] And something like his approach, making 'fragile, corporeal existence into the key to a version of humanism' has already been explored in relation to the Holocaust.

PLANETARY HUMANISM AND *THE HUMAN RACE*

Robert Antelme's *L'Espèce humaine* (1947) offers striking parallels to Gilroy's work. A French communist, Antelme was at Gandersheim, a subcamp of Buchenwald, then survived on a death march and was finally liberated at Dachau. His book is centrally concerned with the way in which the 'calling into question of our quality as men provokes an almost biological claim of belonging to the human race . . . and finally—above all—it brings us to a clear vision of its indivisible oneness'.[39] This refrain goes throughout the book: towards the end of the book, for example, Antelme writes that, even though he and his fellow inmates look like animals, 'we're still men, and we shall not end otherwise than men. The distance separating us from another species is still intact' (*HR* 219). If

at the moment when the subjection of some and the power of others have attained such limits as to seem frozen into supernatural distinctions; if, facing nature, or death, we can perceive no substantial difference between the SS and

---

[36] Gilroy, *Between Camps*, 117.   [37] Ibid. 41.
[38] Ibid.
[39] Robert Antelme, *The Human Race*, tr. Jeffrey Haight and Annie Mahler (Marlboro, Vt.: Marlboro Press, 1992), 5–6. This will be abbreviated to *HR* in the text.

ourselves, then we have to say that there is only one human race . . . everything in the world that masks this unity . . . is false and mad.   (*HR* 219–20)

It is 'because we're men like them that the SS will finally prove power-less before us' (*HR* 219). Even death reaffirms this since 'the worst of victims cannot do otherwise than establish that, in its worst exercise, the executioner's power cannot be other than one of the powers men have, the power of murder. He can kill a man, but he can't change him into something else' (*HR* 220). Levinas's account of murder, discussed in Chapter 9, seems to echo this when he talks of the 'impossibility of killing' (*TI* 199). Antelme's testimony—and his response to the destruction of the 'human'— was extremely influential in post-war France.[40] For Maurice Blanchot, this book was the 'simplest, the purest', and the closest to the 'absolute' of the camps.[41] He argues that it illustrates a basic truth about being, that the human reduced to its need, to 'naked life', reveals that the human is 'one who has need of nothing other than need in order to maintain the human relation in its primacy, negating what negates him'.[42] In *The Human Race*, Antelme describes how even the most basic human actions, walking, urinating, excreting, eating even scraps, celebrate humanity. For Blanchot, in a reading that unsurprisingly echoes Levinas's approach, the human becomes an 'egoism without ego' and other to his (or her) own self: life becomes 'impersonal'.[43] This most basic level affirms a sacredness to life beyond 'being human' for Blanchot. In turn, then, this bears a rela-tion to the act of writing or speaking. Blanchot suggests that it is not simply a question of 'telling the story' (that is, relating facts) but of speaking, of speaking to another human being. And this is the tension Blanchot finds in *The Human Race*: a book about the way humanity is taken away which is at the same time reasserting humanity: thus its 'choking or 'smothered' words.

For Sarah Kofman, Antelme's book offers a way to think about the dilemmas of the Holocaust. Her book, *Smothered Words* is a medita-tion on Anteleme's account—the title is from the first page of *The Human Race* and describes how survivors describe their experiences—

---

[40] For its influence on Perec, see Dan Stone, 'Perec's Antelme', *French Cultural Studies*, 10 (1999), 161–72.

[41] Maurice Blanchot, *Friendship,* tr. Elizabeth Rottenberg (Stanford, Calif.: Stanford University Press, 1997), 110.

[42] Maurice Blanchot, *The Blanchot Reader*, ed. Michael Holland (Oxford: Blackwell, 1995), 238.

[43] Ibid. 239.

and is explicitly influenced by Blanchot and by the deportation and murder of her father by the Nazis. She suggests that his book does not simply celebrate an 'old-fashioned' humanism, but rather marks the limits of the human and the communal, and so begins a new humanism. For Kofman, by 'showing that the abject dispossession suffered by the deportees signifies the indestructibility of alterity, its absolute character, by establishing the possibility of a new kind of "we", he founds without founding—for this "we" is always already undone, destabilised—the possibility of a new ethics'.[44] The unity of the species relies not on 'any specific difference or on a shared essence—reason—but on a shared power to choose . . . the power to kill and the power to respect'.[45] She cites Nietzsche—'man is the yet undetermined animal'—and suggests that for Antleme this is false if it means that 'a transformation of the species is possible' (it is an 'SS fantasy to believe that we have a historical mission to change species, and as this mutation is occurring too slowly, they kill').[46] However, it is true if it means that 'in man is a multiplicity of powers' and the 'irreducibility of man reduced to the irreducible'.[47]

Blanchot's and Kofman's reflections on Antelme suggest that both the animal and the human survive the Holocaust, and this survival reveals that there is still something more than a bare animality, that our 'fragile, corporeal existence' has a meaning. However, this 'ethical' moment needs a political rereading, too, which makes it seem much less certain. This is to follow Gilroy and, in a wider sense, the movement from ethics to reason and from reason to ethics, between universal and particular, that I have stressed occurs in the work of Derrida and Levinas.

As James Young writes, each victim saw—'i.e. understood and witnessed—his predicament differently, depending on his own historical past, religious paradigms, and ideological explanations', and Antelme is no exception.[48] To follow his testimony is to follow one particular version of events. Antelme was not in a death camp, nor was he condemned to death for as a Jew. He himself writes that the

---

[44] Sarah Kofman, *Smothered Words*, tr. Madeleine Dobere (Evanston, Ill.: Northwestern University Press, 1998), 73.

[45] Ibid. 72–3.   [46] Ibid. 70; *HR* 219.

[47] Kofman, *Smothered Words*, 72–3.

[48] James Young, *Writing and Rewriting the Holocaust: Narrative and the Consequences of Interpretation* (Bloomington: Indiana University Press, 1990), 26.

horror in it is not gigantic. At Gandersheim there was no gas chamber, no crematorium. The horror there was darkness, absolute lack of any kind of landmark, solitude, unending oppression, slow annihilation. The motivation underlying our struggle could only have been a furious desire, itself almost always experienced in solitude; a furious desire to remain me, down to the very end. (HR 5)

A desire to 'remain me' is not the same, perhaps as the desire to remain alive: in this, his experience is different from, for example, Levi's or Wiesel's or Leitner's. This is a crucial influence on his perspective on the Holocaust. This is also reflected in one of the themes of the book, how prisoners 'sell out' and become Kapos, or collaborate in other ways with the fascists. Collaboration for Antelme is not just weakness: it is political and national betrayal. This is not least because Antelme, like David Rousset whose *L'Univers concentrationnaire* (1945) is almost contemporaneous with *The Human Race*, was a communist: their politics were their 'ideological/narrative framework', the 'epistemological climate' within which they understood the camps and this is another crucial influence.[49] For Rousset, the camps represented the 'gangrene of a whole economic and social system' and 'sprang from the economic and social foundations of capitalism and imperialism'.[50] For him, the balance of the camps was 'by no means negative' as they provide 'a marvellous armoury' for the revolution to come.[51] His book, too, is concerned with how men—specifically men and often comrades—were corrupted. There was, for him, 'no fundamental difference' between death extermination camps and other concentration camps: 'only a difference in degree' (however, not that much was known, in Western Europe, about the death camps when this was written).[52] Antelme is not as explicit as this, but this idea—the indivisible unity of the species at the basis of his revolutionary Marxist ideals— underlies his work. In the final pages, he shares a cigarette with a Russian survivor: a sign of the 'brotherhood of men' and of the Russian-inspired revolution to come. Ironically, they speak in their common language, German.

Finally, and in a odd paradox bearing in mind the more universal claims, national identity is also a ground for Antelme's resistance and a central influence on his testimony: just as, in many testimonies, the

[49] Michael André Bernstein, *Foregone Conclusions: Against Apocalyptic History* (London: University of California Press, 1994), 49.

[50] David Rousset, *A World Apart*, tr.Yvonne Mayse and Roger Senhouse (London: Secker and Warburg, 1951), 110, 112.

[51] Ibid. 111, 112.   [52] Ibid. 27.

Russians' reliance on Stalin appears again and again, so Antelme's French identity supports him time after time. For example, a rail car from the SNCF (the French national railway) raises the spirits of his colleagues: 'the wind which wafts the west into our faces double crosses the SS, so do the four letters SNCF which he didn't even notice' (*HR* 45). A comrade, Gaston, declares that 'France is free but the war is still continuing, it's continuing right here, too. If sometimes we don't recognise ourselves, that's what this war is costing, and we have got to hang on . . . the end is in sight' (*HR* 196). And at liberation, when the prisoners are commanded in German, they shout, 'You sons of bitches, we're free! Talk to us in French!' (*HR* 290) and, like Fenelon in *Playing for Time*, they sing the Marseillaise. Indeed, this nationalism is not unusual: in his account of Arthur Dodds, a British POW in Auschwitz, Colin Rushton describes the cheers of British prisoners as an RAF reconnaissance plane flew over and dipped its wings.[53] Remaining human, seems to be, for Antelme, the sense of belonging to a nation at war with the Germans. Not only does this simply raise nationalism to be a universal principle and a model for all human beings, but also seems to stress how this sense was, of course, denied the Jews, deprived of their statehood and the trappings of their cultural identity, interpellated according to Nazi propaganda and condemned to death as a community. Moreover, for the Polish and other Eastern European Jews who survived, there was, simply, nothing to return to: for the French, France and French culture remained.

Thus, the reflections of Blanchot, Kofman, and others which draw on Antelme draw on a testimony that offers a fixed and strong national identity, a place to return to safely after the War, and is not by a prisoner specifically selected for death by work or by gas chamber (or by disease, beating, shooting, and so on: the forms of death in the Holocaust are not a short list). Most importantly, in the context of the human, Antelme's testimony presupposes the unity of the human species even if that 'solidity and stability of the species is being put to the test' (*HR* 62). This is to say, really, that the model of what it was to be human is the model of what it is to be French: every nationalism is an anthropology. This is not to say that Blanchot or Kofman are wrong in seeing the ethical moment, but to say that if they took Antelme's testimony to be the only, or the central testimony, as seems to be the case (Kofman's *Smothered Words*, Blanchot's praise), and if that was the

[53] Colin Rushton, *Spectator in Hell* (London: Pharaoh Press, 1998), 112.

principal textual source through which they engaged with the Holocaust, they were also engaging—implicitly—with Antelme's own paradigms and 'epistemological climate'.[54] It could be that it is Antelme's belief that they are reflecting when they discuss the 'indivisible oneness' of the human, and a belief that something comes from that, that there is some bond, even if denuded of the trappings of 'humanness' and stemming from the experience of 'bare life'.

CONCLUSION: TO HOPE WITHOUT FINDING

Beginning with the suggestion that the core of postmodern discussions of the human is not really those obsessed by technology, and instead reflects a strand of thought about the hypocrisy of humanism in the light of the Holocaust and colonialism, this chapter turned to Heidegger's immediate post-war reflections which oriented discussion of the human. In a sense, the crucial development of Heidegger's thought by others such as Agamben stresses the difference between the human animal and *humanitas*. However, what inexorably links these two is the process of identification. It is the way that this process, which is both internal and external, works that is at issue. Moreover, it is almost impossible to discuss in the abstract, as it always works differently in different historical circumstances. For example, it is possible to say that Browning offers an account of how 'Ordinary men' both became 'identified' and 'identified themselves' as mass murderers in occupied Poland, but that this account is not like a laboratory experiment capable of being more generally applicable to other events. However, this process lies at the heart of the political, the aesthetic, and the idea of the human and explains the link between them.

Central to the murders of the Holocaust was the 'de-propriation' or 'disappropriation' of identity. One response to this is simply to find each at war with each, each self-identified nation at war with each other nation. Yet, for Arendt, this is an incorrect counsel of despair, and Levinas explores the grounds for even the possibility of identification. This 'ground of possibility' is taken up as the basis for a new, fragile, and aware postmodern humanism, by, for example, Paul Gilroy, with its eyes open to the hypocrisies and failures, especially over race, of the humanisms that preceded it. Robert Antelme's book,

---

[54] Young, *Writing and Rewriting*, 26.

The Human Race and the commentary illustrate this. While it is taken as a book that embodies or traces an ethical moment of a new humanism, it is at the same time an example of the survival of both nationalist and communist ideas that serve both to alienate and to reduce what is other (to nationalism, say) to the same (all peoples must have nationalism: thus the paradox of an international nationalism). In Levinas's terms, it is both *saying*, responding to the humanism of the other man, the 'human' beyond humanism, and *said*, recapturing this moment in an array of pre-existing themes and philosophies.

However, this double motion, which both accepts the possibility of a human and is open to its inevitable failures and limits, is what makes up a postmodern response. This movement finds its meaning not in an essence in the animal, nor in the social, the human, but in the interplay between the two: what is most important does not lie inside the human but in the interaction of humans, which is why culture in its broadest sense is so important. It is in culture that the process of identification inexorably takes place, and in culture where there are shifts of appropriation. This process itself might be as morally neutral as looking at the sky, yet it underlies attempts both to build human solidarity and to sow race-based dissent and hatred. One role, perhaps, of 'postmodern humanism' is continually to monitor itself, with a terrifying and shuddering regard for its own fragility and potential hypocrisy. A part of this will involve thinking and analysing what this process is in more detail, and trying to see how its particular and universal mechanics work in each instance. Another role, and again aware of the process of identification, lies in the increasing humanization of the world, what Derrida names 'messianic telepoesis': Gilroy writes that that our 'challenge should now be to bring even more powerful visions of planetary humanity from the future into the present and to reconnect them with democratic and cosmopolitan traditions'.[55] This is the attempt to make the distant future real, offering that which is not the opposite of war, but beyond it, the hope of peace.

[55] Gilroy, *Between Camps*, 356.

Conclusion

Having traumatised a vast number of individuals, the Holocaust was also the occasion of a collective historical trauma. Hence, while coming to terms with its reality and ramifications was initially delayed, it can now be said to have projected its impact both forward *and backward* in time, an explosion of destructive energy at the heart of Western Civilisation that compels us to rethink our assumptions about the nature of humanity and culture, history and progress, politics and morality[1]

And as, since the beginning of this lecture, we have been speaking of nothing but the 'translation' of these thoughts and discourses into what are commonly called the 'events' of 'history' and of 'politics' (I put quotation marks around all these obscure words), it would also be necessary to 'translate' what such an exchange of places can imply in its most radical possibility. This 'translation' appears to be both indispensable and for the moment impossible. It therefore calls for quite other protocols, those in view of which I have proposed this reading. What I am aiming at here is, obviously enough, anything but abstract. We are talking about past, present and future events, a composition of forces and discourses which seem to have been waging merciless war on each other (for example from 1933 to our time).[2]

In this complex quotation, Derrida is addressing the relationship between Heidegger's thought and 'events' of Nazism. More widely, it asks about the ways 'thoughts' and 'discourses' become events. Reversing this, exploring how 'events' become 'thoughts' and 'discourses', the three parts of this book have been about how the event of the Holocaust has been responded to—'translated'—through what might roughly be called a 'postmodern turn' in contemporary thought, focusing on testimony, literature, history, historiography, and philosophy.

---

[1] Omer Bartov, *Mirrors of Destruction* (Oxford: Oxford University Press, 2000), 165
[2] Jacques Derrida, *Of Spirit: Heidegger and the Question*, tr. Geoffrey Bennington and Rachel Bowlby (London: University of Chicago Press, 1987), 109.

To write that the Holocaust has changed 'how we are' and 'how the world is for us' is a cliché. However, to think through what this cliché might really mean, what world is revealed after the Holocaust, is harder. It is, as Adorno says, in fact, to try to measure thought and culture by these acts to which the word violence is not descriptive enough. Not to think this, to push 'aside at the outset that which thought should address' means that what we do 'cannot really be called thought at all'.[3] I have argued that the constellation of ideas called postmodernism—centrally but not exclusively inspired by the European post-phenomenological tradition in which Levinas and Derrida are major figures—is the most profound attempt to do this, principally because it has its roots in the experience of and thought about the Holocaust, though these are often unacknowledged. This tradition has ethics at its core, not least in the way in which it resists or points up gaps in the metaphysics of comprehension, in omnivorous thought's aim to assimilate what is other to it. In testimony and literature, the process of identification in reading; in history, the process of 'normalization' in the writing of historical accounts; in philosophy, the seeking of limits, answers, and solutions; all these embodiments of the metaphysics of comprehension seek to overcode or assimilate the events of the Holocaust in the very act of engaging with them. Each must be questioned in different ways. The interlinked ideas of 'genre' or 'discipline' or 'phrase-regimens' or 'language games', meaning, specific systems of thought, is both where and how this happens and a mechanism to interrogate it.

In order to build a dyke, in Levi's words, against this assimilation and respond to its odd but strong affective power, I argued that testimony had to be seen in a genre of its own and that its texts have their own internal as well as external conventions. The Wilkomirski and Demidenko affairs showed both the significance and the inherent risks of this, in that the genre existed enough to be parodied and abused. Second-generation memoirs, too, displayed some similar characteristics, and offered a fragile, contingent hope, albeit one that resisted closure, in relation to the Holocaust. (The fragility and ambivalence of this hope is made clear in, among others, the works of Levi, Lengyel, Hart, Delbo, Kertész, and Weisel.) Understanding more conventional literary responses to the Holocaust involved a rethinking of the categories and ideas that more usually structure literary responses, asking new questions and raising new difficulties.

[3] Theodor Adorno, *Metaphysics: Concepts and Problems*, ed. Rolf Tiedemann, tr. Edmund Jephcott (Cambridge: Polity, 2000), 111.

In response to the Holocaust, historical writing has been forced to reflect on itself intensely and perhaps has challenged some of its assumptions. I argued that, by thinking through the nature of the truth which history aspires to tell, history is revealed as involved with a more fundamental sense of truth than truth as correspondence. History is entangled with a delicate process of inextricably and ineluctably inter-weaving what can be proved or disproved with the existential ethical grounds that make proof or disproof possible. Saul Friedländer's work and intellectual career exemplify a conscious engagement the these issues. This delicate process leads to problems and controversy—an irresolvable but revealing debate between Goldhagen and Browning—but also to clarity: those who would claim the status of historians can be shown to be liars and propagandists.

In philosophy, attempting Adorno's measure with suffering has involved trying to think about the meaning of the 'bedrock', those things upon which philosophy rests, about those things that have been excluded from philosophy, and about reason and the limits of reason. (Though, while the Holocaust has focused attention on an array of hitherto less important areas and thrown up new questions, it might be argued that philosophy has constantly involved this running up against its limits: it is because of this that, as even Fackenheim admits, in part pre-Holocaust philosophy is salvageable.) This has meant eschewing answers for problems (another irritating but accurate cliché, easy to say, hard to do) and avoiding explanation for finding the limits of explanation. Even when suggesting a fragile hope and humanism (say, in readings of Antelme's testimony), it at the same time questions this (in finding false solace there). Yet this process itself offers a sense of hope and community.

In trying to show how those ideas characterized as postmodern are a response to the Holocaust, I have tried to shown what they can con-tribute to continuing debates. For example, throughout, the idea of identity and identification has emerged as a central axis for debate—as befits responding to an event that asks us who we are. Identification, as a both a literary and aesthetic process and a political and socio-cultural process (these two are clearly linked), is unavoid-able yet problematic. I have tried to show that these discourses make things less straightforward, and indeed, part of responding to the Holocaust, in years to come, will be a constant attempt to maintain the inability to come to terms with it, and to trace this through Western culture and thought.

It seems right that a book about the Holocaust ends not with answers but with questions. Briefly, I want to suggest some ways in which the Holocaust and its aftermath still need to be thought and is still 'being translated'.[4] One of the most significant forms of translation is the most concrete but hardest to pin down: the continuing development of memory and memorialization individually, in terms of academic disciplines and communally. This emerges both in the private sphere, as testimony and postmemory, and in the public sphere, with pressing questions of how to preserve sites and remember, and questions about how to teach and study the Holocaust. The production of testimonies, either written—the Valentine Mitchell Library of Holocaust Testimonies, for example—or in other media—such as the Fortunoff archive at Yale—are one area where both these spheres converge. There is more historical work to be done on the Holocaust, especially as archives in Eastern Europe and the former USSR open up and are explored, and there is also more metahistorical work to be done, in finding ways to record this history and looking at the context and frameworks by which the interpretations are oriented. But there is also an even wider public sphere, in which acts of genocide regularly take place: there is no magic solution to prevent these, and, while invoking 'Never Again' is clearly in the right spirit, the slogan covers up as much as it illuminates. Under the pressure of memory, as it were, there is a need to respond to particular cases in the contemporary and future world.

The Holocaust and its aftermath have become an unavoidable part of what is 'confusedly called culture, or the world of the spirit', the intellectual architecture, for, at least, the West.[5] It is still being translated in time. It is relevant not only as a warning from the past, not only as a case study of atrocity, as an object of our research: it is relevant because so many of the discourses and areas of contemporary life are (or ought to be) shaped and marked by the Holocaust. 'Ethnic cleansing', genocide, human rights, and the treatment of refugees and asylum-seekers are clear examples of this, but more diffuse examples exist. Debates over genetics, too, and much of the interpretation of Darwin's legacy should take place under the shadow of the Holocaust. Indeed, all the discourses that already presuppose ideas of who we take

[4] On this, see also Berel Lang, The Future of the Holocaust (London: Cornell University Press, 1999).

[5] Jacques Derrida, Of Spirit: Heidegger and the Question, tr. Geoffrey Bennington and Rachel Bowlby (London: University of Chicago Press, 1987), 109–10.

ourselves to be, questions of representation and of ethics, are interwoven with the Holocaust. It is 'in the back of our minds' in responding to with these problems and issues.

There is much work to be done, too, in the area of what Gillian Rose calls 'Holocaust Ethnography'—the 'exploration of the representation of fascism . . . pursued across the production, distribution and reception of cultural works'.[6] This is not only to chart, and sometimes to question, the contemporary understandings of the Holocaust but also because, as Saul Friedländer puts it, 'contemporary reelaboration presents the reality of the past in a way that sometimes reveals previously unsuspected aspects'.[7] But more than this, the work of engaging with Holocaust texts (centrally testimony), including an awareness of their specificity and difference, opens up ways of engaging with other forms of texts on suffering in ways we are only beginning to understand. In philosophical and religious discourse, too, there is more to be said.

Another contemporary area that needs much work, both academic and more typically political, is on the relationship between the aftermath of the Holocaust and the postcolonial or globalized world, and its divergent histories, knowledges, and politics. Omer Bartov's point, that the impact of the Holocaust projected backwards in time, is extremely illuminating. Postmodernism, as well as having an origin in the Holocaust, is in no small part the result of anti- and postcolonial struggles of different sorts as well as other struggles for liberation. These, in turn, are also understood in the wake of the Holocaust. The colonial genocides of the Native Americans, First Australians, and the Herero in Namibia are now interpreted as genocides: the term dates only to 1944, after all. The link between colonialism and the Holocaust has been made tentatively several times. Victor Klemperer wrote that

Strafexpedition is the first term which I recognised as being specifically National Socialist . . . For me the word . . . was the embodiment of brutal arrogance and contempt for people who are in any way different, it sounded so colonial, you could see the encircled Negro village, you could hear the cracking of the hippopotamus whip.[8]

---

[6] Gillian Rose, *Mourning Becomes the Law* (Cambridge: Cambridge University Press, 1996), 41.

[7] Saul Friedländer, *Reflections on Nazism: An Essay on Kitsch and Death*, tr. Thomas Weyr (Bloomington: Indiana University Press, rev. edn., 1993), 18.

[8] Victor Kemperer, *The Language of the Third Reich*, tr. Martin Brady (London: Continuum, 2000), 43.

Hannah Arendt drew cautious parallels when she wrote of imperialism that some 'of the fundamental aspects of this time appear so close to totalitarian phenomena of the twentieth century that it may be justifiable to consider the whole period a preparatory stage for coming catastrophes'.[9] Colonization in its nineteenth- and twentieth-century forms, as Arendt argues, relies on a discourse of race and racism in its grand justifications and for its day-to-day needs (porterage, for example). However, imperialism did not stem from racism, but from the idea of expansion as the continuous and ultimate aim of politics. The relevance for this, for the Holocaust, is only beginning to become clear in empirical research. Ulrich Herbert summarizes recent Holocaust research, and suggests that two lines of development that led to genocide:

First there were those programmatic schemes that, when implemented as a continental imperialistic policy, regarded the fates of independent ethnic populations as qualitatively negligible, embraced an amoral utilitarianism, and manifested themselves in a myriad of ways according to the circumstances. Second, there was that racist brand of anti-Semitism that set as its goal the expulsion . . . and ultimately the murder of some or all of the Jews. Although each of these two factors has its own traditions, their histories are closely intertwined, involving, one the one hand, policies pursued by Germany and the other great powers in their (especially African) colonies and the long tra- dition of planning for a German, quasi-colonial Hinterland in eastern and south eastern Europe, and, on the other hand the tradition of modern anti- semitism.[10]

Thus, while anti-Semitism played the dominant role in who suffered, the logic of colonialism led, in no small part, to the establishment of the camps. As Fanon wrote,

At first thought it may seem strange that the anti-Semite's outlook should be related to that of the Negrophobe. It was my philosophy professor, a native of the Antilles, who recalled the fact to me one day: 'Whenever you hear anyone abuse the Jews, pay attention, because he is talking about you'. And I found that he was universally right—by which I mean that I was answerable in my

---

[9] Hannah Arendt, *The Origins of Totalitarianism*, new edn. (New York: Harcourt, Brace & World, 1966), 123.
[10] Ulrich Herbert, 'Extermination Policy', in Herbert (ed.), *National Socialist- Extermination Policies: Contemporary German Perspectives and Controversies* (Oxford: Berghahn Books, 2000), 1–52, 14.

body and in my heart for what was done to my brother. Later I realised hat he meant, quite simply, an anti-Semite is inevitably anti-Negro.[11]

This is absolutely not to say that the sufferings of colonized peoples were not recognized at the time, but only that, as a result of the colonial hypocrisy of European nations, they did not have the power to throw over the paradigms of thought that supported them. To put this another way: the Holocaust did not *enable* Fanon, who fought in the Second World War, to write of the hypocrisy and violence of Europe (it was obvious to him): however, the Holocaust *did bring crashing home* to Europeans reading him their own hypocrisy and complicity in atrocity. Likewise, it is the Holocaust that underlies the temporal inversion that empowers, for a Western reader, Aimé Césaire's famous comment on Nazism, that the people of Europe

tolerated Nazism before it was inflicted on them . . . they absolved it, shut their eyes to it, legitimised it because, until then, it had been applied only to non-European peoples; . . . they . . . cultivated that Nazism . . . they are responsible for it . . . before engulfing the whole of Western, Christian civilisation in its reddened waters, it oozes, seeps and trickles from every crack.[12]

This idea of 'backward projection' is not meant to create a tasteless equivalence, or a measuring scale of suffering: such attempts are at best intellectually dubious. Instead, part of the aim of this thought, again, taken from Levinas, is to recognize the inextinguishable singularity of each instance of suffering. It is part of the creation of a way of seeing, an 'optics', and this, again, takes the Holocaust as a central point of reference.[13]

All the tasks above, and the many other ways in which this event has to be thought, are a form of witnessing and so taking responsibility. David Cesarani points out that 'one quality of the Holocaust is that you can say almost anything about it and sound either profound or

[11] Franz Fanon, *Black Skin White Masks*, tr. Charles Lam Markmann (London: Pluto Press, 1986), 122. This point was bloodily made in 1999, 500 m. from where I sit writing, by David Copeland, the neo-fascist 'Brixton Bomber'. He bombed London's Afro-Caribbean, Asian, and gay and lesbian communities. Before he was caught by the police, he had been planning to bomb other minorities, including London's Jewish community. His court case came just after David Irving's in the spring of 2000.
[12] Aimé Césaire, *Discourse on Colonialism*, tr. Joan Pinkham (New York: Monthly Review Press, 1972, orig. 1955), 14.
[13] On this, see A. Dirk Moses, 'Conceptual Blockages and Definitional Dilemmas in the "racial century": Genocides of Indigenous Peoples and the Holocaust', in *Patterns of Prejudice*, 36 (2002), 7–36.

provocative'.[14] Moreover, after a very short while, both profundities and provocations sound first banal and then stunningly inadequate: they become slogans, 'said' in Levinas's terms, and when they should create explosions they become only 'normalized' moves in conversations about sorrow, suffering, and death on such a huge scale. But to remember and think through the banalities is important: Levinas, for example, draws out the philosophical significance in simply saying 'Good morning'. To think through why they become banalities, and what this means, is important too.

'All the tasks above, and the many other ways in which this event has to be thought, are a form of witnessing and so taking responsibility.' Not witnessing through the imagination, but as a culture, both Western and, perhaps, world. Moreover, this witnessing and responsibility is not just at the level of content, recalling specific instances: though, to choose only one from countless atrocities, the murder of Isabella Leitner's baby sister Potyo at Auschwitz has haunted me every day since I first read about it. This form of witnessing takes place too at the level of framework, of how we think and how we think about thinking. The Holocaust changed our intellectual maps of the world: some things it has given us to see in a different way (in part, for example, the Western colonial genocides of other peoples), other things it has covered up or shown to be empty (the idea of a universal, essential humanism and consequent limits to behaviour). It focuses our attention on the processes of identification in all its forms: legal, religious, cultural, memorial, and others. There has been a constant process of coming to terms with this, of trying to see, ever since, and this has been done most significantly, it seems to me, at the level of the form and structure of our thinking. In this way are we best reminded of the tiny shudder or hesitation that is hope, and that in the triumphs we achieve, we stand on cinders.

[14] David Cesarani, 'Holocaust on the Right Side of Kitsch', *Times Higher Education Supplement* (7 July 2000), 20.

Select Bibliography

Adorno, Theodor, *Metaphysics: Concepts and Problems*, ed. Rolf Tiedemann, tr. Edmund Jephcott (Cambridge: Polity, 2000).
—— *Minima Moralia,* tr. E. F. N. Jephcott (London: Verso, 1978).
—— *Negative Dialectics*, tr. E. B. Ashton (London: Routledge, 1973).
—— *Notes to Literature, II*, ed. Rolf Tiedemann, tr. Shierry Weber Nicholson (New York: Columbia University Press, 1993).
Agamben, Giorgio, *Homo Sacer,* tr. Daniel Heller-Roazen (Stanford, Calif.: Stanford University Press, 1998).
—— *Potentialities*, tr. Daniel Heller-Roazen (Stanford, Calif.: Stanford University Press, 1999).
—— *Remnants of Auschwitz,* tr. Daniel Heller-Roazen (New York: Zone Books, 1999).
Ajzenstat, Oona, *Driven Back to the Text* (Pittsburgh: Duquesne University Press, 2001).
Améry, Jean, *At the Mind's Limits*, tr. Sidney Rosenfeld and Stella P. Rosenfeld (London: Granta Books, 1999).
Ankersmit, F. R., *Historical Representation* (Stanford, Calif.: Stanford University Press, 2001).
Anteleme, Robert, *The Human Condition*, tr. Jefrey Haight and Annie Mahler (Marlboro, Vt.: Marlboro Press, 1992).
Arendt, Hannah, *The Origins of Totalitarianism* (London: Harcourt Brace, 1973).
Aristotle, 'On the Art of Poetry', in *Classical Literary Criticism*, tr. T. S. Dorsch (London: Penguin, 1965).
Ashcroft, Bill, and Pal Ahluwalia, *Edward Said: The Paradox of Identity* (London: Routledge, 1999).
Auster, Paul, *The Invention of Solitude* (London: Faber & Faber, 1989).
Bacall-Zwirin, Alina, and Jared Stark (eds.), *No Common Place* (London: University of Nebraska Press, 1999).
Badiou, Alain, *Ethics*, tr. Peter Halliward (London: Verso, 2001).
—— *Manifesto for Philosophy,* tr. Norman Madarazs (Albany, NY: State University of New York Press, 1999).
Badmington, Neil (ed.), *Posthumanism* (London: Palgrave, 2000).
Baldwin, Peter (ed.), *Reworking the Past: Hitler, the Holocaust and the Historian's Debate* (Boston: Beacon Press, 1990).
Banks, Iain, *Dead Air* (London: Little Brown, 2002).

Banner, Gillian, *Holocaust Literature: Schulz, Levi, Spiegleman and the Memory of the Offence* (London: Valentine Mitchell, 2000).

Barthes, Roland, *A Lover's Discourse,* tr. Richard Howard (London: Penguin, 1990).

Bartov, Omer, *Mirrors of Destruction* (Oxford: Oxford University Press, 2000).

Bauer, Yehuda, *Rethinking the Holocaust* (London: Yale University Press, 2002).

Bauman, Zygmunt, *Modernity and the Holocaust* (New York: Cornell University Press, 1991).

Beer, Edith Hahn, with Susan Dworkin, *The Nazi Officer's Wife* (London: Perennial, 2000).

BenGershôm, Ezra, *David: Testimony of a Holocaust Survivor,* tr. J. A. Underwood (Oxford: Oswald Wolff Books, 1988).

Benjamin, Walter, *Illuminations,* tr. Harry Zorn (London; Pimlico, 1999 edn.).

Bennett, Rab, *Under the Shadow of the Swastika: The Moral Dilemmas of Resistance and Collaboration in Hitler's Europe* (London: Macmillan, 1999).

Bennington, Geoffrey, and Jacques Derrida, *Jacques Derrida* (London: University of Chicago Press, 1993).

Berenbaum, Michael, and Abraham J. Peck (eds.), *The Holocaust and History* (Bloomington: Indiana University Press, 1998).

Berger, Alan, *Crisis and Covenant* (Albany, NY: State University of New York Press, 1985).

Berger, James, *After the End: Representations of the Post-Apocalypse* (London: University of Minnesota Press, 1999).

Berlin, Isaiah, *The Proper Study of Mankind,* ed. Henry Hardy and Roger Hausheer (London: Pimlico, 1998).

Bernard-Donals, Michael, and Richard Glejzer, *Between Witness and Testimony: The Holocaust and the Limits of Representation* (Albany, NY: State University of New York Press, 2001).

Bernasconi, Robert, *Heidegger in Question* (Atlantic Highlands, NJ: Humanities Press, 1993).

—— 'The Ethics of Suspicion', *Research in Phenomenology,* 20 (1990), 3–18.

—— and David Wood (eds.), *The Provocation of Levinas* (London: Routledge, 1988).

Bernstein, J. M., *The Fate of Art* (London: Polity, 1992).

Bernstein, Michael André, *Foregone Conclusions: Against Apocalyptic History* (London: University of California Press, 1994).

Bernstein, Richard, *Radical Evil* (Cambridge: Polity, 2002).

Bhabha, Homi, *The Location of Culture* (London: Routledge, 1994).

Blackburn, Simon, and Keith Simons (eds.), *Truth* (Oxford: Oxford University Press, 1999).

Blanchot, Maurice, *Friendship,* tr. Elizabeth Rottenberg (Stanford, Calif.: Stanford University Press, 1997).

—— *The Blanchot Reader*, ed. Michael Holland (Oxford: Blackwell, 1995).

—— and Jacques Derrida, *The Instant of my Death/Demeure*, tr. Elizabeth Rottenberg (Stanford, Calif.: Stanford University Press, 2000).

Bloss, Thomas (ed.), *Obedience to Authority: Current Perspectives on the Milgram Paradigm* (London: Lawrence Erlbaum Assoc., 2000).

Bloxham, Donald, *Genocide on Trial* (Oxford: Oxford University Press, 2001).

Borowshi, Tadeusz, *This Way for the Gas, Ladies and Gentlemen*, tr. Barbara Vedder (London: Penguin, 1976).

Bowie, Andrew, *From Romanticism to Critical Theory* (London: Routledge, 1997).

Boyarin, Jonathan, *Storm from Paradise: The Politics of Jewish Memory* (Minneapolis: University of Minnesota Press, 1992).

Braiterman, Zachary, 'Against Holocaust-Sublime: Naive Reference and the Generation of Memory', *History and Memory,* 12 (2000), 7–28.

Brett, Lily, *In Full View* (Sydney: Picador, 1998).

—— *Too Many Men* (New York: William Morrow, 2001).

Browning, Christopher, *Nazi Policy, Jewish Workers, German Killers* (Cambridge: Cambridge University Press, 2000).

—— *Ordinary Men: Reserve Police Battalion 101 and the Final Solution* (London: Harper Collins, 2nd edn., 1998).

—— *The Path to Genocide* (Cambridge: Cambridge University Press, 1992).

Burleigh, Michael, *Death and Deliverance* (London: Pan, 1994).

—— *The Third Reich: A New History* (London: Macmillan, 2000).

Burns, Robert, and Hugh Rayment-Pickard, *Philosophies of History: From Enlightenment to Postmodernism* (Oxford: Blackwell, 2000).

Camon, Ferdinando, *Conversations with Primo Levi*, tr. John Stepney (Marlboro, Vt.: Marlboro Press, 1989).

Caruth, Cathy, *Trauma: Explorations in Memory* (London: Johns Hopkins University Press, 1995).

—— *Unclaimed Experience: Trauma, Narrative and History* (London: John Hopkins University Press, 1996).

Caygill, Howard, *Levinas and the Political* (London: Routledge, 2002).

—— 'Levinas's Political Judgement: The *Esprit* Articles 1934–1983', *Radical Philosophy,* 104 (2000), 6–15.

Césaire, Aimé, *Discourse on Colonialism*, tr. Joan Pinkham (New York: Monthly Review Press, 1972).

Cesarani, David, 'Holocaust on the Right Side of Kitsch', *Times Higher Education Supplement* (7 July 2000), 20.

Chalier, Catherine, and Miguel Abensour (eds.), *L'Herne Emmanuel Levinas* (Paris: Éditions de l'Herne, 1991).

Chanter, Tina, *Time, Death and the Feminine* (Stanford, Calif.: Stanford University Press, 2001).

Cheyette, Bryan, and Laura Marcus (eds.), *Modernity, Culture and the Jew* (London: Polity Press, 1998).

Clendinnen, Inga, *Reading the Holocaust* (Cambridge: Cambridge University Press, 1999).

Coetzee, J. M., *Elizabeth Costello* (London: Secker & Warburg, 2003).

Cohen, Arthur, *The Tremendum: A Theological Interpretation of the Holocaust* (New York: Crossroad, 1988).

Cohen, Josh, *Interrupting Auschwitz* (London: Continuum, 2003), 105.

Cohen, Richard A. (ed.), *Face to Face with Levinas* (Albany, NY: State University of New York Press, 1986).

Cohen, Richard, *Ethics, Exegesis and Philosophy: Interpretation after Levinas* (Cambridge: Cambridge University Press, 2001).

Cohen, Stanley, *States of Denial* (London: Polity, 2001), 50.

Cole, Tim, *Images of the Holocaust: The Myth of the 'Shoah Business'* (London: Duckworth, 1999).

Committee of Public Safety, ' "My Place in the Sun": Reflections on the Thought of Emmanuel Levinas', *Diacritics,* 26/1 (1996), 3–10.

Cornell, Drucilla, Michael Rosenfeld, and David Gray Carlson (eds.), *Deconstruction and the Possibility of Justice* (London: Routledge, 1992).

Cornwell, John, *Hitler's Pope* (London: Penguin, 1999).

Critchley, Simon, *Very Little . . . Almost Nothing* (London: Routledge, 1997).

—— and Robert Bernasconi (eds.), *The Cambridge Companion to Levinas* (Cambridge: Cambridge University Press, 2002).

Dahlstrom, Daniel O., *Heidegger's Concept of Truth* (Cambridge: Cambridge University Press, 2001).

Dallery, A. B., and C. E. Scott (eds.), *The Question of the Other* (Albany, NY: State University of New York Press, 1989).

Davidson, Donald, *Inquiries into Truth and Interpretation* (Oxford: Oxford University Press, 2001).

Davis, Colin, *Ethical Issues in Twentieth Century French Fiction: Killing the Other* (London: Macmillan, 2000).

de Bolla, Peter, *Art Matters* (London: Harvard University Press, 2001).

de Certeau, Michael, *The Writing of History*, tr. Tom Conley (New York: Columbia University Press, 1988).

Decoste, F. C., and Bernard Schwartz (eds.), *The Holocaust's Ghost* (Edmonton: University of Alberta Press, 2000).

Delbo, Charlotte, *Auschwitz and After*, tr. Rosette C. Lamont (London: Yale University Press, 1995).

—— *Days and Memory*, tr. Rosette Lamont (Marlboro, Vt.: Marlboro Press, 1990).

Derrida, Jacques, *Adieu to Emmanuel Levinas*, tr. Pascale-Anne Brault and Michael Naas (Stanford, Calif.: Stanford University Press, 1999).

—— *Cinders*, tr. and ed. Ned Lukacher (London: University of Nebraska Press, 1991).

—— 'Like the Sound of the Sea Deep within a Shell: Paul de Man's War', *Critical Inquiry*, 14 (1988), 590–652.

—— *Limited Inc.*, tr. Samuel Weber (Evanston, Ill.: Northwestern University Press, 1988).

—— *Of Grammatology*, tr. Gayatri Chakravorty Spivak (London: Johns Hopkins University Press, 1976).

—— *Of Spirit: Heidegger and the Question*, tr. Geoffrey Bennington and Rachel Bowlby (London: University of Chicago Press, 1987).

—— *On Cosmopolitanism and Forgiveness,* tr. Mark Hughes (London: Routledge, 2001).

—— 'On Reading Heidegger: An Outline of Remarks to the Essex Colloquium', *Research in Phenomenology* (1987), 171–88.

—— *Positions*, tr. Alan Bass (London: Athlone Press, 1981).

—— 'Shibboleth: For Paul Celan', tr. Joshua Wilner, in Aris Fioretos (ed.), *Wordtraces: Reading of Paul Celan* (London: Johns Hopkins University Press, 1994).

—— *Spectres of Marx*, tr. Peggy Kamuf (London: Routledge, 1994).

—— *The Gift of Death,* tr. David Wills (Chicago: Chicago University Press, 1992).

—— *The Politics of Friendship,* tr. George Collins (London: Verso, 1997).

—— *Writing and Difference*, tr. Alan Bass (London: Routledge & Kegan Paul, 1978).

—— and Maurizio Ferraris, *A Taste for the Secret*, tr. Giacomo Donis, ed. Giacomo Donis and David Webb (London: Polity, 2001).

Des Pres, Terence, *The Survivor* (New York: Oxford University Press, 1976).

DiCenso, James, *Hermeneutics and the Disclosure of Truth: A Study in the Work of Heidegger, Gadamer and Ricoeur* (Charlottesville, Va.: University Press of Virginia, 1990).

Diner, Dan, 'Between Aporia and Apology: On the Limits of Historicizing National Socialism', *History and Memory,* 9 (1997), 301–21.

—— *Beyond the Conceivable* (London: University of California Press, 2000).

Dintenfass, Michael, 'Truth's Other: The History of the Holocaust and Historiographical Theory after the Linguistic Turn', *History and Theory,* 39 (2000), 1–20.

Dummett, Michael, *On Immigration and Refugees* (London: Routledge, 2001).

—— *Truth and Other Enigmas* (London: Duckworth, 1978).

Düttmann, Alexander Garcia, *The Memory of Thought*, tr. Nicolas Walker (London: Continuum, 2002).

Eagleton, Terry, *Ideology* (London: Verso, 1991).

Elton, Geoffrey, *The Practice of History* (London: Collins, 1967).

Epstein, Helen, *Children of the Holocaust: Conversations with Sons and Daughters of Survivors* (London; Penguin, 1988).

Eskin, Blake, *A Life in Pieces: The Making and Unmaking of Binjamin Wilkomirski* (New York: W. W. Norton, 2002).

Eskin, Michael, *Ethics and Dialogue* (Oxford: Oxford University Press, 2000), 24.

Evans, Richard, 'History, Memory and the Law: The Historian as Expert Witness', *History and Theory,* 41 (2002), 326–45.

—— *In Defence of History* (London: Granta, 1997).

—— *In Hitler's Shadow: West German Historians and the Attempt to Escape from the Nazi Past* (London: I. B. Tauris & Co., 1989).

—— *Lying about Hitler* (London: Basic Books, 2001), 250–1.

—— 'Truth Lost in Vain Views', *Times Higher Education Supplement* (12 Sept. 1997), 18.

Fackenheim, Emil, *To Mend the World: Foundations of Jewish Thought* (New York: Schocken Books, 1982).

—— and Raphael Jospe (eds.), *Jewish Philosophy and the Academy* (London: Associated University Presses, 1996).

Fanon, Frantz, *Black Skin White Masks,* tr. Charles Lam Markmann (London: Pluto Press, 1986).

—— *The Wretched of the Earth*, tr. Constance Farrington (Harmondsworth: Penguin, 1990).

Farias, Victor, *Heidegger and Nazism,* ed. Joseph Margolis and Tom Rockmore, tr. Paul Burrell and Gabriel Ricci (Philadelphia: Temple Press, 1989).

Felman, Shoshona, and Dori Laub, *Testimony: Crises of Witnessing in Literature, Psychoanalysis, and History* (London: Routledge, 1992).

Fénelon, Fania, with Marcelle Routier, *Playing for Time*, tr. Judith Landry (New York: Syracuse University Press, 1977).

Fine, Robert, and Charles Turner (eds.), *Social Theory after the Holocaust* (Liverpool: Liverpool University Press, 2000).

Finkelstein, Norman, *The Holocaust Industry* (London: Verso, 2000).

Finkielkraut, Alain, *L'Avenir d'une négation: Réflexion sur la question du genocide* (Paris: Seuil, 1982).

—— *The Imaginary Jew*, tr. Kevin O'Neill and David Suckoff (London: University of Nebraska Press, 1994).

—— *The Undoing of Thought*, tr. Dennis O'Keeffe (London: Claridge, 1988).

Flanzbaum, Hilene (ed.), *The Americanisation of the Holocaust* (London: Johns Hopkins University Press, 1999).

Foer, Jonathan Safran, *Everything is Illuminated* (London: Penguin, 2002).

Foley, Barbara, 'Fact, Fiction, Fascism: Testimony and Mimesis in Holocaust Narratives', *Comparative Literature*, 34 (1982), 330–60.

Forester, C. S., *The Hostage* (London: New English Library, 1970).

Foucault, Michel, *Language, Counter-Memory, Practice,* ed. Donald Bouchard and tr. Donald Bouchard and Sherry Simon (New York: Cornell University Press, 1977).

—— *The Order of Things* (London: Tavistock/Routledge, 2nd edn., 1989).

Frankel, Neftali, with Roman Palazon Bertra, *I Survived Hell: The Testimony of a Survivor of the Nazi Extermination Camps (Prisoner Number 161040)* (New York: Vintage Press, 1991).

Fridman, Lea Wernick, *Words and Witness* (Albany, NY: State University of New York Press, 2000).

Friedlander, Judith, *Vilna on the Seine: Jewish Intellectuals in France since 1968* (London: Yale University Press, 1990).

Friedländer, Saul, *Memory, History and the Extermination of the Jews of Europe* (Bloomington: Indiana Universoty Press, 1993).

—— *Nazi Germany and the Jews* (London: Weidenfeld & Nicolson, 1997).

—— *Pius XII and the Third Reich,* tr. Charles Fullman (London: Chatto & Windus, 1966).

—— *Prelude to Downfall: Hitler and the United States*, tr. Aline B. Werth and Alexander Werth (London: Chatto & Windus, 1967).

—— (ed.), *Probing the Limits of Representation* (London: Harvard University Press, 1992).

—— *Reflections on Nazism: An Essay on Kitsch and Death,* tr. Thomas Weyr (Bloomington: Indiana University Press, rev. edn., 1993).

—— *The Counterfeit Nazi: The Ambiguity of Good,* tr. Charles Fullman (London: Weidenfeld & Nicolson, 1969).

—— 'Trauma, Transference and "Working through" in Writing the History of the *Shoah*', *History and Memory,* 4 (1992), 39–59.

—— *When Memory Comes,* tr. Helen R. Lane (New York: Discus Books, 1980).

Friedrich, Otto, *The Kingdom of Auschwitz* (London: Penguin, 1996).

Frister, Roman, *The Cap, or the Price of a Life*, tr. Hillel Halkin (London: Weidenfeld & Nicolson, 1999).

Fuss, Diana, *Identification Papers* (London: Routledge, 1995).

Gedi, Noa, and Yigal Elam, 'Collective Memory: What is it?', *History and Memory,* 8/1 (1996), 30–50.

Geertz, Clifford, *The Interpretation of Cultures* (London: Fontana Press, 1993).

Gershom, Yonassan, *Beyond the Ashes: Cases of Reincarnation from the Holocaust* (Virginia Beach, Va.: A. R. E. Press, 1992).

Giardina, Andrea (ed.), *The Romans*, tr. Lydia Cochrane (London: Chicago University Press, 1993).

Gilbert, Martin, *Holocaust Journey: Travelling in Search of the Past* (London: Weidenfeld & Nicolson, 1997).

Gilroy, Paul, *Between Camps* (London Penguin, 2000).

Goldhagen, Daniel Jonah, *Hitler's Willing Executioners: Ordinary Germans and the Holocaust* (London: Abacus, 1997).

—— Christopher Browning, and Leon Wieseltier, *The 'Willing Executioners/Ordinary Men' Debate* (Washington, DC: United States Holocaust Research Institute, 1996).

Golob, Eugene, 'The Irony of Nihilism', *History and Theory*, 19/4 (1980), 55–65.

Gould, C. C., and R. S. Cohen (eds.), *Artefacts, Representations and Social Practice* (London: Kluwer Academic Publishers, 1994).

Gourevitch, Philip, 'The Memory Thief', *The New Yorker* (14 June 1999), 48–68.

Griffin Roger (ed.), *International Fascism* (London: Arnold, 1998).

Grossman, David, *See Under: Love*, tr. Betsy Rosenberg (New York: Noonday Press Farrar Strauss Girouz, 1989).

Gryn, Hugo, with Naomi Gryn, *Chasing Shadows* (London: Penguin, 2001).

Grzyb, Amanda, 'Jacques Derrida and the Holocaust: Cinders, Deconstruction and Excessive Responsibility', unpublished MA thesis, University of Western Ontario, 1996.

Guttenplan, D. D., *The Holocaust on Trial* (London: Granta, 2001).

Hacking, Ian, *Rewriting the Soul: Multiple Personality and the Sciences of Memory* (Princeton: Princeton University Press, 1995).

Halbwachs, Maurice, *On Collective Memory*, tr. Lewis A. Caser (London: University of Chicago Press, 1992).

Halpérin, Jean, and Nelly Hasson (eds.), *Difficile Justice: Dans la trace d'Emmanuel Levinas* (Paris: Albin Michel, 1998).

Ham, Jennifer, and Matthew Senior (eds.), *Animal Acts* (London: Routledge, 1997).

Haraway, Donna, *Simians, Cyborgs, and Women* (London: Free Association Books, 1991).

Harris, Robert, *Fatherland* (London: Arrow, 1993).

Hart, Kitty, *I am Alive* (London: Abelard-Schuman, 1961).

—— *Return to Auschwitz* (London: Panther, 1983).

Hartman, Geoffrey (ed.), *Holocaust Remembrance: The Shapes of Memory* (Oxford: Blackwell, 1994).

—— *The Longest Shadow* (Basingstoke: Palgrave Macmillan, 2002).

—— *The Sympathy Paradox: Poetry, Feeling and Modern Cultural Morality* (Austin, Tex.: Harry Ransom Humanity Research Centre, 1996).

Hass, Aaron, *In the Shadow of the Holocaust: The Second Generation* (Cambridge: Cambridge University Press, 1996).

Heidegger, Martin, *Basic Writings*, ed. David Farrell Krell (London: Harper & Row, 1977).

—— *Being and Time*, tr. John Macquarrie and Edward Robinson (Oxford: Blackwell, 1962).

—— *On Time and Being* (New York: Harper, 1972).

Heinemann, M. E., *Gender and Destiny: Women Writers and the Holocaust* (London: Greenwood, 1986).

Herbert, Ulrich (ed.), *National Socialist-Extermination Policies: Contemporary German Perspectives and Controversies* (Oxford: Berghahn Books, 2000).

Herman, Judith Lewis, *Trauma and Recovery* (London: Pandora, 1992).

Hilberg, Raul, *Perpetrators Victims Bystanders: The Jewish Catastrophe 1933–1945* (London: Harper Perennial, 1992).

—— *Sources of Holocaust Research* (Chicago: Ivan R. Dee, 2001).

—— *The Destruction of the European Jews* (London: Holmes & Meier, 1985).

—— *The Politics of Memory* (Chicago: Ivan R. Dee, 1996).

Hilene Flanzbaum, *The Americanisation of the Holocaust* (London: John Hopkins University Press, 1999), 83–101.

Hirsch, Marianne, *Family Frames: Photographs, Narrative and Postmemory* (London: Harvard University Press, 1997).

Hodge, Joanna, *Heidegger and Ethics* (London: Routledge, 1995).

Horowitz, Rosemary, *Literary and Cultural Transmission in the Reading, Writing and Remembering of Jewish Memorial Books* (London: Austin & Winfield, 1998).

Ignatieff, Michael, *Isaiah Berlin: A Life* (London: Chatto & Windus, 1998).

Isaacson, Judith Magyar, *Seed of Sarah: Memoirs of a Survivor* (Chicago; University of Illinois Press, 2nd edn., 1991).

Jacobson, Dan, 'The Downfall of David Irving', *Times Literary Supplement* (21 April 2000), 12–15.

Jacobus, Mary, *Psychoanalysis and the Scene of Reading* (Oxford: Oxford University Press, 1999).

Jenkins, Keith, *On 'What is History?'* (London: Routledge, 1995).

—— 'Why Bother with the Past?', *Rethinking History,* 1 (1997).

—— (ed.), *The Postmodern History Reader* (London: Routledge, 1997).

Jonas, Hans, *Mortality and Morality: A Search for the Good after Auschwitz*, ed. Lawrence Vogel (Evanston, Ill.: Northwestern University Press, 1999).

Kant, Emmanuel, *Critique of Pure Reason*, tr. Norman Kemp Smith (London: Macmillan, 1929).

Karpf, Anne, *The War After* (London: Minerva, 1996).

Katz, Robert, *Empathy: Its Nature and Uses* (London: Free Press of Glencoe, 1963).

Ka-Tzetnik 135633, *Atrocity* (New York: Lyle Stuart, 1963).

—— *House of Dolls,* tr. Moshe M. Kohn (New York: Simon & Schuster, 1955).

—— (as Yehiel De-Nur), *Shivitti: A Vision,* tr. Eliyah Nike De-Nur and Lisa Herman (San Francisco: Harper Row, 1989).

Kearney, Richard, *Dialogues with Contemporary Continental Thinkers: The Phenomenological Heritage* (Manchester: Manchester University Press, 1984).

Kelley, Donald R., *Faces of History* (London: Yale University Press, 1998).

Kellner, Hans, 'A Bedrock of Order: Hayden White's Linguistic Humanism', *History and Theory*, 19 (1980), 1–29.

Kemperer, Victor, *The Language of the Third Reich*, tr. Martin Brady (London: Continuum, 2000).

Kermode, Frank, *The Genesis of Secrecy: On the Interpretation of Narrative* (London: Harvard University Press, 1979).

Kertész, Imre, *Fateless,* tr. Christopher C. Wilson and Katharina M. Wilson (Evanston, Ill.: Northwestern University Press, 1992).

—— *Kaddish for a Child Not Born*, tr. Christopher C. Wilson and Katharina M. Wilson (Evanston, Ill.: Northwestern University Press, 1997).

King, Nicola, *Memory, Narrative, Identity: Remembering the Self* (Edinburgh: Edinburgh University Press, 2000).

Kirkegaard, Soren, *Papers and Journals*, tr. Alastair Hannay (London: Penguin Books, 1996).

Klein, Kerwin Lee, 'On the Emergence of Memory in Historical Discourse', *Representations,* 69 (2000), 127–50.

Kofman, Sarah, *Rue Ordener Rue Labat,* tr. Ann Smock (London: University of Nebraska Press, 1996).

—— *Smothered Words*, tr. Madeleine Dobere (Evanston, Ill.: Northwestern University Press, 1998).

Kołakowski, Leszek, *Metaphysical Horror*, ed. Agnieszka Kołakowska (London: Penguin, 2001).

Kolitz, Zvi, *Yosl Rakover Talks to God*, tr. Carol Brown Janeway (London: Jonathan Cape, 1999).

Kremer, Lillian, *Witness through the Imagination* (Detroit: Wayne State University Press, 1989).

Kritzman, Lawrence (ed.), *Auschwitz and After: Race, Culture and 'the Jewish Question' in France* (London: Routledge, 1995).

Kushner, Tony, *The Holocaust and the Liberal Imagination* (Oxford: Blackwell, 1994).

LaCapra, Dominick, *Representing the Holocaust: History, Theory, Trauma* (New York: Cornell University Press, 1994).

—— *Writing History, Writing Trauma* (London: Johns Hopkins University Press, 2001).

Lacoue-Labarthe, Philippe, *Heidegger, Art and Politics: The Fiction of the Political*, tr. Chris Turner (Oxford: Blackwell, 1990).

—— and Jean-Luc Nancy, 'The Nazi Myth', *Critical Inquiry,* 16 (Winter 1990), 291–312.

Lang, Berel, *Heidegger's Silence* (London: Athlone, 1996).

—— *The Future of the Holocaust* (London: Cornell University Press, 1999).

Langer, Lawrence (ed.), *Art from the Ashes* (Oxford: Oxford University Press, 1995).

—— *Holocaust Testimonies: The Ruins of Memory* (London: Yale University Press, 1991).

—— *Pre-empting the Holocaust* (London: Yale University Press, 1998).

Langerwey, Mary D., *Reading Auschwitz* (London: Sage, 1998).

Langsdorf, Lenore, and Stephen Watson, with E. Matya Bower (eds.), *Phenomenology, Interpretation, and Community* (Albany, NY: State University of New York Press, 1996).

Lappin, Elena, 'The Man with Two Heads', *Granta,* 66 (1999), 7–65.

Leak, Andrew, and George Paizis (eds.), *The Holocaust and the Text* (London: Macmillan, 2000).

Lee, Michael, 'A Witness in Court', *Perspective: Journal of the Holocaust Centre,* Beth Shalom 3/2 (2000), 8–9.

Leitner, Isabella, *Fragments of Isabella: A Memoir of Auschwitz,* ed. and tr. Irving Leitner (New York: New English Library, 1978).

Lengyl, Olga, *Five Chimneys* (London: Panther, 1959).

Lescourret, Marie-Anne, *Emmanuel Levinas* (Paris: Flammarion, 1994).

Levi, Primo, *If This is a Man and The Truce,* tr. Stuart Woolf (London: Abacus, 1979).

—— *Other People's Trades,* tr. Raymond Rosenthal (London: Abacus, 1989).

—— *The Drowned and the Saved,* tr. Raymond Rosenthal (London: Abacus, 1988).

Levinas, Emmanuel, *Alterity and Transcendence,* tr. Michel B. Smith (London: Athlone Press, 1999).

—— 'As if Consenting to Horror', tr. Paula Wissing, *Critical Inquiry,* 15 (Winter 1989).

—— *Collected Philosophical Papers,* tr. Alphonso Lingis (Dordrecht: Kluwer Academic Publishers, 1987).

—— *Difficult Freedom,* tr. Seàn Hand (London: Athlone, 1990).

—— *Ethics and Infinity: Conversations with Philippe Nemo,* tr. Richard A. Cohen (Pittsburgh: Duquesne University Press, 1985).

—— *Existence and Existents,* tr. Alphonso Lingis (London: Kluwer Academic Publishers, 1978).

—— *God, Death and Time,* tr. Bettina Bergo (Stanford, Calif.: Stanford University Press, 2000).

—— *Is it Righteous to Be? Interviews with Emmanuel Levinas,* ed. Jill Robbins (Stanford, Calif.: Stanford University Press, 2001).

—— *Nine Talmudic Readings,* tr. Annette Aronowicz (Bloomington: Indiana University Press, 1990).

—— *Otherwise than Being: Or, Beyond Essence,* tr. Alphonso Lingis (The Hague: Martinus Nijhoff, 1981).

—— 'Reflection on the Philosophy of Hitlerism', tr. Seàn Hand, *Critical Inquiry,* 17 (1990), 62–71.

Levinas, Emmanuel, *Totality and Infinity*, tr. Alphonso Lingis (London: Kluwer Academic Publishers, 1991).

Levine, George, *The Realist Imagination: English Fiction from Frankenstein to Lady Chatterly* (Chicago: University of Chicago Press, 1981).

Levinson, Julian, 'Transmitting Yiddishkeit: Irving Howe and Jewish American Culture', *Jewish Culture and History*, 2/2 (1999), 42–65.

Lipstadt, Deborah, *Denying the Holocaust: The Growing Assault on Truth and Memory* (London: Penguin, 1994).

Littell, Franklin H. (ed.) *Hyping the Holocaust: Scholars Answer Goldhagen* (Philadelphia: Merion Westfield Press International, 1997).

Llewelyn, John, *The HypoCritical Imagination* (London: Routledge, 2000).

Longerich, Peter, *Policy of Destruction: Nazi Anti-Jewish Policy and the Genesis of the 'Final Solution'* (Washington, DC: United States Holocaust Research Institute, 1999).

—— *The Unwritten Order: Hitler's Role in the Final Solution* (Stroud: Tempus Publishing, 2001).

Lowenthal, David, *The Past is a Different Country* (Cambridge: Cambridge University Press, 1985).

Lustig, Arnost, *Night and Hope*, tr. George Theiner (Washington, DC: Inscape Publishers, 1976).

—— *Lovely Green Eyes,* tr. Eward Osers (London: Harvill Press, 2001).

Lyotard, Jean-François, *The Differend: Phrases in Dispute*, tr. Georges Van Den Abbeele (Manchester: Manchester University Press, 1988).

—— and Jean-Loup Thébaud, *Just Gaming*, tr. Wlad Godzich (Minneapolis: University of Minnesota Press, 1985).

McCaffery, Steve, *Prior to Meaning: Protosemantics and Poetics* (Evanston, Ill.: Northwestern University Press, 2001).

McCarthy, Thomas J., *Relations of Sympathy: The Writer and Reader in British Romanticism* (Aldershot: Scolar Press, 1997).

McCullagh, Bethan C., *The Truth of History* (London: Routledge, 1998).

MacDonnell, Diane, *Theories of Discourse* (Oxford: Blackwell, 1986).

Macey, David, *Frantz Fanon* (London: Granta, 2000).

Macksey, Richard, and Eugenio Donato (eds.), *The Language of Criticism and the Science of Man* (London: Johns Hopkins University Press, 1970).

Madison, Gary B., and Marty Fairbairn, *The Ethics of Postmodernity* (Evanston, Ill.: Northwestern University Press, 1999).

Maechler, Stefan, *The Wilkomirski Affair: A Study in Biographical Truth*, tr. John E. Woods (London: Picador, 2001).

Maier, Charles, *The Unmasterable Past* (London: Harvard University Press, 1988).

Malamud, Bernard, *The Complete Stories* (London: Vintage, 1998).

Malka, Salomon, *Lire Levinas* (Paris: Les Éditions du Cerf, 1984), 103.

Mann, Michael, 'Were the Perpetrators of Genocide "Ordinary Men" or "Real Nazis"? Results from Fifteen Hundred Biographies', *Holocaust and Genocide Studies,* 14/3 (2000), 331–66.

Marchitello, Howard (ed.), *What Happens to History: The Renewal of Ethics in Contemporary Thought* (London: Routledge, 2001).

Marrali-Guénoun, Pada, *La Genèse et la trace* (London: Kluwer Academic Publishing, 1990).

Matthews, Eric, *Twentieth Century French Philosophy* (Oxford: Oxford University Press, 1996).

Michaels, Anne, *Fugitive Pieces* (London: Bloomsbury, 1997).

—— 'Lake of Two Rivers', *The Weight of Oranges* (Toronto: Coach House Press, 1985).

—— *Miner's Pond* (Toronto: McClelland & Stewart, 1991).

—— *Skindivers* (London: Bloomsbury, 1999).

—— *The Weight of Oranges* (Toronto: Coach House Press, 1985).

Michman, Dan, *Holocaust Historiography: A Jewish Perspective* (London: Vallentine Mitchell, 2003).

Middleton, Peter, and Tim Woods, *Literatures of Memory: History, Time and Space in Postwar Writing* (Manchester: Manchester University Press, 2000).

Midgley, Mary, *Utopias, Dolphins and Computers* (London: Routledge, 1996).

—— *Wickedness* (London: Routledge, 1984).

Miele, Frank, 'Giving the Devil his Due: Holocaust Revisionism as a Test Case for Free Speech and the Sceptical Ethic', *Skeptic,* 2/4 (1994), 58–70.

Milchman, Alan, and Alan Rosenberg (eds.), *Martin Heidegger and the Holocaust* (Atlantic Highlands, NJ: Humanities Press, 1996).

Milgram, Stanley, *Obedience to Authority: An Experimental View* (New York: Harper Row, 1974).

Morgan, Michael L. (ed.), *Beyond Auschwitz: Post Holocaust Jewish Thought in America* (Oxford: Oxford University Press, 2001).

Morris, Meaghan, and Paul Patton (eds.), *Michael Foucault: Power/Truth/Strategy* (Sydney: Feral Publications, 1979).

Morrison, Karl, *'I am You': The Hermeneutics of Empathy in Western Theory, Literature and Art* (Princeton: Princeton University Press, 1988).

Moses, Dirk, 'Conceptual Blockages and Definitional Dilemmas in the "Racial Century": Genocides of Indigenous Peoples and the Holocaust', *Patterns of Prejudice,* 36 (2002), 7–36.

Mouffe, Chantal (ed.), *Deconstruction and Pragmatism* (London: Routledge, 1996).

Müller, Filip, *Eyewitness Auschwitz: Three Years in the Gas Chamber*, with Helmut Freitag, tr. Susanne Flatouer (Chicago: Ivan R. Dee, 1979).

Munslow, Alun, *Deconstructing History* (London: Routledge, 1997).

Neusner, Jacob, *Stranger at Home: The Holocaust, Zionism and American Judaism* (Chicago; University of Chicago Press, 1981).

Nietzsche, Fredrich, *Beyond Good and Evil,* tr. R. J. Hollingdale (London: Penguin, 1973).

Novick, Peter, *That Noble Dream: The 'Objectivity Question' and the American Historical Profession* (Cambridge: Cambridge University Press, 1988).

—— *The Holocaust and Collective Memory* (London: Bloomsbury, 2000).

Nussbaum, Martha, *Love's Knowledge: Essays on Philosophy and Literature* (Oxford: Oxford University Press, 1990), p. 143.

Nyiszli, Miklos, *Auschwitz,* tr. Tibere Kremer and Richard Seaver (London: Grafton, 1963).

Ofer, Dalia, and Lenore J. Weitzman (eds.), *Women in the Holocaust* (London: Yale University Press, 1998).

Office of United States Chief of Counsel for Prosecution of Axis Criminality, *Nazi Conspiracy and Aggression,* iv (Washington, DC: United States Government Printing Office, 1946).

Ofrat, Gideon, *The Jewish Derrida,* tr. Peretz Kidron (Syracuse, NY: Syracuse University Press, 2001).

Ott, Hugo, *Martin Heidegger: A Political Life,* tr. Allan Blunden (London: Fontanta Press, 1994).

Patterson, David, *Sun Turned to Darkness* (Syracuse, NY: Syracuse University Press, 1998).

—— Alan L. Berger, and Sarita Cargas (eds.), *Encyclopaedia of Holocaust Literature* (Westport, Conn.: Oryx Press, 2002).

Peperzak, Adriaan T. (ed.), *Ethics as First Philosophy* (London: Routledge, 1995).

Perec, Georges, *W, or the Memory of Childhood,* tr. David Bellos (London: Havill Press, 1996).

Peters, Gary, 'The Rhythm of Alterity: Levinas and Aesthetics', *Radical Philosophy,* 82 (1997), 9–16.

Plato, *The Republic,* tr. H. D. P. Lee (London: Penguin, 1955).

Popper, Karl, *The Poverty of Historicism* (London: Routledge, 1986).

Prager, Emily, *A Visit from the Footbinder* (London: Vintage, 1992).

—— *Eve's Tattoo* (London: Vintage, 1999).

Prager, Jeffrey, *Presenting the Past: Psychoanalysis and the Sociology of Misremembering* (London: Harvard University Press, 1998).

Proust, Marcel, *Remembrance of Things Past,* tr. C. K. Scott Moncrieff and Terence Kilmartin (Harmondsworth: Penguin, 1983).

Putnam, Hilary, *Reason, Truth and History* (Cambridge: Cambridge University Press, 1981).

—— *The Many Faces of Realism* (LaSalle, Ill.: Open Court, 1987).

Raczymow, Henri, 'Memory Shot through with Holes', *Yale French Studies,* 85 (1994), 98–105.

Rand, Richard (ed.), *Logomachia: The Contest of the Faculties* (London: University of Nebraska Press, 1992).

Rée, Jonathan, *Heidegger: History and Truth in Being and Time* (London: Pheonix, 1998).

—— *I See a Voice* (London: Harper Collins, 1999).

Reiter, Andrea, *Narrating the Holocaust*, tr. Patrick Camiler (London: Continuum, 2000).

Ricoeur, Paul, *Time and Narrative*, iii, tr. Kathleen McLaughlin and David Pellauer (London: University of Chicago Press, 1988).

Riley, Denise, '*Am I That Name?': Feminism and the Category of 'Women' in History* (Basingstoke: Macmillan, 1988).

Rittner, Carol, and John K. Roth (eds.) *Different Voices: Women and the Holocaust* (New York: Paragon House, 1993).

Robbins, Jill, *Altered Reading* (Chicago: Chicago University Press, 1999).

Rogers, Kim Lacy, Selma Leydesdorft, and Graham Dawson, *Trauma and Life Stories* (London: Routledge, 1999).

Rorty, Richard, *Essays on Heidegger and Others* (Cambridge: Cambridge University Press, 1991).

Rose, Gillian, *Judaism and Modernity* (Oxford: Blackwell, 1993).

—— *Mourning Becomes the Law* (Cambridge: Cambridge University Press, 1996).

—— *The Broken Middle* (Oxford: Blackwell, 1992).

Roseman, Mark, *The Past in Hiding* (London: Allen Lane, 2000).

Rosen, Norma, *Accidents of Influence: Writing as a Woman and a Jew in America* (Albany, NY: State University of New York Press, 1992).

Rosenfeld, Alvin, *A Double Dying: Reflections on Holocaust Literature* (Bloomington: Indiana University Press, 1988).

Roth, John (ed.), *Ethics after the Holocaust* (St John, Minn.: Paragon House, 1999).

Roth, Michael S. (ed.), *The Ironist's Cage: Memory, Trauma and the Construction of History* (New York: Columbia University Press, 1995).

Rothberg, Michael, *Traumatic Realism: The Demands of Holocaust Representation* (London: University of Minnesota Press, 2000).

Rousset, David, *A World Apart*, tr. Yvonne Mayse and Roger Senhouse (London: Secker & Warburg, 1951).

Rowland, Anthony, *Tony Harrison and the Holocaust* (Liverpool: Liverpool University Press, 2001).

Rüsen, Jörn, 'The Logic of Historicization', tr. William Templer, *History and Memory*, 9 (1997), 113–44.

Rushton, Colin, *Spectator in Hell* (London: Pharaoh Press, 1998).

Safranski, Rüdiger, *Martin Heidegger: Between Good and Evil*, tr. Ewald Osers (Cambridge, Mass.: Harvard University Press, 1998).

Sammon, Paul M., *Future Noir: The Making of Blade Runner* (London: Orion, 1996).

Schwarz, Daniel, *Imagining the Holocaust* (New York: St Martin's Griffin, 1999).

Schwartz-Bart, André, *The Last of the Just*, tr. Stephen Becker (New York: Overlook Press, 2000).

Searleman, Alan, and Douglas Herrman (eds.), *Memory from a Broader Perspective* (New York: McGraw Hill, 1994).

Seidel, Gill, *The Holocaust Denial: Antisemitism, Racism and the New Right* (Leeds: Beyond the Pale Collective, 1986).

Seiffert, Rachel, *The Dark Room* (London: Vintage, 2002).

Semprun, Jorge, *Literature or Life*, tr. Linda Coverdale (London: Viking, 1997).

—— *The Long Voyage*, tr. Richard Seaver (London: Penguin, 1997).

—— *What a Beautiful Sunday!*, tr. Alan Sheridan (London: Secker & Warburg, 1983).

Sereny, Gitta, *Albert Speer: His Battle with Truth* (London: Picador, 1995).

—— *Into That Darkness* (London: Pimlico, 1974).

—— *The German Trauma: Experiences and Reflections 1938–2000* (Harmondsworth: Allen Lane, 2000).

Shandley, Robert (ed.), *Unwilling Germans: The Goldhagen Debate* (Minneapolis: University of Minnesota Press, 1998).

Shermer, Michael, and Alex Grobman, *Denying History* (London: University of California Press, 2002).

Sicher, Efraim (ed.), *Breaking Crystal: Writing and Memory after Auschwitz* (Chicago: University of Illinois Press, 1998).

Silverman, Max, *Facing Postmodernity: Contemporary French Thought on Culture and Society* (London: Routledge, 1999).

Singer, Isaac Bashevis, *The Manor* (London: Penguin, 1975).

Sluga, Hans, *Heidegger's Crisis* (London: Harvard University Press, 1993).

Steinberg, Paul, *Speak You Also*, tr. Linda Coverdale with Bill Ford (London: Penguin, 2001).

Stone, Dan, 'Paul Ricoeur, Hayden White and Holocaust Historiography', in Jorn Stuckrath and Zurg Zbinden (eds.), *Metageschichte: Hayden White und Paul Ricoeur* (Baden-Baden: Nomos Verlagsgesellschaft, 1997), 254–74.

—— 'Perec's Antelme', *French Cultural Studies*, 10 (1999), 161–72.

Strawson, P. F., *The Bounds of Sense* (London: Routledge, 1966).

Taylor, Kressmann, *Address Unknown* (London: Souvenir Press, 2002).

Thomas, D. M., *The White Hotel* (London: Penguin, 1981).

Thomas, Julian, *Time, Culture and Identity* (London: Routledge, 1996).

Trotter, David, *The Making of the Reader* (London: Macmillan, 1984).

Van Pelt, Jan, *The Science of Holocaust Research and the Art of Holocaust Denial* (Waterloo: Department of Geography, University of Waterloo, 1999).

—— and Debórah Dwork, *Auschwitz: 1270 to the Present* (London: Yale University Press, 1996).

Vice, Sue, *Holocaust Fiction* (London: Routledge, 2000)

—— (ed.), *Representing the Holocaust* (London: Vallentine Mitchell, 2003).

Vidal-Naquet, Pierre, *Assassins of Memory: Essays on the Denial of the Holocaust*, tr. Jefrey Mehlman (New York: Columbia University Press, 1993).

—— *Les Assassins de Mémoire* (Paris: Éditions de la Découverte, 1987).

—— and Limar Yagil, *Holocaust Denial in France* (Tel Aviv: Tel Aviv Faculty of Humanities, Project for the Study of Anti-Semitism, 1996).

Vlasopolos, Anca, *No Return Address: A Memoir of Displacement* (New York: Colombia University Press, 2000).

Vrba, Rudolf, and Alan Bestic, *I Cannot Forgive* (London: Sidgwick & Jackson and Anthony Gibbs & Phillips, 1963).

Wardi, Dina, *Memorial Candles: Children of the Holocaust*, tr. Naomi Goldblum (London: Tavistock/Routledge, 1992).

Warnock, Mary, *Memory* (London: Faber & Faber, 1987).

Weiss, John, 'Daniel Jonah Goldhagen's *Hitler's Willing Executioners*: An Historian's View', *Journal of Genocide Research*, 1/2 (1999), 257–72.

—— *Ideology of Death* (Chicago: I. R. Dee, 1996).

White, Hayden, 'An Old Question Raised Again: Is Historiography Art or Science? (Response to Iggers)', *Rethinking History*, 4/3 (2000), 391–406.

—— *Metahistory* (London: Johns Hopkins University Press, 1973).

—— 'The Burden of History', *History and Theory*, 5 (1966), 111–34.

—— *The Content of the Form* (Baltimore: Johns Hopkins University Press, 1987).

Whitebrook, Maureen, *Identity, Narrative and Politics* (London: Routledge, 2001).

Wiesel, Elie, *All Rivers Run to the Sea* (London: Harper Collins, 1996).

—— *Conversations*, ed. Robert Franciosi (Jackson: University of Mississippi Press, 2002).

—— *Night*, tr. Stella Rodway (London: Penguin, 1981).

—— 'The Holocaust as Literary Inspiration', in *Dimensions of the Holocaust* (Evanston, Ill.: Northwestern Univerity Press, 1990).

Wieseltier, Leon, *Kaddish* (London: Picador, 2000).

Wiesenthal, Simon, *The Sunflower* (New York: Schocken Books, 1997).

Wilkomirski, Binjamin, *Fragments*, tr. Carol Brown Janeway (London: Picador, 1996).

Williams, Bernard, *Truth and Truthfulness* (Princeton: Princeton University Press, 2002).

Wittgenstein, Ludwig, *Philosophical Investigations*, tr. G. E. M. Anscombe (Oxford: Blackwell, 1963).

Wood, Nancy, *Vectors of Memory: Legacies of Trauma in Post-War Europe* (Oxford: Berg, 1999).

Wright, Tamra, *The Twilight of Jewish Philosophy* (London: Harwood Academic Publishers 1997).

Wyschogord, Edith, *An Ethics of Remembering: History, Heterology and the Nameless Others* (London: Chicago University Press, 1998).

—— 'God and "Being's Move", in the Philosophy of Emmanuel Levinas', *Journal of Religion*, 62 (1982), 145–55.

Wyszogrod, Morris, *A Brush with Death: An Artist in the Death Camps* (Albany, NY: State University of New York Press, 1999).

Yerushalmi, Yosef Hayim, *Zakhor: Jewish History and Jewish Memory* (London: University of Washington Press, 1983).

Young, James, 'Between History and Memory: The Uncanny Voices of the Historian and Survivor', *History and Memory*, 9 (1997), 47–58.

—— 'Interpreting Literary Testimony: A Preface to Rereading Holocaust Diaries and Memoirs', *New Literary History*, 18 (1986–7), 403–23.

—— *The Texture of Memory; Holocaust Memorials and their Meaning* (London: Yale University Press, 1993).

—— *Writing and Rewriting the Holocaust: Narrative and the Consequences of Interpretation* (Bloomington: Indiana University Press, 1990).

Young, Robert, *Postcolonialism: An Historical Introduction* (Oxford: Blackwell, 2001).

—— *White Mythologies* (London: Routledge, 1990).

Zeitlin, Froma I., 'The Vicarious Witness: Belated Memory and Authorial Presence in Recent Holocaust Literature', *History and Memory*, 10/2 (1992), 5–42.

Zelizer, Barbie (ed.), *Visual Culture and the Holocaust* (London: Athlone Press, 2001).

Index

21783502R00210

Printed in Great Britain
by Amazon